ASHOKA

Also by Charles Allen

Plain Tales from the Raj

Tales from the Dark Continent

Tales from the South China Seas

Raj Scrapbook

The Savage Wars of Peace

Thunder and Lightning

Lives of the Indian Princes

A Soldier of the Company

A Glimpse of the Burning Plain

Kipling's Kingdom

A Mountain in Tibet

The Search for Shangri-La

The Buddha and the Sahibs

Soldier Sahibs

Duel in the Snows

God's Terrorists

Kipling Sahib

The Buddha and Dr Führer

ASHOKA

The Search for India's Lost Emperor

CHARLES ALLEN

THE OVERLOOK PRESS
NEW YORK, NY

The whole earth is the sepulchre of famous men. They are honoured not only by columns and inscriptions in their own land, but in foreign nations on memorials graven not on stone but in the hearts and minds of men.

Thucydides, *History of the Peloponnesian War,* 404 BCE

Contents

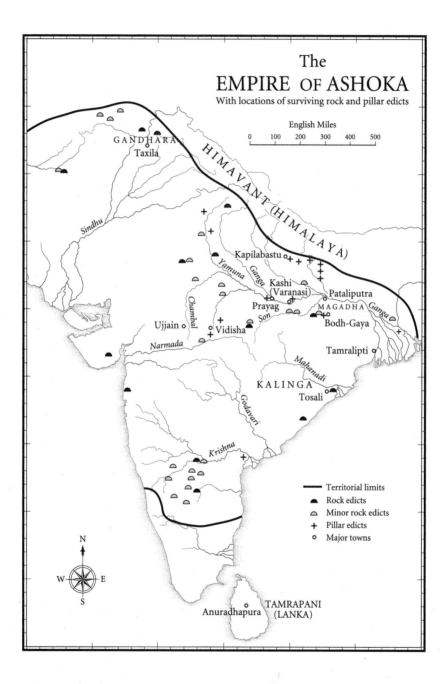

The
EMPIRE OF ASHOKA
With locations of surviving rock and pillar edicts

English Miles

| 0 | 100 | 200 | 300 | 400 | 500 |

GANDHARA
Taxila

HIMAVANT (HIMALAYA)

Sindhu

Kapilabastu

Yamuna *Ganga*

Kashi
(Varanasi) Pataliputra

Chambal Prayag MAGADHA *Ganga*
Son
Ujjain Bodh-Gaya
Vidisha

Narmada Tamralipti

Mahanadi

KALINGA
Tosali

Godavari

Krishna

—— Territorial limits
◗ Rock edicts
◖ Minor rock edicts
+ Pillar edicts
○ Major towns

N
W — E
S

TAMRAPANI
Anuradhapura (LANKA)

Preface

The King Without Sorrow

The emperor listed in the ancient Brahmanical *Puranas* as *Ashoka raja*, 'The King Without Sorrow', ruled over a united India some 2250 years ago. In the course of some forty years Ashoka unified the subcontinent under one government, transformed a minor religious sect into a world religion and introduced moral concepts whose impact on Asia can be felt to this day. Ashoka may be said to be India's founding father, being the first ruler to forge India into a single nation state. As if that were not enough, long before Mahatma Gandhi, Emperor Ashoka espoused non-violence and the utterly novel concept of conquest by moral force alone – and he was very probably the first ruler in history to establish a welfare state. Ashoka is also the first in India's ancient dynasties of kings with a distinctive, identifiable voice – and no ordinary voice at that, for what he had to say was and remains absolutely, unequivocally unique as a statement of governing principles.

The words of what might justifiably be called Ashoka's Song – more prosaically referred to as the Ashokan Rock or Pillar Edicts – were inscribed in India's first written script, Ashoka Brahmi. They were chiselled on hundreds of rock surfaces and on scores of polished pillars of stone throughout the Indian subcontinent, so that his song could be heard loud and clear from Kandahar to the mouths of the Irrawady and from Cape Cormorin at the tip of southern India to the Himalayas. From this heartland that same message spread out in ripples on all sides until it was heard in the furthest corners of Asia.

Only a precious few of these edicts have survived the vicissitudes of time and human violence in readable form: some seven edict rocks, eleven edict pillars, another nineteen more modest sites bearing what are usually referred to as the Minor Rock Edicts and perhaps a dozen more inscriptions in various forms that can be attributed to Ashoka. Together they constitute the earliest surviving written records of India's ancient history. Yet it is a remarkable and little-known fact that they and the emperor who composed them were all but lost to history for the better part of two thousand years.

The religious tolerance that Emperor Ashoka called for in his seventh Rock Edict (RE 7), where he spoke of his desire 'that all religions should reside everywhere', lay at the heart of the new thinking that Ashoka's religious ministers promoted within the borders of his empire and his missionaries beyond. But even in his own time this message was perceived as a threat by those who believed that they and they alone had the authority to dictate what religious codes people should follow.

British historians and archaeologists working in India in the nineteenth century were quick to blame the eclipse of Buddhism there on the Muslim conquests. For seven centuries zealots did indeed inflict horrendous human and cultural damage on India in the name of Islam, yet the fact is that Buddhism in India was in terminal decline long before Mahmud of Ghazni first crossed the Indus in the year

1008 CE.* Already by the ninth century Buddhism as practised by its adherents in India had become so esoteric, so isolated from the wider community as to be unable to compete with revitalised, devotional Hinduism as promoted by the ninth-century reformer Adi Shankaracharya and his followers. However, there is another equally important reason for the failure of Buddhism in India – one that few followers of the Hindutva nationalist movement (which believes that the only good Indian is a Hindu Indian) are prepared to accept: Brahmanical intolerance, which at times was as unbending in its hatred of heresy and heretics as later Muslim hardliners were in their jihads against unbelief and unbelievers.

Much of the evidence for this Brahmanical oppression comes from India's Buddhist neighbours in Tibet, Nepal, Burma and Ceylon. However, there are also Brahmanical texts that demonstrate an implacable hostility towards Buddhists and record their persecution at the hands of orthodox Hindu rulers. And there is the evidence of archaeology.

The politicians who in 1991 egged on the mob that destroyed Babur's mosque at Ayodhya on the grounds that it was built over the Hindu warrior-god Rama's fort may be surprised to know that some of the most famous Hindu temples in India almost certainly began as Buddhist structures, often incorporating Buddhist icons, either in the form of images of deities or as lingams. Four likely examples – selected simply because they come from the four corners of the subcontinent – are the Badrinath shrine in the far north Garhwal Himal, the Jagannath temple at Puri on the east coast, the Ayyappa shrine at Sabarimala in Kerala and the Vithalla shrine at Pandharpur in Western Maharashtra.

---

* The terms 'CE' and 'BCE', standing for 'of the common era' and 'before the common era', have superseded AD and BC.

The triumph of Brahmanism (the lion) over Buddhism (the elephant), as photographed in 1890. The giant lion is one of a pair that guard the entrance to the great temple of the sun god Surya, a sublime example of Hindu architecture in India.[1] (APAC, British Library)

However, the most striking evidence of Brahmanical hostility towards Buddhism comes in the form of silence: the way in which India's Buddhist history, extending over large parts of the country and lasting for many centuries, was excised from the historical record. It was by this simple act of omission – the historical revisionism of generations of pious Brahman pundits and genealogists – that Ashoka's Song was silenced, and Emperor

Ashoka himself all but erased from India's history. In its call for religious tolerance, its wish that all living beings should live together in harmony and without violence, Ashoka's Song spoke to all. But by promoting the Buddhist heresy throughout the land, Ashoka directly challenged the caste-based authority of the Brahman order. He and his beliefs could not be tolerated.

Religious intolerance knows no frontiers. When the Mughal Emperor Shah Jehan was pulling down Hindu temples in Benares, Puritans in England were busying themselves smashing medieval stained glass and destroying idols in churches up and down the country. Historians who deny or conceal such uncomfortable truths do us no favours. Herein lies part of the reason for writing this book about a long-forgotten emperor whose song was silenced.

But there are other and happier reasons, too – one being the means by which India's lost pre-Muslim history was rediscovered in the late eighteenth century and early nineteenth century. It is an astonishing tale of painstaking detective work begun by European Orientalists – a species vilified by the late Professor Edward Said and his followers.[2] Yet anyone who values the advancement of learning has cause to be grateful for these pioneer Orientalists-cum-antiquarians-cum-Indologists – call them what you will. In recounting how the rediscovery of Ashoka and his world came about I hope that even the most ardent Indian nationalist will accept that these foreign enthusiasts and scholars played a progressive role in the advancement of modern India, for all that some were part of the colonial exploitation of India.

That process of rediscovery was first sketched out by the historian John Keay in 1981 in his undervalued book *India Discovered*. I myself explored some aspects in greater detail in *The Buddha and the Sahibs* and *The Buddha and Dr Führer*. Here

I have taken it further in charting step by step the rediscovery
of India's lost Ashokan history by a combination of archaeology
and sheer dogged scholarship.

However, this rediscovery makes no sense without examin-
ing how it was that ancient India – and Ashoka with it – came
to be lost to the outside world; a process exemplifed by the
destruction of the great Buddhist university of Nalanda in
1193–4. A brief account of that dreadful visitation provides this
book's opening chapter. Plenty of Muslim historians were present to chronicle these and subsequent events but they were,
with two notable exceptions, blinded to any history that did
not form part of the advance of Islam. Brahmanical omission
was now compounded by Muslim single-mindedness. The
links with India's past were broken, its pre-Islamic history all
but forgotten. Only in the last quarter of the eighteenth century could the process of recovery begin, thanks to a new spirit
of enquiry originating in Europe, which manifested itself in
India in the Orientalist movement.

It will by now have dawned on the reader that this is no
straightforward biography. The first generation of Orientalists in
India – the 'dead white men in periwigs' so despised by Edward
Said – were very few in number, had no idea what they were
looking for and had few tools other than their enthusiasm – and
the driving force of reason. But there were clues, scattered like
pieces of jigsaw far and wide across the Indian landscape, and it
was by finding these clues, recognising them as such and then
painstakingly piecing them together, with many false starts and
blind alleys, that these enthusiasts reconstructed India's pre-
Islamic history. This process of reassembly extended over more
than two centuries, and it ended with the identity of Emperor
Ashoka far from complete, but with enough of him for us to

understand who he was, what he was like and how enormously important a figure he had been in the shaping of Asia.

The process may have been initiated by Europeans but it was far from one-sided. Very recently I had the pleasure of sitting quite literally at the feet of the Venerable Waskaduwe Mahindawansa Maha Nayako, elder and abbot of the Buddhist monastery of Rajaguru Sri Subuthi Maha Vihara, situated beside the sea on the road between Colombo and Galle in Sri Lanka. There I was shown some of the extensive correspondence that had taken place between Venerable Waskaduwe's predecessor the distinguished Pali scholar Venerable Subuthi and three generations of British Orientalists, beginning with letters written by the newly appointed Director-General of the Archaeological Survey of India, General Sir Alexander Cunningham, from the Bharhut excavation site in 1861, continuing with letters from the Ceylon Civil Servant turned Pali scholar Robert Childers from the 1870s into the 1890s, and ending with letters from the Indian Civil Servant and future historian Vincent Smith, sent from Bihar in 1898.

To replicate this process of reassembly, I have tried to stay in context, so that at each stage the reader knows little more than did the savants at the time. In the same way I have tried to make my illustrations as contemporaneous as possible and I make no apologies for the quality of some of the early photographs. This withholding of information may baffle and even at times frustrate you, the reader, but I hope it will better allow you to share in the process of the discovery of Ashoka, clue by clue.

With that recovery completed I have devoted the final chapter to an account of the man and his dynasty: a potted biography based on what little hard evidence we have together with a reasonable degree of conjecture.

I have avoided academic usage in my spelling: for example, Ashoka rather than *Aśoka*, *raja* rather than *rāja*, *chakra* and not *cakra* and so on. I have also given precedence in my own (as opposed to quoted) text to Sanskrit over Pali, thus *Dharma* rather than *Dhamma*. To this day blurring persists in Indian speech between the soft and hard 's' (think of Simla and Shimla), 'b' and 'v' (Baranasi and Varanasi), and to a lesser extent between 'l' and 'r', 'd' and 'th'; an unconscious hangover from soft Sanskrit and harder Pali. Philologists may quibble but these differences really don't matter.

The ancient texts consulted and quoted come in three interrelated languages – Prakrit, Sanskrit and Pali – and two main alphabets – Brahmi lipi and Kharosthi. An explanatory note on these languages and alphabets is given at the start of the Notes (p. 427).

Finally, a note about my usage of two words: *Brahman* and *Dharma*. A Brahmin – the Anglicised form of the Sanskrit *Brahmana* – is a member of the priestly caste, the highest of the four *varnas* that make up Hindu society. The religion over which this sacerdotal caste presided at the time of Ashoka was very different from the popular Hinduism we know today, as was the authority of that same caste. I have differentiated between Brahmanism then and Hinduism today by referring to the priestly caste then as Brahmans and their descendants today as Brahmins.

The word *Dharma* is closely associated with the name of Ashoka and Buddhism but has its roots in the Proto-Indo-European verb *dhr*, 'to hold', used to describe the cosmic law underpinning the universe. Hindus, Buddhists, Jains and Sikhs alike use the word to describe, at one level, the proper practice of one's religion and, on a higher plane, ultimate reality. In Hindu usage the meaning of the word has been extended to embrace a wide spectrum of ideas ranging from the correct performance of religious rituals and application of caste rules to ethical conduct and the application of civil and criminal law.

However, in the fifth century BCE the Buddhists gave the word a new and more specific meaning. In the spoken Prakrit of the time the form used was *Dhammo*, which became *Dhamma* in Pali, *Dharma* in Sanskrit. In the Buddhist context it came to mean the ultimate truth as contained in the body of teachings expounded by Sakyamuni Buddha. The Emperor Ashoka, who afterwards became known throughout the Buddhist world as *Ashokadharma* (Sanskrit) or *Asokodhamma* (Pali) used the word repeatedly in his Pillar and Rock Edicts. On the bilingual Ashokan edict found in Kandahar in 1958 the word appears in Greek as ευσέβεια (*eusebeia*), usually translated as 'piety'. Arguments continue among academics over what precise meaning was intended but the details contained in his Rock and Pillar Edicts suggest that Ashoka intended his Dharma to be inclusive, that it represented 'a religiously founded civil ethics for all state citizens of the Maurya empire as well as a specific religion usually identified as the Buddhist dharma'.[3]

The Orientalists whose activities make up such a large part of this story could never quite get their heads round the concept of Dharma. They began by translating the word as 'Religion' and afterwards tended to stick with 'the Law'. That still falls short but for ease of reading I am calling it the Moral Law.

Charles Allen, Somerset, August 2011

I

The Breaking of Idols

Part of the ruins of the *Mahavihara*, or 'Great Monastery', of Nalanda, for centuries a beacon of learning in South Asia. A photograph of the partially uncovered remains of the Baladitya Temple soon after the first excavations had begun, photographed by the archaeologist Joseph Beglar in 1872. (APAC, British Library)

At the start of the winter campaigning season of 1193–4 two hundred armed horsemen crossed the Ganges at Varanasi in search of booty. They were mostly Khilji slaves, including the war lord who led them and who shared their bread and their loot. His name was Muhammad Bakhtiyar, 'impetuous, enterprising, bold, sagacious and expert', the most daring of the military commanders serving Qutb-ud-din Aybak – who was himself a slave, his master being Sultan Muhammad of Ghor, celebrated by his compatriots as *Jahanzos*, the 'World-Burner'.

Twelve years earlier the World-Burning Sultan had captured the city of Lahore, which had become the springboard for his further advance into India. The subsequent progress of his armies under the generalship of Qutb-ud-din Aybak had been recorded in detail by the sultan's chroniclers, among them the Persian Sadruddin Muhammad Hasan Nizami:

> He purged by his sword the land of Hind from the filth of infidelity ... and the impurity of idol-worship, and left not one temple standing ... When he arrived at Mirat [Meerut] all the idol temples were converted into mosques. He then marched and encamped under the fort of Delhi. The city and its vicinity were freed from idols and idol-worship, and in the sanctuaries, mosques were raised by the worshippers of one God. The royal army proceeded towards Benares, which is the centre of the country of Hind, and here they destroyed nearly one thousand temples. The temples were converted into mosques and abodes of goodness, and the ejaculations of bead-counters and voices of summoners to prayer ascended to high heaven, and the very name of idolatry was annihilated.[1]

It was at this point, with the upper Gangetic plains secured for Islam, that Muhammad Bakhtiyar was given permission to push on with his small band of mujahideen. Hardened by years of campaigning, inspired by the belief that they were engaged in jihad, he and they gave no thought to their own comfort. We may imagine them whipping their ponies on, intent on covering the 160 miles to their goal as fast as humanly possible. They carried little other than swords, spears and shields, knowing that God would provide.

Their immediate goal was Bihar, which was both the name of the plains country they rode through and the seat of the last of the Pala dynasty of kings. The riders were probably unaware that the very name of Bihar was derived from the numerous Buddhist *viharas*, or monastic centres, scattered across the countryside. They may not even have known that an hour's ride west of Bihar fort was a second seat of power; one without ramparts or garrison but presenting a direct challenge to their belief in the oneness of God. This was the *Mahavihara*, or 'Great Monastery', of Nalanda, known throughout the Buddhist world as the *Dharmaganja*, or 'Treasury of the Moral Law'.

For centuries Nalanda had been the most important seat of learning in Asia. It contained the most extensive repository of Buddhist knowledge in the world, housed in three multi-storeyed libraries: the *Ratnasagara*, or 'Sea of Jewels'; the *Ratnadadhi*, or 'Ocean of Jewels'; and the *Ratnaranjaka*, or 'Jewels of Delight'. Generation upon generation of the Buddhist world's most gifted scholars had come here to study and teach the sacred texts of the Buddhist canon.

Nalanda's glory days had long gone but the great library still drew students from a dozen countries – none of whom could have been unaware that a new and terrifying military power

had descended on the Indian plains from the north, had
scattered to the winds every army sent against it and was even
now working its way down the Ganges crushing all before it.

Surprise and terror were the twin pillars of Muhammad
Bakhtiyar's success as a military commander. He took the
fortress of Bihar before most of its occupants even knew they
were under attack. He then turned his attentions on Nalanda –
but not before sending a messenger to enquire if its libraries
contained a copy of the *Quran*. On learning that they did not,
he ordered the destruction of the Great Monastery and all it
contained.

What followed was chronicled by Minhaj-ud-din, a judge of
Ghor who had accompanied Muhammad of Ghor's invading
army into India:

> The greater number of the inhabitants of that place were
> Brahmans ... and they were all slain. There were a great
> number of books there; and when all these books came
> under the observation of the Musalmans they summoned a
> number of Hindus that they might give them information
> respecting the import of these books; but the whole of the
> Hindus had been killed ... When that victory was effected,
> Muhammad-i-Bakhtyar returned with great booty, and came
> to the presence of the beneficent Sultan Kutb-ud-Din Ibak,
> and received great honour and distinction.[2]

But Minhaj-ud-din was wrong in thinking that Nalanda's
inhabitants were Hindus. They were, of course, Buddhist
monks, whose numbers included many Indians of the Brahman caste. Nor did Minhaj-ud-din trouble to mention that the
raiders put the entire site, extending over many acres, to the

torch or that the task of burning the library took them several months, during which time 'smoke from burning manuscripts hung for days like a dark pall over the low hills'.[3]

There were at this time three major centres of Buddhist learning in Bihar and two more in Bengal. Nalanda was the first to go up in flames, quickly followed by the nearby monastery of Odantapuri, then the larger site at Vikramashila, on the north bank of the Ganges. A decade later Muhammad Bakhtiyar completed the work begun in Bihar by staging another of his lightning strikes on the capital of the Sena kings of Bengal at Nuddia. Here, too, he applied fire and sword to the last two remaining Buddhist Great Monasteries at Somapura and Jagadalala on the banks of the lower Ganges, and to as many lesser monastic sites as he could find.[4]

Muhammad Bakhtiyar was afterwards assassinated in his bed, but he lived to see Muslim dominion extended over Bihar and Bengal. The destruction he wrought at Nalanda and the other great Buddhist libraries has a superficial parallel in the burning of the great royal library at Alexandria – but there is a crucial difference in that what was lost at Alexandria occurred by stages over many centuries.[5] What Muhammad Bakhtiyar did at Nalanda and the other Great Monasteries in Bihar and Bengal was once and for all. For Buddhism in northern India it was the final *coup de grâce* and its consequences were catastrophic: the virtual obliteration of every page of a thousand years of Buddhist history on the subcontinent. Thus India's Buddhist past was all but lost – and very soon forgotten.

2

The Golden Column
of Firoz Shah

The ruins of Sultan Firoz Shah's *kotla*, drawn by a Delhi artist
in about 1820. It shows admirers standing on the upper floor of
the ruins of the palace to examine the golden pillar that its
builder had made the central feature: Firoz Shah's Lat. The
mosque on the right still stands but much of the original fortress
was subsequently demolished to make room for the cricket
stadium. (Metcalfe Album, APAC, British Library)

In India today the IPL Twenty20 Cricket League is the hottest thing there is; a brash, brazen affair in which eight teams composed of the best that money can buy meet in eight cities to slog it out over a series of twenty-over matches played under floodlights. Each team has its own home base and in Delhi that means the Delhi Daredevils occupying the Feroz Shah Kotla Stadium. The word *kotla* means 'fort' but the walls of that fortress are long gone. Cricket has been played here since 1883 and for most Indians Firoz Shah Kotla means one thing: cricket – and nothing else. Few associate the name with Delhi's Muslim past and fewer still are aware that the huddle of ruins in the shadow of the stadium from which it takes its name contains one of India's most ancient and most extraordinary relics.

Sultan Firoz Shah was the builder of the sixth of the many cities of Delhi. The first is the most doubtful: Indraprastha, celebrated in the *Mahabharata* epic of ancient India as the capital of the five battling brothers known as the Pandavas. Its supposed remains are said to underpin the *Purana Qila*, or 'Ancient Fort', next to Delhi Zoo. However, the less imposing jumble of ruins to the south and west known as the *Lal Kot*, or the 'Red Fort', has a more credible claim for it was here that Qutb-ud-din Aybak – that same ferocious slave-general who had overseen his slave Muhammad Bakhtiyar's conquest of Bihar and Bengal – chose to establish the seat of the first Muslim Sultanate of Delhi.

To celebrate his victory over the massed armies of the Hindus in 1193 Qutb-ud-din built a mosque he named the 'Might of Islam', constructed by slave-artisans from the stones of twenty-seven Hindu and Jain temples. Beside the mosque he added a victory tower in the form of the truly monumental Qutb al-minar: a vast, tapering minaret of red sandstone with a base diameter approaching fifty feet. He intended it to be the largest and highest tower in the Islamic world, but by the time Qutb-ud-din met his death under the hooves of a polo pony, only the first of five planned storeys, ninety feet high, had been completed.

A century later a third Delhi rose at Siri, north-west of the Red Fort. This was the work of Sultan Ala-ud-din Khalji and it was largely financed by his plunder of the Deccan memori-alised in Arab legend as Ala-ud-din's Cave. He, too, began to build a victory tower, intended to be twice as big as the minar begun by Qutb-ud-din. But again death intervened, in the form of poison administered by one of his generals, so only the first stage of the tower was raised.

Two decades later a fourth Delhi rose nearby: the fortress of Tughluqabad built by Ghias-ud-din Tughlaq. His celebrated end – smothered to death under a welcoming pavilion erected by his son Muhammad bin Tughluq – brought his son to the throne of Delhi in 1325. This highly eccentric patricide styled himself 'The Warrior in the Cause of God' but was better known to his subjects as *al-Khuni*, 'the Blood-Soaked', chiefly on account of his disastrous decision to move his capital and its entire population seven hundred miles south to Daulatabad in the Deccan – and then back again two years later. On his return to Delhi he founded but then abandoned a fifth Delhi: *Jahanpanah*, or 'Refuge of the World'.

In the spring of 1351 Muhammad the Blood-Soaked caught fever by the banks of the Indus and died. It was four days before his cousin Firoz Shah Tughluq could be persuaded to face his destiny. The mild-mannered Firoz Shah was not cut out to be a despot. Born of a Hindu mother and raised by her in iso-lation after the early death of his father, Firoz Shah must have seemed easy prey to those who raised him to the Sultanate of Delhi. Without friends or funds he had little option but to buy his way out of trouble, using an 'infidel tax' as his chief method of fund-raising. He also had to placate the many religious puritans at court by periodically cracking down on idolators.

It follows that the sultan's record is far from spotless. He was responsible for a notorious assault made on the famous Jagannath temple on the coast of Kalinga (now Orissa) in 1360, leading to a popular uprising, brutally suppressed. This episode allowed his biographers to present Sultan Firoz Shah as a pillar of the faith. Thanks to a central workforce of slave labour said to number one hundred and eighty thousand, Firoz Shah was able to construct madrassas, hospitals, bridges, canals, reservoirs and public buildings up and down the land, none of more far-reaching benefit than the 150-mile West Jumna Canal, which transformed a vast tract of arid land into the granary of Hindustan.

But Firoz Shah was equally keen on restoration – and it was here that he was able, very discreetly, to give expression to another side of his character by displaying a degree of religious tolerance that bordered on the heretical. In 1326 a lightning strike had brought down the two upper storeys of Qutb-ud-din's victory tower, which gave the sultan the excuse to make his own mark on what was already a major religious complex. He restored the great tower – but he may also have added a unique trophy of his own: a twenty-four-foot high pillar of solid iron that had once stood in the forecourt of a Hindu temple.

Hundreds of such pillars, usually made of stone and surmounted by a bronze image of a Garuda sun-bird (vehicle of the god Vishnu), had once stood in temple forecourts across northern India. Many had been overthrown in the preceding centuries and their attendant Garuda images melted down for the value of their metal. Where this particular pillar came from is not recorded, but it was unmistakably a Hindu totem.[1] And yet the sultan may well have caused this infidel pillar to be erected at the centre of the public praying area of the Might of Islam mosque, directly in front of the screen and the niche indicating the direction of Mecca – a blatant act of sacrilege that probably explains why the mosque was abandoned as a place of Friday prayer at about this same time.

But then Sultan Firoz Shah clearly had a fascination for infidel pillars, for one of his first acts on securing the Sultanate of Delhi was to erect his own more modest version of a victory tower at the scene of that triumph: Hisar, about a hundred miles north-west of Delhi. By happy chance a ready-made tower was available close at hand: a handsome stone column approximately thirty feet high, hewn from a single block of stone. This he caused to be re-erected in the prayer court of his new mosque with the addition of an inscription in Persian setting out the history of his dynasty up to Sultan Firoz Shah's glorious accession.

Soon afterwards, while out hunting near the village of Topra further to the east, in the upper region of the Doab (the lands between the Jumna and Ganges rivers), the sultan came upon another standing stone pillar. This also had been cut from a single block of stone but was far grander than the first, being forty-two feet in length and weighing more than twenty-five tons. It was also in much finer condition, with a lustrous, polished or glazed red surface that caused it to shine like gold. Furthermore, it was but one of two columns – the other located to the east of Delhi at Meerut. 'These columns', noted a contemporary, 'had stood in those places from the days of the Pandavas, but had never attracted the attention of any of the kings who sat upon the throne of Delhi, till Sultan Firoz noticed them.'[2]

In fact, other stone columns *had* attracted the attention of earlier Muslim conquerors, but Firoz Shah was the first who thought to preserve rather than destroy them. He also wanted to understand their significance. He made exhaustive enquiries among the Brahman *pandits* (literally, one who has memorised the ancient texts known as the *Vedas* but used more generally to describe a learned Brahman) and discovered that according to local legend, the two columns at Topra and Meerut were 'the walking sticks of the accursed Bhim [one of the five Pandava brothers, a giant of massive strength], a man of great stature and size ... When Bhim died these two columns were left standing as memorials to him.' Filled with admiration, Firoz Shah decided to remove them with great care as trophies to Delhi.

The contemporary who witnessed these events and afterwards wrote about them was twelve-year-old Shams-i Siraj 'Afif, who grew up to serve Sultan Firoz Shah and chronicle his life. Shams-i Siraj observed the feat of engineering, apparently supervised by the sultan himself, by which the two columns were transported to Delhi and then re-erected. The first was the column from Topra, which Firoz Shah named the *minara-i zarin*, or 'column of gold', on account of its wonderful sheen:

Directions were issued for bringing parcels of the cotton of the Sembal [cotton wood tree]. Quantities of this cotton were placed round the column, and when the earth at its base was removed, it fell gently on the bed prepared for it. The cotton was then removed by degrees, and after some days the pillar lay safe upon the ground ... The pillar was then encased from top to bottom in reeds and raw skins, so that no damage might accrue to it. A carriage, with forty-two wheels, was constructed, and ropes were attached to each wheel. Thousands of men hauled at each rope, and after great labour and difficulty the pillar was raised on to the carriage.

The column of gold was dragged down to the banks of the Jumna, where it was loaded aboard a number of large boats lashed together before being floated downriver to Delhi.

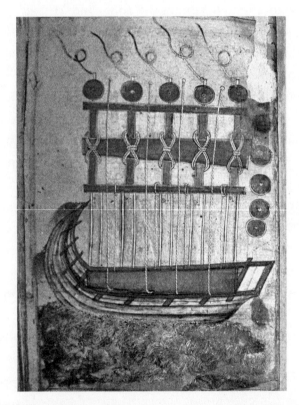

Sultan Firoz Shah's golden column, from a unique illustrated copy of the *Sirat-i Firoz Shahi*. The stone column is loaded aboard a barge before being towed down the Yamuna River. (Khuda Bakhsh Oriental Public Library, Patna)

The sultan was at this time building his own capital with the help of an army of artisan slaves. This new Delhi he established north of the earlier cities raised by previous rulers and named Firozabad. Because its stones were subsequently cannibalised by Firoz Shah's successors, few traces of Firozabad remain today other than the remains of Firoz Shah's fort – and the golden column surmounting it at the centre. To raise that great pillar into position further engineering ingenuity had been required. According to a second biographical source, possibly dictated by Firoz Shah himself, this remarkable totem was then given a new religious purpose: 'After it had remained an object of worship of the polytheists and infidels for so many thousands of years, through the efforts of Sultan Firoz Shah and by the grace of God, it became the *minar* [tower] of a place of worship for the Faithful.'[3]

The second of the giant Bhim's walking sticks secured by Firoz Shah underwent the same process. Men ferried it downriver and re-erected it to become the centrepiece of a hunting pavilion, sited on a low ridge some miles to the north of Firozabad (today known as Delhi Ridge, just beyond the city walls of Old Delhi). Both here and at Firoz Shah's palace the stone column became the central feature, so that the top of each pillar could be seen from a distance rising above the building.

After visiting the remains of the hunting lodge in about 1610, the English traveller William Finch described it as 'a auncient hunting house' out of which rose 'a stone pillar, which, passing through three stories [*sic*], is higher than all twenty foure foot, having at the top a globe and a halfe moone over it. This stone, they say ... hath inscriptions.'[4]

In fact, both the Delhi columns bore inscriptions, which so excited Sultan Firoz Shah's curiosity that he made extensive enquiries about their origins and meaning, but without success: 'Many Brahmans and Hindu devotees were invited to read them but no one was able.' No one, it seems, had any idea what was written on the two pillars – or who had originally caused them to be raised.

What the sultan's official biographer Shams-i Siraj 'Afif never understood – or was reluctant to state – was how large the column of gold and its less splendid twin loomed in the life and imagination of Firoz Shah. That only became apparent many centuries later when a previously unknown account of Firoz Shah's life was found: a manuscript entitled *Sirat-i Firoz Shahi*, which may well have been written or dictated by the sultan himself. It sets out in great detail and with a series of remarkable accompanying illustrations, the engineering skills employed in removing the stone column from its original location, transporting it to the banks of the Jumna, floating it down to Delhi and re-erecting it within its own special building beside the mosque.

Even more remarkably, the same manuscript contains a poem written by Firoz Shah celebrating his column of gold. 'No bird, neither eagle, nor crane, can fly up to its top,' the sultan declares with characteristic Persian hyperbole. He goes on to wonder how it was built and erected, and how its makers were able 'to paint it all over with gold so as to make the people think it to be the golden dawn?' He ends by asking what precisely the column of gold is, without finding any answers: 'Is it the *Tuba* [the Lote-tree of Paradise] which the angels have planted on the earth, or is it the *Sidya* [the Plum-tree of Paradise] which men have taken to be a mountain?'[5]

Sultan Firoz Shah's death in 1388 precipitated a decade of internecine warfare between his descendants. His eldest son

Fateh Khan briefly won the sultanate and celebrated by founding the city of Fatehabad, or 'Victory city', a short distance
north-west of Hisar. He also removed the upper portion of the
pillar at Hisar containing his father's memorial to the Tughlaq
dynasty and re-erected it at Fatehabad.

Fateh Khan's death was soon followed by the eruption of the
Turco-Mongols under the leadership of Amir Timur of
Khorasan, also known as 'Timur the Lame' (Tamberlaine),
great-grandson of Genghis Khan and founder of the Timurid
dynasty, which gave rise to the Mughals. Timur the Lame
swept through the Punjab looting and burning, pausing briefly
at Hisar to destroy what was left of Firoz Shah's pillar.[6]
According to Shams-i Siraj 'Afif, Timur ordered every horseman in his army to gather two loads of firewood. This was
heaped round the pillar and set on fire. The pillar still stands
beside the mosque at Hisar, its lower section so badly fire-dam-
aged that nothing remains of whatever pre-Muslim inscriptions
it may once have carried.

Having slaughtered one hundred thousand infidel prisoners
who were slowing him down, Timur proceeded to assault and
sack Delhi, acquiring so many new prisoners in the process that
each man in his army came away with fifty to a hundred of
them; men, women and children. 'The pen of destiny had
written down this fate for the people of this city ... for it was
the will of God that this calamity should fall upon the city.'[7]
These are the words of Timur himself, set down in his auto-
biography.

One of the few buildings to survive the sacking was Firoz
Shah's fort and mosque, where Timur came to give thanks to
God and went away full of admiration for the column of gold
and its twin, declaring that 'in all the countries he had

traversed he had never seen any monument comparable to these'. After subduing Meerut and other centres of resistance, Timur ordered his army to begin the journey home 'towards Samarkand, my capital and paradise'.

Two and a half centuries later the trader William Finch was among the first Englishmen to prostrate themselves before the 'Great Mogul', Emperor Jehangir. Like his predecessors, Jehangir was a restless ruler and his court essentially peripatetic, which meant that those who wished the light of the Emperor's countenance to shine upon them had to follow in his train. In doing so Finch got the opportunity to visit the new Delhi being laid out just to the north of the ruins of Firozabad (a city completed by Jehangir's son Shah Jehan and named Shahjehanabad, better known today as Old Delhi). Here Finch and his companions inspected the column of gold, by now known as Firoz Shah's Lat or 'staff', and concluded that its unintelligible lettering was some form of Greek, most likely set there by Alexander the Great to mark his victory over the Indian ruler Poros.

When Emperor Jehangir and his court moved on downriver Finch followed, in due course arriving at the ancient town of Prayag, situated at the confluence of the Ganges and Jumna rivers. The emperor had renamed the town Allahabad and was in the process of converting into a fortress. Within its walls Finch was shown a pillar very similar in height, girth and appearance to Firoz Shah's Lat in Delhi, which he ascribed to the same originator, describing it as 'a piller [*sic*] of stone fiftie cubits above ground so deeply placed within the ground that no end can be found, which by circumstances of the Indians seemeth to have beene placed by Alexander or some other great conqueror'.[8]

In 1670 it was the turn of another Englishman, twenty-six-year-old John Marshall, to record the existence of more monumental stone columns in the northern plains of India. Marshall had come out to India as a factor or trade agent in the employ of the still insignificant British mercantile concern known as the East India Company (EICo). In 1670 he was posted to one of the EICo's more remote 'factories' or trading posts at Singhiya, set on the east bank of the River Gandaki, about fifteen miles upstream of the point where that river joined the Ganges above Patna (a settlement since washed away in one of the Gandaki's frequent changes of course). His surviving papers show that at Singhiya the isolated Marshall began to study Hindu religion and philosophy, leading on to a wider enquiry into Indian astrology, medicine and science. This qualifies him as the first of that maligned species, the Orientalists.

Some months after Marshall's arrival at Singhiya he made an expedition into the hinterland, in response to a report of a curious standing pillar. His journal records that he set out northwards from Singhiya on 29 July and walked twelve miles to the village of Bannia, where he spent the night under a large tree. The next day he walked another six miles to reach his objective: a place known locally as Brinkalattee, which he understood to mean the 'Staff of Brim' – more accurately the giant Pandava Bhim. There Marshall was shown 'a Piller of one stone as I conceive. On the top of this piller or Lattee is placed a Tyger ingraven, the neatliest that I have scene [*sic*] in India. His face looks North North East, ½ Easterly.' He learned that the giant Bhim had long ago lived here and that 'this pillar was his Stick to walk with, which is said to be twise [*sic*] as much under as above ground. Oft [when] man came into the world Brin did see them [as] so very little creatures and yet so cunning and so far exceeding him that hee was much troubled thereat, and went into the Tartarian Mountains and there betwixt two great mountains lay down and dyed and was covered with snow.'⁹

The 'Tyger ingraven' capital and stone column seen by John Marshall in North Bihar, as drawn by an unidentified artist – probably Thomas Law – in about 1783. The column is today known as the Lauriya-Nandangarh pillar. (Royal Asiatic Society)

Here was another of the great stone columns ascribed by Hindus to the giant Pandava Bhim. However, Marshall's account of the giant Bhim going towards the Himalayas and dying between two mountains is a distant echo of the circumstances surrounding the death of Sakyamuni Buddha who fell fatally ill as he made his way homewards towards Kapilavastu and died lying between two great sal trees.

In November 1676 Marshall was moved to a more senior post in Balasore in Bengal, where he died eight months later of a raging distemper that killed most of his colleagues and many towns-people. In his will Marshall left his manuscripts concerning India to two friends at Christ's College, Cambridge (now part of the Harleian Collection at the British Museum). These papers included the first English translation of the *Bhagavad Gita* and had Marshall or his friends gone into print the beginnings of Indian studies would have been advanced by the better part of a century.

John Marshall's brief sojourn in Bihar occured at a time when Emperor Jehangir's puritanical grandson Aurangzeb was proving himself the most zealous of his line in the suppression of idola-try. As the centre of Shaivite Hinduism, the city of Varanasi was an obvious target for Aurangzeb's iconoclasm. Already partially cleansed by Muslim rulers on four previous occasions,[10] Varanasi was now subjected to a fifth round of demolitions on Aurangzeb's orders. Hundreds of shrines were demolished, a number of tem-ples replaced by mosques and the city renamed Muhammadabad.

One of these temples was the ancient shrine of Bhairava ('The Terrible One', a wrathful manifestation of Shiva, the pre-siding deity of Varanasi), sited on the northern outskirts of the city and perhaps the most revered Shaivite temple in the city on account of the mighty stone lingam in its courtyard, worshipped for centuries as the *Lath Bhairava*, or 'Staff of Shiva'. Aurangzeb had most of the temple demolished to make way for a mosque – and yet, unaccountably, left the great stone column standing, so prominently so that the new mosque became known as the *Lath Imambarah*, or 'Mosque of the Staff'.

When John Marshall's contemporary, the Frenchman Jean
Baptiste Tavernier, visited Varanasi in the mid-1670s, he found
the stone column set on a raised platform beside a new-built
mosque. Since there were several Muslim tombs in the vicinity, Tavernier assumed the pillar to be some form of obelisk:

> In the middle of this platform you see a column of 32 to 35
> feet in height, all of a piece, and which three men could with
> difficulty embrace. It is of sandstone, so hard that I could not
> scratch it with my knife. All sides of this tomb are covered
> with figures of animals cut in relief on the stone, and it has
> been higher above the ground than now appears, several of
> the old men who guard these tombs having assured me that
> since fifty years it has subsided more than 30 feet. They add
> that it is the tomb of one of the kings of Bhutan, who was
> interred there after he had left his country to conquer this
> kingdom, from which he was subsequently driven by the
> descendants of Tamerlane.[11]

The clue misunderstood by Tavernier lies in the word Bhutan,
which contains the Sanskrit root word *budh*, meaning 'awaken',
as in *Buddha*, the 'Awaked One'.

Emperor Aurangzeb died in 1707 unlamented by the bulk of
his subjects, and with his death the authority of the Mughals
began to crumble, a process assisted by the power struggles
between his sons, grandsons and great-grandsons. At some
point in the next two decades the explosion of a powder mag-
azine blew the pillar at Firoz Shah's hunting lodge north of
Delhi into fragments (painstakingly reassembled two and a half
centuries later, with one neat slice missing – now in the British
Museum in London). As the Mughals declined, other powers

moved in to fill the political vacuum: most notably, the Sikhs from the Punjab, the Marathas from the Deccan and the EICo from Bengal.

Under the patronage of the Maratha warlords and the saintly widow of one of their number, Rani Ahilya Bai Holkar of Indore, the city of Muhammadabad very soon reverted to Varanasi and underwent a spectacular rebirth. The colourful waterfront of temples and bathing ghats that tourists admire today owes its existence almost entirely to the plunder secured by the Maratha chiefs of the eighteenth century – and to their religiosity.

It was at this time, as Varanasi's Hindu majority set out to reclaim their city's Shaivite identity, that the stone pillar seen by Jean Baptiste Tavernier in the courtyard of the Mosque of the Staff became the focus of an increasingly popular fertility cult and the scene of an annual festival known as the 'marriage of Shiva's lat'. It led, almost inevitably, to growing friction between the city's Hindu and Muslim communities, which came to a head in the autumn of 1805 during the Muslim celebration of the Moharam festival. 'It was under such a state of excited zeal', wrote a local historian, 'that a congregation at the *Lat'h Imambareh*, in 1805, was urged by some fanatic preacher to overthrow and defile the pillar and images of Hindu worship at the place.'[12] The mob pulled the Staff of Shiva to the ground and broke it into several pieces.

The enraged Hindus responded by setting fire to the great mosque erected by Aurangzeb beside the river, after which rioting engulfed much of the city. Varanasi's young acting magistrate, William Bird, employed his police and two companies of sepoys as best he could but was unable to prevent mobs of Hindus from attacking the Muslim quarters of the town. In the

words of the *Benares Gazetteer*, 'The whole of Benares was in
the most terrible confusion, as several bazaars were in flames
and all of the Julaha quarter was a scene of plunder and violence. Order was not restored by the troops until some fifty
mosques had been destroyed and several hundred persons had
lost their lives.'[13]

When the Reverend Reginald Heber, Bishop of Calcutta,
visited Varanasi in 1823 he found the Staff of Shiva 'defaced
and prostrate',[14] and guarded by Brahmin sepoys. At some time
during the following three decades what was probably the
largest surviving section of the broken column (or possibly its
stump still *in situ*), measuring some seven or eight feet in
height, was encased in a copper sheath and placed under
armed guard. So it remains to this day, still unexamined by
scholars, for tensions between the two communities in Varanasi
remain as bad as ever.

In the year of Aurangzeb's death, 1707, a Capuchin mission
reached Lhasa on the Tibetan Plateau, despatched from
Portuguese Goa in the belief that deviant Christians were to be
found north of the Himalayas. Eight years later the disappointed Capuchins were ejected from Tibet and settled in
Nepal's Kathmandu Valley, where they maintained a mission
for over half a century until again expelled. This second expulsion came by order of the new ruler of Nepal, the Hindu
Prithvi Narayan Shah of Gorkha, who was not one for religious
tolerance and initiated a programme of caste discrimination
that saw his country's non-Hindu communities reduced to the
status of outcastes or slaves.

The Capuchins and their few converts found refuge near the
town of Bettiah in the plains of Bihar, about 150 miles north-east

of Varanasi. This now became the centre of the Tibet-Hindustan Mission of the Congregation of the Propagation of the Faith in Rome under the leadership of the scholarly Italian Father Marco della Tomba.

In about 1769 Father della Tomba reported the existence of two stone columns in the vicinity, both carrying inscriptions and both topped by carved stone lions (one being the Tirhut 'tyger' seen by Marshall a century earlier):

They stand 27 cubits high up to the capital, on the top of which there is a lion, which looks very natural. The circumference of the column is 7 cubits, as I myself measured. The column seems to consist of a single stone. I struck it several times with a hatchet, and fired some bullets without being able to make out that it was otherwise. These two columns are as if covered with a certain writing, which I traced on paper and then sent to the Hindu Academy of Benares and to some Tibetan scholars; but not one of them could read or understand a word of them ... These characters appear to be some ancient Greek.[15]

This same period saw the doughty Jesuit priest Joseph Tiefenthaler criss-crossing the Gangetic plains, nominally as a propagator of the Gospel but with scholarship as his prime motivation. After the Pope's suppression of the Jesuit order in the mid-1750s, Tiefenthaler had stayed on in India to devote himself to the study of India's languages, religions and natural sciences. He was most probably the first European to learn Sanskrit, the hermetic language in which all the sacred texts of the Hindus were written – hermetic in that it was considered the language of the gods and thus accessible only to Brahmins by virtue of their god-ordained status as intermediaries between the gods and men.

In 1756 Tiefenthaler made the first known copy of what he believed to be the oldest inscription on Firoz Shah's golden pillar, afterwards despatched with other papers to his fellow pioneer Indologist the Frenchman Abraham Anquetil du Perron. However, du Perron was then in the process of being expelled from India along with all his countrymen following the EICo's capture of Pondicherry. As a result it was not until long after Tiefenthaler's death that his scholarship became known through the publication of du Perron's three-volume *Recherches historiques et géographie sur l'Inde,* published in 1786.[16]

Tiefenthaler and du Perron together brought the first seeds of the European Enlightenment to the shores of India. But with France's imperial ambitions baulked by growing British naval superiority on the high seas, it fell to the latter power to continue that process – in the person of a Welsh polymath. It was William 'Oriental' Jones, jurist, scholar and philologist extraordinaire who now laid the ground for those same seeds to germinate.

The son of a well-known mathematician, William Jones was a child prodigy gifted with a quite breathtaking capacity for learning languages. By the time he graduated from Oxford in 1768, Jones was fluent in thirteen languages and familiar with another twenty-eight. Like his father before him, he turned to the aristocracy for patronage, becoming tutor to the young son and heir of Lord Spencer. Having taught himself Arabic and Persian, he embarked on a number of translations that earned him the sobriquet of 'Persian' or 'Oriental' Jones and led him to declare that the works of Persian poets such as Firdusi were as worthy of admiration as the works of Homer.

A constant shortage of funds led Jones to enrol at the Middle

Temple but failed to stifle his ambition. By the time he was called to the Bar in 1774, 'Harmonious' Jones – to give him his third popular title – had become one of the leading lights of the Royal Society and of Samuel Johnson's club at the Turk's Head in Soho, to say nothing of his entanglement in Whig politics. His ambition suffered a severe setback when he failed to secure the professorship of Arabic at Oxford, which he believed to be rightly his. It forced him to look further afield, leading to his acceptance of a seat on the bench of the newly established Supreme Court in Bengal.

From the European perspective India was considered at this time to be little more than a charnel house, a fatal shore from which few returned. Furthermore, Jones shared the Whig view that the EICo was a corrupt and despotic institution best dismantled. What helped William Jones overcome his scruples was the salary. The newly created post of supreme court judge in Bengal paid £6000 a year (worth some £200,000 today), which by Jones's calculation meant that even if he lived very comfortably in India he could return home in ten years' time 'still a young man with thirty thousand pounds in my pocket'.[17] The post also made it possible for Jones to marry the clergyman's daughter he had been courting since his days as an undergraduate – and it came with a knighthood.

But what also attracted Jones was that India presented possibilities all but undreamed of in England. Captain Cook's three voyages to the Pacific had shown what could be accomplished and the companion of Cook's first voyage, Joseph Banks, had demonstrated how a system of scientific endeavour on the grand scale might be set up – provided there was patronage, sufficient men of like mind and someone capable of directing that enquiry at the centre.

Sir William Jones shortly before his untimely death in 1794. An engraving from a drawing by the Calcutta artist Arthur Devis.

So it came about that in September 1783 Sir William Jones stepped ashore at Calcutta as the very embodiment of the European Enlightenment. He was aged thirty-six, newly married, newly knighted and carried two lists in his coat pocket. The first set out sixteen 'Objects of Enquiry during my Residence in India', while the second concentrated on how those objectives might be achieved: by the setting up in India of a learned body modelled on the Royal Society, its brief to enquire into man and nature in general and Asia in particular, including the investigation of 'the annals, and even traditions, of those nations, who from time to time have peopled or desolated it', so as to 'bring to light their various forms of government, with their institutions, civil and religious'.[18]

A new chapter in India's history had begun. The light of reason would now be brought to bear on each of Jones's sixteen objects of enquiry, leading to a new understanding of Mother India as 'the nurse of sciences, the inventress of delightful and useful arts, the scene of glorious actions, fertile in the productions of human genius'. And included in that new understanding would be the recovery of India's pre-Muslim history, its long-forgotten past.

3
Objects of Enquiry

A Brahmin pandit expounding the *Puranas* in a Hindu temple in
Varanasi. A lithograph by James Prinsep from his drawing made
in the 1820s and published by him in his *Benares Illustrated*.

In 1888 the up-and-coming young journalist Rudyard Kipling visited Calcutta as part of a series of articles on Bengal he was writing for the Allahabad newspaper *The Pioneer*. His preoccupation with death and disease led him to the city's largest Christian cemetery, located at the wrong end of Park Street. 'The tombs are small houses,' he afterwards wrote. 'It is as though we walked down the streets of a town, so tall are they and so closely do they stand – a town shrivelled by fire, and scarred by frost and siege. Men must have been afraid of their friends rising up before the due time that they weighted them with such cruel mounds of masonry.'[1]

Under one of the most monumental of Kipling's 'cruel mounds', in the form of a towering sixty-foot high obelisk (today cleaned and whitewashed thanks to the combined efforts of the Indian National Trust for Art and Cultural Heritage (INTACH) and the British Association for Cemeteries in South Asia (BACSA)), lie the mortal remains of Sir William Jones, 'who feared God, but not death ... who thought none below him but the base and unjust, none above him but the wise and virtuous'. The words were self-penned and give no hint of the extraordinary part their author had played in initiating the recovery of India's history and culture, a work that had been cruelly cut short by his death on 27 April 1794 at the age of forty-seven.

As a senior judge on the bench of Calcutta's Supreme Court, Sir William Jones had exploited his elevated position to the full. It had given easy access to the EICo's Governor General, Warren Hastings, an autocrat who nonetheless held enlightened views on the nature of British rule in India that Jones was happy to embrace. The two men found in each other a kindred spirit and within weeks Hastings and the man today recognised as the 'father of Indian studies' had co-founded the Asiatick

Society (afterwards the Asiatic Society of Bengal, without the archaic 'k'), so creating the machinery by which information of every kind could be gathered, centralised, cross-referenced, examined and interpreted, and the results disseminated through the Society's journal *Asiatick Researches* (afterwards *Asiatic Researches*).

Bengal's reputation as a land of nabobs where younger sons of the English gentry came to bleed the locals dry had been well earned. They were there to 'shake the pagoda tree' (of its gold 'pagoda' coins). They were happy to embrace the local women but otherwise had little time for the native peoples over whom they found themselves in ever increasing authority. Even among those few who saw it as their duty to 'secure the gratitude and affection of the natives', the feeling was that they were dealing with a people crushed by centuries of oriental despotism and shackled by superstition, their minds 'untaught by learning and experience, unstored by science and literature, and uncheered by a warm and benevolent religion'.[2]

And yet, as news of Jones's new enterprise and Hastings's patronage spread, a handful of free-thinkers came forward to offer their support: fellow Orientalists who hitherto had followed their pursuits alone and often to the scorn of colleagues. Under the guidance of Sir William Jones as the Society's first President, this small band of individuals applied themselves to the novel discipline of sharing the fruits of their researches, initially in the form of papers read at monthly meetings held in the Grand Jury Room of Calcutta's Supreme Court building. By these means a long-lost India began to reveal itself, albeit slowly and by many small stages.

The Supreme Court sat for eight months in the year, which allowed Sir William Jones four months away from the bench.

He and his wife spent the first of these vacations in Benares but subsequently made a country home for themselves in a thatch bungalow in the district of Krishnagur, north of Calcutta. 'Here,' as a colleague of Jones later put it, 'away from the strife of plaintiff and defendant, his mind went forth unrestrained on the pursuits that were dearest to it. The earnest investigation of Sanscrit lore, the study of botany and the conduct of literary and scientific correspondence never left him a vacant hour.'3

At Krishnagur William and Anna Maria Jones embraced all things Indian with an openness of heart that dismayed as many of Jones's colleagues on the bench of the High Court as it delighted the pandits and other Indians with whom Jones came into contact outside the courts. His closest friend in India, Sir John Shore, afterwards remarked on how unusual this was: 'His intercourse with the Indian natives of character and abilities was extensive: he liberally rewarded those by whom he was served and assisted, and his dependants were treated by him as friends.'4

The Joneses' romance with India began with its music, the sophistication of which quite escaped their friends, but it soon widened to embrace Hindu and Muslim Sufi devotional literature, chiefly as revealed through Persian translations. 'I am', wrote William in an early letter to his fellow enthusiast Warren Hastings, now retired to England, 'in love with the *Gopia* [the maiden cowherds with whom the mischievous god Krishna dallies], charmed with *Crishen* [Krishna], an enthusiastic admirer of Ram [hero of the *Ramayana*] and a devout admirer of *Brimha-bishen-mehais* [the Hindu trinity of Brahma, Vishnu and Shiva]; not to mention that Judishteir, Arjen, Corno, and the other warriors of the *M'gab'harat* [*Mahabharat*] appear greater

in my eyes than Agamemnon, Ajax, and Achilles appeared
when I first read the Iliad.'[5]

That admiration led on to a desire to read these texts in the
original, which became a reality when Sir William Jones
secured the services of Pandit Ramlochan, who was himself
highly unusual in that he was not a Brahmin but an agricul-
turalist of the Vaisya caste who had learned Sanskrit in the
course of studying medicine. Within months Jones was declaring himself to be a delighted trespasser upon 'the untrodden
paths of Hindu learning'.

Jones's timing could not have been better. Five years earlier
two of his old acquaintances from Oxford, Nathaniel Halhed
and Charles Wilkins, had together produced the first Bengali
typeface, which made possible the publication of Halhed's
Grammar of the Bengali Language. Hitherto they had faced a
seemingly impenetrable wall of hostility from the Brahmin
community whenever they had enquired into the sacred texts
of the Hindus. It was not simply that Sanskrit was too sacred
to be read or spoken by non-Brahmins. Centuries of subjugation to Mughal emperors and their predecessors had turned the
Brahmins in on themselves. Their monopoly of Sanskrit was
one of the few remaining vestiges of their authority and they
had no intention of making it available to the latest representatives of the Mughal Emperors of Delhi – for at this stage the
EICo ruled Bengal in the name of Emperor Shah Alam.

That hostility ended with the appearance of the *Bengali
Grammar* and the setting up of Wilkins's vernacular press. The
more far-sighted pandits in Bengal were aware that Brahmanical learning was in decline and Sanskrit itself in danger of
becoming the language of ritual and nothing more. The same
Brahmins who had turned Wilkins away now returned with

offers to teach him Sanskrit, resulting in the publication within a year of the first English–Sanskrit Grammar. Under guidance, Wilkins had then set to work translating the Hindu scriptures, beginning with *Bhagavad Gita* – a work that was still far from complete when ill-health forced Wilkins to retire to England.

It was Jones who now stepped in to take Wilkins's place, his prodigious intellect enabling him to make such rapid progress that he was soon pronouncing Sanskrit to be precisely what the Brahmins claimed for it. And not only was it the language of the gods, it was a language with a close affinity to Latin and Greek – too close to have been produced by accident: 'So strong, indeed, that no philologist could examine all three without believing them to have sprung from some common source.'[6] Assisted by Pandit Ramlochan and a second Brahmin, Pandit Radhacant, who had previously worked for Warren Hastings, Jones went on to bring into the public arena the first works of a vast corpus of sacred and semi-sacred literature hitherto unknown to the Western world.

It was also part of Jones's self-imposed brief to shed light on India's unknown pre-Muslim history. The first obstacle he encountered was the absence of historical records as understood by European and Muslim historians. He was familiar with the histories of Muslim India written by Al-Biruni and the sixteenth-century Persian historian Firishta, but there seemed to be nothing comparable from the other side of the religious divide. The best that the Brahmans could offer were a collection of some eighteen *puranic*, or 'ancient times', religious texts known collectively as the *Puranas*, which concerned themselves chiefly with creation myths, Hindu cosmography and the activities of deities and quasi-mythical heroes of the Hindu pantheon. However, a number of the

Puranas also included genealogical lists of the various gods, demi-gods and humans who since the beginning of time had ruled over the Indian subcontinent – known in early texts as Jambudwipa or 'Blackberry Island'. From these genealogies Jones assembled what he described as 'a concise account of Indian Chronology'.

The human element of this chronology began with Manu, son of the god Brahma, whose posterity had divided into two branches: the *Suryavanshi*, or 'Children of the Sun', and *Chandravanshi*, or 'Children of the Moon'. 'The lineal male descendants in both these families', wrote Jones, 'are supposed to have reigned in the cities of Ayodhya, or Audh, and Partihara, or Vitora, respectively till the thousandth year of the present age, and the names of all the princes have been diligently collected by Radhacant from several *Puranas*.'

This chronology showed that for centuries successive dynasties of Indian rajas had ruled kingdoms known as *janapadas* or footholds. There were traditionally fifteen such footholds in Blackberry Island, of which one stood out above the rest as being the most powerful and the longest-lasting: Magadha, a region that Jones had no difficulty in identifying as the western province of Bengal known as Bihar and the central Gangetic plains region centred on the city of Patna, today capital of Bihar State. According to the *Puranas*, the kingdom of Magadha had been established by King Brihadratha, whose descendants ruled over Magadha for a thousand years before giving way to the Pradotyas, who had ruled for 137 years before being replaced by the Haryankas. They had been replaced by the Shishungas, ten of whom had ruled until overthrown by the base-born Nandas. The first Nanda was a *Sudra*, lowest of the four *varnas* of the Hindu caste system. By usurping the throne of the Kshatriya king Shishunaga, this Nanda had upset the natural order of kingship by which only Kshatriyas (and very occasionally Brahmans) could rule. However, the *Puranas* were couched as prophesies and they foretold that the Nanda line would be overthrown by a righteous Brahman named Chanakya, who would select and anoint one Chandragupta as the lawful sovereign of Magadha.

The name Nanda was already familiar to Jones from his extensive reading. 'This prince,' he wrote, 'of whom frequent mention is made in the Sanscrit books, is said to have been murdered, after a reign of a hundred years, by a very learned and ingenious, but passionate and vindictive Brahman, whose name was Chanacya, and who raised to the throne a man of the Maurya race, named Chandragupta.'

King Chandragupta had founded the dynasty of the Mauryas, consisting of ten monarchs who together ruled Magadha for 137 years. Chandragupta had ruled for twenty-four years and his son – listed variously as Varisara, Vindusara or Bindusara (but hereafter referred to as Bindusara) – for twenty-five years. The third of these Mauryan kings was Chandragupta's grandson Ashoka – sometimes referred to as *Ashokavardhana*, 'Ashoka the Great', who had ruled for thirty-six or thirty-seven years. As far as Brahmanical history was concerned, this Ashoka was unimportant. The compilers of the *Puranas* offered no explanation as to why he should have been named 'great', nor had they anything to say about any Mauryan ruler listed after Ashoka. Indeed (as the following genealogical tables show), the compilers of the *Puranas* seemed unable to agree as to who exactly had followed Ashoka to the throne of Magadha, only finding general agreement when it came to the last two rulers of the Mauryan dynasty:

Vishnu Purana	Matsya Purana	Vayu and Brahmananda Puranas
Chandragupta	Chandragupta	Chandragupta
Bindusara	Bindusara	Bindusara
Ashoka	Ashoka	Ashoka
Suyashas		Kunala
Dasharatha	Dasharatha	Bandhupalita
Samgata	Samprati	Indrapalita
Salishuka		Devavarma
Somavarman		
Shatadhanvan	Shatadhanvan	Shatadhanas
Brihadratha	Brihadratha	Brihadratha

All the genealogical tables agreed that Mauryan dynastic rule had ended with the assassination of the tenth and last of their line, Brihadratha, who had been killed in a parade-ground coup staged by his commander-in-chief, a Brahman named Pushyamitra Shunga. The latter had then established the Brahman Shunga dynasty, consisting of ten rulers who ruled altogether for 112 years until the last was assassinated by his minister Vasudeva Canna. The Canna dynasty apparently ruled for 345 years before being replaced by the Andhras, who lasted for 452 years, ending with the death of King Chandrabija – at which point, Sir William Jones noted, 'we hear no more of Magadha as an independent kingdom'. Taking these statistics at their face value Jones computed that the Mauryan dynasty had ruled Magadha from 1492 to 1365 years before the birth of Christ.

Greatly encouraged by his discovery of the 'common source' of Sanskrit and the European languages, Jones now began to look for further evidence of shared origins in these genealogical charts. For all his learning, Jones had been brought up to regard the Old Testament, with its stories of Adam, Noah and the Flood, as gospel truth. Convincing himself that India's past was bound up with ancient Egypt and the Old Testament, he contrived a comparative chronology of Indian and biblical history in which the Indian Manu corresponded to the biblical Adam. This error led Jones and others into believing that Sakyamuni Buddha was an African conqueror and it would bedevil Indian studies for some decades.

Reports of a religion in the Indies involving a warrior, prophet or philosopher named variously as Boudha, Bodh, Sakyamuni, Gautama, Godama or Fo had circulated in Europe since the return of Marco Polo. Yet in India itself there was no evidence to suggest that the worship of this deity – whose popular name Jones finally settled on as 'Buddha' – had anything to do with that country. The Hindu texts did indeed make occasional reference to one such Buddha but there were certainly no Buddhists in India and no Buddhist literature. Nor, it appeared, was there any known Buddhist monument.

This state of ignorance soon began to change as the Asiatic Society gained more members, many of them stationed up-country: amateur antiquarians such as Thomas Law and John Harrington, who had both joined the EICo as teenage writers in the 1770s and went on to became part of the Company's first generation of civil servants. Both had been posted to the province of Bihar to learn the ropes. In 1783 Law was made Collector of Gaya District in Bihar, where he endeared himself to the local Hindus by abolishing the pilgrim tax. He also drew up the first fixed settlement scheme upon which landowners were taxed, afterwards introduced as part of the land reforms known as the Cornwallis Permanent Settlement of 1789.[8]

At one of the first meetings of the Asiatic Society Thomas Law presented a paper entitled 'A Short Account of Two Pillars to the North of Patna',[9] illustrated with his own drawings. These were the same two pillars described by the Capuchin Father della Tomba, and Law now located one at Nandangarh, some seventeen miles to the north of the town of Bettiah, and the other at Araraj, approximately the same distance south of Bettiah. The first still had its capital, in the form of a seated lion (see illustration, p. 18), while the second was now bare. Both columns carried inscriptions written in characters that Law had never seen before. His paper led Jones to call for accurate copies of these Lat or pillar inscriptions to be made.

John Harrington's contribution concerned caves rather than pillars. He had explored two groups of hills lying about midway between Patna and Gaya in South Bihar. At the first, the Barabar Hills, he had been shown a number of rock-cut caves known locally as the 'seven houses', all with arched roofs, their polished surfaces covered in soot, their appearance being 'very dismal even when lighted'.[10] The entrance to one of the caves had an ornately carved doorway 'very curiously wrought with elephants and other ornaments, of which I hope in a short time to present a drawing to the Society'.

What Harrington overlooked at the Barabar Hills were a number of inscriptions cut into the rock beside the cave entrances. He did better when he moved on to the Nagarjuni Hills nearby, where he spotted two such inscriptions, 'which my Moonshee [*munshi*, language teacher and interpreter] took off in the course of three days, with much trouble and sufficient accuracy'. The first inscription was in medieval Devanagri, which the interpreter had no trouble in reading. The second

(Above) A party of Europeans on the Gaya–Patna road, with the Barabar and Nagarjuni Hills in the background. A pen and ink drawing by Sir Charles D'Oyly, dated 1825. (APAC, British Library) (Below) The doorway of the rock-cut cave that became known as the Lomas Rishi Cave, or 'Cave of the Long-haired Saint'. This early photograph was taken by the archaeologist Joseph Beglar in 1872–3. (APAC, British Library)

was 'unfortunately of a different character, and remains still unintelligible'. Harrington's report excited little interest.[11] It was the monumental inscribed stone columns that had caught the imagination of Jones and his fellow antiquarians – and the curious script carved thereon.

Jones's call for rubbings of the pillar inscriptions had been heard by the Swiss mercenary Colonel Antoine Polier, who had taken service with the Mughal Emperor in Delhi only to find his employer, the ill-starred Shah Alam II, so assailed by Marathas, Sikhs and Afghan Rohillas as to leave him 'tossed about, like a child's toy, from one usurper to another – a tool during their prosperity, a scapegoat in adversity'.[12] Having seen the writing on the wall, Polier had booked a passage to Europe and was in the process of liquidating his assets and bidding farewell to his many local wives. However, before abandoning his begums and his employer to their fate – Shah Alam was blinded at the hands of the insane Afghan chief Ghulam Qadir and his Red Fort sacked – Polier took a rubbing of the inscriptions on Firoz Shah's Lat and sent it to Sir William Jones in Calcutta.[13]

Jones's excitement at having the rubbing in his hands turned to disappointment and frustration when he found himself quite unable to decipher what was clearly the oldest of the three sets of inscriptions cut into Firoz Shah's Lat. 'The Nagari inscriptions are easy & modern,' Jones declared in a letter to a friend, 'but all the old ones on the staff of Firuz-Shah drive me to despair.'[14]

This unreadable inscription was written in an alphabet made up of some thirty or so clearly defined characters that at first glance could be mistaken for Greek but patently were not. Jones's Brahmin pandits who examined the script declared it to be *Brahmi lipi*, or 'writing of the god Brahma' – a suitably romantic appellation that failed to catch on among the Europeans until well into the next century.

What Jones was able to establish was that the alphabet used on Firoz Shah's Lat was the same as that found by Harrington at the Nagarjuni cave and on another set of rubbings sent to the Asiatic Society by a senior civil servant from western India. These had been taken from the walls of a number of man-made cave temples at Ellora, in the mountains inland from Bombay.[15]

For no good reason, Jones now concluded that all three sets of inscriptions must in some way be associated with a conqueror or law-giver from Ethiopia: 'I believe them to be Ethiopian, and to have been imported about a thousand years before Christ by the Bauddhas or priests and soldiers of the conqueror Sisac, whom the Hindus call the Lion of Sacya.' This same Sisac or Sakya had, he supposed, travelled to India from Ethiopia 'about a thousand years before Christ', his title of Buddha, indicating an enlightened person, suggesting that he was 'rather a benefactor than a destroyer of his species'.[16]

What Jones also discovered was that his Brahmin pandits held strong views about this same Sakya or Buddha, declaring him to be not only a heretical leader of a false sect but also the ninth *avatar* or incarnation of the god Vishnu. This mirrored exactly what the Arab historian Abu al-Fazl had written in his *Ain-i-Akbari*, where he had remarked, 'The Brahmans called Boodh the ninth Avatar, but assert that the religion which is ascribed to him is false.'

This paradox greatly puzzled Jones: 'He [Buddha] seems to have been a follower of doctrines contained in the *Vedas*; and though his good nature led him to censure these ancient books,

because they enjoined sacrifices of cattle, yet he is admitted as
the ninth Avatar, even by the Brahmens of Casi [Kashi, the
ancient sobriquet for Varanasi].'[17] His solution was to propose
that there had been two Buddhas: the first a revolutionary who
'attempted to overturn the system of the Brahmans, and was
the cause of their persecution of the Baudhas'; the second a
Buddha who came later, 'assuming the name and character of
the first'.

Jones's tentative thoughts on Buddha and Buddhism
appeared in the first two issues of the *Asiatick Researches*, many
times delayed but finally published in 1789. They provoked a
flood of responses from friends and correspondents: among
them, John Marsden in Sumatra, Captain Mahony in Ceylon,
William Chambers in Madras, Lieutenant Francis Wilford in
Varanasi, Henry Colebrooke in Mirzapur, John Harrington in
Calcutta, and Francis Buchanan also in Bengal. These diverse
correspondents were able to cite ancient Buddhist texts
obtained in countries to the north, east and south of India,
some written in Sanskrit but others in a language known as
Pali, thought to have the same origins as Sanskrit, both apparently derived from a spoken language called Prakrit,
'consisting of provincial dialects, which are less refined, and
have a more imperfect grammar'.[18]

All these foreign texts agreed that Buddhism had originated
in India; specifically, the country of Magadha, 'for above two
thousand years a seat of learning, civilisation and trade', and
'the cradle of the religion of one of the most powerful and
extensive sects of the world'.[19] There was further agreement
that the founder of Buddhism was a historical figure named
Sakyamuni or Gautama Buddha who had lived and died in that
same country of Magadha. And if these sources were correct,

this Buddha's death had occurred not in the eleventh century BCE, as Jones had suggested, but as late as the fifth century BCE. This new evidence also suggested that despite being 'branded as atheists, and persecuted as heretics, by the Brahmans',[20] and despite persecution by various Hindu rulers, the Buddhists had not only flourished in India for many centuries but had continued to survive in some parts of the subcontinent as late as the twelfth century.[21]

At this same time supporting evidence for Buddhism's Indian roots began to emerge from the central Gangetic plain itself, beginning with an inscription found at a ruined temple known locally as Buddha-gaya just south of the town of Gaya in southern Bihar. It recorded a tenth-century donation made to the 'house of Bood-dha', honouring the 'Supreme Being, Bood-dha' who had 'appeared here with a portion of his divine nature'.[22] In Varanasi, too, startling evidence emerged suggesting that this most orthodox of Hindu cities had at one time contended with a rival religion.

Varanasi in the 1780s was in the process of being Anglicised into Benares under the new authority of the EICo. In 1788 the Company appointed as its Resident and superintendent in that city thirty-two-year-old Jonathan Duncan, part of a select band of administrators known as 'Warren Hastings's young men' and one of that minority whose empathy for Indian culture was combined with intellectual curiosity – the twin attributes of the Orientalist. Duncan shared Hastings's view that to interfere with India's ancient laws or its religious views would be an 'unwanted tyranny', while at the same time regarding it as his duty to oppose abuses of what would today be called human rights. These included the custom of female infanticide widely practised by the Rajput class, the most powerful landowners in

and around Benares. By demonstrating to the leading landown-
ers that it contravened the Hindu scriptures, Duncan was able
to convince them to stop the practice. However, the city's more
conservative Brahmin class had also to be won over, which
Duncan achieved by lobbying for a Sanskrit College in
Benares, 'for the preservation and cultivation of the Laws,
Literature and Religion of the Nation at the Centre of their
Faith'.[23]

By such diplomacy Duncan won the support of all sections
of the city. It meant that when in 1794 a green marble urn was
unearthed from some ruins just north of Benares, it was
brought to Duncan and his advice sought. The urn had come
to light when a complex of ruins known as Sarnath was being
excavated for building material.[24] It contained cremated bone
fragments, which was against Hindu custom, leading Duncan
to speculate that the remains must have belonged to 'one of
the worshippers of Buddha, a set of Indian heretics, who
having no reverence for the Ganges, used to deposit their
remains in the earth, instead of committing them to that river'.

Duncan's surmise was confirmed when in the same ruins 'a
statue or idol of Buddha' was uncovered bearing an inscription
which, when translated by his friends from the Sanskrit
College, proved to be a record of an eleventh-century donation
made by Basantapala, King of Gaur, who with his brother had
come to worship there and had 'ordered all those who did not
follow the Buddhas, to embrace that sect'. Here was clear evidence that Buddhism had flourished under royal patronage in
Upper Bengal well into the eleventh century.

But what was now all too apparent to Sir William Jones and
his fellow savants was that the recovery of India's pre-Muslim
past was being held up by the lack of what Jones called 'the

grand desideratum in oriental literature, Chronology';[25] specifically, some name or event which could be tied to European history – a methodology known today as synchronology. Perhaps sensing that he was getting nowhere with his biblical correlations, Jones turned to the classics of his childhood. He knew his Herodotus, his Strabo, and his Megasthenes; he had read Arrian's *Anabapsis*, Ptolemy's *Geographia* and Quintus Curtius Rufus's *Historiae Alexandri Magni* in the original Greek and Latin – and much else besides. He now subjected these texts to the closest re-examination for any light they could throw on early Indian history, particularly with regard to the Indian kings encountered by Alexander the Great in the course of his invasion of India and by Alexander's Macedonian successors in the east. He was convinced that hidden in these accounts was the key that would provide the missing synchronicity: a name or event common to both the Greeks and the Indians that could be identified and by doing so would unlock the past.

4

Enter Alexander

A silver coin issued by Alexander the Great *c.*324 BCE on his return to Babylon to celebrate his victories in India. On the obverse (left) Nike, goddess of victory, holds a garland of laurels over Alexander, clad in full armour and Persian helmet. This is the only known image of Alexander to survive from his lifetime. On the reverse (right) a horseman engages in battle with two men mounted on an elephant showing the moment in the battle of Hydaspes when the Indian king Poros was wounded by a Greek Cavalryman. (British Museum)

Alexander's invasion of India had begun in the winter of 327–326 BCE. Over the preceding twenty months he had destroyed Darius, the last Achaemenid emperor, and proclaimed himself king of kings in his stead. He had hunted down and executed the rebel Bactrian satrap Bessos, who had killed Darius. Wherever he set foot he had planted new cities named after himself, including Alexandria in Arachiosa (modern Kandahar, more properly Iskandahar), Alexandria under Kaukasos (modern Begram, south of the Hindu Kush), and Alexandria *Eschate*, or 'Furthest' (in modern Tajikistan). But it was not enough, and his thoughts had turned to India – according to the historian Herodotus, the most populous nation in the known world and the richest.

No army had ever been so well educated as that which marched to Alexander's drum, particularly those cavalry officers known as the Companions who commanded the royal wing and the eight other squadrons of horse, and the infantry commanders known as the Shield-Bearers who spearheaded the right phalanx of Alexander's army. Some had been friends of Alexander since childhood and had attended the school at Mieza at which the philosopher Aristotle of Stagira had presided over Alexander's education, tutoring him from the age of thirteen in philosophy, morals, logic, science, mathematics, medicine and art. At Mieza Alexander had learned that what distinguished Greeks and Macedonians from other men was the spirit of enquiry. But his education had been cut short when his father King Philip went away to wage war against Byzantium. From that time onwards Alexander had been too busy either defending or enlarging Philip's kingdom to give much thought to Aristotelian ethics.

There was nothing morally uplifting about Alexander's extraordinary advance into Asia but it did at least accord with

Aristotle's assertion that 'All men by nature desire to know'. No less than sixteen of those who accompanied Alexander are known to have written accounts of that extraordinary journey eastwards. None of these eyewitness accounts have survived in the original but enough material was still accessible in the days of late republican and imperial Rome for Greek and Roman historians to plunder them for their own versions of Alexander's eastern adventure, of which five survived to be read by Sir William Jones, together providing a detailed, if contradictory, account of Alexander's invasion of India.[1]

Having made his decision to press on, Alexander had sent envoys to all the local rulers calling on them to submit to his authority. Those whose territories lay in the plains had had ample time to reflect on Alexander's relentless advance across Asia and responded with alacrity. There were even protestations of the warmest friendship from an Indian king whom the Greeks came to know as Omphis of Taxila, whose territories extended east from the River Indus to the River Hydaspes (the modern Jhelum). So eager was King Omphis to show his good-will that he crossed the Indus to meet Alexander, bringing offerings that included twenty-five war elephants – no mean gift, for these were the battle tanks of the day.

However, the mountain tribes of the Aspasioi and Assakenoi – names probably derived from Sanskrit *aswa*, or 'horse', and *aswa-senis*, 'horse-fighters', thus 'horse-people', and 'horse-warriors' – refused to submit. Alexander thereupon divided his army, sending one force down through the defile known today as the Khyber Pass to the winter capital of Gandhara at Peukelaotis (Pushkalavati, now Charsadda, just above the confluences of Swat River and Kabul River) while he himself led the best of his troops on a more northerly route into the mountains.

The winter campaign that followed was swift and brutal in the Alexandrian manner. The first Aspasian town that lay across Alexander's path failed to surrender and every inhabitant was put to the sword; the second held out only briefly before opening its gates. The Greeks renamed this second city Nysa, because it was overlooked by an ivy- and vine-covered mountain that reminded them of the mountain sacred to their god Dionysus. The historians Arrian, Justin and Curtius all tell the same story, which was that Nysa stood at the foot of a mountain called Meros, the summit of which was then occupied by Alexander's forces for ten days of bacchanalian revelry. With his men thoroughly rested, Alexander continued his mountain campaign, which ended with his assault on the great rock of Aornos, a supposedly impregnable mountain that was said to have defeated Heracles himself. Here the last of the Aspasioi and Assakenoi had gathered to make a final stand.

The name given to this great massif may come from the Greek *aornos*, 'birdless', but more probably derives from the Sanskrit *awara*, meaning 'stockade'; thus the Fortress Mountain. Described by Arrian as 'a mighty mass of rock ... said to have a circuit of about 200 *stadia* [1 stadium = 607 feet] and at its lowest elevation a height of 11 stadia',[2] the Aornos massif overlooked the plains of Gandhara and the River Indus at its most northerly crossing-point. It meant that Aornos had to be taken before Alexander could contemplate going any further east.

Alexander duly set about besieging the Fortress Mountain, building up an earthwork to bridge a ravine on one side while a party led by Ptolemy, one of the commanders of Alexander's Shield-Bearers, set about scaling the cliffs at a second point. By the third day the earthwork was complete and Alexander himself led the main assault, resulting in a rout and a massacre.

'Alexander thus became master of the rock,' declares Arrian. 'He sacrificed upon it and built a fort, giving the command of its garrison to Sisikottos, who long before had in Bactria deserted from the Indians to Bessos, but after Alexander had conquered the Bactrian land served in his army, and showed himself a man worthy of confidence.'[3]

The Indian deserter deputed to govern Aornos 'Greekified' by Arrian as Sisikottos is Romanised by Curtius into Sisocostus. The two are clearly one and the same, for the Roman historian ends his account of the taking of Aornos in much the same way as the Greek: 'Upon the rock the king erected altars dedicated to Minerva and Victory. To the guides who had shown the way ... he honourably paid the stipulated recompense ... The defence of the rock and the country surrounding was entrusted to Sisocostus.'[4]

All the surviving accounts record that Indian mercenaries were employed by the Aspasioi, Assakenoi and other mountain peoples and showed no scruples in switching sides. Alexander made extensive use of their military skills before coming to see them as a threat, at which point he disposed of them so ruthlessly as to lead Plutarch to accuse him of an act of treachery: 'As the Indian mercenary troops, consisting, as they did, of the best soldiers to be found in the country, flocked to the cities which he attacked, he thus incurred serious losses, and accordingly concluded a treaty of peace with them; but afterwards, as they were going away, set upon them while they were on the road, and killed them all.'[5]

Sisikottos/Sisocostus was one such Indian mercenary, initially fighting for the Persian satrap Bessos in Bactria against Alexander before switching sides to soldier for the Greeks, where his qualities of leadership evidently recommended him to Alexander as 'a man worthy of confidence'. The significance of his name was missed by Sir William Jones, as it was by many students of Indo-Greek history who came after Jones.

With Mount Aornos taken and his line of supply secured, Alexander was able to reunite his forces and cross the Indus, where he made the customary sacrificial offerings before marching on to Taxila, a 'great and flourishing city, the greatest indeed of all the cities which lay between the river Indus and the Hydaspes'.[6] Here he and his Macedonians were made welcome by King Omphis and his people, the Indian king showering upon Alexander gifts that included another fifty-six elephants, a number of sheep of extraordinary size, three thousand bulls, quantities of corn, gold crowns and eighty talents of coined silver. So gratified was Alexander by the Taxilan king's generosity that he returned his gifts with thanks and added 'a thousand talents from the spoils which he carried, along with many banqueting vessels of gold and silver, a vast quantity of Persian drapery, and thirty chargers from his own stalls' – an act of statesmanship that, according to Quintus, caused 'the deepest offence to his own friends'.

For all Alexander's ruthlessness, his wine-soaked rages and his growing megalomania, he was still a student of Aristotle, as the historian Arrian conceded in describing how he went out of his way to learn about the several different kinds of religious sects in Indian society, of which the most important were said to be the *Brachmanes* and *Sarmanes*. The former were held in the highest esteem and William Jones had no difficulty in identifying them with the Brahman priestly caste. However, the Sarmanes were less easy to understand (the word being derived from the Sanskrit *shramana*, or 'wandering ascetic', a term covering all sorts from Buddhists and Jains to Hindu *saddhus* and atheistic Ajivikas). Unlike the Brachmanes, these Sarmanes were celibate and the most respected among them lived away from centres of population, dressing in rags and living on leaves and wild fruits.

With Omphis secured as his local ally, Alexander continued his eastward advance to the banks of the River Hydaspes, beyond which lay the great plains ruled over by the Indian king known to the Greeks as Poros. His response to Alexander's order to meet him on the banks of the Hydaspes and make his submission was to say that he would indeed meet him there – but with an army many times mightier than Alexander's. Not in the least discouraged, Alexander outmanoeuvred Poros into concentrating his troops at one point while his own main force crossed the river at another under cover of a rainstorm. This gave him time to draw up his battle line and attack before the Indian king could reorder his troops. As the Greeks advanced, the sight of Poros's war elephants caused some wavering in the ranks. However, the real threat came from Poros's front line: four thousand cavalry and a hundred four-horse chariots, each carrying two archers, two shield-bearers and two charioteers armed with darts. But it soon became clear that the chariots were too heavy to move over the wet ground, whereupon Alexander's cavalry saw their chance and charged, forcing the Indian cavalry back upon the elephants.

Whenever the elephants tried to break out Alexander's cavalry harried them with darts, forcing them to fall back. Their retreat allowed Alexander to bring his infantry phalanxes forward, their shields linked together. First the Indian cavalary and then the infantry were cut to pieces, 'since the Macedonians were now pressing upon them from every side. Upon this all turned to flight.'[7]

Among those who fled was King Poros, wounded in the shoulder. Seeing his elephant leaving the field, Alexander sent King Omphis of Taxila after him as a peace-maker, as Arrian recounts: 'Taxiles [Omphis], who was on horseback, approached as near the elephant which carried Poros as seemed safe, and entreated him to stop his elephant and listen to the message he brought from Alexander. But Poros, on finding that the speaker was his old enemy Taxiles, turned round and prepared to smite him with his javelin.' Despite this rebuff, Alexander continued to send one messenger after another to King Poros, 'and last of all Meroes, an Indian, as he had learned that Poros and this Meroes were old friends'.

It was Meroes the Indian who finally won King Poros over and persuaded him to surrender. All the surviving accounts relate how the king's dignity in defeat so moved Alexander that he not only appointed Poros governor of his former kingdom but added to his territory.

Nothing more is heard of the Indian Meroes. However, his name can be read as the genitive 'of Mero', suggesting that he was an Indian mercenary from the mountain region of Meros, the scene of the Greeks' ten-day long bacchanale. And as Meroes the Indian disappears from the battlefield so the Indian mercenary Sisikottos reappears, for as Alexander regrouped after the battle, he received news of a revolt in the mountain country he had only recently subdued. This report came from Sisikottos, the Indian mercenary appointed local administrator of the Mount Aornos country. Alexander's response was to send a military column under one of his best generals, Philippos, to restore order to the province.

The Assakenian revolt failed to weaken Alexander's resolve to continue eastwards until he had reached the furthest sea. But as he prepared to push on across the Punjab he was warned that the entire country beyond the River Hyphasis (the modern Beas) was ruled over by a single all-powerful monarch, named by the Sicilian-Greek historian Diodoros Siculos as Xandrames and by Curtius as Aggrames. He ruled over two peoples, the Gangaridae and the Prasii, who lived on either side of the River Ganges, and he maintained a vast standing army: '20,000 cavalry and 200,000 infantry, besides 2000 four-horsed chariots, and, most formidable of all, a troop of elephants which he said ran up to the number of 3000'.

When Alexander asked Poros for his opinion, Poros declared the information to be correct, adding this all-powerful Indian king was 'a man of quite worthless character, and held in no respect, as he was thought to be the son of a barber'.[8] This barber had become the lover of the queen and had conspired with her to murder the king and seize the throne, after which he had murdered all the royal princes. He had then been suc-ceeded by his son Xandrames.

After his Macedonians refused to cross the Hyphasis, Alexander sulked Achilles-like in his tent for two days before emerging to order twelve altars of squared stone to be erected as a monument of his expedition. He then embarked his army aboard a fleet of ships built by his admiral Nearchos to begin his return journey by way of the Hydaspes and Indus Rivers. 'Designing now to make for the ocean with a thousand ships,' writes Plutarch, 'he left Porus and Taxiles ... in friendly rela-tions with each other, strengthened by a marriage alliance, and ... he confirmed each in his sovereignty.' He also left behind two of his best fighting generals: his old friend Philippos as governor of Gandhara, and Eudemos, senior com-mander of his Shield-Bearers, to support King Omphis of Taxila and, no doubt, to keep an eye on him.

More Indian tribes had to be subdued and more cities sacked before Alexander and his men reached the (Arabian) sea, at which point Alexander made the near fatal decision to march his men through the deserts of Gedrosia (modern Sind), suffering great loss of life, so that it was a thoroughly demoralised army that finally reached the safety of Karmania (modern southeast Persia) in the last months of the year 325 BCE.

Despite the revels with which his men marked their return to Persia, Alexander had few reasons to celebrate. From every quarter came news that the Greek satraps he had left behind as local governors had either abused their authority or had declared themselves independent rulers. But the worst news was that his old friend Philippos, governor of Gandhara, had been killed: 'The satrap of the Indian country', writes Arrian, 'had been plotted against by the mercenaries and treacherously murdered.' Alexander then wrote to Eudemos and King Omphis of Taxila, directing them to assume the administration of Gandhara. He also wrote to all the governors and military commanders throughout his empire, ordering them to dismiss all the mercenaries in their pay immediately.

One of these mercenaries was the Indian Sisikottos, who had been serving as local administrator of Aornos under Philippos and may well have been involved in his death.

As Alexander made his way westwards through Persia his column was swelled by many of the military contingents he had earlier left behind as garrisons. At Persepolis he revisited the remains of the royal palace and expressed his regret at the destruction he had earlier caused there. He then marched on to Susa, greatest of the three Persian capitals, where in the late spring of 324 BCE he organised a mass wedding in the Persian manner for himself and his Companions in a bid to integrate his Macedonian officers into the Persian nobility. Alexander himself married the eldest daughter of King Darius, Roxane, and his closest companion Hephaeston married a younger sister. Other daughters of the Persian and Medean royal families and related aristocracy were married to no less than eighty of Alexander's Companions. Macedonian soldiers who had married local wives were ordered to come forward to have their marriages registered, and no less than ten thousand did so.

Among those who participated at the mass marriage at Susa was the Macedonian general Seleukos, by every account a strong and courageous man who had fought alongside Alexander in many of his fiercest engagements and, by Arrian's account, had led the Shield-Bearers against King Poros. Seleukos's reward was to be given the hand of Apama, daughter of Spitamenes, the most formidable of the Persian chiefs to have opposed Alexander in the Oxus and Jaxartes campaigns.[9]

Alexander was now no more than thirty-one but already showing marked signs of physical and mental decline, brought about as much by his heavy drinking as the many wounds he had suffered. Within fourteen months he was dead, his death at Babylon in the summer of 323 BCE most likely due to malaria or typhoid. Perdiccas, commander of the Companions' cavalry, then appointed a number of his colleagues to govern various provinces in the name of Alexander's heir, Alexander IV, born to Roxane two months after his father's death. These satrapies became the power bases from which each general launched his own bid for ascendancy. With the assassination of Perdiccas in 321 BCE by his own officers, all semblance of Macedonian unity collapsed, and the forty-year Wars of the *Diadochi*, or 'Successors', began.

Meanwhile, on the eastern border of Alexander's empire Eudemos remained in power in Gandhara, initially sharing control of the Punjab with his ally King Poros before securing Poros's death by treachery.[10] He and his fellow Macedonian Peithon, satrap of the lower Indus region, hung on but with each passing year their authority diminished until finally both generals withdrew with their armies into Persia in order to participate in the ongoing power struggle for Alexander's empire.

The winner in the east was Seleukos, afterwards known as *Nikator*, or 'the Victor'. In 305 BCE, having secured 'the whole region from Phrygia to the Indus', Seleukos the Victor felt strong enough to proclaim himself king of Mesopotamia and Persia. He then set about reclaiming Alexander's territories beyond the Indus, which had long since reverted to Indian rule.

What followed is summarised by the historians Appian, Justin and Plutarch. According to the first: 'He [Seleukos the Victor] crossed the Indus and waged war with Androkottos, king of the Indians, who dwelt on the banks of that stream.'[11] Justin gives a slightly longer account: 'He first took Babylon, and then with his force augmented by victory subjugated the Bactrians. He then passed over into India, which after Alexander's death, as if the yoke of servitude had been shaken off from its neck, had put his prefects to death. Sandrocottus was the leader who achieved their freedom.'[12] Plutarch has more to add on this new Indian ruler: 'Androkottos, who had by that time mounted the throne, presented Seleukos with 500 elephants, and overran and subdued the whole of India with an army of 600,000 . . . *Androkottos himself, when he was but a youth, saw Alexander himself,* and afterwards used to declare that Alexander could easily have taken the country since the king was hated and despised by his subjects for the wickedness of his disposition and the meanness of his origin.'[13] Clearly, Androkottos and Sandrocottus are one and the same.

It is at this juncture, after a lapse of some twenty years, that the Indian mercenary Sisikottos/Sisocostus and the more shadowy Meroes give way to Sandrocottus (Justin), Androkottos (Appian and Plutarch), Sandrakottos (Pliny the Elder), Sandrokottos (Strabo), and – most accurately of all – Sandrocoptus (mentioned by the third-century CE Greek philosopher Athenaios in a fleeting reference)[14] – referred to hereafter by the core name of Sandrokoptos, no longer a mercenary but king of India.

Of this new ruler Sandrokoptos, king of the Ganderites and Praesians, and his relations with the Macedonian Seleukos the Victor, king of Mesopotamia and Persia – no one is more forthcoming than Justin, even if he adds some fanciful details about the latter's rise to power:

He [Sandrokoptos] was born in humble life, but was prompted to aspire to royalty by an omen significant of an august destiny. For when by his insolence he had offended Nandrus, and was ordered by that king to be put to death, he sought safety by a speedy flight. When he lay down overcome with fatigue and had fallen into a deep sleep, a lion of enormous size, approaching the slumberer licked with its tongue the sweat which oozed profusely from his body, and, when he awoke, quietly took its departure. It was this prodigy which first inspired him with the hope of winning the throne, and so, having collected a band of robbers, he instigated the Indians to overthrow the existing government. When he was thereafter preparing to attack Alexander's prefects, a wild elephant of monstrous size approached him, and, kneeling submissively like a tame elephant, received him on to its back and fought vigorously in front of the army. Sandrocottus, having thus won the throne, was reigning over India, when Seleukos was laying the foundations of his future greatness.[15]

Here the Indian king whom Sandrokoptos offended is named not Xandrames or Aggrames (as given by Alexander's historians) but more correctly as Nandrus. By this account – and ignoring the giant lion and elephant, ancient symbols of royalty and strength – Sandrokoptos offends King Nandrus and flees for his life. He then collects allies, themselves outlaws, and subsequently turns the local Indian population against Alexander's local satraps in Gandhara – Alexander's murdered governor Philippos and his successors Eudemos and Peithon – before going on to win the throne of India. All this is achieved before Seleukos the Victor had secured his position as basileus; that is to say, some years before 305 BCE, when Seleukos launched his attack across the Indus.

That attack took Seleukos deep into the Gangetic plains, perhaps even as far as Sandrokoptos's capital, known to the Greeks as Palibothra or Palimbothra. The latter's forces then counter-attacked and drove Seleukos back across the Indus and deep into his own territories. The war was then concluded with a peace treaty, under the terms of which the Macedonian king relinquished all claims to India in return for five hundred war elephants, cemented with a marriage. The Greek historians are unusually taciturn on the finer details of this treaty, and only Pliny admits to the loss of Greek territory: 'The Indians afterwards held a large part of Ariane [a satrapy of the Persian empire encompassing what is now eastern Iran, south-western

Afghanistan and Baluchistan] which they had received from
the Macedonians, entering into marriage relations with him,
and giving in return five hundred elephants, of which
Sandrakottos had nine thousand.'[16]

Coin of Seleukos Nikator as *basileus*; on the reverse some of his
Indian war elephants presented to him by the Indian king
Sandrokoptos together with their Indian *mahouts* or drivers. The
elephants are here shown in battle armour and drawing Nike,
goddess of victory, in a war chariot. (British Museum)

In return for five hundred elephants – which the Indian ruler
Sandrokoptos could well afford to lose – Seleukos surrendered
not only all the lands conquered by Alexander east of the Indus
but also Gandhara and Ariana. This was an unequal treaty,
which Seleukos had to accept because he needed his eastern
border settled so that he could move his troops to take on
Antigonos, his one remaining rival west of Mesopotamia.
The concluding marriage settlement between the two monarchs was also unequal, in that it was the loser who gave his
daughter to the victor rather than the other way round. The

Greeks and Romans are silent on the details, which further suggests that it was Seleukos who gave a daughter in marriage to Sandrokoptos – or to the son and heir of Sandrokoptos.

Basileus Seleukos the Victor and King Sandrokoptos subsequently remained on good terms, but the former was much preoccupied in destroying Antigonos and securing Asia Minor for himself and for his son Antiochos. Yet Seleukos sent embassies to the Indian king's capital at Palimbothra, a practice that would be continued by his son and successor Antiochos – whose sister would by then be either a queen or a princess at the Indian court. The first two of these ambassadors were Megasthenes, who was present at the court of King Sandrokoptos, and Deimachos, who, it will be seen, knew Sandrokoptos's son and successor – identified by Strabo as King Allitrochades and by Athenaios as King Amitrochates.

Only fragments of Megasthenes' *India* survive but the writings of both men provided valuable source material for Arrian, Diodorus, Pliny the Elder and Strabo. The ambassadors observed Indian society at first hand, and what they noted down remained the best account of India available to Western Europe for more than fifteen hundred years. Like all good diplomats they gathered intelligence, taking careful note of the administration and how it worked, the strength and running of its army, the class structure of the country, its economy and natural resources. They also observed how the capital city of Palimbothra was defended, where it was located and how far it was from their own frontier.

According to Strabo, Megasthenes placed the city of Palimbothra at the junction of the River Ganges and another great river, the Erranoboas, 'the Ganges being the largest of rivers, and the Erranoboas being perhaps the third largest ... At the

meeting of this river [Ganges] and the other is situated
Palibothra, a city eighty stadia in length and fifteen in breadth.'
Arrian enlarges on the details of Sandrokoptos's capital: 'The
largest city in India, named Palimbothra, is in the land of the
Prasians, where is the confluence of the river Erannoboas and
the Ganges ... Megasthenes says that on one side where it is
longest this city extends ten miles in length, and that its
breadth is one and three-quarters miles; that the city has been
surrounded with a ditch in breadth 600 feet, and in depth 45
feet; and that its wall has 570 towers and 64 gates.'[17]

By 281 BCE Seleukos the Victor had outlived all his rival successors to become, at seventy-seven years of age, the last of the
Macedonian generals who had fought alongside Alexander. In
that year he set out to take possession of Macedonia and Thrace
for his son and heir Antiochos, only to be outwitted and
murdered by one of the sons of his now deceased friend-
turned-adversary Ptolemy of Egypt. The Successor Wars then
gave way to the Syrian Wars, waged between the Seleucid
Empire and the Ptolemaic Kingdom. With the death of
Seleukos's grandson Antiochos II in 246 BCE the Seleucid
Empire began to fall apart. His successor Seleukos II was
defeated by Ptolemy III and his authority contested by his
younger brother. This allowed Diodotos Soter, satrap of Bactria,
to break away to become the independent ruler of Bactria.

Diodotos Soter and his successors prospered. By about
240 BCE the Graeco-Bactrians had annexed a hefty slice of
Indian territory east of the Indus. Meanwhile, Parthia to the
north had also broken away and under the Parthian chief
Arsaces had formed an alliance with the Bactrians that prevented Seleukos II from reclaiming his great-grandfather's
eastern territories. With the rise of the Parthians the overland

links established by Alexander between the Mediterranean world and India were all but severed.

Here was the sum of the information available to Sir William Jones from the Greek side. To achieve that much desired point of synchronicity he had now to link this to something in the new material emerging from his researches into the Sanskrit record. He knew that the war between Seleukos and Sandrokoptos must have taken place in or very soon after 305 BCE, the year in which the former declared himself ruler of Alexander's Persian empire. 'If we can fix on an Indian prince, contemporary with Seleucus',[18] he declared, they would have that common fixed point in history.

The shoreline at Patna, drawn from the terrace of the Patna Customs House, looking upstream towards Bankipore. A pen-and-ink drawing by the EICo's Opium Agent, Sir Charles D'Oyly, dated 24 October 1824. (APAC, British Library)

One of the many authorities consulted by Sir William Jones before he set sail for India was the geographer, map-maker and pioneer oceanographer Major James Rennell, known today as the 'father of Indian geography'. Rennell had been forced to retire in 1776 when in his early thirties after being attacked and badly injured by a group of Hindu fanatics while surveying on the Bhutan frontier. Most of his thirteen years in India had been spent mapping the EICo's newly acquired territories in Bengal, in the course of which Rennel had built up a unique understanding of its terrain and the forces that had shaped it. When Jones had last seen him in his house just off Portland Place in London he had been in the process of completing what would be the first accurate map of India. Now in 1787, just as Jones began his search for the missing link between India and ancient Greece, he received a letter from Rennell concerning the identity and location of ancient Palimbothra. This was the city about which Megasthenes and his successors had written in such detail, placing it 425 miles downstream from the confluence of the rivers Ganges and Yamuna, 638 miles upstream from the mouth of the Ganges, and, quite specifically, at a confluence 'where the Ganges and the Erranoboas unite'.

Jones and his pandits had searched in vain in their Sanskrit texts for any mention of a city named Palimbothra or the river Erranoboas. What they had found, however, were frequent references to the great city of Pataliputra, for centuries the capital city of Magadha.[19] Then came Rennell's letter, containing his account of how while surveying in and about the modern town of Patna more than a decade earlier, he had learned from the local townspeople that an ancient city named 'Patelpoot-her' had once stood there but had long ago been washed away.

Rennell's subsequent surveys had then revealed that the

EICo's new civil and military lines of Bankipore, which were then in the course of being built alongside the Ganges just upstream of the 'native' city of Patna, were being laid out over an old river bed (a disastrous bit of civic planning that continues to bedevil modern Patna every year when the monsoon rains begin). This former river bed, he realised, must have been the original course of the River Soane (today written Sone), which now entered the Ganges twenty-two miles further upstream. What Rennell had also discovered was that this original course of the River Soane had at one time split just before joining the Ganges, so as to create a long oval-shaped island, the length and breadth of which were large enough to contain the rectangular walls of the city of Palimbothra as described by Megasthenes, as well as providing the city's wide moat. Furthermore, the proportions of the mileages given by Megasthenes fitted, placing the ancient city roughly where the modern town of Patna now stood. Was it possible, Rennel wanted to know, that Patna, Pataliputra and Palimbothra were all one and the same?[20]

Yet Rennel's theory failed on one count – why the Greeks had named the river that flowed into the Ganges at Palimbothra the Erranoboas. The explanation came to Sir William Jones from a quite serendipitous reading of a hitherto unread Sanskrit text. In it the River Soane was described as *Hiranyabahu*, or 'golden armed'. This, he realised, had been 'Greekified' by Megasthenes into *Erranoboas*, or 'the river with a lovely murmur'. Here was literary proof that the rivers Soane and Erranboas were one and the same, and that modern Patna was indeed the site of the Greeks' Palimbothra and ancient India's Pataliputra.

This first discovery led on directly to a second, also found in

two hitherto unread Sanskrit texts. One took the form of a
'very long chain of instructive and agreeable stories' written in
verse by a poet named Somadeva. It told the story of 'the
famed revolution at Pataliputra by the murder of King Nanda,
with his eight sons, and the usurpation of Chandragupta'.[21]
The other text was a verse drama entitled *The Coronation of
Chandra* and it dealt with precisely the same subject, the
Chandra of the title being 'the abbreviated name of that able
and adventurous usurper Chandragupta'. This was in fact the
first half of a much longer verse drama entitled *Mudrarakshasa*,
or 'The Minister's Signet Ring', written by a fifth-century play-
wright named Vishakhadatta.

  The Minister's Signet Ring told the story of two rival ministers,
Rakshasa and Chanakya, both serving King Nanda, ruler of
Magadha. King Nanda has become a tyrant in his old age, lead-
ing Chanakya to accede to the plans of the ambitious prince
Chandragupta to usurp the king. Nanda learns of the plot and
sends Chandragupta into exile, together with his eight friends.
Chandragupta finds sanctuary with the lord of the Himalayas,
Parvateswar, who has allies among the Yavans (Greeks), Sacas
(Scythians), Cambojans (Gandharans) and Ciratas (Kashmiris).
Parvateswar provides Chandragupta and his friends with
money and troops in return for half the empire of King Nanda.
They advance on King Nanda's capital of Pataliputra, which
falls after a brief battle. Chandragupta kills all his half-brothers and he and Parvateswar divide up Nanda's kingdom
between them. Parvateswar is then poisoned by Nanda's
daughter and is succeeded by his son Malayaketu, who with
the advice of Nanda's former minister Rakshasa attacks
Chandragupta at Pataliputra. However, Chandragupta fortifies
the city with his Greek allies, while Chanakya uses his guile to

bring Rakshasa over to Chandragupta's camp. Malayaketu's coalition collapses and Chandragupta goes on to reign over Magadha 'for many years, with justice and equity, and adored by his subjects'.

This was a play about Brahmans putting things right, written by a Brahman for Brahmans. But from Jones's point of view the real value of *The Minister's Signet Ring* was that it was based on a real historical event: the overthrow of the Nanda dynasty by Chandragupta Maurya. He already knew the bare bones of the story from his readings of the *Puranas*, but what the play added was detail; in particular, the fact that the exiled prince Chandragupta had overthrown Nanda after forming an alliance with a king from the mountains and a number of peoples from India's North-West frontier. That was precisely what Sandrokoptos had done. Patently, the Greek Sandrokoptos was the Indian king Chandragupta.

The final confirmation – the clincher – came with the later recognition that the two names Sisikottos and Sandrokoptos were both Greek versions of the same name: Chandragupta. The meaning of Chandragupta was plain to every Sanskrit scholar, being derived from two words: *chandra*, 'moon'; and *gupta*, 'protected'. Sisikottos, less obviously, was a Greek rendering of *Sashigupta*, which also meant 'moon-protected', *sashi* being an alternative Sanskrit word for 'moon'. The young Indian exile and mercenary Sashigupta had simply evolved with age into the older monarch Chandragupta.

Obvious as these connections seem today, it had taken a happy combination of chance and scholarship on the part of Sir William Jones to make the all-important breakthrough. 'I cannot help mentioning a discovery which accident threw in my way,' he announced in a now-famous speech marking the

Asiatic Society's tenth anniversary, delivered in Calcutta on 28 February 1793. He first announced the resolution of the Palibothra-Pataliputra-Patna puzzle, then went on to describe how this had led on to an even greater discovery: 'Chandragupta, who, from a military adventurer, became the sovereign of Upper Hindustan ... was none other than that very Sandrocottus who concluded a treaty with Seleucus Nicator.'[22]

With this breakthrough ancient Indian history secured its first positive dating from which to develop its own internal dateline and a contemporaneous chronology. Alexander the Great had died in Babylon in 323 BCE. By the time Seleukos the Victor had begun his Indian campaign in 305 BCE, Chandragupta Maurya was already firmly established as a great king of northern India. He must therefore have won the Nanda throne after the death of Alexander in 323 BCE and before Alexander's satraps Eudemos and Peithon had been forced to withdraw from the conquered Indian territories in 317 BCE. Jones plumped for the latter date.

According to the Puranic 'Table of the Kings of Magadha, Emperors of India' as published in *Asiatick Researches*,[23] Chandragupta had reigned for twenty-four years. Assuming the length of reigns given in the *Puranas* to be correct, it followed that Chandragupta had ruled from about 317 to 293 BCE. His son Bindusara had ruled for twenty-five years, giving him a period of rule from about 292 to 268 BCE. Bindusara had been followed by his son Ashoka, who had ruled for thirty-six or thirty-seven years, so about 267–230 BCE. The Mauryan dynasty had lasted for a total of 137 years, so approximately 317–180 BCE.

In the two centuries and two decades since these datings were first arrived at, little has changed to question their general validity.

5

Furious Orientalists

A carved slab from Amaravati, showing a highly decorated stupa and its surrounding colonnade and four gateways. This was one of a number of drawings made by Colin Mackenzie's draftsmen following his partial excavation of the site in 1816. (APAC, British Library)

The dramatic progress in Indian studies that had been achieved since the arrival of Sir William Jones in Calcutta came to a sudden halt on 27 April 1795.

Jones had agreed to serve a term of ten years and no more, and that ten years was completed in November 1794 – by which time both William and Anna Maria Jones were seriously unwell. However, Jones was determined to complete his *Digest of Hindu and Muslim Law* on which he had been working inter-mittently for some years and which he considered to be his most important legacy. The idea of helping the 'twenty-four millions of black British subjects in these provinces ... by giving them their own laws', was, he wrote, 'more flattering to me than the thanks of the King'.[1] Anna Maria was too ill to stay on and she sailed with the autumn fleet, but her husband remained in Calcutta, despite suffering severe pain from an inflammation of the liver. On 20 April 1795 he called on Lord Hastings's successor as Governor General, his old friend Sir John Shore, but felt too unwell to stay long. A week later Shore was sent for and reached Jones's mansion on Garden Reach in time to see Jones breathe his last.

No one was better placed to appreciate what Jones's death meant than his friend and disciple Henry Colebrooke: 'His premature death leaves the result of his researches unarranged, and must lose to the world much that was com-mitted to memory ... None of those who are now engaged in Oriental researches are so fully informed ... and I fear that in the progress of their enquiries none will be found to have such comprehensive views.'[2]

These fears proved to be well founded. The death of Sir William Jones left the Asiatic Society like a ship at sea without a navigator. Presidents, secretaries and editors came and went while the Society drifted for want of a guiding hand at the helm. Yet its scattered correspondents continued to gather information and *Asiatick Researches* continued to be published, albeit less frequently. These contributors included a Captain James Hoare, who presented the Society with a book of drawings of the Firoz Shah's Lat in Delhi and the Lat at Allahabad, together with eye-copies of their inscriptions.

This was fortuitous because very soon after Hoare's visit to Allahabad the stone column was 'wantonly taken down by that enemy to Hindustani architecture, Colonel Kyd, at which time the capital of it was destroyed'.[3] The EICo had sent troops to garrison the fort at Allahabad following a devious treaty of alliance drawn up with the Nawab of Oude. Then in 1801 the Nawab had formally ceded Allahabad to the EICo, and its military engineers had moved in under the command of Colonel Kyd to strengthen the fort's defences. In doing so Colonel Kyd and his military engineers had not only uprooted the pillar but had left it broken and in pieces by the roadside.

Captain Hoare was dead of fever before his report could be read to the Asiatic Society but in 1800 his copies were examined by Henry Colebrooke, who was now the only European in Calcutta with a thorough knowledge of Sanskrit. But when presented with Hoare's eye-copies of the Delhi and Allahabad pillar inscriptions Colebrooke had to confess that he could make no more sense of their pseudo-Greek characters than his distinguished predecessor.[4]

By 1800 the EICo had rid itself of the worst of the abuses that had made it a byword for corruption, but these reforms had failed to halt the growing power of the EICo's Indian Army, a power that the ambitious Lord Wellesley, appointed Governor General in 1798, now exploited to the full. It was said of Lord Wellesley that 'he was instructed not to engage, if possible, in hostilities with any native power; and yet he waged deadly war with every one of them. He was desired not to add by conquest a single acre to the Company's territory, and he subdued for them all India from the Himmaleh to Cape Comorin.'[5] After using the French Jacobin threat as a pretext to overthrow Tipu Sultan in Mysore, he took on the Marathas of the northern Deccan in what became a hard-fought struggle for power in central India.

In the course of what became known as the Second Maratha War, Lord Wellesley's equally ambitious younger brother Arthur Wellesley – the future Duke of Wellington – secured a famous victory that helped break the Maratha confederacy. Fought on 23 September 1803, the battle of Assaye was, in the opinion of the victor, the bloodiest and the finest he ever won. Five days later his battered army brought their wounded north to the little village of Ajanta, at the very heartland of India, where a small mud-walled fort was put to use as a field hospital. The army remained in and around Ajanta for a month, and soon rumours were heard in the officers' messes of wonderful things to be seen in the caves less than a mile to the south, where a small river had worn through the rock to create a narrow, winding gorge. Known locally as 'Tiger Valley', this gorge was said to be the haunt of tigers and best avoided, which may be why the caves and their contents had remained undisturbed for centuries. Then the army moved north, a peace treaty was signed and the caves of Ajanta were forgotten.

Unashamed imperialist though he was, Lord Wellesley was also determined that India should have administrators who knew the country they were sent to govern. Behind the backs of the EICo's Court of Directors in London he set up a college in a corner of Calcutta's Fort William where new recruits to the Indian Civil Service (ICS) could study Indian languages and customs. By 1818 no fewer than a hundred Indian linguists were employed at Fort William College, providing, in Wellesley's words, 'the best method of acquiring a knowledge of the manners and customs of the natives of India'. The college had also built up the finest oriental library in the world, amounting to almost twelve thousand printed books and manuscripts. But what Wellesley could never have anticipated was the impact his college had on Bengal itself, where it helped initiate what became known as the Bengal Renaissance, inspiring men such as Ram Mohan Roy to work for reforms that would eventually bring about the end of British rule in India.

Among those closely associated with Fort William College in its early days, as Professor of Sanskrit and Hindu Law, was Henry Colebrooke. In 1801 he was elected President of the Asiatic Society and held that position until he retired from India in 1814. It was during his tenure that the natural heir to Sir William Jones arrived in Calcutta: John Leyden, a shepherd's son from the Scottish borders who had studied for the ministry but had shown more aptitude for languages than for theology. Leyden's friends had found him a position as an EICo surgeon in Madras, where it soon became clear that his talents lay elsewhere. 'I had determined at all events to become a furious Orientalist', he wrote to a friend in Scotland two years after his arrival in India.[6] His opportunity came when he was appointed medical assistant to the Mysore survey, with a brief 'to carry on inquiries concerning the natural history of the country, and the manners and languages, &c., of the natives of Mysore'. In the course of his duties Leyden found time to teach himself thirteen Indian languages in as many months.

Leyden was a curious character. A 'disposition to egotism'[7] was accompanied by uncouth manners, a grating voice and a Scots brogue so broad that only his fellow countrymen could fully understand him. Yet his evident genius won the patronage of Lord Wellesley's successor, Lord Minto, and he was appointed Professor of Hindustani at Fort William College. A second post as Assay Master of the Calcutta Mint provided him with the means to devote himself to his Indian studies. 'I may die in the attempt,' he wrote to a friend, 'but if I die without surpassing Sir William Jones a hundred fold in oriental learning, let never a tear for me profane the eye of a borderer.' These were brave words, coming as they did from a man who suffered one bout of sickness after another.

After completing the first translation into English of the Mughal emperor Babur's autobiographical *Baburnama*, John Leyden was asked by Henry Colebrooke to take on the Secretaryship of the Asiatic Society, since the then incumbent was about to retire. The post was unpaid but it had become the Society's most important position and it would allow Leyden to step into the shoes of his idol, the late Sir William Jones. However, at this point the fate that Leyden had so boldly challenged intervened: he was invited by Lord Minto to accompany him to Java as his interpreter. Arriving at the Dutch settlement of Batavia on 25 August 1811 Leyden lost no time in visiting a library reputed to contain rare Indian manuscripts. He emerged shivering and declared the atmosphere of the room to be enough to give any mortal a fever. Three days later he was dead.

With the best candidate gone Henry Colebrooke now had to cast about for someone to take his place. Leyden's place as Assay Master of the Calcutta Mint had been filled by his deputy, a bright twenty-three-year-old assistant surgeon named Horace

Hayman Wilson. Amiable, gentlemanly and well connected, Dr Wilson was the antithesis of Leyden in almost every respect, having come to India with no more than a solid grounding in medicine, chemistry and assaying. He was an inappropriate choice for the Secretaryship of the Asiatic Society, but on accepting the post Wilson set about proving himself worthy of the task.

Wilson's duties as Secretary led him to Sir William Jones's Sanskrit translations. Wishing to understand his work a little better he cast around for a Sanskrit–English dictionary and found there was none, which led him to conclude that his only course was to write his own dictionary. It took him the best part of a decade, but it led to his gaining such a mastery of the language that he could eventually lay claim to be the leading Sanskritist of the age.

But that pre-eminence came at a price, which was that Dr Horace Hayman Wilson held the post of Secretary of the Asiatic Society for almost twenty-two years. After Colebrooke retired from India in 1814, other Presidents of the Society came and went but none with real authority, so that Wilson's position was never challenged, allowing him free rein to order the Asiatic Society's affairs from its impressive new building at the corner of Chowringhee and Park Street very much as he thought fit. A tireless advocate for Indian rights, Wilson opened the membership of the Asiatic Society to Indians and worked no less zealously to promote his twin interests: Sanskrit and amateur theatricals – this last hobby reinforced by his marriage to the granddaughter of the actress Sarah Siddons.

Among Wilson's many accomplishments was the setting up of a Sanskrit college in Calcutta, established in 1824, to match that in Benares. However, his main claims to fame rest with his *Sanskrit Grammar*, his translations of a number of ancient verse dramas and his work on the eighteen *Puranas*. These last were supposed to have been written by Veda Vyasa, the compiler of the *Vedas*, but Wilson's scholarship showed them to be Brahmanical reinterpretations of early history presented as prophecy, none written earlier than the second century of the Christian era. Drawing on earlier dynastic records, the composers of the *Puranas* had highlighted the deeds of those who had abided by the rules of kingship as laid down in the ancient texts, which decreed that monarchs be drawn from the Kshatriya warrior caste but always under the guidance of Brahman ministers, the Kshatriyas representing the arms of the Hindu body politic, the Brahmans the head. When these caste rules of kingship were broken, divine retribution invariably followed, as in the notorious case of the usurping low-caste Nandas.

Wilson is also remembered for his discovery and translation of a long-forgotten document: the *Rajatarangini*, or 'River of Kings', a chronicle of the kings of Kashmir written in the form of a poem in 118 verses by a twelfth-century Brahman poet named Kalhana. Although mostly devoted to events that had occurred during or just before the poet's lifetime, Kalhana had also drawn on earlier historical sources to write about Kashmir prior to the Muslim invasions. And if these sources were to be believed, the 'heretical faith of Bauddha'[8] had at one time dominated that region.

According to the *River of Kings*, Buddhism had been introduced to Kashmir by a king named Ashoka. This King Ashoka had founded the city of Shrinagar in the Kashmir valley, built numerous temples in the valley and caused Buddhism to be taken to adjoining countries, including Tartary. Yet the author of the *River of Kings* displayed a marked hostility towards Ashoka, in striking contrast to his regard for Ashoka's son and successor Jalauka, a 'prince of great prowess' who after becoming a devout worshipper of Shiva 'overcame the assertions of the Bauddha heresies, and quickly expelled the *Mlecchas* [foreigners without caste] from the country'. However, even King Jalauka had turned out to be a less than model ruler, for towards the end of his reign he had begun to look favourably upon the Buddhists, an attitude his son and successor King Damodara had then enlarged on to such a degree that he had incurred the 'the enmity of the Brahmanical order'.

If this King Ashoka who had brought Buddhism to Kashmir was the same as the Ashoka listed in the dynastic tables of the *Puranas* as the third ruler of the Mauryan dynasty of Magadha, then he was patently a powerful ruler, with enough authority to challenge the established order of Kashmir with his heretical religion. The puzzle, for Wilson, was that neither Jalauka nor Damodara, nor Ashoka's named father and grandfather, were listed in any of the Puranic tables.

It was now clear that the authors of the *River of Kings* and the *Puranas* had a common Brahmanical aversion to Buddhism and Buddhist rulers. Indeed, something of that prejudice seemed to colour their translator's thinking, for Horace Hayman Wilson showed little enthusiasm for areas of scholarship that fell outside his own pet subject: Brahmanical Sanskrit. For all his virtues, he lacked the breadth of vision that had made possible the great advances achieved under Sir William Jones. During his long Secretaryship of the Asiatic Society, the network of correspondents that had been such an important factor in the days of Jones and Colebrooke simply fell apart for lack of a directing force at the centre. New discoveries in the field came and went without acknowledgement, with little attempt made to assess their significance or to relate them to what had gone before.

This was particularly true of Buddhist studies, despite the
fact that many hitherto unknown religious texts were now
coming to light in China, Ceylon and Burma, both canonical
works and collections of Buddhist tales such as the *Divyavadana*, or 'Divine Stories'. All added substance to the earlier
suppositions of Orientalists that Buddhism had Indian origins.
Gautama Sakyamuni Buddha, the Sage of the Sakyas, had now
emerged from the realms of myth and was shown to have lived
in the kingdom of Magadha in the central Gangetic plains,
where after attaining a state of enlightenment at the age of
thirty-five, he had preached for forty-five years, proclaiming his
message of *Dharma*, or 'Moral Law', so as to 'bring salvation to
all living beings'. At the age of eighty-two he had expired – a
state described in Buddhist texts as the *Mahaparinirvana*, or
'Great Final Extinguishing' – an event that had apparently
taken place in the year 544 BCE.[9]

This last dating was the work of a Scots surgeon-cum-
botanist named Francis Buchanan.[10] Few individuals played a
greater part in the rediscovery of Buddhism's Indian roots than
Buchanan and none has been so undeservedly neglected. As
a young surgeon attached to diplomatic missions to Burma
and Nepal, Buchanan had the luck to observe two markedly
different forms of living Buddhism at first hand. He was subsequently employed by the EICo to make surveys of territories
newly acquired by the EICo in Madras. Then in 1809 he began
a second round of surveying, this time in Bihar, newly added as
a province to the EICo's Bengal Presidency.

This survey took Buchanan seven years to complete and
showed Bihar to be strewn with ruins of great antiquity. One of
these was the temple of Buddha-Gaya (today the Mahabodhi
temple at Bodhgaya), eighty miles due south of Patna. Here

Buchanan found what was to all appearances a dilapidated Hindu temple, occupied by a group of Hindu devotees and surrounded by scores of stone images of apparently Hindu deities. The devotees showed particular interest in two objects: a stone platform, which they referred to as the 'Feet of Vishnu', and a pipal tree said to have been planted by the great god Brahma.

The Mahabodhi temple at Bodhgaya, drawn by Sir Charles D'Oyly in December 1824. The artist and his contemporaries had no idea of the significance of the temple or of the pipal tree growing beside it. 'The Temple', wrote D'Oyly, 'is situated on a broad terrace, at the West corner of which is one of the finest Pepul Trees in the country ... It is chiefly here that the Pilgrims offer up their prayers.'[11] (APAC, British Library)

Quite by chance Buchanan met a local man who claimed to be a Buddhist. He had been converted some years earlier by two Burmese pilgrims, agents of the king of Ava, who were travelling through India 'in search of the holy places made remarkable by the actions of Gautama'.[12] These Burmese had told the convert that Gautama was a 'lawgiver' who long ago had resided at Buddha-Gaya under the protection of a king named Dharma Asoka, that the temple had once been 'the centre of religion in India', and that it was still held in the highest veneration by the people of Ava. Indeed, the temple's stone platform and the pipal tree beside it had been revered by Buddhists long before the Hindus had ever claimed them. Furthermore, both platform and tree pre-dated the building of the Buddha-Gaya temple, which itself was the work of the king Dharma Asoka: 'It was agreed by both the parties that came from Ava, that Gautama resided at Buddh Gaya, and that at his desire a temple was built by Dharma Asoka, king of Padaripuk [Pataliputra], who held his court at the place.'

Upon examination, most of the stone images that the Hindu devotees had appropriated proved to be the same as the Buddhist statues Buchanan had seen in Burma and Kathmandu. Patently, the Dharma Asoka temple at Buddha-Gaya had indeed been a Buddhist temple.

As Buchanan continued his survey of South Bihar it became increasingly obvious that the Buddhist convert's claims had some basis in fact: that the area had indeed been a centre of Buddhism. Three days' march north of Bodhgaya was the town of Rajgir, or 'House of Kings', named in the *Puranas* as the home of King Jarasandha, first king of Magadha. But, according to Buchanan's Buddhist informant, Rajgir was equally important to Buddhists as the capital of a monarch named Bimbisara, during whose lifetime Sakyamuni Buddha had taught his creed.

From Rajgir Buchanan led his survey party to the all but deserted town of Bihar and its fort, and then westwards to the little village of Baragang (today Baragaum). Here Buchanan 'observed an immense mass of ruins, through which may be traced the foundations of many brick walls and buildings, among which rise several conical mounds that seem to have been temples'. The convert was unable to offer any explanations but a Jain monk came forward to inform Buchanan that these were the remains of the palace of a Raja Srenik and his ancestors: 'The priest says that at the time of Srenik [Sen], the bulk of the people worshipped the Buddhas, and he disclaims all the images and ruins as belonging to those infidels.'

Buchanan and his men set about surveying the most conspicuous of the ruins, 'an immense range of building running north and south, near the west side of the above mentioned mass, for about 2000 feet, and in general 240 feet wide. It has consisted of nearly regular quadrangular courts, surrounded by buildings ... It has for ages been a quarry for bricks, and the devastation goes rapidly on, but still great quantities remain.'[13] Poking out from the larger cone-shaped mounds were a number of statues, the best-preserved of which Buchanan's draftsmen sketched before the party moved on. What they had unwittingly discovered were the ruins of the Great Monastery of Nalanda, the once-famous Buddhist university burned to the ground by Muhammad Bakhtiyar and his mujahideen 518 years earlier.

In 1814 ill-health forced Buchanan to cut short his survey work. He had been led to believe that the post of Superintendent of the EICo's botanic gardens at Calcutta was his for the asking, but a quarrel with the Governor General over the ownership of his papers led to his resignation. He returned to Scotland empty-handed, leaving his reports, journals and drawings to be filed away in the Writers' Building in Calcutta, where they remained unread for the next twenty-two years.

Much the same fate befell Buchanan's equally industrious contemporary and fellow Scot, the military engineer and mapmaker Colin Mackenzie, who over this same period was making important advances in the field of Jain studies in South India. Mackenzie had joined the EICo as an engineer officer at the unusually late age of twenty-eight and after the overthrow of Tipu Sultan of Mysore in 1799 had spent a decade leading a team of translators, draughtsmen and mapmakers on a survey of the newly won territory of Mysore and the Deccan. Like Jones before him, Mackenzie was quick to acknowledge the debt he owed to the devoted Brahmin pandits and Jains who served as his assistants, and to whom he was no less devoted. 'The connexion then formed with one person, a native and a Bramin,' he afterwards wrote of the start of this relationship, 'was the first step of my introduction into the portal of Indian knowledge; devoid of any knowledge of the languages myself, I owe to the happy genius of this individual the encouragement and the means of obtaining what I so long sought.'[14]

The Brahmin in question was a twenty-year-old named Cavelli Venkata Boria, a scholar 'of the quickest genius' who spent seven years at Mackenzie's side before dying of a fever: 'From the moment the talents of the lamented Boria were applied, a new avenue of Hindoo knowledge was opened, and though I was deprived of him at an early age, his example and his instructions were so happily followed up by his bretheren and disciples, that an establishment was gradually formed, by which the whole of our provinces might be gradually analyzed on the method thus fortuitously begun.' This happy 'establishment', made up of Indians and a number of British draughtsmen and paid for by Mackenzie out of his own pocket, allowed him to indulge in his passion for collecting old manuscripts, coins, drawings, sculptures and anything else that caught his antiquarian eye.

One of the many Jain texts collected by Mackenzie was the *Parisishtaparvan*, the work of a twelfth-century polymath named Acharya Hemachandra that might be freely translated as *The Lives of the Jain Elders*.[15] This threw new light on the founder of the Mauryan dynasty kings of Magadha, in the form of a detailed account of Chandragupta's rise to power with the help of the Brahman Chanakya. In this Jain version of events Chandragupta's mother is from a community that keeps royal peacocks, *mora* in Pali; *mayura* in Sanskrit. Her chieftan husband is killed and she is forced to go into hiding with the infant Chandragupta. One day the boy is seen by a Jain ascetic, who is the Brahman Chanakya in disguise. Chanakya has been humiliated by King Nanda of Magadha and has been forced to flee his wrath, and is now plotting revenge. Seeing Chandragupta lording it over other village boys, he recognises in him all the qualities of leadership required of a monarch, so he kidnaps him and educates him to take on that role. Chanakya and Chandragupta together launch an attack on Pataliputra that fails. Chanakya recognises his mistake in attacking Nanda directly and after retreating to the Himalayan regions he forms a military alliance with the mountain king Parvataka. The allies then embark on a long military campaign taking region by region until finally capturing Pataliputra and forcing King Nanda into exile.

Chandragupta marries one of King Nanda's daughters and Parvataka another, but the latter is accidentally poisoned by his new bride, leaving Chandragupta as the sole ruler and with Chanakya as his chief minister. This event is said to have taken

place 155 years after the death of Sakyamuni Buddha's contemporary Mahavira, the founder of Jainism.

Here was the story of Chandragupta's rise to power very
much as told in the verse drama *The Minister's Signet Ring*,
except that the Jain text had more to say on Chandragupta's
rule. By this account a Jain saint named Bhadrabahu guides
King Chandragupta through a period of lawlessness and a
twelve-year famine. He also leads the king away from heretical teachers – in this context, religions other than Jainism,
since *The Lives of the Jain Elders* and other Jain texts all agree
that the great emperor Chandragupta ended his life as a Jain
devotee, abdicating his throne in order to become a disciple of
Bhadrabahu and following him to South India.[16]

Colin Mackenzie flanked by his Jain and Brahmin pandits. A detail
from an oil painting by Thomas Hickey executed after Mackenzie's
appointment as Surveyor General. (APAC, British Library)

Mackenzie's close contacts with Brahmins and Jains help to explain why he remained all but unaware of India's Buddhist past until very late in his life. However, in February 1797, while making a topographic survey of the country south of the Krishna River (in eastern Andhra Pradesh), Mackenzie received a report of 'antiquities' uncovered by a local raja while collecting building material. He lost no time in diverting to the place he initially named Amarapoor – but better known today as Amaravati. The antiquities had come to light when the raja's workmen had begun to dig into a vast circular mound composed almost entirely of large bricks. They had found the mound to be encircled by a ring of large marble pillars and slabs, the latter carrying carvings in bas-relief that showed quite exceptional artistry and sophistication. Mackenzie left the site empty-handed, but not before he had had an opportunity to view some of the decorated slabs. One in particular, showing a king on an elephant directing an armed assault on a fortified town, was judged by Mackenzie to be the finest carving he had ever seen in India.[17]

His professional duties kept Mackenzie occupied elsewhere for the next seventeen years, but in December 1813 he took some local leave and travelled up the Ganges on what was his own version of the Grand Tour, visiting sites of antiquarian interest and, as always, employing his own draughtsmen to make drawings and watercolours. At Delhi he visited Firoz Shah's Lat and what remained of its companion on Delhi Ridge. At Allahabad he saw his third column – and then a fourth at Bakhra (Vaishali) in northern Bihar. At Benares he visited the ruins at Sarnath, still quite unaware that they were Buddhist. By now one of the two cenotaph-like structures that had been there in Jonathan Duncan's time had been demolished for its building material. The remaining structure was described to Mackenzie as 'the Samaudh [cenotaph] of Rajah Booth-Sain at Sara-Nath'. Its general shape was not unlike what he had seen at Amaravati in 1797 but he failed to make the connection.

The brick and stone monument at Sarnath as drawn by Shaikh Abdullah for Colin Mackenzie in January 1814. Described as the 'Samaudh [cenotaph] of Rajah Booth-Sain', it is better known today as the Dharmekh stupa. (APAC, British Library)

When Colin Mackenzie next returned to Madras it was as the EICo's first Surveyor General and with the rank of a full colonel. He now had the authority and the resources to do more or less as he pleased and in March 1816 he returned to the mound at Amaravati with an eleven-strong team of draughts-men and surveyors. Mackenzie still believed it to be an early Jain monument, but his travels had now alerted him to the pos-sibility that he might be wrong. To his dismay, he found the site all but gutted, its entire central core dug out to make a hundred-foot-square 'tank' or reservoir. In the process, three-quarters of its decorated stone surround had gone, leaving only one segment untouched. Of the sculptured slabs that he had seen being uncovered in 1797, some had been used to construct a flight of steps at a nearby tank, others as building material at three temple structures and some mosques: 'In short,' Mackenzie complained, 'these valuable stones of antiquity have been used in various buildings both public and private; those in particular applied to Mussulman mosques have first been carefully divested of every carving by rubbing them on harder stones.'[18]

From what little remained Mackenzie was able to make out that the structure must originally have resembled the cenotaph he had seen at Sarnath – but on a far grander scale, and with the addition of an encircling processional pathway with an inner and an outer stone railing. From the remaining section of this railing he and his men extracted more than a hundred exquisitely carved stone slabs and pillars, many portraying complex scenes from history or mythical scenes involving not only kings and queens but also the worship of a quite remarkable range of objects: trees, thrones, parasols, cartwheels, pairs of footprints, deities seated under the protection of cobras and, above all, great dome-like structures similar to the edifice Mackenzie had seen at Sarnath and which appeared to be modelled on the Amaravati mound itself as it might have appeared in its heyday.

Fortunately for posterity, Mackenzie's draughtsmen made some excellent drawings (now preserved in the British Library in one album) before they moved on, while Mackenzie himself arranged for some eighty-two slabs and pillars to be moved down to Masulipatam for shipment on to Calcutta. Seven reached the Asiatic Society's museum, many of the remainder being commandeered by the Assistant Collector of Masulipatam

One of some ninety drawings of the Amaravati sculptures made
by Murugesa Moodaliar in Madras in 1853. It shows three
objects of worship: a stupa (top), a *Dharmachakra*, or 'Wheel of
the Moral Law' (middle), and the Bodhi tree with the *Vajrasana*,
or 'Diamond Throne', at its base. (APAC, British Library)

to decorate a curious structure in the town square that became
known as 'Mr Robertson's Mount'. By the time the next antiquarian visited Amaravati, much of what remained had been
'carried away and burnt into lime'.[19]

It was left to future generations to establish the full significance
of Amaravati, perhaps the finest Buddhist monument ever erected
in India. Mackenzie and his contemporaries had no idea what to

make of the iconography shown on its magnificent sculptures. They also failed to note that many of the earliest of the decorated slabs had been recycled, turned over and new scenes carved on their backs, so that the earlier scenes were hidden from view.

One of these early slabs is now in the Musée Guimet in Paris (see below). Although badly damaged and incomplete, enough survives to show a king flanked by two lesser male figures who face him with their hands pressed together in the

The defaced *Chakravartin* bas-relief, showing a 'Wheel-turning Monarch' bestowing universal good government based on the Dharma. (Musée Guimet, Paris)

anjali mudra, the 'gesture of reverence'. The king – who quite clearly has something of a beer-belly hanging over his waist-cloth – has assumed a striking pose, with his right hand raised and his left clenched by his breast. A multi-spoked cartwheel is displayed behind him on the top of a pillar, together with a second, far taller pillar broken at the top but closely resembling Firoz Shah's Lat and other such columns. A saddled but riderless horse stands at the king's feet. On one side part of a shrine-like structure and part of the figure of a buxom woman grasping the branch of a tree have survived. The faces of all three male figures appear to have been deliberately defaced.

A simpler version of this curious scene is shown in a wash drawing by a local draftsman, Murugesa Moodaliar. In the upper panel, a king is shown supported by two male figures on his left and two female figures on his right, with an elephant and a horse in attendance. The king has his right hand raised and his left fist clenched, just as in the first carving. Here, too, his face has been defaced. The acute observer will note other similarities. In the lower panel a king is seated on a throne with a queen below him, with an umbrella bearer in attendance (the parasol denotes royalty). What we should now call the *Dharmachakra*, or 'Wheel of the Moral Law', is displayed behind him and at his feet two monks present a begging bowl which he has filled. Again, an elephant and a horse are in attendance. Clearly, there is a link between the upper and lower panels.

The importance of these particular slabs as historical documents only began to be realised after a much later round of excavations at Amaravati and the surrounding region, carried out by the professional archaeologist James Burgess in the early

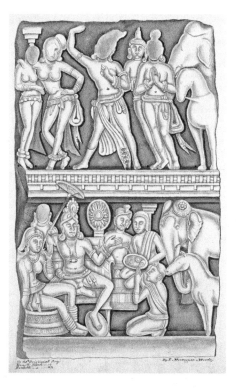

Two panels from the Great Stupa at Amaravati, drawn by
Murugesa Moodaliar in Madras in 1853. The original bas-relief
is in the Chennai Museum. (APAC, British Library)

1880s. It was he who first noted that a number of the remaining stone slabs had been carved on both sides and that the
structure itself had suffered 'some violent destruction' at an
early stage, probably in the second century BCE when the
Satavahana dynasty was in the process of moving in to fill the
vacuum left by the Mauryas. The monument had then been
restored and a surrounding colonnade with four gates added,
only to be further enlarged some centuries later when the
nearby city of Dhanyakataka had become the capital of the
Satavahana rulers of Andra.

Disappointed by what he had found at Amaravati, Burgess moved on to survey the extensive ruins found on both banks of the Krishna River upstream of Amaravati. Many turned out to be Buddhist monastic sites which, in Burgess's opinion, had suffered the same fate as the Amaravati stupa. One Buddhist monument at Jaggayyapeta, some thirty miles upstream of Amaravati, was less damaged than the rest. Known locally as the 'Hill of Wealth', it proved to be a smaller version of the Amaravati structure. Its four gateways, surrounding colonnade and most of its slabs had gone, but a number of slabs that had fallen flat had been overlooked. 'On a few', wrote Burgess in the briefest of reports, 'there were carvings in very low relief and of an archaic type ... Some letters on other slabs are of the Maurya type and must date about 200 to 170 B.C.'[20]

Burgess made a drawing of the best of these carved slabs which he added to his official report. It is a far more sophisticated version of the scenes shown on the damaged slab from Amaravati in the Musée Guimet and on the upper panel of the Amaravati slab in the Chennai Museum.

These three scenes all portray a *Chakravartin* or 'Wheel-turning Monarch'. The concept of the world-conquering Wheel-turning Monarch has its roots in early Vedic literature as the sovereign who creates an age, and from whom flows moral order, happiness and power based on the cosmic law underpinning the universe. In the Brahmanical context he wields a *chakra*, a disc-like weapon, to destroy his enemies, which becomes the instrument of Vishnu with the evolution of Hinduism. However, these images from Amaravati and surrounds show the Wheel-turning Monarch as taken over by the Buddhists and made their own. Here the Chakravartin is a

The Jaggayyapeta bas-relief shows a *Chakravartin*, or 'Wheel-turning Monarch', surrounded by various symbols: at his feet, a saddled horse and elephant, both symbolising the Buddha; over his head an umbrella symbolising royalty; on his left his counsellor and treasurer; on his right a *yakshi* fertility figure; and in the background a *Dharmachakra* wheel on a pillar and a Buddhist *ratna* or jewel symbol on a second pillar. The Chakravartin has raised his hand to cause gold to fall from the clouds.

secular counterpart to the Buddha who by following his Dharma conquers by moral force alone.[21]

A fourth slab from Amaravati completes the picture. This now forms part of the Amaravati marbles gallery at the British Museum and dates from Amaravati's last phase. Here the Wheel-turning

Monarch is magnificently ornamented and wears a cloak of the finest filigree or gauze, his status indicated by the royal umbrella held by the female attendant behind him. Now he has only one counsellor and his queen has been outranked by the fly-whisk-bearing *yakshi*, or fertility goddess, who stands at the king's left shoulder.

What is different about this portrayal of the Wheel-turning Monarch is that he is shown in an act of reverence – and he is facing outwards, towards the viewer. The object of his reverence is missing. That was carved on the panel directly above him – which has failed to survive the damage done to Amaravati.

The Chakravartin bas-relief, probably dating from the first century CE, a masterpiece now in the British Museum's Amaravati marbles gallery. (British Museum)

This magnificent piece of marble first went on display at the
Paris Exhibition in 1867 but its full significance only became
apparent sixty years later.

What these surviving images from Amaravati tell us is that
the cult of the Wheel-turning Monarch was well established
within the Mahayana Buddhist tradition in India at an early
age. From India it would spread north to China and beyond.

6

The Long Shadow of Horace Hayman Wilson

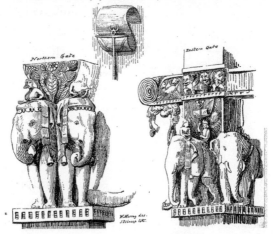

The so-called Great Tope at Sanchi, with details, as drawn by William Murray and engraved by James Prinsep for publication in the *Journal of the Asiatic Society of Bengal* in 1837.

The old fortress at Jaffna, on the northernmost tip of Sri Lanka, was once said to be the strongest in Asia. Today it lies in ruins, having suffered bombardment from land, sea and air. It had been built originally by the Portuguese to control the sea lanes leading to and from the Spice Islands of the East Indies, including the island of Lanka itself – which they renamed *Ceilao*, from the local *Sinhalana* or 'Land of the Lion'. In 1658, Portuguese survivors of the siege of Colombo briefly found refuge here before being expelled from the island by its new rulers, the Vereenigde Oost-Indische Compagnie, known to the British as the Dutch East India Company. The Dutch further strengthened the fortifications, so that by the time the British took over in 1796 there was very little for them to do but change flags.

What became known as the Dutch Fort remained in an excellent state of preservation until the insurgency initiated in July 1983 by the separatists popularly known as the Tamil Tigers developed into a civil war. Jaffna and its fort became the scene of some of the fiercest fighting, twice changing hands in the course of a bitter, long-drawn-out war that only finally came to an end in May 2009.

Somewhere in all the rubble is the grave of Major the Hon. George Turnour, the younger son of an Irish earl, Lord Winterton. George Turnour had taken part in the capture of Jaffna from the Dutch as a lieutenant in the 73rd Regiment of Foot and had stayed on as the fort adjutant. He had married the daughter of a refugee French aristocrat and in March 1799 their son, also the Hon. George, was born in Jaffna Fort. Here the boy remained for some years before being sent to England to be educated. The father stayed on.

When the British took possession of the island they

Anglicised Ceilao into Ceylon. It might have become part of
the EICo's Indian possessions but for the scruples of the
British government, increasingly vexed by its inability to rein
in its Governors General in India. So Ceylon became a crown
colony with its own administration, the Ceylon Civil Service,
which was fortunate in having as its first governor the Hon.
Frederick North. Like his contemporary in India, Marquess
Wellesley, North was an aristocrat and an Eton and Christ
Church, Oxford, man, and although he lacked Wellesley's
ambition he shared his view that the best administrators were
men who aspired to work with the natives rather than over
them. These included the French botanist Joseph de Joinville,
the first foreigner to make a study of Buddhism in Ceylon, and
Captain George Turnour himself, who served as a local administrator in and around Jaffna until his death in 1813 at the age
of forty-five.

Another able member of North's administration was the
lawyer Alexander Johnston, Ceylon's first advocate general and
later chief justice, a man of great erudition but incapable of
uttering a single sentence when two or three would do.
Johnston might with some justification be termed Ceylon's
answer to Sir William Jones. He had spent his boyhood up to
the age of eleven in Madras and Madurai and at one stage had
been tutored informally by Colin Mackenzie, which may
explain why as an adult in Ceylon he was said to have had an
'insatiable curiosity about Tamil Saivism and Sinhalese
Buddhism'.[1] As advocate general, Johnston played the leading
role in the abolition of the slave trade on the island and the
establishment of trial by jury, and he paved the way for universal education. Like Jones in Calcutta, he was determined
that local law should have its place within the judicial system

and to this end he made a study of 'all the customary laws of the various religions and casts [*sic*] of Ceylon', before drawing up what became the Ceylon Judicial Code.

In the course of pushing through his reforms Johnston formed a close friendship with a former slave-owner named Rajah Pakse, said to be the most powerful man on the island. When Johnston needed the cooperation of the elders of the Buddhist *Sangha*, or church, it was Rajah Pakse who interceded on his behalf and who afterwards secured for him three manuscripts together said to contain 'the most genuine account which is extant of the origin of the Budhu religion, of its doctrines, of its introduction into Ceylon, and of the effects, moral and political, which those doctrines had produced upon the native government'.[2]

Two of these texts were written in Sinhalese (today Sinhala) but the third – called by Johnston the *Mahavansi*, but more correctly the *Mahavamsa*, or 'Great Dynastic Chronicle' – was in the original Pali. When Sir Alexander Johnston retired from Ceylon in 1819 these gifts went with him.

This same period saw the arrival of the first Protestant missionaries on the island. They included the Reverend William Buckly Fox, a Wesleyan who made it his business to translate biblical tracts into the local tongues and to this end assembled a *Dictionary of the Ceylon-Portuguese, Singalese and English Languages*, published in 1819. When he returned to England in 1823 Fox was declared by Johnston to be 'the best European Pali and Singhalese scholar at present in Europe'. But how he had acquired his knowledge of Pali – if indeed he could read Pali at all – is a mystery, since Pali was at that time as hermetic a language as Sanskrit had been in India before the Wilkins–Halhead breakthrough, although in this case it was the Sinhalese Buddhist

monks who refused to share its secrets. Nevertheless, it was Fox
to whom Johnston turned when it was decided that his three
Ceylonese texts should be published in English.

Fox's purported translation of the *Great Dynastic Chronicle*
was duly published in England in 1833 as the first volume of
*The Mahavansi, the Raja-Ratnacari and the Raja-vali, forming the
Sacred and Historical Books of Ceylon*. However, the only name
to appear on the book's title page was that of its publisher,
Edward Upham, who had died the year before – and to further
muddy the waters, the Reverend Fox himself died within
months of the book's appearance. For reasons that have never
been explained, Fox's translation attracted very little public
notice in Britain. It may be that the project's chief supporter,
Sir Alexander Johnston, had begun to have doubts. Yet the fact
remains that here was the first published English translation of
that Lankan epic, the *Great Dynastic Chronicle* – albeit one made
from what was almost certainly a Sinhalese translation of an
imperfect copy of the original Pali.

Even more remarkably, this translation stated that in the
very earliest days of the island's history a strong connection had
existed between a Lankan king, named by the chronicle's
translator as 'Petissa the Second', and an Indian monarch,
'King Darmasoca of Jambu-dwipa [the Indian mainland]'.
These two rulers had 'lived in friendship, and loved each
other'. They had exchanged gifts and letters, and the Indian
king Darmasoca had written to Petissa to say that he kept the
commandments of 'Budhu' and desired the king of Lanka to
do the same. The consequences of this royal friendship had, it
seems, been profound, for it was during the reign of these two
monarchs that Buddhism had been established in Lanka,
changing the entire course of that island's history.

As a demonstration of the importance of this alliance, the compilers of the *Great Dynastic Chronicle* had devoted several chapters to the Indian monarchs who had ruled over Magadha from the time of Sakyamuni Buddha down to the reign of King Darmasoca. Indeed, the chronicle's fifth chapter was entirely given over to an account of Darmasoca's rule, beginning with an account of the rise to power of his grandfather Chandragupta with the help of the Brahman Chanakya very much as given in the Sanskrit verse-drama *The Minister's Signet Ring* translated by Sir William Jones. It went on to describe how Chandragupta's son Bindusara had appointed as his heir his eldest son, Prince Sumana, but that among King Bindusara's other ninety-nine children was a son called Priyadase. According to Fox's summary, this prince Priyadase had as a youth been sent away by his father to the city of Wettisa [Vidisha], where he 'married the princess, called Wettisa, of the royal family called Sacca [Sakya] . . . and became king of the city Udeny [Ujjain]: he had one son and a daughter by this Queen Wettisa. As this king was very prosperous in every thing, he was styled Asoca Prince.'

This single passage established a clear link that no one at the time noticed, which was that King Bindusara's eldest son by his second queen was named 'Priyadase' but later came to be known as 'Asoca'. As told in Fox's summary, this same Prince Priyadase/Asoca had gone on to sieze the throne of Magadha for himself following the death of his father. Whereupon his brother Prince Sumana 'made war against the new king, called Asoca of Cusumepura, and Asoka was the conqueror. This conqueror became sovereign king over the whole Jambu-Dweepa.'

Five further chapters of the *Great Dynastic Chronicle* were devoted to the close relationship between King Petissa the

Second of Lanka and King Asoca of India, in his later years
styled Darmasoca. In the last chapter King Asoca's reign of
forty-four years had been summarised in one succinct
paragraph:

> He had first conquered his enemies, and reigned four years
> without being crowned; and, after he was crowned, he had
> been succouring 60,000 impostors for three years; and on the
> fourth year that he was crowned, he was converted by the
> grand priest Niggroda, and embraced the religion of
> Budhu ... and he had also commenced to build in the same
> year 84,000 temples, at the expense of ninety-six kelles in
> gold, which temples he completed within the time of three
> years. On the sixth year that he was crowned, he caused his
> son, the priest Mihindu, and his daughter Sangamittrah, to
> be created priest and priestess ... On the seventeenth year,
> he caused to be compiled the law of Budhu, and had
> restored it to its original purity. On the eighteenth year that
> he was crowned, he had sent the bough of the holy tree to
> Ceylon. On the twelfth year after this, he solemnised the
> funeral ceremony of his Queen Asandimittrah by burning
> her corpse. On the fourth year after that, he was again mar-
> ried to a young queen, called Tissahraccah. On the third year
> of his second marriage, this Queen Tissahraccah, through
> malice, had pierced a prickle, called mandoe, in the holy
> tree, to kill it, after which he reigned but four years only.

This remarkable story was first set down in print in England in
1833 – and ignored. However, notice of its appearance was
published in Ceylon, where the news came as a shattering
blow to a young Ceylon Civil Servant named George Turnour.

George Turnour had returned to the land of his birth as a twenty-year-old Ceylon Civil Service cadet in 1820 and had spent his first six years as a junior administrator in a variety of posts in and around Colombo, the island's capital. He had then been promoted to be Government Agent in the province of Saffragan, with his headquarters at the town of Ratnapura, a centre of Sinhalese Buddhist culture. He was by then thoroughly at ease with vernacular and written Sinhalese but not with its main root, Pali, the language in which the island's Buddhist texts were written. Despite the opposition of the local monks, Turnour began to study Pali and within a year of his arrival was reading that ancient language. In the course of his studies he came to hear of a much-prized but rarely read Pali text, the *Mahavamsa*, said to detail the reigns of fifty-four Lankan kings of the Great Dynasty – the *Mahavamsa* of the title – and one hundred and eleven sovereigns of the *Sulavamsa* or Lesser Dynasty.

Finding a copy of this *Great Dynastic Chronicle* was not the problem, since most monasteries on the island possessed what they claimed to be authentic copies. The difficulty was that the text had been so overlaid with mystical hyperbole that even the best Pali readers among the Buddhist priests found it well-nigh unintelligible. Hearing of Turnour's quest, a Buddhist priest named Gallé came to him and explained that what was required was a *tika* or 'commentary' that could be applied to the poem to demystify it and transform it into a coherent narrative. Gallé then made it his business to find such a commentary, eventually tracking down a copy in the ancient rock monastery of Mulkirigalla, near Tangalle in the south of Ceylon.

With this commentary and an authentic copy of the *Great Dynastic Chronicle* obtained from the same monastic source,

Turnour was now able to cut through the verbiage to get to the heart of the matter: a coherent narrative of the Buddhist history of Lanka extending over a period of more than two thousand years. Turnour also discovered that to compile the earliest section of the island's history the authors of the *Great Dynastic Chronicle* had drawn on an earlier chronicle known as the *Dipavamsa*, or 'Island Chronicle', subsequently described by Turnour as 'the principal historical record in Ceylon ... comprising the history of Ceylon from B.C. 543 to A.D. 301'.

At Turnour's behest, Gallé began a second search, which resulted in the discovery of a copy of the *Island Chronicle*. Thus armed, George Turnour in 1827 began to work on an accurate English translation of the *Great Dynastic Chronicle* – a project that he had frequently to put to one side as his official duties took him from Ratnagiri to Tamankudawa and then on to Kandy, where he served as revenue commissioner for four years from 1828 to 1832.

The first that Turnour knew of Reverend Fox's supposed translation of the *Great Dynastic Chronicle* was when he read an article in the *Transactions of the Royal Asiatic Society* in the form of 'Remarks furnished by Captain J. J. Chapman of the R. E. upon the ancient City of Anarajapura or Anaradhepura, and the Hill Temple of Mehentale, in Ceylon', published in 1834. While on a shooting trip in the great wilderness that made up the central plains to the north of Kandy, Captain Chapman had taken the opportunity to explore a series of man-made reservoirs and ruins that extended for many miles. The lakes alone, he declared, 'rivalled the most remarkable labours of antiquity', pointing to 'an amount of population and a state of prosperity infinitely superior to what exists at present'.[3] Another striking feature of this ruinous landscape was a number of bell-like brick mounds all buried in undergrowth, some standing more than 250 feet high.

These were the remains of the ancient city of Anuradha-pura, which had been known of for some years but had remained largely unexplored. Chapman had been amazed by what he saw and what he learned from the priests of the one functioning temple at Anuradhapura, a modest structure directly associated with one of the oldest legends of the island: the sacred Bo-tree under which Sakyamuni Buddha had attained enlightenment and which, it seems, had been mirac-ulously transported from India to the island. Chapman was told that this was no miracle but historical fact, as set down in the island's ancient chronicle, the *Great Dynastic Chronicle*, excerpts from which he now quoted. He had read Fox's translation in its proof stage and had been given permission by its publisher to quote from it.

We can only imagine what George Turnour must have felt when he first saw in print and in English a text he had spent the better part of six years translating, much of those years passed in isolation and with 'the absence of all sympathy with his pursuits on the part of those around him'.[4] He had himself just published a digest of the *Great Dynastic Chronicle* in the *Ceylon Almanac for 1833*, but it was just that, an outline, and it had excited little interest outside Ceylon. His response was to abandon his plans to publish his own translation of the *Great Dynastic Chronicle*.

Over the previous two decades the armies of the EICo had continued to push ever deeper into the Indian interior in a series of campaigns: against the Marathas and the marauding gangs known as the Pindaris in central India south and west of the Gangetic plains; and against the Gorkhas of Nepal along the foothills of the Himalayas. It was from among their ranks that the next round of discoveries was made.

In March 1814 two columns of troops entered North Bihar with orders to drive the Nepalese back into the Himalayan foothills. Their line of march took them past the stone column at Lauriya-Araraj, which was recorded for posterity in a water-colour drawn by Lieutenant J. Harris of the 24th Regiment of Foot. A peace treaty was subsequently signed which required the Nepalese to surrender North Bihar to the EICo and to accept the presence of a British Resident in Kathmandu.

In 1818 a more striking discovery took place in central India when a military force led by Colonel Henry Taylor made camp under a small, neatly rounded hill in the open country north-east of Bhopal, not far from the village of Bhilsa (today Vidisha). The hill was known locally as the *chaitya giri*, or 'hill of shrines', but is today better known as Sanchi. As was the custom, Taylor's officers ended the day with a spot of hunting to liven the pot. On climbing Sanchi hill to its summit they found themselves surrounded by the remains of a number of astonishingly well-preserved structures of brick and plaster of a kind generally spoken of as *topes*, a corruption of the Sanskrit *stupa* and the Pali *thupa*. The largest of these so-called topes was in the form of a hemispherical dome surrounded by a processional pathway enclosed within a massive balustrade of red stone. This balustrade was divided into four quadrants by entrances at the cardinal points, each adorned by an intricately ornamented gateway. Three of these magnificent gateways were still standing and they were covered on every surface with 'exquisitely finished sculptures'.

At least three of the officers returned to make sketches of what they initially took to be a Jain temple, one of them – Lieutenant John Bagnold of the 14th Bengal Native Infantry – observing that a number of the stone images that littered the site appeared to have been deliberately defaced. However, it was the central monument's magnificent gateways that chiefly caught Bagnold's eye. On one such drawing he listed the main figures shown:

A winged tiger . . . elephants male drawing a female seated behind . . . winged antelopes . . . and elephant . . . devee [*devi*, 'goddess'] bathed by elephants . . . a wheel or sun on pedestal worshipped . . . figures on lions couchant . . . representations of the Building & 2 trees . . . trees & crowd of worshippers . . . procession in the centre a car drawn by four horses a crowd of armed men about it . . . A devee on a lotus . . . wheel or sun 2 females worshiping . . . figures on Bulls couchant . . . Building surrounded by worshippers . . . a female under a tree . . . figures having clubs on their shoulders . . . numbers of deities under them a train of worshippers . . . four elephants supporting a wheel.[5]

For one of Bagnold's superior officers, Major William Franklin, the chief attraction seems to have been the carved scenes on the gateway on the southern side of what they now named the Great Tope. This gateway had fallen, leaving its decorated pillars and cross-beams broken and scattered over the ground, making them more accessible than the others. Franklin evidently sat down to draw the panoramic scene depicted on one of these architraves, quite unaware that it was a key piece in the Ashokan jigsaw. His drawing shows a king in a horse-drawn chariot approaching a monument shaped rather like the dome of St Paul's Cathedral with a pair of angels hovering above. On the other side a number of men and women wearing elaborate turbans appear to be making obeisance to the monument.

'Sculptures at a Jeyne Temple in the province of Malwah AD 1820'; Major William Franklin's watercolour based on a drawing made during his earlier visit to Sanchi. (Royal Asiatic Society)

In that same year of 1818 a very different kind of discovery was made by a young administrator named Andrew Stirling in the district of Bhubaneshwar in Orissa, on the eastern coast of the subcontinent between Calcutta and Visakhapatnam. While on his official duties Stirling had come to a hill named Khandagiri five miles west of the Hindu holy city of Bhubaneshwar. It was honeycombed with rock-cut caves, many occupied by Jain and Hindu ascetics who informed Stirling that 'the place had its origin in the time of Buddha, and that it was last inhabited by the Rani of the famous Raja Lalat Indra Kesari, a favourer of the Buddhist religion'.[6] Halfway up the hill, on the overhanging brow of a natural rock cave known locally as the *Hathigumpha* or 'Elephant's Cave', Stirling spotted that an area fifteen feet across and ten feet high had been smoothed and polished to create a base for an inscription extending over seventeen lines. He informed the Surveyor General, Colonel Colin Mackenzie. 'The Brahmins refer to the inscription with shuddering and disgust', Stirling wrote, 'and to the Budh Ka Amel, or time when the Buddhist doctrines prevailed, and are reluctant even to speak on the subject. I have in vain also applied to the Jains of the district for an explanation.'

Some months after Stirling's discovery, Colin Mackenzie came to see the Elephant's Cave inscription for himself and at once recognised the writing to be 'in the very identical character which occurs on the pillars at Delhi'. Under his direction, Stirling made an eye-copy of the inscription, noting that the same writing was now being reported on a number of ancient monuments scattered far and wide across India: 'Any reader who will take the trouble of comparing the Khandgiri inscription with that on Firoz Shah's Lat at Delhi, on the column at Allahabad, on the Lat of Bhim Sen, in Sarun, a part of the Elephanta, and a part of the Ellora inscriptions, will find that the characters are identically the same.'

Tucked away in this same account by Stirling is a reference to an enormous stone pillar seen by him inside the Hindu temple of Bhaskareshvara in Bhubaneshwar. It appeared to Stirling that the temple had been constructed around the stone column, which he described as being forty feet high. When the Bhaskareshvara lingam was next reported on, in the 1880s, it had shrunk to a mere stump, rising no more than four feet in height. Its significance might have been forgotten but for the discovery that would come in 1929 of the head and shoulders of a stone lion in a pit just forty feet north of the Bhaskareshvara temple, followed by the further recovery of a stone bell-capital and fragments of a pillar temple from an old tank or reservoir

two miles west of Bhaskareshvara. These would add weight to
the claim that all were parts of the same pillar, which had once
stood on the site now occupied by the Bhaskareshvara temple.[7]
The sensitivities of the temple authorities have prevented the
matter from being taken any further.

It had always been Colin Mackenzie's intention to publish
a major work on the Amaravati stupa and much else besides,
drawing on the hoard of manuscripts, coins, statuary, inscribed
copper plates, drawings and copies of inscriptions he and his
assistants had accumulated over the years. But he was already
a sick man when he visited Stirling's Elephant Cave on
Khandagiri Hill. As the Hot Weather of 1821 came on he was
advised to take in the sea air, and it was as he sailed down the
Hoogly River towards the Bay of Bengal that Colin Mackenzie
died. He was aged sixty-one.

Thanks to the efforts of his friends and admirers Mackenzie's
collection was bought from his young widow for the then
extraordinary sum of £10,000, the purchaser being Horace
Hayman Wilson, acting on the instructions of the EICo. But
Wilson's only interest lay in the classical Sanskrit texts that
formed the bulk of Mackenzie's fifteen hundred manuscripts.
The remainder, including 152 volumes of inscriptions and
translations, 2630 drawings and 6218 coins, was stored away in
the Asiatic Society's basement, where it was allowed to moul-
der for decades before being sent to the EICo's museum at its
London headquarters in Leadenhall Street. Many of these documents fell victim to termites, but one that survived was an
eye-copy made of an inscription carved on a rock above a water-
hole in the countryside between the district capitals of Bellary
and Kurnool in Madras Presidency, having been collected by
Colin Mackenzie during his time as surveyor of the Madras

region in the 1790s. The significance of the inscription would not be recognised until 1946, when the document caught the eye of a researcher who passed the details on to the government epigraphist for India. Thanks to the directions attached to the eye-copy the original rock inscription would be located in 1952, leading to the discovery of a hitherto unknown Ashokan Minor Rock Edict.[8]

Another victim of Wilson's telescopic vision was Major James Tod, who in the course of eighteen years' service as Political Agent in the region known at this time as Rajputana (today Rajasthan) amassed a collection second only to Colin Mackenzie's. Tod's main focus of interest was the Rajput ruling clans of central India, but in his latter years of service he began collecting ancient coins, even going so far as to employ agents who during the rainy season went to Mathura and other cities located beside the Ganges to 'collect all that were brought to light by the action of the water, while tearing up old foundations, and levelling mouldering walls. In this manner, I accumulated about 20,000 coins, of all denominations.'[9]

In 1823 Tod was advised to leave India for the sake of his health. He chose to make his way down to Bombay by a circuitous route that took him to the celebrated Jain temples on the holy mountain of Girnar in the Kathiawar peninsula on the western seaboard. Here on its lower slopes he and his entourage came upon 'a huge hemispherical mass of dark granite' shaped rather like a kneeling elephant, almost its entire surface covered in writing.

'The memorial in question', Tod noted, 'is divided into compartments or parallelograms, within which are inscriptions in the usual antique character ... Each letter is about two inches long, most symmetrically formed, and in perfect preservation ... I may well call it a book; for the rock is covered with these characters, so uniform in execution, that we may safely pronounce all those of the most ancient class, which I designate the "Pandu character", to be the work of one man. But who was this man?'[10]

The Girnar edict rock. A lithograph engraved by Captain Markham Kittoe, from a drawing by Lieutenant Postans, and published in the *JASB* in 1837.

Like Stirling and Mackenzie at Bhubaneshwar, Tod was immediately struck by the writing's affinity to 'the inscriptions on the triumphal pillars at Delhi'. With the help of his Jain interpreter he copied down two sections of text.

Tod's notice to the Secretary of the Asiatic Society of his discovery failed to elicit any response. This was particularly unfortunate, since Andrew Stirling had just published at his own expense an illustrated account of his Elephant Cave inscription discovered at Khandagiri in Orissa on the eastern seaboard. As a result, thirteen years passed before anyone in India became aware of the close affinities between these two rock inscriptions on opposite sides of the Indian subcontinent.

Tod took his entire collection with him when he returned to England, where he wrote a ground-breaking article on India's Hellenistic coinage. However, he professed himself baffled by the writing on the coins of those who had succeeded the Greeks as rulers in north-west India. 'The characters have the appearance of a rude provincial Greek,' Tod wrote. 'That they belonged to Parthian and Indo-Scythic kings, who had sovereignties within the Indus, there cannot be a doubt.'[11] This article Tod published not in *Asiatic Researches* but in the first transactions of a new learned society set up in England, supposedly to complement the Asiatic Society but to all intents a rival body.

This new body was the Royal Asiatic Society of Great Britain and Northern Ireland (RAS), founded in 1823 following a meeting held at the London home of Henry Colebrooke, who since his retirement from India had gathered about him a circle of other retired 'Indians' who shared his Orientalist interests. At the inaugural meeting of the RAS, held at the Thatched House Tavern in St James's Street on 7 June 1823, Henry Colebrooke followed the example of his mentor Sir William Jones in delivering his own 'discourse' on the new society's aims, declaring that since the origins of Western civilisation were to be found in Asia and England's success as a world power owed so much to India, it followed that England had a duty to repay this debt. This included making a study of Asia in all its aspects.

Among the many luminaries present on that occasion were the pioneer Sanskritist Charles Wilkins, the Ceylon jurist Sir

Alexander Johnston and the retired Colonel James Tod, who
agreed to serve as the RAS's first Librarian. Tod's first concern
was to write up his monumental two-volume *Annals and
Antiquities of Rajasthan*, which took him the best part of five
years. Ill-health then prevented him from completing his *Travels
in Western India*, which was not published until four years after
his death in 1835. It meant that Tod's remarkable discovery of
the Girnar rock inscription would remain unknown until 1839.

There is nothing in the records of either the Asiatic Society
or the RAS that suggests a rift between these two learned
bodies. Indeed, it can be argued that the founding of the RAS
in England in 1823 was in direct response to the establishment
of the Société Asiatique in France in 1822, and that having two
societies that concerned themselves with Asian affairs was
better than having one. But there are hints that suggest a distinct *froideur* between the two societies, one being a brief
notice in the journal of the older body that it had rejected a
proposal from the younger that it should rename itself the
'Asiatic Society of Bengal' and become affiliated to the RAS,
another a note in the first issue of the RAS's journal that copies
of its aims had been sent to the EICo's Madras and Bombay
Presidencies – but not to Bengal.

Despite their differences, these two learned bodies were
united in their opposition to the creeping Anglicisation that
was now taking place in India, under pressure from the evangelical movement and other reformers. Milords Hastings and
Wellesley – both founder members of the RAS – and their successors as Governors General had stood firm against the
thunderings of the Claphamite Sect and its determination to
exchange India's 'dark and bloody superstition for the genial
influence of Christian light and truth'.[12] But with the passing

of the India Act in 1813 the evangelicals got their way. Calcutta became a bishopric and the missionaries began to stream in. 'The thin edge of the wedge being thus fairly inserted in the stronghold of idolatry, the force of truth drove it home,' was how a contemporary evangelical historian put it, using words that might equally have come from a Muslim historian writing centuries earlier. 'The Scriptures were now openly distributed. Toleration was no longer conceded only to Hindooism and other idolatries.'[13]

Female infanticide, slavery and *sati* (the practice of immolating widows on their husbands' funeral pyres) were now prohibited by law, but such reforms went hand in hand with a growing contempt for Indian culture in general. In a despatch written by the EICo's Court of Directors in London in 1821 to Lord Hastings (serving a second term as Governor General), Hastings was warned that 'in teaching mere Hindoo or Mohammedan learning, you bind yourselves to teach a great deal of what is frivolous, not a little of what is purely mischievous, and a small remainder indeed in which utility is in any way encouraged'. Nine years later the Court of Directors proposed that the 'Oriental scheme of education' should be replaced by English: 'We think it highly advisable to enable and encourage a large number of natives to acquire a thorough knowledge of English, being convinced that the high tone and better spirit of European literature can produce their full effect only on those who become familiar with them in the original language.'[14]

Orientalists and their allies both in England and in India resisted these moves vociferously, but they were few in number and became fewer still with each passing decade.

At this time fresh accounts began to circulate once more in military circles of caves filled with wondrous paintings on the eastern frontiers of the Bombay Presidency. The rumours were finally confirmed in 1824 when a young cavalry lieutenant, James Alexander of the 16th Lancers, returned to his regiment with news of just such a site: at Ajanta, some sixty miles north-east of Aurangabad. He had taken local leave to go hunting and, ignoring local warnings, had entered the tiger-infested gorge below Ajanta town, accompanied by a local guide. He had soon found himself on the floor of a natural amphitheatre formed by a great bend in the River Waghewa. Above were a series of twenty-six rock-cut caves set into a cliff face of black basalt in two tiers like rows of boxes in a theatre.

Clambering up the face of the cliff, Alexander and his guide reached the lower tier of the caves, occupied only by bats. The branch of a conveniently sited tree gave Alexander access to the upper tier, where the largest and most elaborately deco-rated caves had been cut. It was clear that they had remained unoccupied for centuries. 'That these excavations served for the retirement of some monastic society I have no doubt,' the young cavalryman would afterwards observe. He had seen something quite similar at the well-known Kanheri caves out-side Bombay. But what set these caves apart only became apparent when he began to explore their interiors by the light of a brushwood torch. The walls and ceilings of virtually every cave were adorned with paintings of astonishing quality, 'as exhibiting the dresses, habits of life, pursuits, general appear-ance and even features of the natives of India perhaps two thousand or two thousand five hundred years ago, well pre-served and highly coloured, and exhibiting in glowing tints, of which light red is the most common, the crisp-haired aborig-ines of the sect of the Buddhists, who were driven from India to Ceylon by the advent of Brahminism'.[15]

(Above) The interior of Cave 10 at Ajanta, dating from the second century BCE. Modelled on a wooden roofed prayer hall, this was the first cave to be cut into the rock in the Waghewa gorge. A lithograph by Thomas Dibdin reproduced in James Fergusson, *Illustrations from the Rock Cut Temples of India*, 1845. (Below) A ruler surrounded by his queens and concubines. A drawing by James Burgess of part of a wall painting in the same Cave 10, from his *Original Drawings from the Buddhist Rock Temples of Ajanta*. (APAC, British Library)

With this discovery Lieutenant Alexander threw open a window into the past to reveal a brightly lit world peopled by gods, demi-gods and lesser beings of flesh and blood, every aspect of whose living and dying was depicted, from the king in his palace harem to the solitary hermit in the jungle: scenes of love and war, triumph and adversity, pageantry and poverty – each crowded scene rendered the more authentic by the details of hairstyle, dress, ornament, utensil, weaponry, musical instrument and much else besides. Many of the paintings had an obvious religious content, showing haloed Buddha figures meditating, teaching and reclining, always watched over by floating beings that could be construed as angels, but the most striking images were those of bare-breasted men and women of exceptional grace and beauty: sad-eyed monarchs clasping lily-flowers in one hand and consorts in the other; queens and princesses riding in state on elephants or being pampered by handmaidens who giggled and gossiped as they went about their duties.

News of Lieutenant Alexander's discovery was initially confined to military circles and for the next five years the site remained undisturbed. Ajanta's extraordinary secret was finally revealed to the wider world when a lecture given by Alexander to his brother officers at Sandhurst Military Academy in August 1828 was reprinted in 1830 in the second volume of *Transactions of the Royal Asiatic Society of Great Britain and Ireland*, the official organ of the RAS – soon afterwards retitled the *Journal of the Royal Asiatic Society* (*JRAS*).

Some six months after Lieutenant Alexander's Sandhurst lecture a Captain Gresley and a Mr Ralph visited the Ajanta caves, coming away with copies of inscriptions from its walls 'which were in vain shewn to the pandits of Benares and to the

Secretary of the College there'. Mr Ralph also jotted down a vivid stream-of-consciousness account of what they had seen, which became the subject of a 'most animated and scenic correspondence'. Who the other party in this correspondence was remains unclear but a later reference suggests that Mr Ralph tried and failed to get the Secretary of the Asiatic Society interested.[16]

It was not until 1837 that the first notice of the Ajanta caves was published in India, in the form of Mr Ralph's colourful account. This appeared in the pages of the *Journal of the Asiatic Society of Bengal*, the new organ of the Asiatic Society, now modernised as the Asiatic Society of Bengal – and under entirely new management, having at last emerged from under the long shadow cast by Horace Hayman Wilson.

7

Prinsep's Ghat

A view of the Ganges from Benares. A lithograph by James Prinsep based on a drawing made during his ten-year residence in Benares as Assay Master of the EICo's Mint in the city. (From Prinsep's *Benares Illustrated*)

Since 1992 an elegant cable-stayed bridge has spanned the River Hooghly, linking the suburb of Howrah and the city of Kolkata, the former Calcutta.[1] Officially known as the Vidyasagar Sethu but usually referred to as the 'second Hooghly bridge', it is named after Ishwar Chandra Vidyasagar, a key figure in the Bengali Renaissance. At the bridge's southern (Kolkata) end its overpass skirts the western bastions and the water gate of Fort William, the old EICo citadel that today serves as the headquarters of the Indian Army's Eastern Command. This was where Lord Wellesley's Fort William College was sited and where in 1841 Vidyasagar became the head Sanskrit pandit, being then but twenty-one years of age and already renowned for his learning. While Vidyasagar went on to greater things the college went into decline, although it survives as a centre of education in the form of the Kendriya Vidyalaya Government School.

Also overshadowed by bridge and overpass is another memorial to the past: a curious Palladian-style structure made up of a number of classical columns supporting a flat roof. It stands on what was once the landing place where young Britons coming out to seek their fortunes in Bengal were ferried ashore from the ships moored in the river. Once erected, it came to be used as a sort of unofficial gateway of India, welcoming incoming viceroys and other dignitaries, being especially conspicuous during the royal visits of 1875, 1905 and 1910. But that was never the structure's intended purpose. This is set out in large letters of bronze laid out across one face of the building. They declare: 'Erected in the honour of JAMES PRINSEP by his fellow citizen' – the final 's' fell off some years ago and was never replaced. No date is given but the memorial is known to have been erected in 1843.

A postcard from the 1860s, showing James Prinsep's memorial
at the *ghat* or landing place beside the River Hoogly.

The intervening years were not particularly kind either to
the man or his memorial. The area originally known as
Prinsep's Ghat became known as Princep Ghat and even
Princes Ghat. Indeed, the little railway station beside the river
is today called Princep Ghat. If the site was known at all it was
as a romantic ruin that frequently served as a backdrop for
advertising or movie shoots.

That has changed in the last decade thanks to the efforts
of INTACH, a national body charged with the preservation
and conservation of India's national heritage. Despite a shortage of funds INTACH has helped alter the perception in
India that monuments associated with the departed British are
unworthy of preservation. In the case of the Prinsep memorial
INTACH proposed that this would make a marvellous venue
for cultural events – as an arena whereon India's own native
traditions could work in harmony with its colonial past. In

January 2008 that vision was realised with the launch of the first Prinsep Ghat dance festival, made possible with the support of an international bank and the goodwill of the Indian Army.

It was here that twenty-year-old James Prinsep was brought ashore in September 1819 and almost exactly twenty years later carried down to the river in a litter to begin his journey home, but as 'an entire wreck ... His overstrained mind ... covered in desolation ... his body sunk into debility.'[2]

Prinsep never recovered his mind or his health and died in England in April 1840. But tragic as his death was, Prinsep's twenty crowded years in India were well spent, and he was particularly fortunate in being in good company as the youngest of three remarkable Englishmen, born within months of each other at the turn of the century, who between them changed the course of Indian studies. Despite their shared interests and exchanged correspondence and the influence they exerted on each other, the three never actually met face to face.

George Turnour was the eldest of the three by a matter of months. The next in seniority was Brian Houghton Hodgson, who came out to join the EICo's civil service in Calcutta in 1818. Hodgson's superiors soon discovered that his fragile state of health was no match for the Indian Hot Weather and found a post for him as Political Assistant and Secretary to the British Resident in Kathmandu in Nepal. Here he would remain almost without a break for the next twenty-six years, initially as a subordinate but from 1829 onwards as the Resident.

The youngest of the three and the last to arrive in the East was James Prinsep, born in Bristol of a father who had made a fortune in Bengal only to lose it in England, as a result of which he was raised in such straitened circumstances that for a time he and a younger brother had to share one pair of breeches. With his blue eyes, pale complexion, blond hair, slight frame and what his sister Emily described as his 'constitutional shyness ... and a timidity of speech',[3] the teenage James appeared to be an unlikely genius. Forced by poor eyesight to give up studying architecture he turned down the offer of a civil service cadetship in India and was eventually offered a post at the EICo's Bengal Mint. Here Prinsep learned all the necessary skills of a metallurgist under the eyes of the Calcutta Mint's Assay Master, Horace Hayman Wilson, the great Sanskritist and grand panjandrum of the Asiatic Society.

The twenty-year-old James Prinsep lectures in Calcutta on the latest scientific advances with 'a set of the most showy experiments'. (Lithograph from a portrait by George Chinnery, 1820)

Eighteen months later Prinsep was posted upriver to manage the EICo's second Mint at Benares, where he turned his scientific expertise to good use in making a census of the city's inhabitants and drawing the first detailed map of the city. He also honed his architectural skills in a series of ambitious civil engineering works, which included building a three-arched bridge, restoring the foundations of the great mosque built by Aurangzeb beside the Ganges and constructing a deep underground tunnel that drained a large swamp in the centre of Benares and became the centrepiece of the city's new drainage system. Prinsep was also a talented artist, and the skills he developed in Benares in etching and lithography were to stand him in very good stead in later years.

The enthusiasm with which Prinsep threw himself into every sort of project for the improvement of the city won him friends in all sections of the community, so that when in 1830 the two main sects within the Jain community were locked in dispute they turned to him for help. Their argument was over whose remains were buried within the great dome-like monument that stood just outside the city boundaries at Sarnath. This might be resolved if he were to use his engineering skills to open the structure, 'that it might be ascertained to which party (Digambari or Swetambari) the enclosed image might belong. My departure from Benares alone prevented my satisfying their curiosity in 1830.'[4] The Jains' request had come too late – but it was not forgotten.

Meanwhile in Kathmandu Brian Hodgson had been using his leisure hours to pursue a quite breathtaking range of intellectual pursuits. The hostility of the rulers of Nepal towards their old enemies, and what Hodgson saw as 'the jealousy of the people in regard to any profanation of their sacred things by a European'[5] meant that throughout his time in Nepal Hodgson was a virtual prisoner within the grounds of the British Residency on the outskirts of Kathmandu. He overcame this restriction as far as he could by recruiting a number of local Nepalis and training them to act as his researchers and artists, all paid for out of his own pocket.

One of Hodgson's earliest objects of enquiry was the Buddhism practised in Kathmandu Valley. It led him to Amrita Nanda Bandya, 'the most learned Buddhist, then or now, living in this country',[6] who soon came into conflict with Hodgson's own pandit, a Brahmin from Benares, after he brought Hodgson a Buddhist text attacking 'the Brahmanical doctrine of caste'.[7] One outcome of their long and fruitful relationship was a growing collection of ancient Buddhist scriptures written in Sanskrit gathered by Amrita Nanda in response to Hodgson's request for information on the Buddhism practised in Nepal.

Through Amrita Nanda Hodgson learned that the original inhabitants of Kathmandu Valley, the Newars, had been among the earliest converts to Buddhism and that many of what appeared to be Hindu temples in Kathmandu and the surrounding towns were in fact Buddhist monasteries, nearly all of them dilapidated structures built around a courtyard dominated by a central dome-like structure known as a *chaitya*, the local equivalent of the stupa, adorned with both Buddha images and Hindu deities. Hodgson's local artists were put to work drawing these structures, leading him to conclude that the simplest of these chaityas were the earliest, particularly those in and around the town of Patan, which were ascribed to *Sri nama Miora*, 'the honoured one named Maurya', or to *Dharmarajya*, 'the Dharma king'.

One of the five ancient stupas said to have been built by King
Ashoka in the city of Patan in Kathmandu Valley. Drawn by one
of William Hodgson's Nepali artists, its caption in Hodgson's
handwriting reads: 'The Ipi Thuda Vihar and Chaitya [monastery
and stupa] at Patan in the Valley of Nepal. Built in the 1000th
year of the Kali era by Sri Nama Miora [the honoured one named
Maurya].' (Royal Asiatic Society)

Between 1820 and 1823 Brian Hodgson sent no less than
218 Sanskrit manuscripts down to the Asiatic Society in
Calcutta, where they were acknowledged by Dr Wilson and
then ignored. Undeterred, Hodgson continued to supply further collections of Buddhists texts, including two complete sets
of the Tibetan canon of Buddhist literature known as the
Kanjur. Again, he received a lukewarm response. He then set
about making what he could of the material still available to
him, the first fruits of which appeared in *Asiatick Researches* in
1828 under the title of 'Notices on the Languages, Literature,
and Religion of the Bauddhas of Nepal and Bhot [Tibet]'.[8]

This was to be the first of fourteen essays published by Hodgson on the subject of Buddhism, and to his great gratification it elicited an enthusiastic response from the illustrious French Orientalist Eugène Burnouf, at that time Europe's leading authority on the Pali language. A friendship developed by correspondence and many more Sanskrit texts followed. This unprompted generosity went down badly with some of Hodgson's compatriots but it led to Burnouf taking up Sanskrit, culminating in the publication in 1844 of his seminal *Introduction à l'histoire du Buddhisme Indien* – probably the most influential work on Buddhism to be published in the nineteenth century.

Horace Hayman Wilson's narrow-mindedness – for it was Wilson whose inaction had so frustrated Hodgson – also blighted the career of that most eccentric of scholars the Hungarian Csoma de Koros, who had spent years travelling through Central Asia in search of the language roots of Hungarian before settling in a Buddhist monastery in Ladakh to learn Tibetan. In 1824 de Koros offered to make the fruits of his researches into Tibetan language and literature freely available to the Asiatic Society, an offer he repeated in 1827. Wilson spurned both offers. After three further years of isolated study in Zanskar, during which he compiled the first Tibetan dictionary and grammar, de Koros applied to the EICo for permission to enter India. Fortunately, this application reached the desk of Governor General Lord Bentinck, who recognised the value of de Koros's work as an aid to trade and saw to it that he and his manuscripts were made welcome at the Asiatic Society. Here he was given a small government salary and put to work by Wilson cataloguing Brian Hodgson's collection of Sanskrit and Tibetan works. This had the advantage of enabling de Koros and Hodgson to continue a correspondence begun while the former was still in Zanskar. Nevertheless, Wilson's hostility towards the Hungarian continued and he refused to sanction the publication of de Koros's *Tibetan Grammar* and *Tibetan–English Dictionary* on the grounds of cost.

However, in 1832 the logjam created by Wilson's long tenure as Secretary of the Asiatic Society at last began to break up when he secured the newly established Boden Chair of Sanskrit at Oxford. Two years earlier James Prinsep had joined him in Calcutta as deputy Assay Master, and had been proposed by him for membership of the Asiatic Society. The two had then collaborated on an article for *Asiatick Researches* on the coins in the Asiatic Society's museum, centred on the lettering on a number of gold and silver coins, 'some of them resembling the characters of the staff of Feroz Shah at Delhi, and on other columns'.[9] The article was illustrated by four plates of engravings of coins, some of which had been acquired by the Italian mercenary General Ventura from his excavation of the Manikyala Tope, a famous landmark beside the *Sadak-e-Azam* or 'Great Highway' (afterwards known as the Grand Trunk Road) running from Peshawar to Calcutta.

These engravings were the work of James Prinsep, whose involvement had the happy effect of leading him to make his own study of Indian coins. Two published articles on Roman and Greek coins found in India were soon followed by others on Indian coinage, each progressively demonstrating Prinsep's growing authority in an area of numismatics about which virtually nothing was known. Unlike Wilson and his predecessors, Prinsep had neither classical learning nor language skills but he made up for these shortcomings by the application of scientific method, a rigour that underpinned all his work.

Prinsep's collaboration with his senior drew him into the heart of the Asiatic Society. Within months he had accepted Wilson's proposal that he succeed him as the Society's Secretary. A double transfer of power then took place as Prinsep took over both as Assay Master at the Calcutta Mint and as Secretary of the Asiatic Society. And no sooner had Prinsep been voted in as the latter than he set about making the position his own with the energy that had characterised his years in Benares. One of his first actions was to propose Csoma de Koros as an honorary member, after which he found quarters for the Hungarian at the Society, doubled his salary and secured funds for the publication of his two books. Prinsep also brought in a native clerk from Fort William College, Babu Ramkomal Sen, to act as his personal secretary – the first Indian to hold a recognised post within the Society. Although opposed to the modernisers led by the Bengali reformer Ram Mohun Roy, Sen was an able Sanskritist and later became principal of Calcutta's Sanskrit College.

Prinsep's main concern was to revitalise the Asiatic Society. It now became the Asiatic Society of Bengal (ASB), while the bulky folio tomes of *Asiatick Researches* were replaced by the more accessible octavo-sized pages of the *Journal of the Asiatic Society of Bengal* (*JASB*), henceforward published in regular monthly issues. Prinsep appointed himself the *JASB*'s editor and in the first issue sent out a rallying cry that was a deliberate echo of the appeals made by Sir William Jones and Henry Colebrooke, calling all 'naturalists, chemists, antiquaries, philologers and men of science, in different parts of Asia' to unite in their efforts and to 'commit their observations in writing and send them to the Asiatic Society in Calcutta'.[10]

It was a calculated attempt to jolt the Orientalist movement

out of the defeatism into which its members had retreated over
the preceding decade, and it worked, initiating a second round
of advances in Indian studies even more dramatic than the
first – made possible by the happy combination of a second
Jones at the centre and some outstanding scholars on the
periphery, extending from Brian Hodgson at one end of the
subcontinent to George Turnour at the other. But it was James
Prinsep upon whom every advance depended, no longer the
creature of 'constitutional shyness' he had been a decade
earlier but an inspirational leader. 'Himself the soul of enthusiasm,' wrote one of his admirers, the botanist Dr Hugh Falconer,
'he transferred a portion of his spirit into every enquirer in
India; he seduced men to observe and to write; they felt as if
he observed and watched over them; and the mere pleasure of
participating in his sympathies and communicating with him,
was in itself a sufficient reward for the task of a laborious and
painful investigation.'[11]

The timing was perfect. That first joint article on the coins
in the Asiatic Society's collection had provoked a flood of
correspondence, much of it coming from the Punjab and
Afghanistan: from foreign mercenaries such as the Italian and
French generals Ventura and Court; travellers such as Lieutenant Alexander 'Bokhara' Burnes, Dr James Gerard and Dr
Martin Honingberger, and adventurers such as the supposed
American from Kentucky who called himself Charles Masson
but whose true identity was James Lewis, a deserter from the
EICo's army, inspired to visit Afghanistan by reports of gigan-
tic statues at Bamiyan.

This correspondence was supported by tangible evidence in
the form of gold, silver and copper coinage, confirming James
Tod's view that Macedonian rule in Bactria and ancient

Gandhara had given way to an equally dynamic 'Indo-Scythian' civilisation that had reached deep into northern India and had embraced Buddhism. Indeed, Buddhism itself had patently flourished throughout that region for centuries prior to the Islamic invasions. Writing to James Prinsep from beyond the Khyber Pass at Jelalabad in December 1833, Dr Gerard reported the existence of scores of 'topes' similar to those found in the Punjab. These stupas were to be found 'along the skirts of the mountain ridges' between Kabul and Jalalabad and 'very thickly planted on both banks of the Kabul river'. Known locally as 'spirit houses', they produced coins, jewels and reliquaries when opened but gave few clues as to who had built them. 'Whether we view them as contemporary with the Grecian dynasty', speculated Gerard, 'or of those subsequent satrapies which emanated from the remains of that kingdom, the same thoughts recur, the same suggestions arise: Who were these kings?'[12]

Meanwhile, in the Punjab, the French soldier of fortune General Claude Auguste Court, engaged to remodel the artillery of Maharaja Ranjit Singh's army along French lines, was spending his leisure hours excavating stupas for their coins and relics and taking note of other ancient monuments – among them a large boulder close to the village of Shahbaz-garhi on the edge of the Vale of Peshawar abutting the mountains of Swat – 'a rock on which there are inscriptions almost effaced by time'.[13] Falling into the old trap of associating the inscription with Alexander and his Macedonian successors, Court tried and failed to decipher its 'Greek' inscription.

To every field report published in the *JASB* Prinsep appended his own notes, based on a better understanding of the early Indian ruling dynasties made possible by the ever-growing numbers of Indian coins now coming his away. The finest of these coins had been inspired by the Mediterranean models first introduced by Alexander's Macedonian satraps and continued by their successors in Bactria and the Gandharan region: coins bearing a regal portrait on the obverse, a variety of human or animal figures on the reverse, and with Greek lettering on one or both faces. Prinsep's studies showed that the later Bactrian coins continued to bear proper Greek characters on the obverse but a different script on the reverse, superficially similar but clearly relating to some other language. This same writing also shared some but not all of the characters of the writing found on Firoz Shah's Lat and on the rock inscriptions found by Major Tod at Girnar and by Andrew Stirling at Khandagiri in Orissa.

Only later did Prinsep realise that what he termed 'Gandharan' writing was in fact a quite separate language altogether – today known as Kharosthi – with its own script and often written from right to left. Indeed, in what was to be one of his last articles he announced that he had identified almost half of the consonants of this unknown language and three of its vowels.[14] Another half-century would pass before philologists realised that Kharosthi was based primarily on Aramaic, the official written and spoken language of the Persian empire. It would take another full century before it was understood that the Brahmi alphabet of the Mauryas was itself a development from Kharosthi, improved to better express Indian language sounds.[15]

Another type of coinage proved even harder to understand: small coins of a type already shown by Colonel Colin Mackenzie to have been used all over India: 'They are of irregular form,' wrote Prinsep, 'being square, angular, round, oval, etc. They bear no inscription, are not infrequently quite plain, and in any case have only a few indistinct and unintelligible symbols.'

These symbols included lions and elephants but most appeared to be more basic, such as radiating suns or crosses. One symbol, in particular, caught Prinsep's eye: 'a pyramidal building, with three tiers of rounded *suras*, spires or domes ... It may be intended to portray some holy hill,' he proposed, in what was a remarkably astute conjecture.[16] Further study led him to conclude – correctly – that what are today known as punch-marked coins must have constituted India's earliest coinage.[17] Prinsep further assumed that these crude and relatively easy to produce punch-marked coins must have given way to the Greek model, as used by the Graeco-Bactrian rulers and their successors, the Scythians and Kushans. In fact, they continued to be minted throughout that period.

Helping Prinsep to sort out his coins was an enthusiastic subaltern engineer Alexander Cunningham, who had arrived in Calcutta in 1833 as a nineteen-year-old military cadet and had found himself at a loose end while he waited for his first posting. When despatched up-country to Benares two years later, Cunningham kept in touch with Prinsep through a correspondence that continued until the latter's death. 'Even at this distance of time,' Cunningham was to write four decades later, 'I feel that his letters still possess the same power of winning my warmest sympathy in all his discoveries, and that his joyous and generous disposition still communicates the same contagious enthusiasm.'[18]

Much of this correspondence concerned their shared interest in Indian coins but there was also Prinsep's unfinished

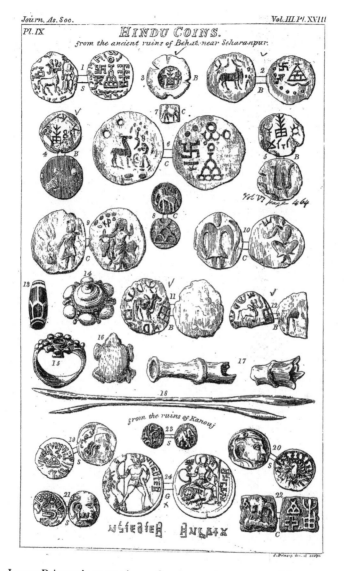

James Prinsep's engravings of various coins recovered from two ancient sites, Behat and Kanouj, in the Gangetic plains, including a number of what are today known as punch-marked coins (e.g. bottom right, number 22). The 'stupa' symbol can be seen on the reverse of several coins (numbers. 1, 5, 8 and 22). (*JASB*, Vol. III, May 1834).

business relating to the great stupa at Sarnath. At Prinsep's request and expense Cunningham hired a team of labourers and, having checked that no religious group would be offended, erected a wooden ramp that gave him access to the top of the 143-foot-high structure, today called the Dharmekh Stupa (see illustration, p. 86). Beginning in January 1835, he and his workmen sank a shaft down through the centre of the monument, a process that took far longer than anticipated as the structure turned out to have been built of blocks of stone secured to each other with iron clamps. Only when they had dug down to a depth of 110 feet did the work become easier, for here the stonework gave way to large flat bricks. The digging then went on until they reached the soil at the base of the structure without producing any result. 'Thus ended my opening of the great tower,' wrote Cunningham, 'after 14 months labour and at a cost of more than five hundred rupees',[19] all he had to show for it was an inscribed slab from the Gupta era (330–550 CE) uncovered at an early stage of the excavation.

However, in the course of the dig Cunningham became friendly with an old man who had been involved in the quarrying of the site reported on by Jonathan Duncan back in 1795. What Cunningham learned was that this quarrying had completely destroyed a second stupa as large as the remaining structure. But it had also uncovered an underground chamber full of stone statues, which had been hastily covered over for fear of disturbing evil spirits. He was able to lead Cunningham to the spot, where his workmen unearthed a cache of 'about 60 statues and bas-reliefs in an upright position, all packed closely together within a small space of less than ten feet square'. All were Buddhist and had been deliberately hidden. From the copious layer of ash overlaying his find Cunningham concluded that some catastrophic fire had brought an end to the Buddhist occupation of the site.

Then duty called and Cunningham was ordered away to join the staff of the Governor General as an aide-de-camp. He just had time to arrange for some twenty of those statues bearing inscriptions to be transported downriver to the Asiatic Society in Calcutta. It was four years before he was able to return to Benares, only to learn that by order of the city magistrate, Mr Davidson, the remaining forty statues together with fifty cart-loads of carved stonework had been thrown into the River Barna to serve as a breakwater for the city's first iron bridge. This vandalism made a deep impression on Cunningham, who in later years became almost obsessive in his calls for the protection of ancient sites.

James Prinsep always acknowledged the help he received from his young correspondent. However, it was his own formidable intelligence that counted. Over the course of six years he wrote a series of increasingly erudite articles on Indian coinage, each illustrated with his own engravings, which together laid the foundations of Indian numismatics up to the post-Gupta period, an achievement eclipsed by his later work on proto-Sanskrit languages. But it was the one that led to the other, for it was his work on the lettering on Indian coins that directed Prinsep towards the inscriptions on Firoz Shah's Lat and the other inscribed columns and rocks.

Prinsep was initially unaware of the efforts made by Sir William Jones, Henry Colebrooke and others, all faithfully recorded in the early volumes of *Asiatick Researches* – and since forgotten. However, during his time in Benares he had visited the fort at Allahabad and had been dismayed to see how the sun and rain were eroding the lettering on the broken pillar lying just inside the fort gates. 'I could not see the highly curious column lying at Allahabad, falling into decay, without wishing to preserve a complete copy of its several inscriptions,' he wrote. 'The Moghul emperor Jehangir was content to engrave his name and proud descent in a belt through the middle of the most ancient inscription – the English would rightly deprecate such profanation, but their own passive neglect has proved in a few short years even more destructive than the barbarous act of the Muhammadan despot.'[20]

The more he looked into the subject the more intrigued Prinsep became by the mystery of the undeciphered script on that fallen column, a script he now termed 'No. 1'. He wrote to one of his correspondents in Allahabad, Lieutenant Thomas Burt of the Bengal Engineers, and within weeks was rewarded with a set of drawings, which he engraved and published in the March issue of the *JASB* in 1834.[21] That article provoked an immediate response from Brian Hodgson in Kathmandu, whose letter Prinsep read to a meeting of the Asiatic Society of Bengal in May.

Hodgson began with a complaint, which was that some years earlier he had sent Horace Wilson drawings of what he called the Mattiah Lat pillar (today better known as the Lauriya-Nandangarh pillar), seen by him on his travels to and from Nepal, together with an eye-copy of the ancient inscription it bore. Dr Wilson had failed to respond. Now he attached drawings of two more pillars he had encountered. These were the three pillars seen and recorded in earlier times by John Marshall, Father Marco della Tomba and others.

Brian Hodgson and Csoma de Koros had each independently established that the Tibetan alphabet was based on written Sanskrit. Hodgson now proposed to Prinsep that his 'No.1' was probably an early written form of the same language: 'When we consider the wide diffusion over all parts of India of these alphabetical signs, we can scarcely doubt their derivation from Deva Nagari, and the inference is equally worthy of attention that the language is Sanscrit.'[22]

Armed with Lieutenant Burt's copies of 'No. 1' from Allahabad and the Asiatic Society's set of copies of 'No. 1' from Firoz Shah's Lat copied four decades earlier by Captain Hoare, James Prinsep now set out to determine if this was indeed the case. He began by making a painstaking analysis of the alphabet: 'I soon perceived that each radical letter was subject to five principal inflections, the same in all, corresponding in their nature with the five vowel marks of the ancient Sanscrit No. 2. This circumstance alone would be sufficient to prove that the alphabet is of the Sanscrit family, whatever the language may be.'

The five inflections Prinsep presumed – correctly – to correspond with the five basic vowel sounds 'a', 'e', 'i', 'o', 'u' found in Sanskrit and other Indo-European root languages. After drawing up a chart showing all the radical letters with their inflections he found that twenty-nine radical characters were employed – less than in modern languages based on Sanskrit, but what might be expected if this was an early form. He went on to highlight one particular group of fifteen characters, which he observed recurring in identical form at the beginning of almost every section or paragraph of text.

Prinsep's conviction that this group of fifteen characters would prove to be the keystone of 'No. 1' grew all the stronger when he retrieved Brian Hodgson's eye-copy of the Mattiah Lat inscription, where each section also began with that same group of fifteen letters. But then as he examined the three sets

of facsimiles from Allahabad, Delhi and Bihar side by side he
made an even more astounding discovery – 'namely, that *all
three inscriptions are identically the same*. Thus the *whole* of the
Bettiah inscription is contained verbatim in that of Feroz's
Lath, published in four consecutive plates in the seventh
volume of the *Asiatick Researches* [Captain Hoare's eye-copies];
and all that remains of the Allahabad inscription can with equal
facility be traced in the same plates.'[23] The italics are Prinsep's.

Prinsep went on to speculate on the implications of this discovery: 'Whether they mark the conquests of some victorious
raja; whether they are as it were the boundary pillars of his
dominions; or whether they are of a religious nature, bearing
some important text from the sacred volumes of the Baud-
dhists or Brahmins, can only be satisfactorily solved by the
discovery of the language.'

The publication of Hodgson's letter and Prinsep's
response in the October 1834 issue of the *JASB* caused a flurry
of excitement among its readers, an excitement intensified
when an eye-copy made by Hodgson of the inscription on
another of the North Bihar columns (today known as the
Lauriya-Araraj pillar)[24] was shown by Prinsep also to be identical to the other three sets: 'So we are now in the possession
of four copies of the same inscription, three of them perfect,
viz. the Delhi, the Matthiah, and the present one, and that of
Allahabad mutilated.'[25]

These revelations led Prinsep to cast around for more examples of No. 1 text. He reprinted in the *JRAS* Captain Edward
Fell's account of a visit to the Great Tope at Sanchi, originally
published in the *Calcutta Journal* back in 1819, together with
an appeal for more drawings from Sanchi and, more importantly, copies of its inscriptions.[26]

It was precisely at this point that George Turnour joined the debate from his distant outpost in Ceylon. What prompted him to resume his work on the island's *Great Dynastic Chronicle* is not known, but after some months of reflection he submitted to James Prinsep in Calcutta a short article on the importance of the *Great Dynastic Chronicle* as an accurate account of early Buddhism. It meant so little to James Prinsep that he unwittingly forwarded it to his former mentor Professor H. H. Wilson in Oxford for comments. Prinsep then added these comments as highly critical footnotes to Turnour's article when it appeared in the *JASB* in September 1836.[27]

Wilson had been one of the sponsors of the two volumes of *The Mahavansi, the Raja-Ratnacari and the Raja-vali, forming the Sacred and Historical Books of Ceylon*, as translated by the Reverend William Fox. He had no time for Turnour's central argument, which was that the *Great Dynastic Chronicle* demonstrated the major role played by the Mauryan king Ashoka in the development of Buddhism, both in India and beyond India's borders, after himself converting to Buddhism. This was nonsense, declared Wilson. It was well known that Ashoka was a worshipper of Shiva, and besides, 'the faith of Asoka is a matter of very little moment, as the prince himself is possibly an ideal personage'. Furthermore, the *Great Dynastic Chronicle* was a thoroughly unreliable document when compared to Brahmanical texts such as the *Puranas* and the poet Kalhana's chronicle of the kings of Kashmir, the *River of Kings*.

This very public rebuke did not go down well with Turnour. He appealed to the Asiatic Society of Bengal for its support in the publication of his translation of the first twenty chapters of the *Great Dynastic Chronicle*. Probably because of his own close ties with Wilson, Prinsep passed this appeal on to the

Reverend William Mill, the Asiatic Society's Vice-President – a wise move as it turned out, for despite being a Unitarian and principal of Calcutta's newly established Bishop's College, Mill was a Sanskritist and a genuine scholar in his own right.

Mill's reading of Turnour's manuscript left him astonished and in no doubt that the *Great Dynastic Chronicle* was, as Turnour claimed, a work of great antiquity and of huge importance as a source document. Not only did it pre-date the *Puranas* by some centuries but it showed every sign of being a far more authentic chronicle of events. Despite the *Great Dynastic Chronicle*'s focus on Ceylon, Mill declared it to be the most valuable historical source yet known relating to the history of India prior to the Muslim invasions. Furthermore, it highlighted 'the peculiarly interesting connection between the history of Ceylon before the Christian era, with that of Magadha' – a connection that extended to the language in which the *Great Dynastic Chronicle* had been written.[28]

That language was Pali, which Turnour had shown to be 'no other than the Magadha Prakrit – the classical form in ancient Bihar'. It appeared that Pali and Sanskrit were both derived from the same source: Magadhan Prakrit.

The Reverend Mill's unequivocal support for Turnour led to a meeting of the Asiatic Society of Bengal held in Calcutta on 4 January 1836, at which those present disregarded the advice of Professor Wilson and voted 'to advocate the patronage by the Government of India of Mr Turnour's intended publication'. That funding enabled George Turnour's *Epitome of the History of Ceylon, Compiled from Native Annals: and the First Twenty Chapters of the Mahawanso* to be published by the Cotta Church Mission Press in Ceylon later in that same year, complete with an introduction in which its author comprehensively demolished many of the claims made by Wilson and others in their studies of early Indian history.[29]

Turnour was able to show that the *Great Dynastic Chronicle*'s early source, the *Dipavamsa* or 'Island Chronicle', contained the oldest account yet known of the life of Gautama Sakyamuni Buddha and the subsequent development of the Buddhist community in India and Ceylon over some seven centuries. Here was a very different slant on historical events hitherto seen only from the perspective of Brahman writers – and one that directly challenged their version of Indian history.

The *Great Dynastic Chronicle* was, first and foremost, a history of the Buddhist Church on the island of Lanka but it included events on the mainland from the time of the Buddha, helpfully backed up with a twin dating system: one based on years since the death of Sakyamuni Buddha, the other on years since the accession of the ruling monarch. Thus, the Sakyamuni's death – year zero in the Buddhist calendar – had taken place in the eighth year of the reign of King Ajatasatru of Magadha. Exactly a century after the Buddha's death the Second Buddhist Council had taken place, that being the tenth year of the reign of King Kalasoko, whose ten sons had ruled for twenty-two years before giving way to the nine Nanda brothers, the last of which was Dhana Nanda, overthrown by the Brahman minister Chanakya.

'Having put him to death,' wrote Turnour in his translation –

Chanako installed in the sovereignty over the whole of Jambudipo [India], a descendant of the dynasty of Moriyan sovereigns, endowed with illustrious and beneficent attributes, named Chandragutto. He reigned thirty-four years. His son Bindusara reigned twenty-eight years. The sons of

Bindusara were one hundred and one, the issue of different mothers. Among them, Asoko [the Pali form of the Sanskrit Ashoka, rendered as Ashoka from here on to avoid confusion] by his piety and supernatural wisdom, became all-powerful. He having put to death one hundred brothers, minus one, born of different mothers, reigned sole sovereign of all Jambudipo. Be it known, that from the period of the death of Buddho, and antecedent to his installation, two hundred and eighteen years had elapsed.

In other words, Ashoka had been anointed king of Magadha 218 years after the death of Sakyamuni Buddha.

Turnour's translation went on to give details of King Ashoka's rise to power. Due to a rumour that he is destined to murder his father and take the throne for himself, Ashoka is sent away to govern the kingdom of Avanti, with its capital city at Ujjain. On his way there Ashoka halts at Vidisha and meets a 'lovely maiden named Devi, the daughter of a merchant. He made her his wife, and she was (afterwards) with child by him and bore in Ujjeni a beautiful boy, Mahindo [Mahinda in Sanskrit, and in that form hereafter], and when two years had passed she bore a daughter, Samghamitta [Sanghamitta in Sanskrit, and in that form hereafter].'[30]

A decade later, while acting as his father's viceroy in Ujjain, Ashoka receives news that King Bindusara is dying. He hastens to Pataliputra and immediately on arrival presents himself at his father's deathbed: 'As soon as his sire expired, seizing the capital for himself, and putting to death his eldest brother in that celebrated city, he usurped the sovereignty.'[31]

Four years pass before Ashoka's position as ruler of Magadha is strong enough to allow his official anointing as king to take place. He appoints his younger brother Tisso (Tissa in Sanskrit, and in that form hereafter), born of the same mother, as his deputy. However, Ashoka's violent conduct earns him the epithet *Candasoka* or 'Angry Ashoka'. He then begins to have religious doubts. His father King Bindusara had been 'of the Brahmanical faith' and had supported sixty thousand Brahmans with alms, a practice which Ashoka follows for three years until the 'despicable' behaviour of the Brahmans at court leads him to order representatives from all religions to come before him separately so that he can question them about their tenets. While this examination is in progress his eye is caught by the calm bearing of a young Buddhist monk passing under his window. The boy's name is Nigrodha, and he turns out to be the orphaned son of Ashoka's eldest half-brother Sumana, whom Ashoka killed in his rise to power. Sitting Nigrodha on his throne, Ashoka questions him on matters of Buddhist doctrine until he is satisfied that this is the true faith – 'and when the lord of the earth had heard him he was won to the doctrine of the Conqueror [i.e. Sakyamuni Buddha]'.[32]

Ashoka now becomes an *upasaka* or 'lay Buddhist', the Brahmans are expelled from court and sixty thousand Buddhist monks take their place. The leading elder of the age, Moggaliputta Tissa (Tissa son of Moggali), becomes King Ashoka's teacher and remains the dominant figure in Ashoka's life until his death in the twenty-sixth year of Ashoka's reign.

Having learned that there are eighty-four thousand discourses on the tenets of Buddhism, King Ashoka orders stupas and monastic institutions to be built in eighty-four thousand places. Outside his capital of Pataliputra he builds the Ashokarama, a major monastic complex bearing his name. The building of these monasteries takes three years and to celebrate their completion Ashoka holds a great festival, bestowing lavish gifts upon the Buddhist Church. On the day of the festival itself he proceeds in state to visit his Ashokarama and is proclaimed Dhammasoko – in Sanskrit *Dharmashoka*, or 'Ashoka of the Moral Law':

> On that day the great king wearing all his adornments with the women of his household, with his ministers and surrounded by the multitude of his troops, went to his own arama, as if cleaving the earth. In the midst of the brotherhood he stood, bowing down to the venerable brotherhood. In the assembly were eighty kotis [millions] of bhikkhus [monks], and ... ninety times one hundred thousand bhikkhunis [nuns] ... These monks and nuns wrought the miracle called the 'unveiling of the world' to the end that the king Dharmashoka might be converted. Candashoka was he called in earlier times, by reason of his evil deeds; he was known as Dharmashoka afterwards because of his pious deeds.[33]

The elder Moggaliputta Tissa acknowledges the king's great generosity towards the Buddhist Sangha but explains that a greater means of gaining merit would be to allow his two children Mahinda and Sanghamitta to enter the Buddhist order. Mahinda is then aged twenty and his sister eighteen. Their ordination takes places in King Dharmashoka's sixth year following his consecration. Dharmashoka's younger brother Tissa then seeks permission to become a monk, which is reluctantly given.

The fortunes of the Buddhists now improve greatly, thanks to the generosity of Dharmashoka. But this success attracts 'heretics' who bring their own false doctrines, leading to great confusion within the Buddhist community and causing Moggaliputta Tissa to describe them as a 'dreadful excrescence on religion, like unto a boil'. These schisms continue for seven years and eventually force the king to act. However, his teacher had gone into a seven-year solitary retreat in the Himalaya, so King Dharmashoka sends one of his ministers to the Ashokarama with orders to settle a particular dispute, resulting in an incident in which a number of monks are killed.

Greatly distressed, King Dharmashoka sends for Moggaliputta Tissa, who finally breaks his retreat when the king despatches a ship up the Ganges to collect him. Ashoka then summons the whole of the Buddhist priesthood to assemble for a special convocation beside the Ashokarama. Each monk expounds the doctrines according to his school, after which sixty thousand are expelled as heretics. Under the direction of Moggaliputta Tissa the remaining Buddhists succeed in making 'a true compilation of the true dharma'.[34] This important event – afterwards known as the Third Buddhist Council – lasts nine months and ends in the seventeenth year of Dharmashoka's reign.

Meanwhile, in 'the celebrated capital Anuradhapura, in the delightful Lanka', the Lankan king Mutasiwo has died after a reign of sixty years. His second son becomes king and takes the name *Dewananpiatisso* or 'Tisso Beloved-of-the-Gods' (Devanamapiyatissa in Sanskrit, and in that form hereafter). He decides that no one is more worthy to receive a gift of such jewels than his friend King Dharmashoka. To escort the jewels he sends his nephew Maha Aritto, who journeys for seven days by sea and then another seven days by land to reach Pataliputra and present the gifts to King Dharmashoka. The Magadhan

king responds with gifts of his own that include sacred water
from the Ganges, 'a royal virgin of great personal charms' and
'one hundred and sixty loads of hill paddy [rice] which had
been brought by parrots'.

Along with these material presents Dharmashoka sends the
gift of 'pious advice' in the form of the following words: 'I have
taken refuge in Buddho, his religion, and his priesthood: I have
avowed myself a devotee in the religion of the descendant of
Sakyo. Ruler of men, imbuing thy mind with the conviction of
the truth of these supreme blessings, with unfeigned faith, do
thou also take refuge in this salvation.'

This first religious contact between the two monarchs is followed by a far more ambitious missionary project, attributed in
the *Great Dynastic Chronicle* not to Ashoka but to his religious
teacher Moggaliputta Tissa, who sends missionaries to every
corner of the Indian subcontinent and beyond. This includes
a deputation of five elders, led by King Dharmashoka's son
Mahinda, who are despatched south with the instruction,
'Establish ye in the delightful land of Lanka, the delightful
religion of the Vanquisher [i.e. Sakyamuni Buddha].'

Understandably, the *Great Dynastic Chronicle* devotes a great
deal of space to Mahinda's mission to Lanka, which takes place
when Mahinda has been a monk for twelve years. Before he
leaves for Lanka, Mahinda goes to Vidisha to say goodbye to
his mother, his party now including his sister Sanghamitta's
son, Sumano. His mother Devi is described as living in a
monastery at Chetiyagiri, or 'the Hill of the Stupa', and being
overjoyed at seeing her beloved son.

After a month at his mother's monastery on the Hill of the
Stupa, Mahinda and his party depart for Lanka – not by land
and sea but by air, alighting on a mountain peak in the centre

of the island. King Devanamapiyatissa of Lanka receives the
missionaries at Mihintale and is converted to Buddhism, along
with his family and his court. Several chapters later Sumano is
asked to return to Pataliputra to beg his great-uncle King
Dharmashoka for relics of the Buddha. Sumano returns to
Magadha to find Dharmashoka engaged in worshipping the
Bodhi tree at Bodhgaya. Having received the Buddha's alms
bowl from him, Sumano proceeds to the Himalayas to collect
two further Buddha relics: a collarbone and an eye-tooth.
These precious relics are transported to Lanka and interred by
King Devanamapiyatissa in a great stupa built for that purpose
at Anuradhapura.

King Devanamapiyatissa's next request is for a cutting from
the sacred Bodhi tree, which is communicated to Dharmashoka
by his daughter Sanghamitta, now a female elder of the new
Buddhist Church in Lanka. The king is greatly troubled as to
how this can be done without harming the tree but performs a
complex ceremony that ends with his taking a cutting from the
Bo tree, potting it and placing it on board a sea-going vessel
under Sanghamitta's care. The boat then sails down the
Ganges to the sea while the king and his army march across the
land for seven days before meeting up with the boat at the port
of Tamalitta (Tamralipti in modern Bengal). Here a final ceremony is held before the king wades into the sea up to his neck
to place the cutting on board and bid it farewell: 'The maharaja
having thus spoken, stood on the shore of the ocean with
uplifted hands; and, gazing on the departing bo-branch, shed
tears in the bitterness of his grief. In the agony of parting with
the bo-branch, the disconsolate Dharmashoka, weeping and
lamenting in loud sobs, departed for his own capital.'[35]

After planting the Bodhi-tree cutting in his pleasure garden at

Anuradhapura the king of Lanka follows his neighbour's example by establishing stupas and monasteries throughout his island.
'Thus this ruler of Lanka, Dewanamapiyatissa [*sic*],' declares the
Great Dynastic Chronicle, 'for the spiritual benefit of the people of
Lanka, executed these undertakings in the first year of his reign;
and delighting in the exercise of his benevolence, during the
whole of his life, realised for himself manifold blessings.' He
reigns for forty years, his death being followed eight years later
by that of Dharmashoka's son Mahinda, 'the light of Lanka'.

From this point onwards the *Great Dynastic Chronicle* has little
more to say about events on the Indian mainland – except for
one ambiguous paragraph at the start of its twentieth chapter,
which tells how in the thirtieth year of King Ashoka's reign his
Buddhist queen Asandhimitra dies, and how four years later he
remarries:

> Dharmashoka, under the influence of carnal passions, raised
> to the dignity of queen consort, an attendant of his former
> wife. In the third year from that date, this malicious and vain
> creature, who thought but of the charms of her own person,
> saying 'this king, neglecting me, lavishes his devotion exclu-
> sively on the bo-tree' – in her rage attempted to destroy the
> great bo with the poisoned fang of a toad. In the fourth year
> from that occurrence [i.e. after the death of Queen Asand-
> himitra, thus thirty-seven years after Ashoka's anointing],
> this highly gifted monarch Dharmashoka fulfilled the lot of
> mortality.

This summary hints that all was not well in King Ashoka's royal
household in the last years of his life. Thirty years after his
anointing his beloved Buddhist queen dies. Four years later he

takes one of his late wife's attendants as his new queen, who becomes so jealous of her husband's devotion to Buddhism that in the thirty-seventh year after his consecration she seeks to destroy the Bodhi tree. Ashoka dies soon afterwards, but he is accorded none of the laudatory remarks that the *Great Dynastic Chronicle* gives his son or his daughter at their deaths. The disappointment is almost palpable. King Devanama-piyatissa's great ally and model sets Buddhism in motion in Lanka, but then at the very end of his life lets himself and the Buddhist cause down.

With Dharmashoka's death the *Great Dynastic Chronicle* loses all interest in the affairs of the mainland. In fact, India as Jambudwipa features only once more, when a later Lankan monarch builds a new relic stupa at Anuradhapura and invites Buddhist monks from all over India and beyond to attend its inauguration. According to the *Great Dynastic Chronicle*, many thousands of monks attend from Rajgir, Isipatana, the Jetavana monastery at Sravasti, the Mahavana monastery at Vaishali, Kosambi, the Ashokarama at Pataliputra, Kashmir, Pallavabhogga, 'Alasanda [Alexandria] the city of the Yonas [probably modern Kandahar]', the 'Vinjha forest mountains', the Bodhimanda monastery, the 'Vanavasa country', and the 'great Kelasa vihara'.[36] It seems that a century after the death of King Dharmashoka Buddhism was flourishing mightily both in Lanka and on the Indian mainland.

George Turnour's *Epitome of the History of Ceylon, Compiled from Native Annals: and the First Twenty Chapters of the Mahawanso* showed beyond all reasonable doubt that King Ashoka was not merely the instrument for the establishment of Buddhism in Lanka but a major figure in Indian history in his own right, whose sovereign authority extended throughout the subcontinent and whose influence as a propagator of Buddhism extended beyond its borders. And for those who cared to look, it provided an important clue as to why the complex of stupas at Sanchi might have some special significance in the Ashoka story. The *Great Dynastic Chronicle* had described how the Prince Ashoka's first wife Devi, whom he had first met at Vidisha, afterwards lived in Chetiyagiri, 'the Hill of the Stupa', so named because of 'the superb Chetiya *wiharo* [monastic complex] which had been erected by herself'. It was from here that their eldest son Mahinda had set out with his fellow missionaries to take the Buddhist teachings to Lanka. There are several hills in close proximity to the town of Vidisha but the nearest is the hill today known as Sanchi. Here, it seems, lay the explanation as to why that particular Buddhist site might have become the object of special attention both during and after Ashoka's lifetime.

With Turnour's revelations the stage was now set for what would be the last act of the mystery of the golden pillar of Firoz Shah: a dramatic denouement that would come in the form of a double revelation.

8

Thus Spake King Piyadasi

James Prinsep's page of engravings of the Sanchi stupa donations, which when brought together gave him the first clues to the deciphering of the Brahmi script. (*JRAS*, Vol. VIII, July 1837)

In Britain the year 1837 is best remembered for the start of the Victorian era. To political historians of India, 1837 represents the black year in which the Orientalist movement, led by Professor H. H. Wilson in Oxford and James Prinsep's elder brother Henry Thoby Prinsep in Calcutta, was finally defeated by the Anglicists and the evangelicals under Thomas Macaulay and Lord Bentinck; a defeat that led to the imposition of English as the chief medium of instruction and the ending of government funding for the printing of works in the vernacular.[1]

But for students of Indian studies the year 1837 will always be remembered as the *annus mirabilis* of Indian historiography and philology; the year in which astonishing revelations came so thick and fast that there was no time to absorb the implications of one before the next had been announced.

The year began with James Prinsep's announcement that he had identified two inscribed stone slabs in the collection of the Asiatic Society of Bengal as stolen property. Some months earlier he had asked a correspondent in Orissa to re-examine the rock inscription at Khandagiri near Bhubaneshwar, first identified by Andrew Stirling twenty years earlier. However, this correspondent had been prevented from carrying out that examination by the local Brahmins, who had complained that some years earlier an English colonel had stolen a number of stone effigies and inscriptions from their temples. That disturbing news provoked Prinsep into searching through the records of the Asiatic Society of Bengal, leading to the unmasking of the culprit as the late General Charles 'Hindoo' Stuart, who a generation earlier had scandalised Calcutta society by adopting Hindu manners and urging English memsahibs for the sake of their health to throw off their tight dresses and wear saris instead.[2] Prinsep arranged for two stone slabs taken by

Stuart from Bhubaneshwar to be sent down the coast to Cuttack, the provincial capital of Orissa, where his contact restored them to their proper owners.[3]

The correspondent concerned was Lieutenant Markham Kittoe of the 6th Native Infantry and he was at this time in disgrace. Kittoe was one of John Company's misfits, a keen young antiquarian who had come out to India in 1825 as a seventeen-year-old military cadet but failed to get along with his brother officers. He had found love in the arms of a colonel's daughter, Emily, whom he had married in 1835 and who had already borne him the first two of their nine children. But he had made the mistake of accusing his commanding officer of oppression, and was at this time awaiting a court martial at which he would be found guilty of 'insubordinate, disrespectful, and litigious conduct, unbecoming of an officer and a gentleman', and discharged from the service. It was James Prinsep who had come to his rescue by finding him temporary employment as secretary of the Coal Committee, a post which allowed him to tour Orissa ostensibly in search of coalfields.

The goodwill engendered by the return of the two stolen slabs now worked to Kittoe's advantage, for he was allowed to make a copy of the Khandagiri rock inscription, but as he did so he heard talk of a second rock inscription, said to be on a hill on the other side of Bhubaneshwar town and on the far side of the River Daya – a name that in Sanskrit means 'compassion', the significance of which would only later become apparent. However, when Kittoe tried to track down this new inscription he was again frustrated, this time by the local inhabitants, the Oriyas. Only the intervention of a passing Hindu religious mendicant from Benares enabled Kittoe to find what he was looking for. 'Such is the aversion the Ooriyahs have of our going near their places of worship', Kittoe afterwards wrote, 'that I was actually decoyed away from the spot, when within a few yards of it, being assured that there was no such place, and had returned for a mile or more, when I met with a man who led me back to the spot by torchlight. I set fire to the *jangal* [jungle] and perceived the inscription, which was completely hidden by it.'[4]

Lieutenant Markham Kittoe, with the Ashokan elephant rock at Dhauli shown behind him and the temple spires of Bhubaneshwar in the distance. (A drawing by Colesworthy Grant published in his *Lithographic Sketches*, 1850)

The hostility experienced by Kittoe remains one of the hazards of Indian archaeology to this day, sometimes inspired by religious prejudice but more often than not arising from the belief that anyone who comes to dig into old ruins is seeking buried treasure, and anything inscribed on rocks or pillars must be the key to those treasures.[5]

When Kittoe returned to the rock the following morning to begin copying the inscription, he was confronted by a she-bear and her two cubs who had made their home at the base of the rock. To evade them, Kittoe scrambled up the rock face, where he found himself confronted by a small elephant – or, rather, 'the fore half of an elephant, four feet high, of superior workmanship ... hewn out of solid rock'. The bear cubs had fled – but not the mother, so Kittoe shot her. Only then was he able to examine the inscription on the rock face below.

The Dhauli Rock Edict inscription, with the head of the Dhauli elephant just visible on the terrace above. This photograph was taken by Alexander Caddy in 1895. (APAC, British Library)

What Kittoe termed the Aswastama[6] rock inscription is
better known today as the Dhauli Rock Edict, taking its name
from the nearby village of Dhauli. These edicts had been chiselled across the face of a rock just below the summit of one of
three low hills overlooking the River Daya: 'The rock has been
hewn and polished for a space of fifteen feet long by ten in
height, and the inscription cut thereon being divided into four
tablets, the first of which appears to have been executed at a
different period from the rest; the letters are much larger and
not so well cut. The fourth tablet is encircled by a deep line,
and is cut with more care than the others.'

The arrival in Calcutta of Kittoe's copy of the Dhauli inscription was opportune, for it coincided with the receipt of two
other sets of facsimiles of inscriptions. The first had been
copied from the great elephant rock at Girnar discovered by
Colonel James Tod back in 1823. This had been taken at
Prinsep's request by a Mr Wathen from an earlier set of facsimiles made by the Reverend Dr John Wilson, a Scots surgeon
and missionary who, besides founding the first school for Indian
girls in Bombay and giving his name to what became Wilson
College, was a keen antiquarian. The other set of inscriptions
had come from the Great Tope at Sanchi, taken by Captain
Edward Smith of the Royal Engineers in answer to Prinsep's
call for copies of its inscriptions and drawings of its sculptures.

Smith's Sanchi inscriptions were accompanied by some lively
drawings showing a number of the sculptures that adorned the
four gateways of the Great Tope, but Prinsep had eyes only for
the former, for in addition to the several pillar inscriptions from
the Gangetic plains, he now had three more different inscriptions
from three widely separated locations in Western, Central and
Eastern India – all of them written in the same 'No. 1' script.

One of the readers who responded to Prinsep's appeal for illustrations of the Sanchi sculptures was Captain William Murray, assistant to the commander of the Saugor and Narbada Territories. He sent in two drawings, both taken from the cross-beams of the fallen South Gateway of the Great Tope. Prinsep selected for reproduction in the *JASB* the more striking of the two scenes, showing a city under attack and what appeared to be a monarch on a huge elephant directing the assault. Unknown to Murray and Prinsep, both scenes were part of the Ashokan story that would not be understood until eighty years later (for an earlier drawing of the upper scene see p. 108, and for a later photograph see p. 240). (Royal Asiatic Society)

'This inscription will be seen to have arrived at a most fortunate moment,' declared Prinsep when he rose to speak at the monthly meeting of the ASB held on 7 June 1837. The minutes of that momentous meeting state quite simply: 'The Secretary read a note on the inscriptions, which had proved of high interest from their enabling him to discover the long-sought alphabet of the ancient Lat character (or No. 1 of Allahabad) – and to read therewith the inscriptions of Delhi, Allahabad, Bettiah, Girnar, and Cuttack [the Dhauli inscription] – all intimately connected, as it turns out, in their origin, and in their purport.'

Prinsep's note was subsequently published in the *JRAS*, providing posterity with a step-by-step explanation of how he came to break the code of No. 1.[7]

The inscriptions from Sanchi were of two sorts. The first two recorded grants of land from the early Gupta dynasty of the fourth century CE. The remaining twenty-three (see illustration, p. 153) consisted of a number of much shorter inscriptions in No. 1 script found on the crosspieces of the pillars that formed the colonnade surrounding the stupa, most of them cut in a rough and ready way that was in marked contrast to the finely wrought sculptures that decorated the four gateways. 'These apparently trivial fragments of rude writing', declared Prinsep, 'have instructed us in the alphabet and the language of those ancient pillars and rock inscriptions which have been the wonder of the learned since the days of Sir William Jones.'

Prinsep went on to explain how, as he set about arranging the inscriptions to appear together as one lithographed plate for publication in the Society's *Journal*, he had been struck by the fact that virtually every one ended in the same two letters: a snake-like squiggle formed by six straight lines, followed by an inverted capital T with a dot on one side:

'Coupling this circumstance,' he continued, 'with their extreme brevity ... it immediately occurred to me that they must record either obituary notices, or more probably, the offerings and presents of votaries.' These two characters were in many cases preceded by a third symbol resembling a double-barbed hook or anchor in which one of the hooks had been distorted to curve downwards rather than up:

$$\mathcal{L}$$

By yet another of those happy conjunctions of timing that surrounded this great breakthrough, Prinsep had only days earlier been working on the coins of Saurashtra in western India.[8] 'Now this [character] I had learned from the Saurashtra coins, deciphered only a day or two before, to be one sign of the genitive case singular, being the *ssa* of the Pali, or *sya* of the Sanskrit.' If that character represented the genitive 'of' (just as the apostrophe 's' in English represents 'of') it was logical to suppose that the rest of each short phrase concerned a donation and the name of the donor: '"Of so-and-so the gift," must then be the form of each brief sentence.'

Both in Sanskrit and Pali the verb 'to give' was *dana* and the noun 'gift' or 'donation' *danam*, sharing the same Indo-European root as the Latin *donare* (to give) and *donus* (gift). This led Prinsep to 'the speedy recognition of the word *danam* (gift), teaching me the very two letters *d* and *n*.' The snake-like squiggle represented the sound 'da', the inverted 'T' the sound 'na' and the single dot the muted 'm', together forming the word *danam*.

With these two letters and the genitive singular understood, all the concentrated study that Prinsep had put in over the previous four years suddenly and dramatically fell into place. It was the eureka moment of Indian philology: 'My

acquaintance with ancient alphabets had become so familiar
that most of the remaining letters in the present examples
could be named at once on re-inspection. In the course of a
few minutes I thus became possessed of the whole alphabet,
which I tested by applying it to the inscription on the Delhi
column.'

Having announced the single most important advance in the
study of Indian history, Prinsep then backed off, explaining
that before he could give the Society his complete translation
of the Firoz Shah Lat inscription he needed to prepare a fount
of type for his alphabet of No. 1, which he was himself in the
process of making. He then sought to mollify those present at
that historic meeting by offering them a few titbits. These
included the statement that the language of the No. 1 inscriptions was 'Magadhi ... the original type whereon the more
complicated structure of the Sanskrit has been founded. If
carefully analyzed, each member of the alphabet will be found
to contain the element of the corresponding number, not only
of the Deva-Nagari, but of the Canouj, the Pali, the Tibetan,
the Hala Canara, and of all the derivates from the Sanskrit
stock.'

In other words, No. 1, the written language of the Maga-
dhans, was the ancestor of most of India's modern languages
and alphabets. Written from left to right, its alphabet consisted
of thirty-three basic letters, each representing a consonant
followed by the 'a' vowel, the other vowels being formed by
the addition of ancilliary glyphs to the base consonant, with
only initial vowel sounds having their own specific characters. It had all the simplicity of an original, developed to give
written expression to a popular spoken language, Prakrit, which
had preceded Sanskrit. Initially, Prinsep called this alphabet

'Indian Pali', but it was later recognised that the early Brahmans had termed it *Brahmi lipi*, the 'language of Brahma'. Today it is best known as Brahmi, with the earliest form often being referred to as Ashokan Brahmi.

Once he had understood how the Brahmi alphabet worked, Prinsep applied it – speedily and triumphantly – to the translation of the twenty-three records of donations from the Sanchi stupa and the names of their donors. Next came translations of the lettering on a number of bilingual Indo-Bactrian coins bearing Greek lettering on the obverse and No.1 on the reverse. A number of short inscriptions from Bodhgaya followed. Only then did Prinsep feel ready to take on the Firoz Shah's Lat inscription, beginning with the fifteen-character phrase that he had earlier found to begin virtually every paragraph at Delhi, Allahabad, Girnar, Dhauli and elsewhere. 'The most usual reading,' he declared, 'and the equivalent according to my alphabet, are as follows:

Devanamapiya piyadasi laja hevam aha

The word *laja* initially threw both Prinsep and his Pali-speaking Sinhalese assistant Ratna Paula, until they realised that this was 'the licence of a loose vernacular orthography' and that the intended word was *raja*. That gave them the opening phrase: 'Beloved-of-the-Gods beloved king'. The last two words – *hevam aha* – translated as 'spake thus', which together gave the complete sentence:

Thus spake King Piyadasi, Beloved-of-the-Gods

These words, professed Prinsep, had every appearance of a
royal edict: 'The simplicity of the form reminds us of the
common expression in our own Scriptures – "Thus spake the
prophet", or in the proclamation of the Persian monarch –
"Thus saith Cyrus, king of Persia".'

Prinsep's first thoughts were that here were 'the doctrines of
some great reformer, such as Shakya [Sakyamuni Buddha]'.
But when he translated the second sentence it immediately
became clear that this could only be the work of a monarch, for
it began *Saddavisati vasa abhisitename* – 'In the twenty-seventh
year of my anointment'[9] – a phrase that was repeated in
another four places of the inscription. Today that sentence is
generally read as 'When I had been consecrated twenty-six
years'[10] or 'twenty-six years after my coronation'.[11]

Who then, Prinsep asked, could this monarch have been –
for he was patently a ruler powerful enough 'to spread his
edicts thus over the continent of India'? So far as Prinsep knew,
no Indian ruler before Akbar the Great had ever ruled over
such a large area as that covered by the pillar and rock inscriptions. He had gone through all the Hindu genealogical tables
and had found no one by the name of Devanamapiya Piyadasi
(more accurately, Devanamapriya Priydarsin, the form most
often used today in academic circles).

Only one contender seemed to fit the bill – but a monarch
from outside India: 'In Mr Turnour's *Epitome of Ceylonese History*,
then, we are presented once, and once only, with the name of
a king, Devenampiatissa [*sic*], as nearly identical with ours as
possible.' George Turnour's translation of the *Great Dynastic
Chronicle* had described how this King Devanamapiyatissa of

Lanka had been converted to Buddhism through the efforts of the Indian king Dharmashoka, who could only be the Mauryan ruler Ashoka. 'Was [it] possible, then, that this Lankan king was the author of the rock edicts', that 'Devanampiyatissa [*sic*], the royal convert, caused, in his zeal, the dogmas of his newly adopted faith to be promulgated far and wide?'

James Prinsep presented his complete translation of the Firoz Shah Lat inscription at the next meeting of the ASB, held in early August 1837.[12] It was, in his view, 'a series of edicts connected with the Buddhist faith issued by Divanamapiya Piyadasi [*sic*], a king of Ceylon', their purpose being to 'proclaim his renunciation of his former faith, and his adoption of the Buddhist persuasion'.

Even though the edicts made no reference to Buddha Sakyamuni, they appeared to be directly associated with Buddhist thinking. The word *dharma* ran through the inscription like a thread: 'The sacred name constantly employed – the true keystone of Shakya's reform – is *Dhamma* or *Dharma*.' This word Prinsep translated – or, rather, mistranslated – as 'virtue' or 'religion'. The promotion of Dharma lay at the heart of these edicts, even though it was quite clear that the real authority lay with the edicts' author, whose name appeared no less than sixteen times on the Delhi column: 'The chief drift of the writing seems to enhance the merits of the author – the continual recurrence of *esa me kate*, "so I have done", arguing a vaunt of his own acts rather than an inculcation of virtue in others'.

Prinsep established that the first of seven edicts – known today as Pillar Edicts 1–7 (PE 1–7) inscribed on Firoz Shah's Lat began on the north side of the column. Here three edicts had been set down within one compartment, each beginning

with the solemn fifteen-letter sentence declaration, 'Thus
spake King Piyadasi, Beloved-of-the-Gods'. The fourth edict
appeared by itself on the west side of the column, the fifth on
the south, the sixth on the east, and the seventh and longest
beginning under the east compartment and continuing right
round the column.

'Thus spake king Devanamapiya Piyadasi', begins Prinsep's
historic translation of Pillar Edict 1 (PE 1, here quoted in its
entirety):

> In the twenty-seventh year of my anointment, I have caused
> this religious edict to be published in writing. I acknowledge
> and confess the faults that have been cherished in my heart.
> From the love of virtue, by the side of which all other things
> are but sins – from the strict scrutiny of sin, and from a fervid
> desire to be told of sin – by the fear of sin and by the very
> enormity of sin – by these may my eyes be strengthened and
> confirmed. The sight of religion and the love of religion of
> their own accord increase and will ever increase: and my
> people whether of the laity, or of the priesthood – all mortal
> beings, are knit together thereby, and prescribe to them-
> selves the same path: and above all having obtained the
> mastery over their passions, they become supremely wise.
> For this is indeed true wisdom: it is upheld and bound by
> religion – by religion which cherishes, religion which teaches
> pious acts, religion which bestows pleasure.

By today's standards of epigraphy, this first translation was very
wide of the mark. Neither Prinsep nor Ratna Paula could fully
grasp the meaning of many sentences, as can be seen when the
above is set beside a modern translation (see Appendix, p. 419):

The second Pillar Edict (PE 2) was easier to translate, although it too was taken up with the meaning of Dharma, here defined by King Piyadasi as the performance of good works that included (in Prinsep's translation) 'the non-omission of many acts: mercy and charity, purity and chastity'. To this end, King Piyadasi had himself performed many acts of benevolence 'towards the poor and afflicted, towards bipeds and quadrupeds, towards the fowls of the air and things that move in the waters'. It closed with an explanation as to why these edicts were being promulgated: 'Let all pay attention to it, and let it endure for ages to come, and he who acts in conformity thereto, the same shall attain eternal happiness.'

James Prinsep's translation of the Pillar Edicts cannot be quoted here in full simply for reasons of space. However, an exception has be made for Prinsep's rendering of the closing sentences of the last of the seven Pillar Edicts (PE 7), where he came closest to catching the essence of its author's call for his message to be read by future generations:

For such an object is all this done, that it may endure to my sons and their sons' sons – as long as the sun and the moon shall last. Wherefore let them follow its injunctions and be obedient thereto – and let it be held in reverence and respect. In the twenty-seventh year of my reign have I caused this edict to be written: so sayeth Devanamapiya – 'Let stone pillars be prepared and let this edict of religion be engraven thereon, that it may endure unto the remotest ages.'

The modern translation may be more precise but no less moving (see Appendix, p. 425).

*

Prinsep's breaking of the Brahmi No. 1 script, his translations
of the Sanchi donations and the seven Pillar Edicts of the Firoz
Shah Lat inscription, and his identification of their author as
Devanamapiya Piyadasi came so fast one upon another that
they gave his fellow Orientalists little respite. But hard on the
heels of Prinsep's first tentative identification of Piyadasi,
Beloved-of-the-Gods as King Devanamapiyatissa of Lanka,
published in the July 1837 issue of the *JASB*, came a dramatic
response from George Turnour in Colombo.

'I have made a most important discovery,' Turnour wrote:
'You will find in the Introduction to my *Epitome* that a valuable
collection of Pali works was brought back to Ceylon from Siam,
by George Nodaris, modliar (chief of the cinnamon department, and then a Buddhist priest) in 1812.'[13] This collection of
Pali texts included a copy of the *Island Chronicle*, the original
chronicle from which the later *Great Dynastic Chronicle* took its
earliest historical material, but in a less corrupted version than
that upon which Turnour had based his translation – and with
crucial differences. While casually turning the leaves of the
manuscript Turnour had hit upon an entirely new passage
relating to the identity of Piyadasi. In translation it read: 'Two
hundred and eighteen years after the beatitude of Buddha was
the inauguration of Piyadassi ... who, the grandson of
Chandragupta, and own son of Bindusara, was at that time
Viceroy of Ujjayani.'

Here was Turnour's revelation. The King Devanamapiya
Piyadasi of the Firoz Shah Lat inscription was not King
Devanamapiyatissa of Lanka, as Prinsep had assumed. He was
his Indian contemporary Ashoka Maurya. The unfortunate
Wesleyan missionary William Fox had published just such a
conclusion four years earlier but had gone to his grave

unacknowledged, so it fell to George Turnour to receive all the plaudits – and rightly so.[14] Thus, the identity of Ashoka Maurya as the author of the Rock and Pillar Edicts was established beyond reasonable doubt – another milestone on the road to the recovery of India's lost history, another missing piece of the jigsaw.

Prinsep announced the next breakthrough in the August issue of *JASB*: his translation of eye-copies of two inscriptions in the Society's collection which had come from the Nagurjuni caves north of Gaya.[15] These were William Harrington's eye-copies, which had been gathering dust for almost forty years. They were in Brahmi and almost identical, except that one referred to the 'Brahman's cave' and the other to the 'Milkman's cave'. According to Prinsep's reading, they had been granted to 'the most devoted sect of Bauddha ascetics' by 'Dasharatha, the Beloved-of-the-Gods, immediately on his ascending the throne'. Dasharatha had used exactly the same epithet as that used by Ashoka in the Pillar Edicts. Furthermore, the name Dasharatha appeared in the lists of kings of Magadha as given in several of the *Puranas*: 'Looking into the Magadha catalogue we find a raja also named Dasharatha next but one below Dharma Asoka, the great champion of the Buddhist faith.' Here was evidence that a grandson of Ashoka had ruled in Magadha and had used the same epithet as Ashoka, perhaps as an expression of identification with him.

What Prinsep declared to be 'another link of the same chain of discovery'[16] came before the end of the year with the arrival in Calcutta of Markham Kittoe's improved version of the Dhauli inscription. Kittoe had been asked to make a second and more accurate copy at Prinsep's request, and had done so at some cost, for not only had he re-encountered the bear cubs, now fully grown, but had also hurt himself by falling off the edict rock: 'Being intent on my interesting task I forgot my ticklish footing; the bearer had also fallen asleep and let go his hold, so that having overbalanced myself I was pitched head foremost down the rock.'[17]

Kittoe's much improved facsimile of the Dhauli inscription arrived just as Prinsep was completing his first reading of an inaccurate eye-copy of the Girnar Rock Edicts. 'I had just groped my way through the Girnar text,' Prinsep afterwards wrote, 'which proved to be, like that of the pillars, a series of edicts promulgated by Asoka ... when I took up the Cuttack [Dhauli] inscriptions of which Lieut. Kittoe had been engaged in making a lithographic copy for my journal. To my surprise and joy I discovered that the greater part of these inscriptions was identical with the inscription at Girnar!'[18]

Despite being located on India's east and west coasts and nine hundred miles apart, these two great rocks bore messages that were for the most part identical, or, as Prinsep put it, 'from the first to the tenth [edict] they keep pace together'.[19] At this point the two diverged, the Girnar rock carrying three edicts not found at Dhauli, and the Dhauli rock two not found at Girnar. In essence, the Girnar rock carries the edicts known today as REs 1–14 but the Dhauli rock omits REs 11–13 and compensates by adding two REs of its own, known today as the Separate Rock Edicts (SREs 1 and 2). Markham Kittoe's two versions of the Dhauli REs also showed that what Prinsep had taken to be his errors of copying were actually differences in language between the western and eastern edicts, pointing to regional dialects of a common language, Prakrit.

The Girnar and Dhauli REs were presented in the same style and shared the same royal author as Firoz Shah's Lat and other PEs from the Gangetic plains to the north, but they were different both in content and in the time of their making.

The Firoz Shah Lat and the other Pillar Edicts had declared themselves to have been written twenty-six years after Ashoka's consecration, whereas the third of the Girnar and Dhauli Rock Edicts began: 'Beloved-of-the-Gods, King Piyadasi, speaks thus. Twelve years after my coronation this has been ordered.'[20] In other words, the Rock Edicts had been cut fourteen years before the Pillar Edicts.

What also became clear to Prinsep as he worked on his translation of this second set of edicts was that the Girnar and Dhauli edicts were significantly less sophisticated than the Pillar Edicts. Indeed, they appeared disorganised, even haphazard, as if they had been dictated off the cuff, with frequent repetitions and asides, seemingly the thoughts of a monarch used to despotic rule, his mind filled with conflicting notions about the nature of the Dharma he had committed himself to implementing and how best he should go about it. This confusion made Prinsep's work of translation doubly difficult.

RE 1 began simply enough: 'Beloved-of-the-Gods, King Piyadasi, has caused this Dharma edict to be written.' It went on to order a ban on the taking of all forms of life and on festivals involving animal sacrifice. It also threw some surprising light on Ashoka's own culinary tastes and his seeming reluctance to give up his favourite meats (in Venerable Shravasti Dhammika's modern translation here and below):

Here in my domain no living beings are to be slaughtered or offered in sacrifice. Nor should festivals be held, for Beloved-of-the-Gods, King Piyadasi, sees much to object to in such festivals, although there are some festivals that

Beloved-of-the-Gods, King Piyadasi, does approve of. Formerly, in the kitchen of Beloved-of-the-Gods, King Piyadasi, hundreds of thousands of animals were killed every day to make curry. But now with the writing of this Dharma edict only three creatures, two peacocks and a deer, are killed, and the deer not always. And in time, not even these three creatures will be killed.[21]

Respect for all living things was a feature of several of the edicts that followed. RE 2 talked about medical aid being provided for both human and animals, as well as wells dug and trees planted beside roads for their benefit. RE 3 called on the king's subjects to respect their parents, show generosity to others and live with moderation. Some edicts were distinctly personal in tone, even to the point of eccentricity, such as RE 6, which ordered that its author was to be kept fully informed at all times:

In the past, state business was not transacted nor were reports delivered to the king at all hours. But now I have given this order, that at any time, whether I am eating, in the women's quarters, the bed chamber, the chariot, the palanquin, in the park or wherever, reporters are to be posted with instructions to report to me the affairs of the people so that I might attend to these affairs wherever I am ... Truly, I consider the welfare of all to be my duty, and the root of this is exertion and the prompt despatch of business.

Yet the central focus of the edicts was always the practice of Dharma, defined in RE 11 in practical rather than spiritual terms:

There is no gift like the gift of the Dharma, no acquaintance like acquaintance with Dharma, no distribution like distribution of Dharma, and no kinship like kinship through Dharma. It consists of this: proper behaviour towards servants and employees, respect for mother and father, generosity to friends, companions, relations, Brahmans and ascetics, and not killing living beings. Therefore a father, a son, a brother, a master, a friend, a companion or a neighbour should say: 'This is good, this should be done.' One benefits in this world and gains great merit in the next by giving the gift of the Dharma.

Ashoka himself was promoting the practice of Dharma throughout his realms and beyond, following religious instruction he had received in the tenth year after his consecration. This was the subject of RE 8: 'In the past kings used to go out on pleasure tours during which there was hunting and other entertainment. But ten years after Beloved-of-the-Gods had been coronated, he went on a tour to Sambodhi and thus instituted Dharma tours.' The Sanskrit term *Sambodhi* means 'proceeding towards enlightenment', which could mean either that Ashoka went to the place of Sakyamuni Buddha's Enlightenment, which was Bodhgaya and its Bodhi-tree, or that he received Buddhist teaching. Either way, it was explicit confirmation that Ashoka had received some form of Buddhist instruction.

To assist the spreading of the Dharma, Ashoka had created a special class of religious officers known as *Dharma Mahamatras*, as explained in RE 5. They had been created thirteen years after his consecration to promote the Dharma not only within his borders but also among his neighbours, for 'They work among the Greeks, the Kambojas, the Gandharas, the Rastikas, the Pitinikas, and other people on the western borders.'

These religious officers also worked among all religions. This toleration was the subject of RE 7 – the briefest of all the edicts: 'Beloved-of-the-Gods, King Piyadasi, desires that all religions should reside everywhere, for all of them desire self-control and purity of heart. But people have various desires and various passions, and they may practise all of what they should or only a part of it.' This principle of freedom of religious expression was also the subject of RE 12 (at Girnar), which encouraged all forms of religious activity. 'One should listen to and respect the doctrines professed by others,' this edict reads in part. It continues (modern translation): 'Beloved-of-the-Gods, King Piyadasi, desires that all should be well-learned in the good doctrines of other religions. Those who are content with their own religion should be told this: Beloved-of-the-Gods, King Piyadasi, does not value gifts and honours as much as he values that there should be growth in the essentials of all religions.'

The final edict, RE 14, explained how and in what form Ashoka's Rock Edicts had been written. Prinsep describes it as 'a kind of summing up of the foregoing. We learn from this edict that the whole was engraved at one time from an authentic copy, issued, doubtless, under the royal mandate, by a scribe and pandit of a name not very easily deciphered. It is somewhat curious to find the same words precisely on the rock in Catak [Dhauli].'22 RE 14 also gave notice to Prinsep and his fellow Orientalists in India that many more edicts were waiting to be found (modern translation):

Beloved-of-the-Gods, King Piyadasi, has had these Dharma edicts written in brief, in medium length, and in extended form. Not all of them occur everywhere, for my domain is vast, but much has been written, and I will have still more written. And also there are some subjects here that have been spoken of again and again because of their sweetness, and so that the people may act in accordance with them. If some things written are incomplete, this is because of the locality, or in consideration of the object, or due to the fault of the scribe.

But this was not all. For Prinsep, the greatest cause for excitement after the discovery of the true identity of Piyadasi was to be found in the extra nuggets of historical detail tucked away in RE 2 and RE 13 (Girnar).

RE 2 concerned itself chiefly with medical provisions made by King Piyadasi, apparently extending beyond his borders into the territories of his immediate neighbour to the west. 'Everywhere within the conquered provinces of raja Piyadasi,' was how Prinsep translated its opening sentences, 'as well as the parts occupied by the faithful, such as Chola, Pida, Satiyaputra and Keralaputra, even as far as Tambapanni – and moreover within the dominions of Antiochus the Greek, of which Antiochus' generals are the rulers – everywhere the heaven-beloved raja Piyadasi's double system of medical aid is established.'[23]

The Cholas and Pandyas (Pida) were South Indian tribes, the Satiyaputras and Keralaputras were from India's south-western seaboard, and Tambapanni was Taproban, the ancient name for Ceylon. But then came the phrase *antiyoke name yona lajaya*, which Prinsep read as 'Antiochus the Greek King'. His

immediate assumption was that this was a reference to the
Graeco-Persian Antiochos Soter, son of the man who had taken
on Ashoka's grandfather Chandragupta and lost. Antiochos had
succeeded his father Seleukos the Victor after his assassination
in 281 BCE and had presided over an ever shrinking empire
until his own death in 261 BCE.

However, the most astonishing revelation was to be found in
the last of the Girnar interpolations, RE 13. It told of King
Ashoka's brutal conquest of the country of Kalinga in the eighth
year after his consecration. The name Kalinga was familiar to
Prinsep, from the fragments of Megasthenes' *India*. It was an
ancient kingdom in central-eastern India known in Prinsep's
time as the province of Orissa, under the authority of the
Bengal Presidency. Megasthenes had written that at the time
of Chandragupta, Kalinga's capital was Parthalis, defended
by an army of sixty thousand foot-soldiers, seven hundred war
elephants and one thousand horsemen. According to the Girnar
rock, those forces had proved no match for Ashoka's army
which, by his own admission, had followed his orders in showing no mercy. So much suffering had ensued in his conquest
of Kalinga that Ashoka had been overcome by remorse and, so
the Rock Edict implied, had become a convert to Buddhism.
RE 13 set this all out in quite remarkable detail. It began (for
the full edict in modern translation see Appendix, p. 413):

> Beloved-of-the-Gods, King Piyadasi, conquered the
> Kalingas eight years after his coronation. One hundred and
> fifty thousand were deported, one hundred thousand were
> killed and many more died from other causes. After the
> Kalingas had been conquered, Beloved-of-the-Gods came to
> feel a strong inclination towards the Dharma, a love for the

Dharma and for instruction in Dharma. Now Beloved-of-the-Gods feels deep remorse for having conquered the Kalingas . . .[24]

It was now clear why that particular edict was missing from the Dhauli rock in Orissa. It had been omitted to spare the feelings of the conquered people of Kalinga. It also helped to explain why the river that flowed past the Dhauli rock was known as the River of Compassion, Daya.

RE 13 closed with a call for Ashoka's descendants to follow his example and to continue to rule by non-violence:

Truly, Beloved-of-the-Gods desires non-injury, restraint and impartiality to all beings, even where wrong has been done. Now it is conquest by Dharma that Beloved-of-the-Gods considers to be the best conquest . . . I have had this Dharma edict written so that my sons and great-grandsons may not consider making new conquests, or that if military conquests are made, that they be done with forbearance and light punishment, or better still, that they consider making conquest by Dharma only, for that bears fruit in this world and the next.

In the middle section of that same RE 13 were still more revelations – except that since Tod's visit in 1823 the Girnar rock had suffered severe damage to one corner after a pious Jain had used gunpowder to widen the pilgrim trail leading up Girnar's sacred mountain. The explosion had blown off a corner of the rock at the point where the left-hand section of RE 13 had been cut, leaving just enough for Prinsep to make out that it listed seven kingdoms within the Indian subcontinent where King Ashoka's conquest by Dharma had been achieved as well as other kingdoms beyond Ashoka's western borders influenced by his Dharma, even as far as 'six hundred *yojanas*', or approximately three thousand miles! The names of five foreign monarchs had originally been inscribed, of which only two were now decipherable: 'Antiochus the ally of Asoka' (already mentioned in RE 1) and 'one of the Ptolemies of Egypt'.

The loss of the remaining three names was deeply frustrating. Even so, the names of Antiochos and Ptolemy allowed Prinsep to speculate as to when the Girnar edicts might have been written, for both must have been ruling at that time. The first he had taken to be Antiochos Soter, son of Seleukos the Victor (281–261 BCE), so it followed that the rule of the king named Ptolemy had to fall within his dates. Ptolemy, founder of the Ptolemaic dynasty of kings of Egypt, had declared himself ruler in 305 BCE. However, this first Ptolemy had died in 285 or 283 BCE – at least two years before Antiochos had succeeded his father in 281 BCE – so the Ptolemy in question had to be Ptolemy II Philadelphos, who had ruled Egypt from 285/283 to 246 BCE. Since Ptolemy II was ruling in Egypt when Antiochos became king in 281 BCE and was still on the throne when the latter died in 261 BCE, it followed that RE 13 must have been inscribed somewhere between those two dates: 281 BCE and 261 BCE. And since the Girnar Rock Edict declared itself to have been cut twelve years after Ashoka's consecration, it further followed that he must have been anointed king of Magadha at some point between 293 and 273 BCE.

This window challenged the dating established by Sir William Jones in 1789, which had placed the year of Chandragupta's accession in 317 BCE or soon after. Chandragupta had ruled for twenty-four years before being succeeded by his son Bindusara, who ruled for twenty-five years before being followed by Ashoka. That had given a provisional dating for Ashoka's consecration as king as the year 266 BCE – which fell outside Prinsep's window by six years.

What Prinsep had failed to take into account was that Ptolemy II had been followed by Ptolemy III – and Antiochos Soter by his son of the same name, Antiochos II. It would take another generation and the discovery of more complete Rock Edicts before the names of the three missing allies of Ashoka would be determined – and with them more exact dating.

This was a rare error among many advances. By the early spring of 1838 Prinsep's work on the Pillar and Rock Edicts had established a rough chronology of events in the rule of King Ashoka: in the eighth year after his consecration he had waged war on Kalinga, effecting such destruction that he had been overcome by remorse and had turned to the Dharma (RE 13); in his tenth year Ashoka had gone on a tour of the holy places of Dharma, which had included 'visits and gifts to Brahmans and ascetics, visits and gift of gold to the aged, visits to people in the countryside, instructing them in the Dharma, and discussing Dharma with them as suitable' (RE 8); in his twelfth year Ashoka had started to have Dharma edicts written in various forms 'for the welfare and happiness of the people, and so that not transgressing them they might grow in the Dharma' (PE 6); in his twelfth and thirteenth years Ashoka had set up a missionary organisation staffed by a new cadre of religious officers for the spreading of the Dharma through his kingdom and beyond (REs 3, 5); and in his twenty-sixth and twenty-seventh years Ashoka had brought out further edicts that were inscribed on pillars rather than rocks (PEs 1, 4, 5, 6 and 7).

Prinsep's translations had also showed that the Rock and Pillar Edicts were unequivocally the work of one omnipotent ruler, Ashoka Maurya, known to his subjects as Piyadasi, Beloved-of-the-Gods. Those edicts had been inscribed in terms that were personal and idiosyncratic, repetitious and heavy-handed, but unquestionably heartfelt. They showed Ashoka to be a man of paradoxes: highly intelligent, self-confident, comfortable in the exercise of power, and believing himself divinely appointed to rule as the father of his people. They also revealed him to be deeply – even obsessively – spiritual, passion-ate in his belief in a higher morality, in showing kindness and helping the poor, in moderation and self-control, in tolerance for all religions, in the sanctity of life, in the virtues of self-exami-nation, truthfulness, purity of heart and, above all, in his love of the Dharma. In sum, the edicts were the work of a ruler like no other – and a revolutionary one at that. 'Conquest by Dharma alone'; for an all-powerful monarch to express such pacific sentiments and make them the central pillar of his rule was without parallel, utterly at odds with the duties of kingship as laid down in the *Vedas* and other texts. And no less revolutionary was Ashoka's call for religious tolerance and his ban on animal sacrifice, for the first undermined the authority of the Brahman priesthood and the second struck at the heart of the cult of blood sacrifice that was a central feature of Brahmanistic religious practice at this time.

Ashokan studies came into existence in the *annus mirabilis* of 1837 – and continued to flourish mightily until the autumn of the following year. But in September 1838 James Prinsep was struck down by paralysing headaches brought on by an inflammation of the brain. It soon extended to the loss of his mental faculties, leading to his removal to England as a help-less, speechless invalid, and his death in London seven months later at the age of forty-one.

This poor quality etching of James Prinsep shows him already in the grip of the illness that would kill him four months later. (Colesworthy Grant, *Lithographic Sketches*, 1850)

Unaware that Prinsep was dying, George Turnour wrote to him on 18 October 1838 enclosing another article for the *JRAS* on the *Great Dynastic Chronicle* and explaining that this would be his last contribution: 'In a few days I leave Kandy for Colombo. The duties of my new office, and my separation from the Buddhist pandits, and the libraries of this place, will prevent, for some time at least, the further prosecution of this examination.'[25]

For Turnour, too, the separation was final. His health destroyed by malaria, he took early retirement and died an invalid in Italy in 1843 at the age of forty-three.

9

Brian Hodgson's Gift

'Ashoka's temple – called Chillundeo – in the centre of Patun'. The central stupa of five said to have been built by Emperor Ashoka in and around the town of Patan in Kathmandu Valley. A water-colour by Dr Henry Oldfield, surgeon at the British Residency, Kathmandu, from 1850 to 1863. (APAC, British Library)

One of the best places in the Eastern Himalayas to view the snows of Kanchenjunga is from Observatory Hill above the town of Darjeeling. When the British authorities in Calcutta decided on Darjeeling as an ideal retreat from the summer heat, they first settled on Observatory Hill's Jalapahar ridge, known as the 'Burning Hill' on account of the rhododendrons that burst into red flower in the spring. The first European-style cottages were built here, among them a house and grounds that for almost a century and a half have been occupied by one of India's oldest public schools, St Paul's.

The school moved here from Calcutta in 1864 after some seventy-five acres had been purchased from the owner, whose house became the home of the school's principal. Today known as the 'Rectory', it may well be the oldest surviving building in Darjeeling. It was originally named 'Brianstone' and until 1858 was the home of Brian Houghton Hodgson.

Of the three English pioneer Indologists born at the turn of the century – James Prinsep, George Turnour and Brian Hodgson – the survivor was the one whose health had always seemed the most precarious. Houghton lived to the age of ninety-four, being described in his late sixties as 'a tall slender aristocratic man, with an air of distinction even in his moustaches, a great hunting man and hence an early riser'[1] – but also as a sad man, with a strong sense of grievance about the way his labours had been 'plagiarised and ignored'.[2]

Following Britain's disastrous adventure into Afghanistan in the form of the First Afghan War of 1838–41 the lightweight Lord Auckland was replaced as Governor General of India by Lord Ellenborough. Knowing how Auckland had allowed his judgement to be swayed by headstrong politicals, Ellenborough was determined to bring them to heel. To this end, he

ordered Brian Houghton Hodgson, still British Resident in
Kathmandu, to cease meddling in Nepal's internal affairs. After
more than two decades' residence in Nepal, Hodgson had
every reason to regard himself as a major influence for good at
the Nepalese court. Time and again he had intervened or
intrigued to foil a militant faction in Nepal intent on provok-
ing a second war against the EICo. He now made what his
biographer, Sir William Hunter, described as 'a somewhat
needlessly emphatic protest against a piece of unfairness in
high places'. His punishment was to be offered a junior post as
assistant commissioner at the fledgling hill-station of Simla. He
promptly resigned and sailed to England with all his papers –
stopping off briefly in France to meet Eugène Burnouf and
donate more manuscripts to the Collège de France.

But Hodgson's long romance with Asia was not yet over.
Unable to settle 'at home', after less than a year he returned to
India, with a young wife, to continue his researches. Forbidden
to re-enter Nepal, he found the next best thing to Kathmandu
at the sanatorium of Darjeeling. Here he settled down in the
estate he named 'Brianstone', now concentrating his efforts
on ethnology, until the declining health of his wife finally
persuaded him to quit India for good in 1858. Despite his
immense contribution to Indian studies, zoology, botany and
other sciences, Hodgson never received any public recognition
from his own government, and it was not until 1889 that he was
belatedly awarded an honorary doctorate from Oxford. Despite
his donations of hundreds of Sanskrit manuscripts and thousands of drawings to the EICo's Library, the Bodleian Library,
the Royal Asiatic Society, the Natural History Museum, the
Zoological Society, the Royal Botanical Gardens at Kew and
other learned bodies in Britain, it seems his countrymen never

forgave Hodgson for his gifts to French scholarship and his acceptance of the Légion d'Honneur.

Brian Houghton Hodgson some years after he returned to England in 1858. A portrait painted by Louis Starr-Canziani at an unknown date, possibly showing Houghton in his old Indian Political Service uniform – but without the button of his Légion d'Honneur. (National Portrait Gallery)

Eugène Burnouf's *Le Lotus de la Bonne Loi*, published posthumously in 1852, was dedicated to Hodgson as 'founder of the study of Buddhism', and with good reason. Burnouf showed that there were two traditions and chronologies within the Buddhist world: a Northern *Mahayana*, or 'Great Vehicle', tradition recorded chiefly in Sanskrit and a Southern *Theravada*, or 'Vehicle of the Elders', tradition set down in Pali. Within the Northern tradition there were conflicting dates regarding the

dating of the 'Great Final Extinguishing' of Sakyamuni Buddha, ranging from 949 BCE (China, Japan and Korea) to 881 BCE
(Tibet and Nepal), with Ashoka anointed ruler a century after
his death. Within the Southern tradition (chiefly Ceylon, Siam
and Burma) there was no such disagreement, it being agreed
that Sakyamuni's death had occurred in the year 544 BCE and
that Ashoka Maurya had been anointed as ruler 218 years after
that death, thus 326 BCE. Burnouf argued that even this date
was too early and a consensus was gradually reached among
Indologists that Sakyamuni Buddha had probably died in
about 486 BCE and that Ashoka had begun his rule not 218
years later but 118 years, so about 268 BCE.

Thanks to Hodgson, Burnouf was also the first Westerner to
have access to a Sanskrit text known as the *Divyavadana*, or
'Divine Stories', made up of thirty-eight *avadanas*, or morality
tales, about the lives of Buddhist saints. One of these was the
Ashokavadana, or 'Legend of King Ashoka', being an account
of the life and death of Emperor Ashoka set out in almost ten
thousand verses.

Hitherto the Western world's nascent understanding of
Ashoka and his times had come from two main sources: the
Ashokan Rock and Pillar Edicts, and George Turnour's translation of the *Great Dynastic Chronicle* – the latter representing
Buddhist history as interpreted within the Southern tradition.
The Theravadin compilers of the *Great Dynastic Chronicle* had
made much of Ashoka as patron and propagator of Buddhism
and as father of two of their local heroes, Mahinda and
Sanghamitta. They had also stressed the dominant role of the
proto-Theravadin elder Moggaliputta Tissa in guiding Ashoka,
sending missionaries to Lanka and elsewhere and managing
the Third Buddhist Council.

The *Legend of King Ashoka*, as revealed by Burnouf, took a very different line. This was a text that belonged to the Mahayana school, which had its origins in the split that came to a head at about the time of the Third Buddhist Council. Initially, both schools preserved by oral transmission the teachings of the Buddha spoken in the Prakrit tongue in the form of the *Tripitaka* or 'Three Baskets'. These Buddhist scriptures were first set down in writing in about the first century CE with both traditions using the same Brahmi script, but whereas the southern Buddhists stuck with Pali the northerners abandoned it in favour of the more refined religious language of the Brahmans, Sanskrit.³

The *Legend of King Ashoka* was therefore set down in Sanskrit and its portrayal of Ashoka is very different from that given in the *Great Dynastic Chronicle* or as revealed in Ashoka's edicts. It makes no reference to the great slaughter at Kalinga or to Ashoka's subsequent remorse and conversion. It has nothing to say about the Third Buddhist Council or the split in the Buddhist Church. There is no mention of the Buddhist elder Moggaliputta Tissa and it is entirely silent on the subject of the propagation of Buddhism abroad. Instead, its focus is on the leading roles played by the elders of its own school in controlling the initial violence of Ashoka and redirecting him to work for the Buddhist Church. The emperor's conversion is now ascribed not to the words of his nephew Nigrodha but to a saintly monk named Samudra and his serenity under torture. In place of Moggaliputta Tissa the Buddhist centre-stage is now occupied by the elder Upagupta. It is Upagupta who advises Ashoka on all spiritual matters as his guide and mentor, and who organises Ashoka's pilgrimage. As for Ashoka himself, the *Legend of King Ashoka* portrays him as a seriously flawed individual, a cruel, hot-tempered oppressor until his conversion to Buddhism. The king's transformation under Buddhist guidance is presented as a Buddhist morality tale, but one that provides some intriguing – although not necessarily reliable – insights into the private life of Ashoka and the seeming nightmare of his dotage and death.

The *Legend of King Ashoka* opens with a long account of Upagupta's saintliness in a previous life before describing how Upagupta is reborn the son of a perfume seller of Mathura and ordained as a Buddhist monk. Only then does Ashoka come into the story, beginning with his previous existence as a boy who meets the Buddha, also in a previous life, on the road and makes him an offering of a handful of dirt – an action with profound karmic consequences. The Buddha accepts the offering and predicts how in consequence the boy will be reborn as Ashoka a hundred years after his own death.

The *Legend of King Ashoka* then lists the kings of Magadha but entirely omits Chandragupta, describing Bindusara simply as the son of Nanda. Ashoka's mother is here named as Subhadrangi, the daughter of a Brahman of Champaran (in North Bihar). The jealousy of the women of the royal household keeps Subhadrangi away from King Bindusara so she trains as a barber. When she finally gets an opportunity to shave the king she explains she is a Brahman and tells her story, whereupon Bindusara makes her his chief queen. The first fruit of their union is named Ashoka, 'without sorrow', because by his birth his mother has emancipated herself from suffering. However, Bindusara rejects the boy because his skin is 'rough and unpleasant to the touch' – a direct consequence of his offering of dirt in his previous birth. Ashoka grows into an unruly youth and is handed over for disciplining to an astrologer, who foretells that he will succeed his father to the throne. This displeases King Bindusara, who favours his eldest son Sushima. The city of Taxila then rebels against King Bindusara, who sees an opportunity to get rid of Ashoka and sends him to deal with it, allowing him an army but no weaponry. However, Ashoka is made welcome by the Taxilans and the rebellion is resolved. The prince then goes on to deal with disturbances in the country of Kashmir, where he wins the support of two powerful mountain warriors – possibly Greek local rulers or mercenaries.

Meanwhile in Pataliputra the heir-apparent Sushima angers his father's (unnamed) chief minister by slapping his bald head in jest, causing the minister to reflect that when Sushima becomes king he will use his sword just as freely. The minister turns all the other ministers, including his own son Radhagupta, against Sushima and for Ashoka. The Taxilans rise in rebellion for a second time and on advice of his chief minister King Bindusara sends Sushima to deal with it. But then Bindusara falls seriously ill and orders Sushima's recall, commanding Ashoka to go in his place. However, the king's ministers delay the king's order to Sushima and smear Ashoka's body with red turmeric to make him appear too sick to travel. When it is clear that Bindusara is dying, Ashoka appears before him dressed in full royal regalia and calls on his father to make him temporary ruler. This makes Bindusara so apoplectic with rage that he vomits blood and dies.

As soon as he hears of his father's death Sushima marches on Pataliputra. Ashoka deploys his two mountain warrior allies to guard two of the city's gates, his ministerial supporter Radhagupta takes charge of a third gate and he himself takes on the defence of the fourth and eastern gate, where Sushima is lured into a trap (given here and below in a modern translation by John Strong):

> Radhagupta set up an artificial elephant, on top of which he placed an image of Ashoka that he had fashioned. All around he dug a ditch, filled it with live coals of acacia wood, covered it with reeds, and camouflaged the whole with dirt. He then went and taunted Susima: 'If you are able to kill Ashoka, you will become king.' Susima immediately rushed to the eastern gate, intending to do battle with his half-brother, but he fell into the ditch full of charcoal, and came to an untimely and painful end.[4]

Once Ashoka has been consecrated as king of Magadha he reveals his true character. When his ministers challenge his order to cut down all fruit and flowering trees he beheads five hundred of their number, and when he learns that his concubines dislike caressing his rough skin he orders them to be burned alive. He also appoints as his executioner one Chandagirika, 'the fierce mountaineer', and builds a prison that is lovely to look at from the outside but contains all the tortures of hell. Chandagirika sets about inflicting the 'five great agonies' on all who enter its portals. But then a Buddhist novice monk named Samudra wanders into Ashoka's 'hell' while begging for alms. Finding the monk impervious to his cruelty, Chandagirika reports this to the king, who comes to see for himself and is confounded by Samudra's fortitude. Samudra then explains that he has been freed 'from the terrors of *samsara*' – the suffering involved in rebirth – thanks to the teachings of Sakyamuni Buddha and goes on to tell Ashoka the Buddha has prophesied that one hundred years after his

Great Final Extinguishing a mighty king named Ashoka will rule in the city of Pataliputra. The king will be a *Chakravartin* or 'Wheel-turning Monarch' who will follow the example of the Buddha's turning of the wheel of the Dharma. He will also be a *Dharmaraja* or 'Righteous King' who will distribute the relics of the Buddha far and wide, building eighty-four thousand *Dharmarajikas* or 'Righteous King's monuments' to contain them. That is what the Buddha has prophesied, says Samudra, 'But instead your majesty has built this place that resembles a hell and where thousands of living beings have been killed.'

So moved is Ashoka by these words that he promises to fulfil Sakyamuni Buddha's prophesy. He converts to Buddhism, destroys his hell prison and Chandagirika with it, and asks Upagupta to become his spiritual mentor, after which issues a proclamation declaring Buddhism to be the official religion of the country.

The reformed king then sets out to perform meritorious acts, including the building of eighty-four thousand 'Righteous King's monuments', containing portions of the Buddha's relics, throughout his empire. This he does with the help of an elder named Yashah, abbot of a monastery outside Pataliputra known as the Kukkutarama, or 'Cock monastery'. At the request of the people of Taxila he causes three and a half thousand million stupas to be built in their country, and by his order the *yakshas*, or semi-deities, build ten million stupas along the subcontinent's seashore. Upagupta then takes Ashoka on a pilgrimage to the holy places of Buddhism, beginning with Lumbini, where Ashoka makes an offering of a hundred thousand pieces of gold and builds a stupa. He repeats the process at Kapilavastu, Bodhgaya, Sarnath and at Kushinagara, where King Ashoka is so overcome with motion that he faints and has to be revived by his attendants.

With this first pilgrimage to the holy places of Buddhism completed, Ashoka is then taken by Upagupta to visit the stupas of the great saints of Buddhism who have followed Sakyamuni Buddha. However, what particularly arouses the faith of the king is the Bodhi tree. When he returns to Bodhgaya to find that the Bodhi tree is dying, he again faints. He learns that the Bodhi tree has been cursed by an act of sorcery instigated by his chief queen, Tishyarakshita, who has been angered by the king's forsaking of the old family religion. The queen realises her mistake, gets the curse lifted and waters the roots of the Bodhi tree with a thousand pitchers of milk a day until it revives, whereupon Ashoka proclaims:

I will twice perform the highest honours;
I will bathe the Bodhi tree
with jars full of fragrant waters,
and I will undertake to honour the sangha
with a great quinquennial festival.

Ashoka then orders a great quinquennial (held every five years) festival to be held outside Pataliputra, attended by monks from every corner of the land and from beyond the Himalayas. He honours the monks gathered there and deputes an elder to preach the true religion throughout his empire

The last section of the *Legend of King Ashoka* is taken up with tales of the emperor's decline and death. It begins with the story of the birth of Ashoka's son Dharmavivardhana by his queen Padmavati. Ashoka is overwhelmed by the beauty of the boy's eyes and on hearing them compared to a Himalayan bird called the *kunala* he renames the boy Kunala. A Buddhist elder foresees that Kunala will lose his eyesight and teaches him about the impermanence of all things. Ashoka's chief queen Tishyarakshita then falls in love with Kunala's eyes. When he rejects her advances and calls her 'mother', Tishyarakshita plots his destruction.

History now seems to repeat itself as Taxila once more rises in revolt against the king. Prince Kunala is sent to deal with the rebellion, and is warmly received by the people of Taxila, who explain that their quarrel is with the king and his arrogant ministers. Ashoka then falls dangerously ill in Pataliputra, with 'an impure substance' oozing from his pores. He sends for Kunala to return to Pataliputra to take over the kingdom, but Queen Tishyarakshita fears that after her indiscretion Kunala will order her killed if he succeeds to the throne. She therefore sets out to find a cure for Ashoka's illness by making enquiries to see if anyone is suffering in the same way as the king. One such victim is found and brought to the queen, who kills him, cuts open his belly and discovers a large worm. She experiments with a succession of remedies, none of which kills the worm until she tries an onion – a vegetable regarded as unclean and therefore avoided by Brahmans and Kshatriyas. She doses the king with onion and cures him, and as a reward asks to be allowed to rule the country for a week. She then takes her revenge on Kunala by sending a message to Taxila in the king's name ordering him to be blinded.

Knowing his fate is preordained, Kunala submits and is blinded. He and his wife then take to the road as beggar musicians. They make their way back to Pataliputra where Ashoka hears Kunala singing outside the walls of his palace and sends for him. He recognises his son and falls to the ground weeping.

He hears Kunala's story and 'burning with the fire of anger' orders Tishyarakshita to be tortured to death. However, Kunala begs for the queen to be forgiven and because he has only compassion for his wicked stepmother his eyesight is restored. His father heeds his call for forgiveness – but still has Tishyarakshita burned to death.

After these events Ashoka teaches his younger brother Vitashoka the nature of suffering and, with the help of the elder Yashah, Vitashoka is ordained as a Buddhist monk. Initially, Vitashoka enters the Cock monastery outside Pataliputra but after finding this too noisy he retreats to the Himalayas. In the meantime, an enemy of Buddhism has circulated a painting of himself with the Buddha lying at his feet, which so angers Ashoka that he puts a price on the man's head. A cowherd then catches sight of Vitashoka, who has allowed his hair and beard to grow, and mistakes him for the blasphemer. The cowherd kills him and brings his head to the king to claim the reward, whereupon Ashoka recognises his younger brother and is deeply grieved. Upagupta explains that the death of his brother is a consequence of Ashoka's cruelty.

According to the *Legend of King Ashoka*, the great emperor's last days are not happy ones. As he becomes increasingly ill and infirm, Ashoka becomes obsessed with giving donations to the Buddhist Church, to the point where the state treasury is in danger of being emptied. Prince Kunala's son Sampadi has been appointed heir-apparent and on the advice of his counsellors he prohibits the state treasurer from disbursing any more state funds. Emperor Ashoka then starts donating his own personal tableware: first his gold dishes, then his silver plates and finally his copper plates, until his food is being served on plates of rough earthenware. He is finally left with nothing of his own but half a *myrobalan*, or cherry plum fruit. This he presents to the Cock monastery as his last gift, with the words:

> He who previously ruled the earth
> Over which he spread his umbrella of sovereignty
> And warmed the world like the noonday sun at its zenith –
> Today that king has seen his fortunes cut off.
> Deceived by his own karmic acts, he finds his glory gone
> like the setting sun at dusk.

The dying Ashoka has the cherry plum fruit mashed and put into a soup for distribution to the community of monks at the Cock monastery. He asks his minister Radhagupta who is lord of the earth and is assured that he is. He then struggles to his feet, turns to each point of the compass and with a gesture of offering declares that he is presenting the whole earth 'to the community of the Blessed One's disciples'. He has these words written on a document that he seals with his teeth – and then dies. With what remains in the state treasury the ministers buy back the late king's dominions from the Buddhist Sangha and Ashoka's grandson Sampadi is consecrated as king.

But this is not quite the end of Ashoka's story as told in the *Ashokavadana*, for a brief epilogue is attached. It begins: 'Sampadi's son was Brhaspati who, in turn, had a son named Vrsasena and Vrsasena had a son named Pushyadharman, and Pushyadharman begot Pushyamitra.' It goes on to relate how King Pushyamitra, wishing his name to be as renowned as that of Ashoka, asks his Brahman priest how he can accomplish this. He is told that there are two ways: one is to do what King Ashoka did and build eighty-four thousand stupas; and the other is to destroy all those same stupas. Pushyamitra decides to follow the latter course and advances with his army on the Cock monastery established by Ashoka outside Pataliputra, where he tells the monks to choose between saving themselves or the monastery. The monks offer to sacrifice themselves but Pushyamitra destroys both the monks and the monastery. He then embarks on a campaign against all Buddhist institutions, offering a reward for the head of every monk brought to him, until finally confronted by a *yaksha* guardian deity who flattens him under a mountain. 'With the death of Pushyamitra,' declares the last line of the *Legend of King Ashoka*, 'the Mauryan lineage came to an end.'

The *Legend of King Ashoka* contains some obvious errors, such as its description of Bindusara as the son of Nanda and the Brahman regicide Pushyamitra as the last of the Mauryas. Its list of names of the Mauryan kings is also seriously at odds with those given in the *Vishnu, Matsya, Vayu* and *Brahmananda Puranas* (see chart , p. 36). However, when this list of Mauryan kings provided by the *Legend of King Ashoka* is set alongside the other lists in the *Puranas*, one thing is very clear: the confusion of Mauryan rulers' names after the death of Ashoka. It points to an empire already falling apart in the great monarch's last years, and then at his death breaking up into two or more warring regions as various claimants fought for supremacy, very much as the Successors had done after the death of Alexander.

Even as Burnouf was completing his work on the history of Buddhism, rumours came from Russia of more previous un-known documents on early Indian Buddhism. They emanated from the Department of Mongolian Language at the University of Kazan on the Volga River, where the students were using a handwritten text translated from the original Tibetan. In 1840 one of those students, Vasili Vasiliev, joined the Russian Orthodox Church Mission in Peking (Beijing), and procured a copy of this same text in the original, printed by woodblock and entitled *Gya-gar Chos-byung*, or *The History of Buddhism in India*, the work of a Tibetan Lama named Taranatha.[5]

Taranatha's *History of Buddhism in India* devotes three of its forty-four chapters to King Ashoka, so adding another twist to the story. Although written as recently as 1608, it had drawn on older sources that included the *Divine Stories* but also two works now lost.[6] These lost sources told the story of Ashoka from a perspective best described as north-eastern, in that it allied itself with the Northern school but promoted the role of the early Buddhist Church in northern Magadha. In this version the great Buddhist instructor who teaches and advises King Ashoka is not Upagupta, the leading apostle of Mathura, as given in the *Legend of King Ashoka*, but Yashah, abbot of King Ashoka's Cock monastery outside Pataliputra – which also features in the *Great Dynastic Chronicle* as the Ashokarama.

Taranatha's *History* has been dismissed by scholars as too garbled to have any credence, but it contains elements that deserve to be considered when reconstructing Ashoka and his time. It describes Ashoka as the son of Nemita, king of Champaran in north Magadha, by a merchant's daughter. Unlike his elder brothers who live in luxury, Prince Ashoka lives simply and sits on the ground to eat. When the mountain people of Kashmir and Nepal revolt he is sent to deal with them and is rewarded by his father by being made governor of Pataliputra. When King Nemita dies his ministers install Ashoka as ruler of Pataliputra, where he worships various mother-goddesses, including Uma Devi, consort of Shiva, and keeps five hundred women in his harem: 'Indulging as he did in lust for several years, he came to be known as Kama Ashoka [*kama* meaning 'love' or 'desire'].'[7]

Ashoka goes to war against his half-brothers and destroys them all to become ruler of 'the whole territory from the Himalaya to the Vindhya'. He grows ever more haughty and cruel, only finding peace of mind when performing violent deeds, so acquiring the name 'Ashoka the Wrathful'. Then a Buddhist novice who is a disciple of the elder Yashah enters Ashoka's torture house by mistake and, just as related in the *Legend of King Ashoka*, survives his ordeal unscathed. Yashah then converts Ashoka, who thereafter 'was full of great reverence and started spending the day and night in pious acts'.

Yashah invites all the Buddhist monks to Pataliputra for a religious festival, for which the king builds a very large hall. Sixty thousand monks attend the festival, which lasts three months. He then embarks on a second round of conquest to bring 'under his rule without bloodshed all the countries including those to the south of the Vindhya ... the northern Himalayas, the snowy ranges beyond Li-yul [Khotan, thus the Tien Shan mountains], the entire land of Jambudvipa bounded on seas on east, south and west, and also fifty small islands.'

Ashoka then follows the advice of Yashah to collect relics of the Buddha and disperse these in eighty-four thousand stupas throughout his empire 'as far as Li-yul in the north'. Taranatha goes on to recount the story of the blinding of Ashoka's favourite son Kunala, but with significant differences from the version found in the *Legend of King Ashoka*, in that here Kunala is rendered unfit to rule by his blindness and becomes a monk.

'That is why,' adds Taranatha, 'though it was his turn to be king, his son Vigatashoka was placed on the throne.'

In Taranatha's *History* Ashoka's end follows much the same general course given in the *Legend of King Ashoka*, although he adds a curious detail concerning Ashoka's last moments. A female attendant who is fanning him falls asleep in the midday heat and drops her yak-tail whisk on his body, angering the dying Ashoka: 'The king thought, "Previously even great kings used to wash my feet. Even the lowest of my servants is insulting me now in this way." Thus he died with anger in mind. Because of this anger, he had to be reborn as a Naga [snake king] in a big lake of Pataliputra.'

Unlike the *Legend of King Ashoka*, Taranatha's *History* contains a brief reference to a link with Lanka, although here the arrival of Buddhism in Lanka owes nothing to Ashoka and everything to an elder named Krishna, who comes to the island at the request of its king, Asana-Simha-Kosa: 'He preached the Doctrine for three months in that island, filled it with monasteries and sanghas and led many people to the "four stages of perfection".' According to Taranatha, this Krishna was succeeded by Sudarshana, who died some years before Ashoka's reign, suggesting that the arrival of Buddhism in Lanka began during Chandragupta's reign rather than Ashoka's – a view shared by some modern historians.

Taranatha lists as the successors to Ashoka his grandson Vigatashoka and his great-grandson Virasena. He tells us that Virasena acquired a vast amount of treasure by propitiating the Hindu goddess of wealth, Lakshmi, suggesting that his loyalties had switched from Buddhism. But he then adds that Virasena 'entertained for three years the monks all around and worshipped at all the caityas in the world with a hundred items of offerings for each'. Perhaps Virasena was doing no more than following Ashoka's doctrine of respecting all religions.

To further confuse matters, Taranatha then introduces a second line of kings he calls the Candras,[8] named after its founder, Candragupta: patently, Chandragupta Maurya. Chandragupta is succeeded by Bindusara, who is followed by Shricandra – perhaps Bindusara's eldest son Sushima – who is followed by Dharmacandra – presumably Ashoka as Dharma Ashoka. Then come eleven names all ending in 'candra' not found in any other genealogical table, the last three said by Taranatha to have been 'very powerful and had reverence for the Three Jewels [Buddhism]'. Taranatha then concludes: 'Soon after Nemacandra ruled the kingdom Brahmana Pusyamitra, the royal priest, revolted against the king and assumed power.' This is, of course, the Brahman Pushyamitra named in the *Puranas* and in the *Legend of King Ashoka* as the army commander who overthrows the last of the Mauryas to found the Shunga dynasty.

Despite the efforts of Vasili Vasiliev, much of the detail contained in Taranatha's *History of Buddhism in India* remained unknown outside Russia and Germany until well into the twentieth century. And despite the scholarship of Eugène Burnouf and Stanislas Julien in France, the *Legend of King Ashoka* was similarly neglected. Indeed, the first English translation of the latter – by Professor John Strong (whose translations have been quoted above) – only appeared in print in 1983.

But for what we must now call the last of the Orientalists and the first of the Indologists, archaeologists, philologists and epigraphists working in India, these omissions scarcely mattered. They were preoccupied with two quite different texts.

The first to appear was Jean-Pierre Abel-Rémusat's *Foé Koué Ki, ou Relations des Royaumes Bouddhiques* ('Records of Buddhist Kingdoms'), his translation into French of the Chinese Buddhist pilgrim Faxian's account of his pilgrimage across India at the start of the fifth century CE, published in 1836.[9] The second was *Histoire de la vie de Hiouen-tsang et de ses voyages dans l'Inde depuis l'an 629 jusqu'en 645* ('History of the Life of Hiouen-tsang and his Travels in India Between the Years 629 and 645'), published in 1853 – this second work being Stanislas Julien's translation into French of the travels of Faxian's more famous and later compatriot Xuanzang.[10]

The publication in France of these two eyewitness accounts of India in the fifth and seventh centuries caused no great stir across the other side of English Channel – except among a handful of Indologists who recognised in them a means of rediscovering India's lost Buddhist landscape. In India James Prinsep welcomed the news of the publication of the French translation of Faxian's travels, finally published in Paris after years of delay – but wondered if he would ever see it. 'Alas!' he lamented, 'When shall we in India have the opportunity of seeing these works at any tolerable period after their publication?'

Even before that statement appeared in print Prinsep had become fatally incapacitated. With his departure and death, it fell to the most devoted of his disciples to take up the challenge. One was Captain Markham Kittoe, discoverer of the Dhauli Rock Edicts – a fine upstanding figure of a man with an unfortunate tendency to upset authority. The other was the military engineer who had assisted Prinsep in his studies of Indian coinage: Captain Alexander Cunningham – short, balding and tending towards plumpness, but as solid as a rock.

10

Records of the Western Regions

The Chinese Buddhist monk Xuanzang, greatest of all the pilgrim-travellers to India, as portrayed in a ninth-century wall painting in the Mogao Caves, Dunhuang. (Wikimedia PD-Art).

In August 1966 China's Cultural Revolution entered its most violent phase. Groups of young men and women in the green uniform of the Red Guards rampaged through town and country-side targeting one or other of the 'Four Olds' – old customs, old culture, old habits, old ideas – that the Great Helmsman Mao had declared to be the targets of the Cultural Revolution. In the suburbs of Xian in China's Shanxi province one such group stormed that city's most beloved building: the ancient seven-storied *Dayan Ta*, or Wild Goose Pagoda. Shouting 'Smash the old world, build a brand-new world',[1] they broke down the doors, pushed aside the monks and began to tie ropes round the heads of the Buddha and Bodhisattva statues in the shrine hall in order to pull them to the ground. At this point a cadre from the State Cultural Relics Bureau arrived with a certificate declaring the statues and the pagoda itself to be national treasures and not to be touched.

But there was no such prohibition order on the Wild Goose Pagoda's most precious treasures: its collection of Buddhist *sutras*, or canonical texts, some of which dated to the construction of the pagoda in the sixth century, and a few of which even pre-dated it. These were gathered into a pyre in the courtyard outside and set alight. The bonfire continued to burn throughout the night.

The first known translation of Buddhist scriptures into Chinese had taken place in 148 CE with the arrival in China of a Parthian prince and missionary who founded Buddhist temples in Loyang and set about translating Sanskrit scriptures into Chinese. By the fourth century Buddhism in China had begun to win imperial favour and as it grew in popularity so the demand increased for more authentic texts from the heartland of Buddhism itself – the Indian subcontinent. It was this that

inspired the Chinese monk Faxian and four companions to set
out from their homes in Shanxi province in 399 CE on what was
to become for Faxian a fifteen-year journey.

Faxian was not the first Chinese Buddhist pilgrim to visit
India but he was the first whose account of his travels survived
to become widely read, appearing under the title of *Foguo-ji*,
or *A Record of Buddhistic Kingdoms*. He was also fortunate in
making his journey at a time when Buddhism in China had just
won its first royal convert.

After following the upper course of the Indus through the
Pamirs with great difficulty, Faxian arrived at the Buddhist
kingdom of *Woo-chang*, or the 'Garden Country' (Mahabun,
today Swat, northern Pakistan), in the spring of 402 CE, finding
it to be a Buddhist demi-paradise where 'the Law of Buddha
is very flourishing'.[2] In the autumn Faxian moved on to the
plains country of Gandhara, noting that here, too, the population was still largely Buddhist, even if mostly Hinayana, with
monks and monasteries in abundance.

Also much in evidence throughout Gandhara were the
memorial mounds containing relics of Buddhist saints known
as stupas. At the city of Purushpura (today Peshawar) Faxian
was pleased to see two vast stupas built by the Kushan king
Kanishka, one housing the alms bowl of Sakyamuni Buddha,
brought back from India by the Kushans as war booty.

But King Kanishka was not the only monarch to have supported Buddhism and to have built stupas. Long before the
invasion of the Kushans a far more powerful monarch had set
the example that King Kanishka had merely followed. This
great king was known to the Chinese as *Wuyou Wang*, or 'The
King Not Feeling Sorrow'. It was King Wuyou who had caused
the blessings of the Dharma to be brought to China and his

name was celebrated and revered throughout the Middle
Kingdom as a Chakravartin, or 'Wheel-turning Monarch'.[3]

King Wuyou was a name that Faxian was to encounter many
times on his Indian travels, making its first appearance as he
crossed the mountains dividing the Garden Country from the
plains, described in his account as 'the place where Dharmavivardhana, the son of Wuyou Wang, ruled'.[4] From this point
on Faxian's references to King Wuyou were nearly always in
the context of stupas that were said to have been built by this
greatest of all stupa builders.

After six months in Gandhara three of Faxian's companions
returned to China. He and the other remaining pilgrims then
journeyed across the Punjab to the city of Mataoulu (Mathura),
at that time under the rule of Indian kings described by Faxian
as firm believers in the Dharma. They were not themselves
Buddhists but showed great respect to the Buddhist monastic
community by making offerings to the monks, removing their
headgear in their presence and offering them food 'with their
own hands'.

Faxian's years in India coincided with the rule of the greatest
of the Gupta rulers: Raja Vikramaditya, or 'Sun of Power', also
known – somewhat confusingly in the context of this book – as
Chandragupta, the 'Moon-Protected', but generally known to
later historians as Chandragupta II so as to avoid confusing him
with Chandragupta Maurya. The Guptas had grown in strength
as the Kushans declined, and by Faxian's time they controlled
a large empire extending from the mouth of the Indus to the
mouth of the Ganges. Despite being listed in Brahmanical texts
as a devout follower of the Hindu god Vishnu, Chandragupta II
patronised all forms of religious expression, only taking a dog-
matic line when it came to matters of caste.

Faxian spent the summer of 404 CE at Sankisa, which he knew of as the place where Sakyamuni Buddha had descended by a triple ladder from the heavenly realms after giving Buddhist teachings to his dead mother.

Sakyamuni Buddha descending to earth at Sankisa, as shown on a second-century BCE bas-relief. The Buddha is represented only by symbols. His footprints can be seen at the top and bottom of the ladder. (Cunningham, *The Stupa of Bharhut*, 1879)

In his *Record of Buddhistic Kingdoms* Faxian reports that here at Sankisa the great monarch King Wuyou had long ago built a monastery 'with a standing image, sixteen cubits in height, right over the middle flight [of the ladder]. Behind the monastery he had erected a stone pillar, about fifty cubits high, with a lion on the top of it.'⁵ This is the earliest known reference to a stone column attributed to the emperor Ashoka – for Wuyou, 'Without Feeling Sorrow', is, of course, a Chinese rendering of the Sanskrit *ashoka*, 'without sorrow'.

Faxian then journeyed east to visit a number of sites associated with the life, death and teachings of Sakyamuni Buddha. These included the four most sacred sites of Buddhism: Lumbini, where Prince Sidhhartha Sakya was born; Bodhgaya, where he achieved enlightenment to become the *Buddha*, or 'Awakened One'; the 'Deer Park' of Sarnath, where he preached the first sermon known as the *Dharmachakra-pravartana*, or 'Turning of the Wheel of the Moral Law'; and Kushinagara, where he achieved his Great Final Extinguishing, with his death. After reaching the first of these auspicious sites Faxian travelled south to cross the Ganges at a point he describes as 'the confluence of the five rivers', just upstream of the capital of the country of Magadha: *Pataliputra*, the 'city of flowers'.

This, Faxian notes, was the very city from which King Wuyou had ruled India. Indeed, his palace and his halls were still to be seen, and his towering city walls and gates still stood, all inlaid with sculpture-work carved 'in a way which no human hands of this world could accomplish', leading Faxian to declare that this was the work of spirits working to King Wuyou's command. Indeed, Pataliputra and its surrounds contained an abundance of sites directly associated with the name of Wuyou Wang. One was a large artificial hill within the city itself, which the king had had specially built for his younger brother, who had wished to find solitude as a Buddhist monk. Another was a large stupa situated just outside the city; one of the original eight stupas that had been raised over the divided remains of Sakyamuni Buddha following his cremation, only to be reopened by King Wuyou as part of his redistribution of the relics throughout the land. The Buddha stupa at Pataliputra was the first of these to be disturbed. Beside it Faxian saw two stone columns ascribed to King Wuyou, the first 'fourteen or fifteen cubits in circumference, and more than thirty cubits high, on which there is an inscription saying, "Wuyou-Wang gave the *Jambudvipa* [the southern continent, India] to the general body of the monks, and then redeemed it from them with money. This he did three times".' The second pillar was of similar height but with a carved lion for a capital. Here the inscription recorded King Wuyou's building of a town and the day, month and year in which it had been built.

Beside King Wuyou's relic stupa was a Mahayana monastery where Faxian studied for three years, learning Sanskrit and copying a number of sutras to take back to China. During this period he also visited the nearby city of Rajagriha, closely associated with the life of the Buddha, as well as the Buddhist 'holy of holies' of Bodhgaya and its Bodhi tree.

At this point in his narrative Faxian adds a chapter devoted to the history of Wuyou Wang very much as set out in the *Divine Stories*, beginning with the story of how as a small boy in a previous existence Wuyou Wang had met an earlier incarnation of the Buddha and had made him an offering of earth for his begging bowl, as a result of which he 'received the recompense of becoming a king of the iron wheel, to rule over Jambudvipa'.

The significance of the iron wheel lay in the Buddhist belief that when a Chakravartin or 'Wheel-turning Monarch', ascended the throne, he received from heaven a *chakra* or wheel, made of gold, silver, copper or iron, its material indicating the length and quality of his reign. King Wuyou, therefore, was a Wheel-turning Monarch, but of the lowest of the three levels, being less than perfect.[6]

In the year 407 CE Faxian began his return journey to China, but by slow stages that occupied another four years, including two spent on the island of Singhala, or the 'Lion Kingdom' (now Sri Lanka). Faxian's departure from India coincided with the arrival of a new group of Central Asian nomads on India's north-west borders, a people known to the Chinese as the *Ye-tai* or *Hoa* – the latter form afterwards reaching Europe as the Huns and India as the Huna. By 410 CE the first wave of these Huns had settled in Bactria and Gandhara, only to be moved on by a second wave of Huns, known to the Indians as the *Sveta Huna*, or 'White Huns'. By the end of the fifth century the White Huns had driven the Gupta rulers of northern India back to their core territories in the mid-Gangetic plains.

In Persia the twentieth Sassanid emperor, the celebrated Khosrau (Chosroes), joined forces with a confederation of nomadic tribes to disperse the White Huns. However, within eastern Gandhara and northern India, isolated pockets of Huns clung on, competing with other nomadic migrants from Central Asia to establish their own petty kingdoms. They adopted the local culture, accepted the religious authority of the Brahmans and, after undergoing various purification rites, emerged as self-proclaimed *Rajputs*, or 'sons of kings', and as fully paid-up Kshatriyas of the warrior caste. The most powerful of these new Rajput clans rose to power under the leadership of Raja Harshavardana, 'Harsha the Great', who established himself at Kannauj on the Ganges in the early years of the sixth century and ruled over the Gangetic plains for some forty years.

Harsha the Great's rise to power coincided with the unification of Arabia under the leadership of the Prophet Muhammad, the start of the Tang dynasty in China, and – on a more humble level – the formation of the Anglo-Saxon petty kingdoms in Britain.

It was during this brief moment of clarity in an otherwise confused period of India's history that a second Chinese monk set out on what was to become the most fruitful journey ever undertaken by a Buddhist pilgrim. Born in eastern China in 602, Xuanzang was ordained as Buddhist monk at the age of twenty at a time when Buddhism in China was experiencing a golden age thanks to the enthusiastic patronage of a succession of emperors, one of whom – Emperor Wu-di of the Liang dynasty (502–49) – consciously modelled himself on the Indian emperor Wuyou Wang and embarked on an extravagant temple-building programme of his own.

Thanks in part to the accounts of Faxian, India had now assumed almost mythical status in China as a 'Western Paradise' where great Wheel-turners such as King Wuyou and King Kanishka had ruled as *Dharmarajas*, or 'Dharma-promoting rulers'. It was this vision of India as the only true source of Buddhist truth that inspired Xuanzang to make his own journey in search of Buddhist sutras. The emperor Taizong, founder of the Tang dynasty, had imposed a ban on foreign travel. Defying the imperial edict, Xuanzang set out for India in the year 629. According to his biographer, he was a tall, handsome man with beautiful eyes and a good complexion, stately in manner, serious expression and zealous in the pursuit of learning.

Following a more northerly route than that taken by his predecessor, Xuanzang crossed the Tien Shan mountains to enter what are now the Central Asian khanates, then dominated by the hostile Gokturks. Crossing the Amur Darya river into less hostile Sassanid territory, he encountered scattered communities of Buddhist monks who had survived the depredations of the Huns. These communities extended as far west as Kangguo (Samarkand), Anguo (Bokhara) and Talaquan (Balkh in western Afghanistan), where Xuanzang paused to study Buddhist scriptures and to collect the first of what became a hugely important collection of Buddhist texts. Xuanzang then picked up Faxian's trail to visit the Buddhist community at Bamiyan, where he admired the two great standing images of Buddha and noted the presence of 'several tens of monasteries with several thousand monks',[7] before moving on to the Gandharan summer capital of Kapisha (Begram), even then governed by a Buddhist king: 'He loves and nurtures his subjects and venerates the Triple Gem [*Triratna*, comprising the Buddha, the Dharma and the Sangha or Buddhist Church].' From Kapisha the Chinese monk crossed 'steep and precipitous' mountains to enter eastern Gandhara and the territory of India.

At this point in his account of his Indian travels Xuanzang breaks off to give a detailed description of the people of India and their customs, this information being added after Xuanzang's return to China by order of Emperor Taizong. In his desire to please his emperor, Xuanzang did his best to match his imagined India with the reality, fudging the details whenever these conflicted with the imperial vision. But nothing could entirely conceal the fact that what Xuanzang found in India was Buddhism in decline and Brahmanism very much in the ascendant. Purushpura, winter capital of Gandhara, had been a thriving centre of Buddhism in Faxian's time, and was now all but abandoned, its great Buddhist monuments in ruins. Only the foundations remained of the famous building that had once housed King Kanishka's most prized Buddhist trophy, the Buddha's alms bowl. The bowl itself had been carried off to Persia.

From Purushpura Xuanzang travelled north over the Malakand mountain range to enter the Garden Country. Here, too, everything lay in ruins: 'Along the two sides of the Subavastu River [Swat River] there were formerly one thousand four hundred monasteries, but most of them are now in desolation.' Moving east, Xuanzang came to the great mountain of Mo-ha-fa-na, a Chinese rendering of the Sanskrit *Mahavana*, or 'Great Forest', later Mahaban. Here he venerated a stupa built by King Wuyou to mark the spot where the Buddha in a previous life had cut a slice of flesh from his body in order to ransom a dove from a hawk.

This is the first mention of Wuyou Wang in Xuanzang's account and from this point onwards his references to the great Indian emperor become ever more frequent. King Wuyou, Xuanzang seems to imply, is still a force to be reckoned with, even though his memorials are often to be found surrounded by scenes of desolation and neglect. To reinforce the point, the Chinese pilgrim adds further detail in the form of tales about King Wuyou, drawing on a number of historical sources that would remain unknown to the Western world for centuries to come – as indeed would Xuanzang's and Faxian's own accounts.

After crossing the Indus Xuanzang came to the once great city of Taxila. Here, too, it was the same story of ruination. In the city's surrounds was a number of stupas attributed by Xuanzang to King Wuyou, including one to the south-east of the city built by him 'at the place where his son, Prince Kunala, had his eyes torn out'. Here Xuanzang takes time out to relate the story of Kunala's blinding at the instigation of his wicked stepmother.

From Taxila Xuanzang moved on to Kashmir to be the guest of its Buddhist ruler. Here, too, the continuing influence of Wuyou Wang is reported in the form of stupas raised and monasteries founded by him, allowing Xuanzang to discourse further on this great 'King Wuyou of Magadha', who 'fostered all creatures of the four forms of birth'. He goes on to tell the curious story of how Wuyou Wang orders five hundred monks who have accepted the heterodox teachings of a Buddhist elder to be drowned in the Ganges. They flee to Kashmir, and when they refuse to return, the king comes in person to apologise for their persecution and causes five hundred monasteries to be built in Kashmir.

After three years spent studying the scriptures in the Himalayas, Xuanzang continued his pilgrimage across the upper Gangetic plains. Everywhere he encountered further evidence of the decline of Buddhism, although his hopes were raised when he reached the country of Kapitha, which in Faxian's time had been known as Sankisa – the scene of the celebrated event in the life of Sakyamuni Buddha when he had returned to earth from heaven by way of a divinely constructed ladder. By the time Xuanzang reached this spot the stairway seen by Faxian had disappeared. 'However, King Wuyou's stone column topped by a lion was still standing' and was reckoned by Xuanzang to be seventy feet high: 'Being dark purple in colour, it is made of a lustrous hard stone with a fine grain, and on its top is a carved lion crouching and facing towards the stairs. On the surface all round the pillar there are engraved various kinds of strange figures.'

The Chinese pilgrim had now arrived at the borders of the most powerful kingdom in India, ruled over by the mighty monarch Harsha the Great. On his arrival at Kannouj in the year 636, Xuanzang was brought before King Harsha and questioned at length about his own country. He subsequently met the king on other occasions and was greatly impressed by his character and the principles upon which he based his rule. To Xuanzang, these principles mirrored those instituted by Wuyou Wang many centuries earlier and were Buddhist in all but name.

And yet, as Xuanzang continued his pilgrimage across what is today Uttar Pradesh and Bihar, the physical evidence of Buddhist decline was undeniable. For all Xuanzang's descriptions of glorious events of long ago, the monuments and monastic institutions associated with them were for the most part ruined and deserted. Huge tracts of countryside appeared to have been abandoned, even if at almost every stage the Chinese monk came across evidence of the legacy of the Wheel-turning Monarch Wuyou Wang. Outside the deserted city of Sravasti he saw two seventy-foot pillars flanking the eastern gate of Sakyamuni Buddha's Jetavana monastery: 'On the top of the left pillar there is carved the wheel sign, and a figure of a bull is engraved on the top of the right one.' On the outskirts of the abandoned city of Kapilivastu, where Sakyamuni Buddha had spent his early years as Prince Sidhhartha, were two more such pillars, both topped by carved lions and carrying inscriptions. At the Lumbini pool nearby a single column and a stupa marked the spot where the prince had been born, although here the pillar had been broken in two by a dragon.

Xuanzang noted more of King Wuyou's stone columns as he made his way southwards across Bihar: one at Kushinagara, where Sakyamuni Buddha entered nirvana, marked by a large stupa and 'a stone pillar with a record of the Tathagata's Nirvana inscribed on it'; one at the Cremation Stupa, where Sakyamuni Buddha's remains were cremated and divided into eight portions; one in Chandu country, surmounted by a lion and inscribed with a record 'of the event of subduing demons'; one at Vaishali, where one of the eight portions of Sakyamuni's ashes had been placed in a stupa by a Licchavi king, a pillar 'fifty or sixty feet tall with the figure of a lion on the top'; and two more pillars outside the city of Varanasi, 'one on the west side of the Varana River, the other on the east'. The first was 'as smooth as a mirror' and stood in front of a hundred-foot-high stupa built by King Wuyou; the other was within the confines of the Deer Park Monastery (Sarnath) where Sakyamuni Buddha had preached his wheel-turning sermon to his first five disciples. 'Within the great enclosure,' Xuanzang writes –

there is a temple over two hundred feet high with a gilt *amra* [mango] fruit carved in relief at the top . . . To the northeast of the temple is a stone stupa built by King Wuyou.[8] Although the foundation has sunk, the remaining trunk is still one hundred feet high. In front of it is erected a stone pillar more than seventy feet tall, which is smooth as jade and as reflective as a mirror. This is the place where the Tathagata ['one who has found the truth', thus Sakyamuni Buddha], after having obtained full enlightenment, first turned the Wheel of the Dharma.

An excursion north brought Xuanzang to the country of
Nepala (Nepal), where he found the country's Licchavi ruler
to be 'a pure Buddhist' and its people a mix of Buddhist and
Hindu: 'the monasteries and deva-temples [Hindu temples]
are so close together that they touch each other'. Xuanzang
then returned to the Indian plains, and after crossing the
Ganges came to Pataliputra – only to find this once mighty city
all but abandoned: 'Of the monasteries, deva-temples and
stupas, there are several hundred remnant sites lying in ruins;
only two or three remain intact.'

These remains allowed Xuanzang to follow Faxian's directions and identify the city as it had been in the days of King
Wuyou, including the site of his notorious 'Hell' prison, now
marked by a pillar several tens of feet in height, and the great
relic stupa south of the city seen and described by Faxian –
which had now sunk on one side so that it resembled an over-
turned alms bowl. The lustrous stone column was still standing
but, notes the Chinese pilgrim, 'the inscription on it has
become incomplete'.

The last royal monument to be visited by Xuanzang at
Pataliputra was the remains of the Kukkutarama, the Cock
monastery sited to the south-east of the old city, built by King
Ashoka soon after his conversion to Buddhism and the scene
of the great council attended by a thousand Buddhists, both
monks and lay-people. This had also been the scene of King
Ashoka's last days, commemorated by a stupa known as the
Amalaka stupa, taking its name from the cherry plum that had
been the dying king's last possession.

Xuanzang's next point of pilgrimage was Bodhgaya, where
he was shocked to find the temple and Bodhi tree all but
engulfed by drifting sand dunes. He comments: 'Some old

people said that when the statues of the Bodhsattva disappear
and become invisible, the Buddha-dharma will come to an end,
and now the statue at the south corner has already sunk down
up to the chest.' He goes on to give details of King Ashoka's
actions not found in the *Legend of King Ashoka*:

> When King Wuyou had just ascended the throne, he
> believed in heretical doctrines and destroyed the sites left
> by the Buddha. He sent his troops and went in person to
> cut the tree. He chopped the roots, stalks, branches, and
> leaves into small pieces and had them heaped up at a spot
> a few tens of paces to the west, where fire-worshipping
> Brahmans were ordered to burn the pile as a sacrifice to
> their god. But before the smoke and flames had vanished,
> two trees grew out of the furious fire and luxurious and
> verdurous leaves.

On seeing this miracle King Wuyou repents, irrigates the
remaining roots with milk and makes offerings to the tree so
conscientiously that he forgets to go home. But then his queen
sets out to finish what her husband failed to complete:

> The queen, being a heretical believer, secretly sent a man to
> fell the tree after nightfall. When King Wuyou went to wor-
> ship the tree at dawn, he was very sad to see only the stump
> of the tree. He prayed earnestly and irrigated the stump with
> sweet milk, and in a few days the tree grew up once again.
> With deep respect and astonishment, the king built a stone
> enclosure to the height of more than ten feet around the
> tree, which is still in existence.

Xuanzang had also to report that the Bodhi tree had once again come under attack, and very recently at that, the assailant being King Sasanka of Bengal, who only recently had murdered King Harsha the Great's elder brother Raja the Great. Described by Xuanzang as a 'wicked king and heretical believer', King Sasanka was a devoted follower of Shiva and an equally ardent enemy of Buddhism. He had set about destroying Buddhist monasteries in Bengal and Bihar, and had made the Bodhi tree at Bodhgaya a special target, first cutting it down and setting fire to it and then digging down to the roots and soaking them in sugarcane juice to prevent them regrowing. 'Several months later,' adds Xuanzang, 'King Purnavarman of Magadha, the last descendant of King Wuyou, heard about the event and said with a sigh of regret, "The Sun of Wisdom has sunk, and only the Buddha's tree remained in the world; now that the tree has been destroyed, what else is there for living things to see?"'

This King Purnavarman irrigates the remaining roots with milk from several thousand cows and the tree grows ten feet in one night. He then builds a new enclosure round the tree to a height of twenty-four feet. 'Thus the Bodhi Tree at present is behind the stone wall,' concludes Xuanzang, 'with over ten feet of its branches growing out over the wall.'

After his visit to Bodhgaya the Chinese pilgrim began an extended period of study of Buddhist texts that lasted for three years, undertaking it at Nalanda, the greatest centre of learning in the Buddhist world, drawing students from the furthest corners of Asia. According to Xuanzang, all these students were brilliant scholars of high learning, whose virtue was esteemed by their contemporaries and whose reputation was known to foreign lands 'amounting to several hundreds'. The fruits of centuries of Buddhist thought and philosophy were contained here and at Nalanda's sister monasteries nearby. It meant that when Xuanzang finally left Magadha in the year 640 he was able to take with him not only a great many Sanskrit works and sutras in manuscript form but a thorough knowledge of the *Yogacara* or 'consciousness' school of Buddhist teaching that through his intervention would spread through China and on to Korea and Japan.

Another three years of travelling passed before Xuanzang finally began to make his way back to China. His return to Xian in Eastern China in the year 645 caused huge excitement and was celebrated throughout much of China. Turning his back on the honours heaped upon him by Emperor Taizong, Xuanzang retired to the newly built Da Chien temple outside Xian to teach and translate. Here he constructed the Wild Goose Pagoda to serve as a library for his Indian sutras and as a translation centre. By the time of Xuanzang's death in 664, the Wild Goose Pagoda had become the most important centre for the diffusion of Buddhism north of the Himalayas, staffed by fifty translators who had all been taught Sanskrit by the head abbot, Xuanzang. At the emperor's command, Xuanzang also found time to write what soon became a popular classic of Chinese literature: *Da Tang Xiyo Ti* or 'Great Tang Records of the Western Regions'.

Under the strong central government of the Tang dynasty Buddhism continued to flourish in China – a happy state of affairs brought to an abrupt end by the events listed in Chinese Buddhist sources as the 'Third Catastrophe': the anti-Buddhist persecutions initiated by the emperor Wu-tsung in 842. In the darker centuries that followed, the persona of the monk Xuanzang underwent a curious transformation by becoming fictionalised as the monk Tripitaka in the much-loved Ming classic novel *Xi You Ji*, or *Journey to the West*, better known in more recent centuries as *The Monkey King*, which in our own time provided the basis for the cult TV series *Monkey*.

However, the insularity of the Middle Kingdom and the disdain of its rulers for the outside world ensured that Xuanzang's *Great Tang Records of the Western Regions*, along with Faxian's *A Record of Buddhistic Kingdoms*, remained unknown and unread outside China until well into the nineteenth century.

In 1841 tantalising excerpts from the travels in India of both Faxian and Xuanzang began to appear in French academic journals.[9] The first to react in India was the late James Prinsep's protégé Captain Alexander Cunningham. In 1842 he triumphantly demonstrated the accuracy of Faxian's account by using his directions to locate the ancient Buddhist site of Sankisa, where Sakyamuni Buddha was said to have descended from the Tushita Heaven by a stairway. Faxian had placed Sankisa seven yojanas north-west of Kannauj. This ancient city, situated east of Agra in the Doab country, was still occupied even though it had fallen on hard times, so Cunningham began his search there. He knew that a yojana was a measure of distance used in ancient India to represent a day's march by a royal army, which he assumed to be about seven miles. After riding out in a north-westerly direction from Kannauj for some fifty miles, Cunningham arrived at the little hamlet of Samkassa. 'The village', he afterwards wrote, 'consists of only fifty or sixty houses, on a high mound which has once been a fort: but all around it for a circuit of six miles there is a succession of high ruined mounds of bricks and earth, which are said to be the walls of the old city.'[10]

Bolstered by this little coup, Cunningham called on the

EICo to appoint an archaeological enquirer, a qualified person 'to tread in the footsteps of the Chinese pilgrims Hwan Thsang [Xuanzang] and Fa Hian [Faxian]'. His appeal fell on deaf years. Four years later he tried again, this time declaring that as the ruling power in India the EICo had a duty to India to protect its ancient monuments, and the sooner the better. 'The discovery and publication', he added, 'of all the existing remains of architecture and sculpture, with coins and inscriptions, would throw more light on the ancient history of India, both public and domestic, than the printing of all the rubbish contained in the 18 *Puranas*.'[11]

Cunningham's jibe about the *Puranas* was aimed directly at the scholar most closely associated with their translation, Professor Horace Hayman Wilson, and it hit its mark. The EICo's Court of Directors in London decided that an archaeological enquirer was indeed required and turned to Professor Wilson for advice on who was best qualified to fill such a post. The position went to another protégé of the late James Prinsep, Captain Markham Kittoe, thanks in part to his translation of the Bhabra rock inscription, better known today as the Bairat-Calcutta Minor Rock Edict. This energetic Captain Thomas Burt of the Royal Engineers had found on a chunk of grey granite lodged at the back of a rock shelter on a hill known as the *bijak ki pahari*, or 'hill of the writing', overlooking the old Jaipur–Delhi road close to the Rajasthan border. One surface of the rock had been smoothed flat and polished, and bore a short eight-line inscription very neatly chiselled in Brahmi characters.

It was this unimpressive-looking rock that initiated a gentlemanly rivalry between Alexander Cunningham and Markham Kittoe. Cunningham was then aged twenty-six, ambitious, well connected and highly thought of within military and political circles, even if he sometimes trod a fine line between his military duties and his Indological pursuits. Kittoe was the older of the two by six years, and by his own admission 'a self-educated man, and no Classic or Sanskrit scholar', his language skills 'woefully deficient'. His court-martial verdict had been quashed by order of the Governor General but he was still viewed with suspicion by the military authorities. Yet it was Markham Kittoe whose star first appeared to be in the ascendant, following the publication of his reading of the Bairat-Calcutta inscription in the *JRAS*.

Kittoe's translation had been made 'with the aid of the learned Pandit Kamala Kanta',[12] and it was subsequently shown to be wildly fanciful, for, learned or not, the pandit had misinterpreted the inscription as a Vedic tract. Kittoe's confusion was understandable, for the Ashokan edicts so far discovered had all been monumental, whether on pillars or boulders, and this eight-line inscription appeared rudimentary by comparison. Furthermore, all the other inscriptions had opened with the declamatory phrase 'Thus spake Piyadasi, Beloved-of-the-Gods', whereas this inscription began *Piyadasi laja magadhe sangham abhivademanam* or 'Piyadasi king of Magadha salutes the Sangha'.

When more accurately translated by the French scholar Eugène Burnouf,[13] it proved to be an order rather than edict, directed specifically at the Buddhist Church, with Ashoka speaking as ruler of Magadha rather than emperor of the Indian subcontinent. After first declaring his reverence for the 'three jewels', of Buddhism, in the shape of the Buddha, the Dharma and the Sangha, the king went on to advise the Sangha to take note of certain Dharma texts as spoken by *Bhagavata Budhena* or 'Lord Buddha'. It then cited seven specific texts by their titles and ordered that these should be constantly listened to and memorised, both by monks and nuns and by members of the Buddhist laity.

Buddhist scholars continue to argue over what specific texts Ashoka was here referring to, but they seem to be relatively minor Buddhist scriptures. That immediately raises the question of why the king of Magadha should have gone to the trouble of publishing such an order, for the implications are unmistakable: this was a royal command directing the Buddhist community to toe the Buddhist line according to Ashoka, king of Magadha.

The Bairat-Calcutta inscription provided the clearest confirmation yet of what scholars like Burnouf already suspected: that Ashoka was not only deeply committed to the Buddhist cause but directly involved in shaping its course, even to the extent of making it known what teachings he thought monks and nuns should be committing to memory (bearing in mind that at this time all religious teachings were passed down from teacher to disciple by oral transmission only). It also referred specifically to Lord Buddha, a fact that even Professor Horace Wilson – when finally confronted by an accurate translation – had to admit did rather suggest that King Piyadasi might be a Buddhist ruler, even though he continued to maintain that, whoever else he was, King Piyadasi was not King Ashoka. What no one could then have known was that this was to be the only location where Ashoka had been found to refer specifically to the Buddha in his edicts, that this was almost certainly one of his earliest rock inscriptions to be put up, and that he hereafter appears to have gone to some pains to present his Dharma as inclusive and not specifically Buddhist.

Although Kittoe's translation of the Bairat-Calcutta rock inscription was wayward, it impressed Horace Wilson – which helps to explain why it was that when Markham Kittoe and Alexander Cunningham competed to follow the trails of the Chinese travellers, the better candidate lost.

So eager was the new archaeological enquirer to steal a march on Cunningham that as soon as he received news of his appointment in May 1846 he set out for Bihar, even though the Hot Weather was well advanced. Kittoe may have been ill-equipped and understaffed but he had what mattered: an English version of Abel-Rémusat's *Foé Koué Ki, ou Relations des Royaumes Bouddhiques*, specially translated for him by an obliging friend at the Asiatic Society of Bengal, J. W. Laidley.[14] The information given by Faxian proved to be astonishingly accurate, allowing Kittoe to locate and identify many of the sites associated with the life of Sakyamuni Buddha in southern Bihar. The big disappointment was Patna, where Kittoe could find no signs of its distinguished past as Pataliputra, capital of Magadha. He fared much better at Rajgir, site of the first Magadhan capital of Rajagriha, where he had no difficulty in identifying many important Buddhist sites associated with the life of Buddha as seen by Faxian.

In the Cold Weather months of 1847–8 Captain Kittoe resumed what he termed his 'rambles through Bihar'. At Bodhgaya he cleared away some of the sand that had buried much of the base of the Buddhist temple there – today known as the Mahabodhi Temple – and in doing so uncovered the remains of a stone railing, the posts of which had been decorated with carved medallions. Without realising the significance of what he had found, Kittoe made drawings of more than forty of these medallions, some of which were purely decorative, depicting a variety of animals and mythical beasts, while others showed human worshippers praying before a range of objects that included stupas, Bodhi trees and Dharma wheels. He went on to make a more careful survey of the rock-cut caves in the Barabar and Nagarjuni Hills, where he identified four new inscriptions in Brahmi script. He sent his eye-copies directly to Eugène Burnouf in Paris, who established that three of the inscriptions had been set there by order of Ashoka, here calling himself simply 'King Piyadasi' without any reference to 'Beloved-of-the-Gods'. Two of the caves had been donated by Ashoka twelve years after his consecration and the third in his nineteenth year. But Burnouf also showed that all three caves had been donated not to the Buddhists but to an order of ascetics known as Ajivikas, who were neither Jain, Buddhist nor Hindu, but a sect of atheists who followed the precepts of their founder Maskarin Gosala, a contemporary of Sakyamuni Buddha and the Jain philosopher Mahavira. Indeed, it now turned out that the two Barabar caves donated by Ashoka's descendant Dasharatha were also donations to the Ajivikas – not to the Buddhists, as Prinsep had thought. So here was Ashoka and his descendant bestowing royal patronage on others besides the Buddhists – very much in line with the sentiments contained in Ashoka's RE 7.

Kittoe continued his survey of Bihar over a second year but his efforts failed to satisfy the authorities and he was ordered to Benares to design and build the city's new Queen's College, which was being built to replace Jonathan Duncan's Sanskrit College. Kittoe hated his new job, confiding to Cunningham that it gave him no time to pursue his archaeological enquires. What was particularly frustrating for Kittoe was that he now knew from his reading of Faxian and Xuanzang what

Cunningham had not known back in 1835 when he had dug into the great Darmekh stupa outside Benares at Sarnath – that this was the site of one of the four most sacred places in Buddhism: the Deer Park where Buddha Sakyamuni had preached the discourse known to all Buddhists as the Turning of the Wheel of the Moral Law. Xuanzang, in particular, had left a detailed account of the two great Ashokan stupas he had seen there, and the Ashokan pillar 'smooth as jade and as reflective as a mirror'.

When, in the Cold Weather season of 1851–2, Kittoe at last got his chance to excavate at Sarnath, he botched it, probably for reasons connected with his failing health. He came away with little more than further evidence of catastrophic destruction: 'All has been sacked and burned – priests, temples, idols, all together; for in some places, bones, iron, wood, and stone, are found in huge masses, and this has happened more than once.'[15]

That was Kittoe's last throw. He began to develop virtually identical symptoms to those experienced by his hero James Prinsep and, like his old patron, he was sent home to die. 'Alas poor Kittoe,' wrote Cunningham when he heard the news of his death, even though it meant the archaeological field was now clear of rivals.

Alexander Cunningham the Great

Lion capitals, broken architraves and other pieces of sculpture
near the Great Tope at Sanchi, photographed by the archaeologist
Joseph Beglar in 1870. (APAC, British Library)

Between 1845 and 1849 the armies of the EICo fought two
wars that ended in the annexation of the Punjab and the exten-
sion of John Company's borders as far north-west as the
Khyber Pass. Major Alexander Cunningham was engaged in
both wars but in the lull between the first and the second he
was despatched to Ladakh as head of a boundary commission,
with orders to demarcate the frontier between India and Tibet
(still disputed to this day). It was onerous work but he still
found time to visit Kashmir and explore the region's distinctive
temple architecture, which he thought far superior to anything
he had seen in the Indian plains and ascribed, quite unreasonably, to the lingering influence of the Greeks. Cunningham
also took the opportunity to climb up to the thousand-foot
summit of the Throne of Solomon peak overlooking the
town of Srinagar in order to explore the Shaivite temple of
Shankaracharya perched on its summit. This ancient temple
was said to have been founded by the ninth-century reformer
of Hinduism who had given it its name, but Cunningham was
pleased to discover that even the local Brahmins ascribed its
erection to King Ashoka's son Jalauka, the Shiva-worshipping
ruler so glorified in the *River of Kings* chronicle for his part in
restoring Hinduism to Kashmir after the heretical excesses of
his Buddhist father.

Cunningham was particularly keen to visit one particular
archaeological site on the northern borders of the Punjab. This
had been the subject of two articles which had recently
appeared in the *JRAS*,[1] the first written by the supposed
American adventurer Charles Masson, the other by the
Assistant Secretary of the RAS, an unassuming, self-taught
philologist named Edwin Norris, who in the course of many
years spent as a humble clerk at the EICo's London office in

Leadenhall Street had moved on from his private study of the Cornish language to specialise in the cuneiform writing of Assyria and Babylon. Both articles concerned a rock inscription on the Punjab frontier, first discovered by the French mercenary General Court back in the 1830s but reported just too late for James Prinsep in Calcutta to do more than note its existence.

In 1838 Charles Masson had travelled to the site at considerable personal risk to take the first impression of the inscriptions, which he found set on two faces of a large rock on a hill about a thousand yards from the village of Shahbazgarhi. His eye-copy and impression, made on two strips of 'fine British calico',[2] after several days spent laboriously cleaning the two sides of the rock, had eventually found its way to England and the RAS. The then director of the RAS – who else but the ubiquitous Professor H. H. Wilson – had found it to be written in an alphabet significantly different from the Brahmi of the known Ashokan Rock and Pillar Edicts, and had passed it on to the Society's Assistant Secretary, Edwin Norris.

After some days' study of the Shahbazgarhi writing, Norris noted 'a group of letters of frequent occurrence representing, according to the value to such of the characters as correspond with those on the coins of Bactria, the word *piyasa* ... preceded by three letters which I could not identify ... A further investigation, and an examination of the list of names in Turnour's *Mahawanso*, convinced me that the word was *Devanampiya*.'[3] The all-important difference was that the word as it appeared here was written, not from left to right, as in Pali and Sanskrit, but from right to left, as in Aramaic.

Realising that this was another Ashokan edict rock Norris turned to another member of the RAS, John Dowson, who had spent some years teaching in India. They together compared the Shahbazgarhi inscription with the RAS's copies of the Girnar Rock Edict and realised that they were dealing with two versions of the same text written in related but different languages and characters. The Shahbazgarhi Rock Edict was written in James Prinsep's 'Bactrian-Pali' – Kharosthi – and it confirmed Prinsep's theory that two distinct sets of characters had co-existed side by side in the north-west corner of the subcontinent, both being used for writing what was essentially the same pre-Sanskrit and pre-Pali tongue of Prakrit.

Norris read his paper on the Shahbazgarhi Rock Edict at a meeting of the RAS only a matter of months before his death. It was subsequently published in the autumn issue of the *JASB* in 1846, accompanied by a note from Wilson, in which he commended Norris's work but reiterated his conviction that this and the other edicts had nothing to do with Ashoka.

Now in January 1847, in an unsanctioned visit about which he remained silent for some years, Cunningham crossed the Indus by way of the bridge of boats at Attock and made his way to the village of Hoti Mardan in the Yusufzai plains north of Nowshera. This was three years before Hoti Mardan became the regimental headquarters of the famous Corps of Guides Cavalry and Infantry raised by Captain Harry Lumsden in 1847,[4] and for good strategic reasons, for the village stood at the crossroads of two important routes: one leading north from Peshawar to the Malakand Pass that gave access to Swat; the other being the ancient east–west trade route known as the *Sadak-e-Azam*, or 'Great Highway', which followed the course of the Kabul River as far as Charsadda before skirting round the foothills of the Mahabun massif to reach the crossing-point of the Indus at the edge of the plains.

The village of Shahbazgarhi straddled the Great Highway a few miles east of Hoti Mardan, at a point where the highway was joined by a road coming down from the mountains of Mahabun by way of the defile known as the Ambeyla Pass. Here, on the side of a hill overlooking the village and the highway, King Ashoka had chosen to display another set of his Rock Edicts in a manner strikingly similar to those at Girnar and Dhauli.

The elephantine rock at Shahbazgarhi, photographed by James Craddock in 1875. Rock Edicts 1–11 are carved on the eastern face of the boulder, as seen above. (APAC, British Library)

'The great inscription of Asoka', Cunningham noted, 'is engraved on a large shapeless mass of trap rock, lying about 80 feet up the slope of the hill, with its western face looking downwards towards the village of Shahbazgarhi. The greater portion of the inscription is on the eastern face of the rock looking up the hill, but all the latter part, which contains the names of the five Greek kings, is on the western face.' Cunningham was mistaken in describing the Shahbazgarhi rock as a 'shapeless mass'. It was, in fact, shaped very like a seated elephant, as were the two Rock Edict sites so far discovered. The fact that these three sites – at Girnar, Dhauli and now Shahbazgarhi – together enclosed a triangle of land that extended to three thousand miles was a striking demonstration of how far Ashoka's authority had extended.

Cunningham had no time to take an impression or make an eye-copy of the edicts but he observed that Shahbazgarhi village was surrounded by the remains of what, according to the local Yusufzai villagers, had once been the capital of the region. They pointed to several mounds of ruins as having been inside the city, and to two well-known spots, named Khaprai and Khapardarh, as the sites of the northern and eastern gates of the city: 'The truth of their statements was confirmed by an examination of the ground within the limits specified, which I found everywhere strewn with broken bricks and pieces of pottery.'5 What Cunningham also learned was that the village had acquired its name – literally in Pashto, 'the home of the king of eagles' – from a shrine on the top of the Rock Edict hill, supposed by some to be the tomb of a Muslim saint but regarded by others as the grave of an unbeliever. That led Cunningham to John Leyden's translation of the memoirs of the first Mughal emperor Babur, *Baburnama*.

In the course of his journey down the old highway in the year 1519 Babur had camped at Shahbazgarhi and had found the prospect from the top of its little hill very beautiful. But he had taken offence at the hilltop shrine and had ordered its destruction: 'It struck me as improper that so charming and delightful a spot should be occupied by the tomb of an unbeliever. I therefore gave orders that the tomb should be pulled down and levelled with the ground.' Babur's actions at Shahbazgarhi raised all sorts of questions in Cunningham's mind but twenty-three years were to pass before he was in a position to provide answers.

On this same journey to the Punjab's north-west frontier Cunningham became aware that another military officer in the area shared his antiquarian interests. He was Major James Abbott, part of the first wave of British political officers brought in to administer the Punjab frontier, initially in alliance with the Sikh government and then replacing it. 'Uncle' Abbott, as he became known, had made his mark as a young cavalry officer with a daring mercy mission to Khiva to rescue some Russian hostages. The bid had cost Abbott two fingers on his sword hand but it led to his selection in 1846 as the right man to impose British authority on Hazara (not the region in Afghanistan known for its much-persecuted Shia inhabitants but the less well-known mountain country east of the Indus River in what is now northern Pakistan). In the course of six years spent among the Hazarawals, Abbott came to identify closely with the mountain tribesmen – too closely for the comfort of his superiors, leading to his removal and transfer. But Abbott got to know the Hazara country better than any European before or since, and being a man of wide interests he explored Hazara's past, beginning with the incursion of Alexander and his Macedonians.

Just across the River Indus from James Abbott's fiefdom of Hazara lay the mountains of Swat and Buner, dominated by the great Mahabun massif. This was hostile country, already notorious as the home of a band of Muslim jihadis known to the British as the 'Hindustani fanatics'.[6] It meant that Abbott never set foot on the Mahabun mountain – which did not prevent him from speculating that it had to be Alexander's Mount Aornos, the rock stronghold where the mountain tribes had made their last stand. 'The whole account of Arrian of the rock Aornos is a faithful picture of the Mahabun,' he wrote, 'a mountain table scarped on the east by tremendous precipices, from which descends one large spur down upon the Indus between Sitana and Umb.'[7] What convinced Abbott that he was right was that Alexander had made his camp below Aornos at a place called Embolina, and on the lower slopes of the Mahabun massif were two modern villages called Amb and Balimah, 'the one in the river valley, the other on the mountain immediately above it'.[8]

Abbott's theory found support from another British officer, Dr Henry Bellew, the first surgeon of Lumsden's Corps of Guides.[9] Dr Bellew spent almost his entire military career in and around the Vale of Peshawar, his facility with local languages and his knowledge of the Yusufzai Pathans making him much more than just a military doctor. He and his commanding officer, Harry Lumsden, were the first Europeans to explore the large Buddhist monastic complex of Takht-i-bahi, nine miles north of Mardan on the road to Swat. Here and elsewhere in the Peshawar Vale they found coins and other antiquities proving 'the successive existence in this country ... of Greeks, Graeco-Bactrians, Indo-Bactrians, Scythians, and Brahmins'.[10] One civilisation after another had flourished here, with Brahmanism ultimately triumphing over Buddhism, only for both to be completely annihilated by Mahmud of Ghazni in the eleventh century: 'Fire appears to have been the chief means of destruction; for most of the ruins that have been excavated bear marks of its action, and show signs of the hasty flight of their former inhabitants.'

Swat and the Mahabun mountain country lay outside British control but Bellew employed scouts to map the area, from which he determined Alexander's route through the mountains to Mount Aornos and on down to the Indus crossing. He learned that on the summit plateau of the Mahabun there still stood 'the ruins of an extensive rock-built fortress, very diffi-cult of access', and that according to local tradition, 'Alexander did cross the Indus by a ford at the foot of the hill alluded to [Mahabun], passing from Amb across to Darband in Hazara. The tradition relates how he gained possession of the hitherto impregnable fortress through the miraculous intervention of a native ascetic he met with on the spot.'

However, for Alexander Cunningham it was the travels of the Chinese pilgrims rather than Alexander that counted. He contributed two largely speculative articles on this subject to the *JASB* before rejoining the Bengal Army and putting his engineering skills to good use when the second round of the Anglo-Sikh War began in December 1848. He was present at the hard-fought battles of Chilianwala and Gujrat and at the surrender that followed in March 1849, leading to the final annexation of the Punjab.

Cunningham had too much self-belief for his own good, which made him reluctant to admit that he was wrong. He was determined to see Greek influences in early Indian sculpture and architecture that weren't there, and his archaeological methods were essentially destructive, but he was also far ahead of his time in grasping the potential of what he termed 'field archaeology', in understanding that excavation went hand in hand with epigraphy and that there was also a need to preserve and conserve. He undertook the first recognisably systematic archaeological excavation in India in 1851, and by the time he had ended his last dig, at Bodhgaya in 1892, he had overseen three decades of archaeological advances as founder and first director of the Archaeological Survey of India (ASI).

This new age of Indian archaeology dawned at Sanchi, thanks to the appointment of Cunningham's younger brother Joseph as Political Agent to the native state of Bhopal in central India. Twenty-five miles north-west of the state capital was Sanchi, with its hill-top complex of stupas dominated by its central stupa. The Great Tope, as it was then called, had been much talked about since James Prinsep's pioneering readings of its inscriptions in 1837, but the geographical isolation that had helped it survive, in Cunningham's words, 'the destructive rancour of the fiery Saivas and the bigoted Musalmans' had long since ended. In 1822 a Captain Johnson, Assistant Political Agent in Bhopal, had torn open the Great Stupa from top to bottom, leaving a vast breach and in the process knocking down part of the surrounding balustrade and the western gateway. He had then compounded his vandalism by hacking his way into the next two largest stupas, afterwards known as Stupa 2 and Stupa 3.

In January 1851 Sanchi became the test bed for a new sort of archaeology, still highly damaging by modern standards but undertaken against a background of widespread destruction of such ancient sites – by local villagers in search of hidden treasure, landowners seeking building material, contractors extracting rubble for the foundations of new roads, railways and bridges, and bored British officers or officials who should have known better. At Sanchi the excavation was mapped, drawn, documented and

analysed. What made this possible was Cunningham's partner-
ship with a fellow engineer, Lieutenant Fred Maisey, a talented
draughtsman and surveyor posted to Bhopal State some two
years earlier specifically to make an illustrated report on Sanchi
and its sculptures and inscriptions. He now found himself
having to defer to Cunningham's superior rank and expertise.

Cunningham began, as at Sarnath, by sinking a shaft down
from the top of the Great Tope and, as before, he found their
efforts unrewarded. It contained no human remains and was
therefore a memorial rather than an ossuary, with a plain
plaster exterior laid over a solid-brick interior. But where the
Sanchi stupa differed from Sarnath was in its surround: its
stone railing that enclosed a processional pathway encircling
the stupa and its four entrance points in the form of elaborate
toranas, or gateways, set at the four cardinal points. Two of the
gateways were still standing, the other two lay in pieces.

'These four gateways are the most picturesque and valuable
objects at Sanchi,' Cunningham wrote in his subsequent
report. 'They are entirely covered with bas-relief, representing
various domestic scenes and religious ceremonies.'[11] The pillars of the four gateways were supported by sets of elephants,
lions and dwarfs, the open spaces between the uprights contained figures of elephant riders and horsemen and on the
outside were what Cunningham described as 'female dancers'.
The faces of the pillars were divided into compartments, each
containing religious or domestic scenes and the crossbeams of
the gateways, in the form of three nineteen-foot architraves
placed one above the other and projecting at both ends, were
similarly decorated with complex panoramic scenes. These
Cunningham assumed to be portrayals of events either from
the life of Sakyamuni Buddha or the *Jataka Tales* – stories from

the lives of the earlier Buddhas who preceded Sakyamuni – as well as numerous depictions of stupa and Bodhi tree worship.

Cunningham left it to his junior colleague to make painstaking drawings of some of the most striking of these scenes, being much more interested in the accompanying inscriptions. As James Prinsep had discovered back in 1837, these were mostly records of donations. Cunningham recorded almost two hundred, showing that the colonnade and the four gateways had been paid for by individual donors, one third of them women, rather than mighty monarchs or religious institutions. The repeated appearance of the archaic form *bhichhu* for 'monk' on the colonnade, as opposed to *bhikku* written on the gateways, showed that the one had come before the other, leading Cunningham to conclude that the colonnade had gone up in Ashoka's time and the four gateways a century later. This appeared to be confirmed by his reading of a donor inscription carved on a stupa at the centre of the panoramic scene shown in the upper architrave of the South Gateway. It read: 'Gift of Ananda, son of the neophyte Vasishtha, in the reign of Sri Satakarni'.[12]

Cunningham took this to refer to King Satakarni I, listed in the *Vishnu Purana* as sixth in the Satavahana dynasty of kings of Andhra. The Satavahanas were well known to Cunningham because they were the first Indian rulers to put their heads on their coinage. They had been feudatories of the Mauryas until the death of Ashoka, after which they had broken away, and under King Satakarni I had defeated the Shungas of North India to extend Satavahani rule over much of central India. Unfortunately for Cunningham, the Satavahana dynasty contained several kings named Satakarni, including a self-declared Buddhist monarch who styled himself Gautamiputra ('son of Gautama') Satakarni and who ruled in the first century CE.

Cunningham either got his dates wrong or muddled these two figures, and on this basis dated the four gateways to the first century CE.

Cunningham's lack of interest in the gateway bas-reliefs meant he failed to note that a number of the scenes shown had been inspired by comparatively recent events, including some which may even have occurred within the living memory of the crafts-men who carved them – particularly in the case of the South Gateway, which now lay scattered on the ground in pieces.

Part of the fallen South Gateway of the Great Tope at Sanchi, with the brick stupa and surrounding railing in the background, and sections of architrave in the foreground. A photograph taken in 1861 by James Waterhouse. (APAC, British Library) (Overleaf) Part of the relief shown on the inner side of the middle architrave, showing a king in his chariot proceeding towards a stupa. A photograph (with cracked glass plate) taken by Raja Deen Dayal in 1881. (APAC, British Library)

Cunningham's descriptions of the scenes depicted on the scattered pillars and architraves of the South Gateway were no more than cursory. He merely noted that one of the extended panoramas depicted a king riding in a chariot approaching a stupa, and on the other side of the stupa the same king appearing to bow before it while a number of Naga snake kings looked on approvingly. Major Franklin had drawn this scene back in 1820 (see p. 108) and Captain Murray in 1837 for James Prinsep to reproduce in the *JASB* (see p. 159). Like them, Cunningham missed the significance of what was portrayed here – and on two other scenes shown on the same gateway's cross-beams, both showing a huge elephant whose mahout, or driver, bears a relic casket on his head.

It was left to Fred Maisey to make drawings of these and other scenes from the South Gateway, the full significance of which would only be understood some seventy years later. One of these scenes would prove to be of crucial importance. It comes from a side panel of one of the gateway's supporting pillars and shows the Bodhi tree at Bodhgaya and the Diamond Throne at its base set within the pavilion-like structure and surrounding wall built for it by King Ashoka. Immediately below it are six figures facing outwards, a king in the centre, indicated by the royal umbrella, and five women. The king appears to be supported by the two women on either side of him.

The Bodhi tree with its Ashokan pavilion and surrounding wall, and below it a king apparently supported by two women. (Frederick Maisey, *Sanchi and its Remains*, 1892)

The other three gateways also showed scenes that Cunningham and his contemporaries failed to fully understand. Of particular interest here are two more sculpted bas-reliefs drawn by Maisey. The first, from a side-panel on one of the pillars of the West Gateway, shows the Bodhi tree without its pavilion and surrounding wall. On the left a very corpulent king is paying homage to the tree surrounded by his womenfolk. The second scene is from a side panel of one of the pillars on the North Gateway. It shows a stupa surrounded by worshippers with a large number of musicians in attendance, in what looks like an inauguration ceremony of some sort. One of the worshippers carries a relic casket.

(Above) One of the panels on a pillar of the West Gateway of the Great Tope at Sanchi. It shows the Bodhi tree unfenced and in its simplest form, surrounded by worshippers headed by an unusually rotund man. (Opposite) Musicians and worshippers clad in decidedly un-Indian dress worship a newly built stupa, from a side panel from the North Gateway. (Maisey, *Sanchi and its Remains*, 1892)

This last image did catch Cunningham's attention. It shows the worshippers clad in short skirts and cloaks, with pointed caps or bands round their heads and wearing sandals laced up to the knee. One of the musicians plays a double flute, another a harp-like instrument. Both the musical instruments and the dress are more Greek than Indian. Everything points to this being the portrayal of the dedication of a stupa in the Taxila or Gandhara region.

From the Great Tope the excavators moved on to its surrounds.

In front of each of the four gateways they found shrines containing Buddha statues, and immediately beside the South Gateway the broken remains of a column of a light-coloured sandstone, displaying that high polish that characterised the stone columns Cunningham had seen in Delhi and Allahabad. It bore an inscription in eight lines of Brahmi, the upper part of which was damaged. 'The opening is nearly obliterated,' wrote Cunningham –

> I think it probable that the first word was *Devanam*; next comes a blank and then *Maga;* and it is possible that the whole line might be read –
> *Devanam (piya) Magadha raja*
> 'Devanampriya, King of Magadha.'
> The second line may be partially restored, thus –
> *(a)bhi(vadema)nam chetiyagiri*
> 'with salutation to the fraternity of Chaityagiri.'

At the end of the third line the word *sangham* or 'Buddhist community' was distinctly visible, as were the words '*bhikhu cha bhikhuni*', 'monks or nuns'. The concluding line of the inscription was also perfectly legible, reading: 'It is my wish that the Sangha community may always be united.'

This was the first of Ashoka's so-called Schism Edicts to be discovered, in which the emperor urged the Buddhist community to avoid dissension and remain united. If Ashoka had caused such an inscription to be erected here it was logical to suppose that similar edict pillars would be found at other major Buddhist sites. To date, only three such Schism Edict pillars have been found: at Sanchi, Sarnath and Kausambi, but there must originally have been many more.

Cunningham worked out that the original height of the

inscribed shaft must have been 31 feet 11 inches. His measurements also demonstrated that the column had been shaped so as to give 'a gentle swell in the middle of the shaft', showing that whoever had cut the pillar had followed the same practice as the Greeks, who perfected this technique. The pillar bore a number of deep cuts where unsuccessful efforts had been made to saw through the shaft, presumably so that those segments could be put to use as rollers.

Further sorting through the mass of stonework covering the site brought to light the bell, abacus and capital that had once crowned the Ashokan pillar. To the delight of the excavators the capital was in the form of four lions 'standing back to back, each four feet in height'. Their heads had been knocked off

Fred Maisey's drawing of the damaged Ashokan lion capital at Sanchi. (Maisey, *Sanchi and its Remains*, 1892)

but their bodies and limbs were still intact, 'so boldly sculpted, and the muscles and claws so accuracy placed, that they might well be placed in comparison with many specimens of Grecian art'. Equally well sculpted was the decoration on the circular abacus on which the four lions stood, with 'some very Grecian-looking foliage, and with four pairs of *chakwas*, or holy Brahmani geese. These birds are always seen in pairs, and are celebrated among the Hindus for their conjugal affection. They are there-fore presented billing, with outstretched necks, and heads lowered towards the ground.'

This abacus was strikingly similar to that supporting the capital of the pillar at Lauriya-Nandangarh in North Bihar, except that here at Sanchi the ducks came in pairs rather than in an extended line.

A second pillar similar in height and shape to the first was found close to the North Gateway, with a capital topped not by lions but a larger than life-size human figure. 'The expression of the face is placid, but cheerful,' wrote Cunningham, 'that places it amongst the finest specimens of Indian sculpture. It probably represents Asoka himself.' However, this was wishful thinking; the statue actually dates from the Gupta era.

Cunningham judged the Great Tope and its surrounds to have been built in three phases – the stupa pre-dating Ashoka, the railings and stone columns being Ashokan, and the four gateways post-Ashokan. He was right only in so far as there were three phases. The brick core of the stupa, the edict pillar and its lion capital are indeed Ashokan, but at the close of the Mauryan period the site had been badly damaged, the most likely culprit being the Brahman Pushyamitra, founder of the Shunga dynasty. One or more of Pushyamitra's successors had then restored and enlarged the stupa, adding stonework and the surrounding balustrade. The four gateways had gone up in the third phase, beginning with the South Gateway, which identifies itself as erected during the reign of the Satavahana king Satakarni – but which Satakarni? Although carved in stone, this and the other three gateways clearly drew on wooden prototypes that may well have preceded them here and at other sites. They mark the moment of transition from building in wood to building in stone. But Cunningham could well have been right in linking them to the empire-building Satakarni I, who ruled for some fifty years before his death in about 125 BCE. If that dating is correct – and there are plenty of scholars who argue that it is too early by a century – then the older stonemasons mong those who worked on the relief carvings would easily have been born in the same century as the great emperor Ashoka.

From the Great Tope Cunningham and Maisey moved on to open another twenty-seven stupas, ten of them on Sanchi hill and the remainder at four Buddhist sites in the surrounding hills. Every excavation led to the discovery of relic boxes containing one or more soapstone reliquaries, each holding ashes and bone fragments, and each inscribed in Brahmi with the name of the Buddhist saint or saints whose remains it contained, in some cases with added background information – such as, for example, 'Relics of the emancipated Kasyapa Gotra the missionary to the whole Hemawanta [Himalayas]'. To the amazement of the excavators, many of these names matched those of early Buddhist elders and missionaries as given in the *Great Dynastic Chronicle*. In what Cunningham had designated 'No. 2 Tope' at Sanchi were found five reliquaries, which together held the remains of 'no less than ten men of the Buddhist Church, during the reign of Ashoka. One of them

[Moggaliputta Tissa] conducted the proceedings of the Third Synod, in 241 B.C., and two were deputed to the Hemawanta country as missionaries, after the meeting of the Synod. From this we may conclude that the date of the Tope cannot be earlier than about 220 B.C., by which time the last of Ashoka's contemporaries would have passed away.'

The relics from 'No. 3 Tope' at Sanchi proved to be equally revealing. They were found to contain the ashes of two even more famous early Buddhists: Sariputra and Mogalana, two of Sakyamuni Buddha's earliest converts and among the closest of his disciples. Further remains of these same two elders were buried in other stupas, showing that the practice of spreading relics had been widespread at the time of Ashoka. 'These discoveries', wrote Cunningham with absolute justification, 'appear to me to be of the greatest importance for the early illustration of the early history of India, for they authenticate in the fullest manner the narrative of the most interesting portions of Ashoka's reign.'[13] More specifically, they corroborated the claims made in Ceylon's *Great Dynastic Chronicle*.

Cunningham concluded that Sanchi and the Bhilsa region (today Vidisha) made up the place identified in the *Great Dynastic Chronicle* as Chetiyagiri, the 'stupa hill', where Ashoka's first wife Devi had come from and where his first two children, Mahinda and Sanghamitta, grew up. That same Devi had either founded or patronised a monastery there and, even though the Great Tope's colonnade and gateways were the work of Ashoka's successors, this site was of particular interest to Ashoka as the starting point of the great missionary programme he had initiated as part of his drive to spread the Dharma throughout Jambudwipa and beyond.

Needless to say, Cunningham's first report on Sanchi was immediately challenged by Professor Horace Wilson, still occupying the Boden Chair of Sanskrit at Oxford and still refusing to accept that the author of the Rock and Pillar Edicts was Ashoka. Cunningham responded by writing *The Bhilsa Topes*, copiously illustrated with Maisey's maps and drawings, which became the model for all subsequent archaeological reports published in British India. He demolished Wilson's arguments point by point, making no secret of his contempt for Wilson's reliance on 'mendacious' Brahmanical testaments. Here, by contrast, was hard archaeological evidence that provided 'the most complete and convincing proof of the authenticity of the history of Asoka, as related in the *Mahawanso*'. The publication of *The Bhilsa Topes* in 1853 effectively silenced Wilson, finally putting an end to the arguments over the identity of Piyadasi and the significance of Ashoka as the champion and propagator of Buddhism in the third century BCE.

Dr Wilson had dominated the Orientalist scene since the 1820s, but not always to its advantage. With his death in 1860 a millstone fell from the neck of Indian studies, even if Wilson's influence continued to linger at Oxford, where the scholar best qualified to succeed him to the Boden Chair, Wilson's young German rival Max Müller, was notoriously passed over in favour of Wilson's former student Monier Williams.

Cunningham believed his discoveries at Sanchi and the Bhilsa region to be equal in importance to those recently made in Mesopotamia by Henry Layard, whose impressive folio volume of *Illustrations of the Monuments of Nineveh* had appeared a few years earlier. But outside India few academics shared his enthusiasm and the British public showed no interest whatsoever. They could respond to the romance of Ancient Egypt, thanks to the army of savants who had accompanied Napoleon's invasion of Egypt in 1798, the decipherment of the Rosetta Stone by Jean François Champollion in 1822 and the rich plunder from its tombs and pyramids that now filled their museums. They could even identify with Nineveh, Nimrod and Babylon through the Old Testament and the Holy Land. But India was something else. John Company now reigned supreme, imposing British values over a land formerly 'cursed from one end to the other by the vice, the ignorance, the oppression, the despotism, the barbarous and cruel customs that have been the growth of ages under every description of Asiatic misrule'.[14] As far as the British public was concerned India had little to offer and never had, a land of picturesque mosques and tumbledown Muslim tombs as portrayed in the prints of the Daniells. Small wonder that a hitherto unheard-of emperor in a far distant past excited little interest. A century and a half later, the situation remains pretty much the same.

Sir Alexander in Excelsis

One of the pillars of the East Gateway of the Bharhut stupa, with adjoining rail and coping, photographed by Joseph Beglar in 1874. (Cunningham, *The Stupa of Bharhut*, 1879)

The uprising known to the British as the Indian Mutiny con-
vulsed the subcontinent from the summer of 1857 through
almost to the end of 1858. It ended East India Company rule
and led to Crown rule, with a Viceroy governing India in the
name of the Queen. Four years later Alexander Cunningham
retired from military service with a colonel's pension. A group
photograph taken at the time of his departure shows him looking every bit his forty-six years.

Alexander Cunningham (centre) at the time of his retirement
from the Indian Army, with other Royal Engineer officers in
October 1862. (Royal Engineers Museum, Chatham)

However, before his departure Cunningham had taken care
to make his case with Lord Canning, the first viceroy, and
within a matter of months he was back – but as a major-general

and archaeological surveyor to the Government of India 'in Behar and elsewhere', together with an equally vague brief to 'make an accurate description of such remains as most deserve notice'. It was the role he had been born to fill.

No financial provision had been made other than Cunningham's official salary of 450 rupees a month and a field allowance of 350 rupees a month. But it was a start and it allowed Cunningham to devote himself full-time to the recovery of ancient India's historical geography, criss-crossing northern India in a series of field-trips during the winter months and then writing up the results over the summer. The fruit of these surveys eventually amounted to twenty-three volumes of *Archaeological Survey Reports*, which to this day make breathtaking reading, as much for their scope as their findings.

The first Cold Weather survey was concentrated on Bihar and the province then known as the North-Western Provinces and Oude (subsequently United Provinces and today the northern Indian state of Uttar Pradesh). Stanislas Julien's two-volume translation of the travels of Xuanzang, *Memoires sur les Contrées Occidental,* had appeared in 1857–8, which meant that Cunningham was now able to conduct his field surveys with copies of both Faxian's and Xuanzang's travels in his knapsack. It enabled him to track down virtually every place visited by the Chinese pilgrims, including such ancient cities as Sravasti, Kosambi and Ayodhya. At Kosambi, west of Allahabad on a bend of the Yamuna River, Cunningham found an Ashokan pillar that Xuanzang had failed to mention, lacking a capital, badly damaged by a recent fire and carrying no Brahmi inscription, but still standing. At Ayodhya, where Xuanzang had seen several ruined monasteries including one 'with an Asoka tope to mark a place at which the Buddha had preached to the devas',[1] Cunningham could find only the bell of an Ashokan capital, inverted to serve as the base of a lingam in the Shaivite temple of Nageshvarnatha.[2]

He did better south of the River Ganges, identifying the extensive ruins first reported on by Francis Buchanan south of the fort of Bihar as the site of the famous monastic university of Nalanda. At Bodhgaya he began clearing the mass of ruins surrounding the great temple and its Bodhi tree to better expose the stone railing that Markham Kittoe had unearthed during his visit to the site back in 1847. He found more of the posts decorated with medallions that Kittoe had drawn, a number of which had been recycled to serve as roof supports for a building beside the main temple now occupied by Hindu devotees.

From the style of the decorations and the accompanying Brahmi inscriptions recording the names of the donors, Cunningham concluded that the railings could not be of much later date than Ashokan.[3] However, he was wrong, as a second round of excavations conducted in 1875 revealed when the remains of a simpler and earlier set of railings was uncovered. Together, they confirmed the essential accuracy of Xuanzang's account, which was that the original Ashokan railings had been destroyed by the anti-Buddhist regicide Pushyamitra and that the second set of railings that had replaced them had themselves been destroyed by King Sasanka of Bengal.

The Bodhi tree was itself a major cause for concern. In 1812 Francis Buchanan had found the tree in full vigour but when Cunningham saw it half a century later it was 'very much decayed', its branches 'barkless and rotten'.[4] By the time of Cunningham's third visit to Bodhgaya in 1876 the tree had gone completely, having been brought down in a storm and removed. During the course of his fourth visit, in the Cold

Weather of 1880–1, it occurred to him that some of the tree's roots might have survived. A dig into the sandy soil just west of the Diamond Throne disinterred two large pieces of 'an Old Pipal Tree'. Conscious that the sacred continuity of the Bodhi tree was now at risk, he took a cutting from the nearest pipal tree and planted it beside the now restored Diamond Throne. It took root and is now venerated by Buddhist pilgrims as the authentic descendant of the original Bodhi tree of Sakyamuni Buddha's time.

In 1864 Cunningham returned to the scene of his first success: Sankisa, the site of the Buddha's descent from heaven. He now had Xuanzang's account and the extra information it provided, including the detail of an Ashokan stone pillar of a 'lustrous violet colour and very hard, with a crouching lion on the top'.[5] The modern village of Samkassa was perched on a large rectangular mound known locally as the *qila* or 'fort'. About three-quarters of a mile south of the fort was a smaller mound, made up of solid brickwork crowned by a modern Hindu temple dedicated to Bisari Devi, described to Cunningham as a goddess of great power. As he made his way across the open ground towards the temple he almost fell over a large boulder-like object. When cleared of the surrounding undergrowth it revealed itself as a capital of an ancient pillar, bearing the figure of an elephant.[6]

Carved in lustrous pale sandstone and standing four feet high, the elephant was incomplete, having lost its trunk, tusks, ears and tail. Even so, Cunningham thought the sculpture 'by far the best representation of that animal that I have seen in any Indian sculpture. The veins of the legs are carefully chiselled, and the toes are well and faithfully represented.' It stood on a round abacus and bell similar in style to that recovered by

The Ashokan elephant capital found by Alexander Cunningham
in a field outside Samkassa village in 1864, as photographed on
site by his assistant Joseph Beglar in the 1870s. The original print
is damaged. (APAC, British Library)

Cunningham at Sanchi, although here decorated with stylised
leaves rather than ducks.

The pillar upon which the elephant had originally stood
could not be found. However, Cunningham had no hesitation
in declaring this to be another of Emperor Ashoka's works and
he speculated that the reason why Xuanzang had reported
seeing a lion capital at Sankisa and not an elephant could have

been because the trunk had already broken off when the Chinese pilgrim saw it and 'the elephant thus disfigured was mistaken for the lion'.

In this same winter season Cunningham returned to Kosambi to look for further remains of the pillar located a year before. He uncovered a short and much mutilated edict almost identical to the Schism Edict found at Sanchi, confirmation that Ashoka had indeed sent out a directive to a number of Buddhist monasteries ordering the Sangha to toe the line.

But not every discovery came from directions supplied by the Chinese pilgrims. Following information provided by a Mr Forrest, Cunningham travelled due north from Delhi as far as the village of Kalsi, just west of the hill-station of Mussoorie at a point where the Jumna River debouched on to the plains. From here Cunningham was directed to a low ridge above the river, upon which rested a large elephantine boulder of distinctive white quartz covered in moss. Three sides had been smoothed and polished and on two of these were neatly set out the fourteen Rock Edicts of Ashoka, all virtually identical in lettering and contents to the Girnar Rock Edict. An added bonus came with the discovery that the northern shoulder of the rock bore the figure of a bull-elephant with large tusks and a curled trunk, neatly cut. Between the elephant's fore and rear legs were four Brahmi characters spelling out the word *gajatame*.

After much puzzling Cunningham had to admit that he had no idea as to what this could mean, other than it might refer to the name of the rock, which like the other three edict rocks so far discovered had clearly been selected because of its elephant-like appearance. The best theory today is that *gajatame* means something like 'best of elephants' – possibly Ashoka's personal

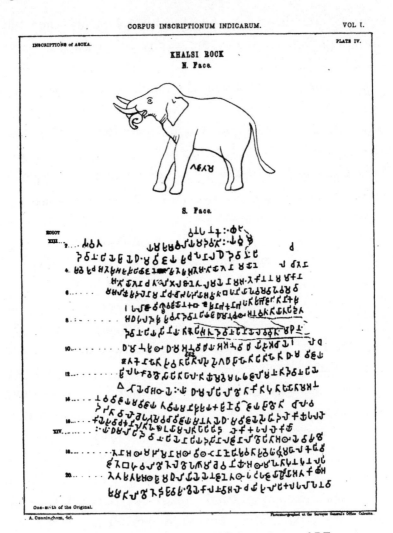

CORPUS INSCRIPTIONUM INDICARUM.   VOL I.

INSCRIPTIONS of ASOKA.   PLATE IV.

KHALSI ROCK
N. Face.

S. Face.

One-sixth of the Original.

A. Cunningham, del.   Photozincographed at the Surveyor General's Office Calcutta.

The Kalsi elephant together with RE 13 and part of RE 14, as drawn and published by Alexander Cunningham in his *Inscriptions of Aśoka*, 1877.

memorial to a favourite elephant but more probably a reference to the elephant as a symbol of the Buddha.[7] The Kalsi elephant was the third such image to be discovered in close proximity to an Ashokan monument, the first being the elephant carved out of the solid rock at Dhauli and the second the elephant capital at Sankisa. All have been cut or carved with remarkable realism.

Under its veneer of moss the Kalsi Rock Edict was in excellent condition. 'I find the Khalsi text to be in a more perfect state than any of them', wrote Cunningham in his report, 'and more specifically in that part which contains the names of the five Greek kings – Antiochus, Ptolemy, Antigonus, Magas, and Alexander.' Now at last the issue of who precisely these names referred to could finally be cleared up, allowing a more accurate dating for Ashoka's inauguration as king to be arrived at.

It had already been established that: firstly, Antigonos was not Antigonos I but his grandson Antigonos II, who had established the Antigonid dynasty in Macedonia in 319 BCE and had died at the age of eighty in 239 BCE; secondly, Antiochos was not Antiochos Soter but his less successful son Antiochos II, who succeeded his father in 262 BCE and was thereafter preoccupied in warring with Ptolemy II of Egypt; and thirdly, that Ptolemy was this same Ptolemy II, who had become king of Ptolemaic Egypt in 283 BCE. Antiochos II and Ptolemy II had concluded a peace treaty in about 250 BCE, and both had died in the same year of 246 BCE.

Of the two last Greek kings now clearly identified on the Kalsi Rock Edict – Magas and Alexander – the first had to be the half-brother of Ptolemy II, who had broken away in about 277 BCE to found Cyrene (approximating to modern Libya), which remained independent of Egypt until Magas's death in about 255 BCE. Finally, the last of the five named rulers could only be Alexander II, who had succeeded his father King Pyrrhas of Epirus (approximating to modern Albania) in 272 BCE and gone on to drive Antigonos II out of Macedonia, which he had then ruled over until it was reclaimed by Antigonos's son Demetrius II.

These five kings provided the following ruling spans:

Antigonos II 319–239 BCE
Antiochos II 262–246 BCE
Ptolemy II 283–246 BCE
Magas 277– c.255 BCE
Alexander II 272– c.254 BCE

Taken together, these five sets of dates showed that the Girnar, Shahbazgarhi and Kalsi Rock Edicts must have been ordered between 262 BCE – when Antiochos II came to the throne – and 255 BCE, the death of Magas.

In RE 12 Ashoka had listed his nearest neighbour to the west, Antiochos II, but – surprisingly – made no mention of the Macedonian satraps Diodotos and Andragoras, who had broken away in or just after the year 255 BCE to rule Bactria and Parthia as independent kings. This strengthened the case that the Rock Edicts must have been inscribed before that date, and since RE 3 stated unambiguously that 'Twelve years after my coronation this has been ordered', it followed that Ashoka had been anointed king of Magadha twelve years before 262–255 BCE, so somewhere between 274–267 BCE. Cunningham plumped for the latter date.

At the start of the Cold Weather months of 1865–6 General Cunningham made his second visit to the northern Punjab. He had hitherto assumed the celebrated Manikyala Tope, dug into by Court, Masson and others, to be the site of the ancient city of Taxila. But after matching the accounts of Alexander's invasion with the details provided of Faxian and Xuanzang, he was able to place Taxila behind the long, curling spur of the Margalla Ridge, which extends southwards into the plains from the mountains of Hazara. Until recently this was a favourite picnic spot for the diplomats and their families at nearby Islamabad. Today it is off-limits, but if you stand on that ridge and look to the west you can see how advantageously the city of Taxila was placed. Besides being protected on three sides by mountains, it controls the Margalla Pass, where the Great Highway (and the more recent railway line) cuts through Margalla Ridge.

At Taxila Cunningham identified three areas of occupation, each enclosed within clearly defined city walls. The best pre-served was Sirsuk, neatly laid out like a Roman town with a street grid, temples on raised platforms, massive cut-stone walls and city gates. However, the oldest and largest of the three cities was Bir, to the east of which stood the largest of a number of stupa mounds, referred to by the local inhabitants as the *Chir*, or 'Split', Tope, because of the way it had been torn open by the French general Claude Auguste Court back in the days when he was employed by Maharaja Ranjit Singh. Over the next fifteen years Taxila continued to draw Cunningham like a magnet, for he was fully aware of its importance in India's early history. He made his last visit in the Cold Weather season of 1878–9, when he was sixty-five – very old for British India where fifty was the usual age for retirement. By then he had developed more sophisticated excavation techniques that took account of lesser objects such as potsherds, fragments of terracotta or even bits of plaster. However, it was the coinage of Taxila that chiefly preoccupied him. The whole area was lit-tered with rectangular copper punch-marked coins, many bearing only a single die stamp, leading him to conclude that this was the earliest form of the Indian punch-marked coin, most probably minted in Taxila and pre-dating the arrival of the Greeks. His discovery of a hoard of punch-marked coins mixed with Greek-type coinage that included coins of the Graeco-Bactrian rulers Pantaleon and Agathocles – probably the sons of Demetrius, who succeeded Euthydemous in about 200 BCE – showed that despite their close contact with Alexander's successors in Gandhara, the Mauryans had kept to their own style of coinage, displaying only punch-marked symbols most probably related to regions or local mints.

If Cunningham hoped to find evidence of Ashoka or his grandfather Chandragupta at Taxila, his expectations were never fulfilled. That was left to a later Director-General, John Marshall, who would spend more than fifteen years excavating at Taxila and so love the place that he would build himself a delightful cottage there. This missing link between Ashoka and the city where he spent some years as his father's viceroy would come in the form of an inscription written in Aramaic, inked and then overcut on to a stone slab, of which only part had survived as a sliver of rock lodged into the wall. It came from Taxila's Sirkap site, where it had been used for building material for the new Greek-styled city established by the Graeco-Bactrian king Demetrius in about 200 BCE.

Half of each line is missing but its references to no killing of living beings, respect for Brahmans and monks, obedience to parents and elders and the performance of good works appear to have affinities with the sentiments expressed in RE 3 and RE 11 as inscribed on the edict rocks at nearby Shahbazgarhi and Mansehra – the latter being the fifth Rock Edict to be identified, discovered in the mid-1880s. Near the bottom of the stone sliver the name of Priyadasi has survived, along with a reference to the sons of Priyadasi.

*

As Cunningham made his way back to the Gangetic plains towards the end of his tour of 1864–5 he had every reason to feel despondent. In four winter seasons he had identified and surveyed more than 160 ancient sites in northern India, more than justifying the faith shown in him by Lord Canning. But the first Viceroy's successor, Lord Lawrence, had come looking for budget cuts and Cunningham returned to Calcutta knowing that his archaeological department had been axed.

Four lean years as a military pensioner in England followed, which Alexander Cunningham put to good use by writing *The Ancient Geography of India: the Buddhist Period*. Then in January 1869 Lord Mayo arrived in Calcutta to replace Lord Lawrence, the political weathercock turned once more and in 1871 the general returned to India as Director-General of the Archaeological Survey of India (ASI) – and as a Knight Commander of the Indian Empire.

Sir Alexander Cunningham's new instructions were to 'superintend a complete search over the whole country and a systematic record and description of all architectural and other remains that are remarkable alike for their antiquity or their beauty, or their historic interest'. These were brave words but in fact Cunningham's new remit did not extend to the Madras and Bombay Presidencies. He was, however, provided with sufficient funds to pay for two assistants: an Armenian engineer from the Bengal Public Works Department named Joseph Beglar; and an Englishman, Archibald Carllyle, who had come out to India to tutor the sons of a minor raja and had stayed on to work as a museum curator.

It is beyond the scope of this book to do justice to the archaeological work undertaken by Cunningham, Beglar, Carllyle and their subordinate staff through the 1870s and

into the 1880s. Only a fraction concerns the further dis-
interring of Ashoka and his times – a process that resumed in
the early months of 1871 with Cunningham's discovery of a
box on a shelf at the Asiatic Society of Bengal's premises in
Calcutta bearing the label 'Rupnath, in Parganah [District]
Salimabad'.

The shrine of Rupnath lies at the very heart of the Indian
subcontinent. The temple itself is a simple structure that
stands in an attractively wooded glade beside one of three
small pools linked by a series of waterfalls descending from
the Kaimur hill range. It is well off the beaten track, some
thirty-five miles north of Jabalpur and fifteen miles due west
of Sleemanabad, which was called Salimabad before the
arrival of Colonel James 'Thugee' Sleeman, the suppressor of
the murderous thugee cult endemic in this part of India in the
1830s.

Pilgrims come to Rupnath to worship the lingam in the
shrine, which has a long association with the Nath order of
ascetics. These Naths follow many different paths but all share
an antipathy towards caste barriers and honour Matyendranath
as their founder, a ninth-century yogi said to have invented
Hatha yoga as a spiritual exercise. Despite claiming Lord Shiva
as their first master, these Naths stand outside the Brahmanical
tradition, representing in their lineage the last phase of
Buddhism in India, when tantric ritual entered the Mahayana
Buddhist mainstream as a means of attaining spiritual perfection.

Nath shrines are generally found in remote mountain
regions and isolated forests, as at Rupnath. Today the waters
that feed the three pools have been dammed, so that a lake
extends out into the plain below the lowest of them, but in

other respects Rupnath has changed very little since the day in the mid-nineteenth century when the servant of a Colonel Ellis came to this spot, probably to attend the annual *mela*, or religious fair, held here on *Shivaratri*, the 'night of Shiva', celebrated in late February–early March. This unnamed servant came away from Rupnath with an eye-copy of an inscription engraved on a rock beside the pool, which he gave to his employer, who passed it on to the Asiatic Society of Bengal in Calcutta – where it was placed in a box and shelved.

It was this box that Sir Alexander came upon in 1871 while rummaging through the Society's shelves. He at once instructed his new senior assistant Joseph Beglar to make a search of the district of Salimabad, between Gaya and Monghyr in Bihar. Beglar duly searched but found nothing. However, the general was not one to let matters rest. He made enquiries and learned of the second Salimabad, now renamed Sleemanabad. Beglar made a new search and soon reported back that he had found both Rupnath and the inscription.

Cunningham immediately set out to see for himself. 'Here a small stream breaks over the crest of the Kaimur range', he afterwards reported, 'and, after three low falls, forms a deep secluded pool at the foot of the scarp. Each of these pools is considered holy, the uppermost being named after Rama, the next after Lakshmana, and the lowest after Sita. The spot, however, is best known by the name of Rupnath, from a linga of Siva which is placed at a narrow cleft of the rocks.' The inscription was carved in five lines on a flat boulder beside the lowest lake, its upper surface 'worn quite smooth by people sitting upon it for hundreds of years at the annual fairs'.

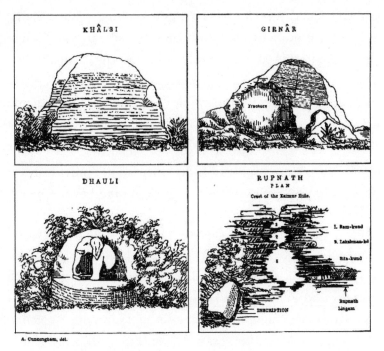

Sir Alexander Cunningham's engraving of the Rupnath rock at the foot of the Kaimur Falls, together with his depictions of three other Ashokan sites. (Reproduced in *Inscriptions of Aśoka*, 1877)

It was an Ashokan edict of the category known today as Minor Rock Edicts (MRE), so clumsily lettered that Cunningham thought it must have been copied by someone with only a rudimentary knowledge of Brahmi lettering. It began in the usual declamatory way – 'Beloved-of-the-Gods speaks thus' – but omitted the personal name *Piyadasi* and the title *raja*. It went on to give some remarkably personal information about Piyadasi's conversion to Buddhism and his relations with the Buddhist Church (modern translation): 'It is now two and a half years since I became a lay-disciple, but until now I have not been very zealous. But now that I have visited the Sangha for more than a year, I have become very zealous.'[8]

The key words here were *upasaka* or 'lay-disciple' and *yamme samghe upeti*, translating literally as 'went to the Sangha'. It seemed to say that Ashoka had initially become a lay Buddhist and then a year and a half later had entered the Buddhist community of monks, the clear implication being that he had undergone the rites that made him an initiate monk, which would have required him to wear monks' robes and live in a monastery.

The edict went on to say how, as a result of Ashoka's new religious zeal, the people of India who had not previously associated with the gods now did so. It then urged everyone to be zealous in supporting the Dharma:

> Even the humble, if they are zealous, can attain heaven. And this proclamation has been made with this aim. Let both humble and great be zealous, let even those on the borders know and let zeal last long. Then this zeal will increase, it will greatly increase, it will increase up to one and a half times. This message has been proclaimed two hundred and fifty-six times by the king while on tour.[9]

These were patently the words of a convert, speaking with all the fervour of the newly converted, eager to share his new-found faith with his subjects – so eager in fact that he appeared to have embarked on a proselytising tour of the country. The words of what is today classified as MRE 1 confirmed Ashoka's conversion to Buddhism as given in the *Great Dynastic Chronicle*, which stated that for three years after his anointing Ashoka had remained in his ancestral faith before coming under the influence of his young nephew Nigrodha, who introduced him to Buddhism. This had led Ashoka to visit the Buddhist community and to invite Buddhist monks to join him in his royal abode, after which he had ordered the dissemination of the

Dharma throughout his kingdom in the form of a massive building programme of monasteries and stupas.

The discovery of the Rupnath MRE led Cunningham to take a fresh look at two other inscriptions found some years earlier. The first had come from a cave overlooking the Grand Trunk Road at Sassaram, midway between Benares and Gaya. In 1839 a rough eye-copy of the inscription had been forwarded to the ASB in Calcutta but too late to be seen by James Prinsep and had lain mouldering on a shelf ever since. Joseph Beglar was ordered to Sassaram to find the cave and its edict, which he duly did. It turned out to be another version of the Rupnath MRE – but with the addition of two crucial sentences at the end: 'And cause ye this matter to be engraved in rocks. And wherever there are stone pillars here (in my dominions), there also cause (it) to be engraved.'[10]

So here was King Ashoka in his home ground of Magadha ordering his remarks about his conversion to Buddhism to be written on rocks and existing pillars throughout the land – the clear implication being that no such Ashokan edicts had existed before. Taken together with the crude craftsmanship and clumsy lettering both here at Sassaram and at Rupnath, it pointed to these two MREs being the earliest of Ashoka's edicts yet found, pre-dating the more extensive and far better written Rock Edicts found at Girnar, Dhauli, Shahbazgarhi and Kalsi – which themselves pre-dated the Pillar Edicts.

The third inscription to be re-examined was the Bairat-Calcutta inscription, the segment of rock found on the northern borders of Rajputana by Captain Burt back in 1840. In content and appearance it was quite different from the Rupnath and Sassaram MREs, being finely chiselled in large, clear letters on a highly polished surface – possibly a rock face but more probably a pillar.[11] Cunningham and his junior assistant Archie Carllyle together explored the site where it had been found, lodged under a large projecting boulder on a hillside south of the village of Bairat, and discovered that the boulder stood beside the remains of two monastic buildings and a stupa on a platform levelled out of the hillside. Clearly the edict and the monastic settlement were linked: 'As the proclamation is specially addressed to the Buddhist assembly of Magadha, we must suppose ... that copies were sent to all the greater Buddhist fraternities for the purpose of recording the enduring firmness of the king's faith in the law of Buddha.'[12]

As Cunningham and Carllyle surveyed the surrounding area the latter's eye was caught by a 'bare, black-looking, pyramidal-shaped, jagged-edged, peaked hill, composed entirely of enormous blocks of porphyritic and basaltic rock'. One of the largest of these blocks, as big as a house, had rolled down the hill and on its underside Carllyle spotted what proved to be the third MRE – today known as the Bairat MRE.

The next significant discovery was far more dramatic. It came at the start of the Cold Weather season of 1873–4 as Alexander Cunningham headed south across the wild country of Bhundelkhand from Allahabad towards Jabalpur in the heart of India. He was, in terms of Buddhist geography, 'on the high road between Ujjain and Bhilsa in the south, and Kosambi and Sravasti in the north, as well as Pataliputra in the east'.[13] As he rode ahead of his party towards the head of the narrow Mahiyar valley, his practised eye was drawn to a stupa-like mound in the distance, out of which protruded what were, unmistakably, the pillars of a stone railing.

At that first sighting Cunningham could do no more than satisfy himself that what he had found was indeed a stupa, similar in size and design to that at Sanchi, but more like Amaravati in that most of its stonework and bricks had already been removed for building material. Three months later he was back with his team of workmen to begin the excavation of what he named the Great Stupa of Bharhut – the unhelpful word 'Tope' at last being considered outmoded.

Ten days of excavation revealed the remains of a monument that in its heyday must have been just as magnificent as the Great Stupa at Sanchi. Sections of two of the four original ceremonial gateways remained, as well as the segment of circular colonnade linking them. Every one of the great stone beams that had formed the crosspieces of these two gateways had been smashed to pieces, but their four uprights were relatively undamaged, as were the thirty-five pillars and eighty crossbars that made up the railings of the surviving quarter of the colonnade. Unlike at Sanchi, these pillars and crossbars of the colonnade were copiously decorated.

The most dramatic feature of these pillars were the thirty almost life-size figures of divine kings and various forms of lesser deities – *naga rajas*, *devas* and *devatas*, *yakshas* and *yakshinis* – carved on three sides, in particular, the devatas and yakshinis: semi-divine goddesses and attendants with exaggerated, melon-like breasts, narrow waists and wide hips, carved with deliberate intent to make them voluptuous, and always shown with one hand raised in the air grasping the branch of a tree, one leg entwined around the same tree and the other hand approaching or even touching their genitals.

These female fertility figures were in striking contrast to the male figures found on other faces of the same pillar, carved as idealised symbols of kingship, their faces stern and serene, their arms crossed as if in meditation – although this was merely the sculptor's way of conveying hands clasped together in the *anjali mudra* or 'gesture of reverence'.

One of the deliberately voluptuous yakshini figures from the Great Stupa at Bharhut – more accurately, *vriksh devatas* or 'tree goddess' embodying female energy and fecundity. These figures are the earliest representations of this central icon of Buddhist art. The tree these goddesses are hugging is the ashoka tree (*Saraca indica*), considered sacred by Hindus, Buddhists and Jains. Photograph by Joseph Beglar, 1874. (Cunningham, *The Stupa of Bharhut*, 1879)

(Left to right) A male yaksha, a female goddess and Chakavaka, King of the Naga snake gods, worshipped as water-spirits. (Cunningham, *The Stupa of Bharhut*, 1879)

But for Alexander Cunningham the most intriguing sculpture of all was that of a warrior: 'His head is bare, and the short curly hair is bound with a broad band or ribbon, which is fastened at the back of the head in a bow, with its long ends streaming in the wind. His dress consists of a tunic with long sleeves, and reaching nearly to the thigh.' The warrior's dress, his sandals and the hair tied in a ribbon marked him out as a Greek, perhaps a mercenary of the sort that had helped both Chandragupta and Ashoka win their thrones. His sword, however, was indisputably Indian. 'We have the description of Arrian,' wrote Cunningham, '"All wear swords of a vast breadth, though scarce exceeding three cubits in length. Those, when they engage in close fight, they clasp with both their hands, that their blow may be the stronger".' This evidence of contacts with India's north-west was strengthened with the discovery that some of the pillars carried mason's marks using Kharosthi rather than Brahmi lettering, showing that some of the sculptors had been brought in from the Gandhara region.

The Greek warrior carved on one of the rail pillars at Bharhut, photographed by Joseph Beglar in 1874 with a local tribal woman seated beside him. (APAC, British Library)

Scarcely less striking were the many scenes of human and sacerdotal activity portrayed on panels, copings, medallions and other elements of the surviving architecture, sculpted in a heavier and less sophisticated style than either at Sanchi or Amaravati – the clearest indication that they pre-dated them.

By now Cunningham was far more knowledgeable about
early Buddhism than he had been when he had excavated at
Sanchi, and he had no difficulty in identifying some twenty of
these scenes as illustrations of the *Jataka Tales*. Others showed
scenes of important incidents in the life of Sakyamuni Buddha –
even though Sakyamuni himself was notable by his absence
throughout, being represented only by such symbols as a turban
resting on an empty throne or an empty saddle on a horse. Just
as at Sanchi and Amaravati, three objects of worship were represented time and time again: the Bodhi tree and its Diamond
Throne, the stupa, and the Dharma in the form of the 'Wheel
of the Moral Law', the *chakra*.

Scenes of the worship of the Bodhi tree and Diamond Throne,
stupas, and the Dharma, in the form of the chakra wheel. Here
all three are shown in a composite photograph of the front and
sides of the same pillar, which Cunningham named the
Prasenajit pillar, since these scenes appeared to show King
Prasenajit worshipping at these three sites. (Cunningham, *The
Stupa of Bharhut*, 1879)

The Bodhi tree was shown sometimes within its protective pavilion and wall but also unadorned, and not only the Bodhi tree, for all forms of trees were well represented, suggesting to Cunningham that Buddhism in the Bharhut region had been allied with some from of tree-worshipping cult, just as at Amaravati the Naga snake cult appeared to be a major element.

All these sculptures were brought into the light of day in the presence of large crowds drawn from the surrounding area. 'The curious sculptures were a source of much wonder,' commented Cunningham, 'a wonder that grew all the greater when it became known that the *lat* sahib [lord sahib] could read the writing that accompanied the carvings.' With every fresh discovery he was asked to say what was the subject of the writing, and was always met with disappointment when he announced the name of a donor or guardian deity: 'Their only idea of such excavations is that they are really intended as a search for hidden treasure.'

As at Sanchi, numerous short donor inscriptions in Brahmi had been appended to the sculptures but there were also inscriptions that were in effect captions, giving the subject of the illustration. The Brahmi script employed exactly the same form as on Ashoka's edicts, but nowhere was the name of Ashoka or Piyadasi to be found.

The excavators broke off in April when it became too hot to continue work and resumed again in November, when enough fragments were recovered to reconstruct much of the East Gateway. Cunningham also took the opportunity to tour the surrounding country and was rewarded by the discovery of two more railing pillars and two bas-reliefs, one 'the missing half of a well-known Jataka tale', which had been 'degraded to the

ignoble position of a washerman's plank'. A third visit to the
Bharhut excavation site in January 1875 produced a pillar from
one of the two missing gateways. Cunningham then took the
decision to move everything so far recovered from Bharhut six
hundred miles to the Indian Museum in Calcutta – an act that
some of his contemporaries in England condemned as having
'an aroma of vandalism' and likened to moving Stonehenge
from Wiltshire to London. But Cunningham was adamant that
he had done the right thing. 'I am willing to accept the aroma',
he wrote, 'since I have saved all the more important sculptures. Of those that were left behind at Bharhut every stone
that was removable has since been "carted away" by the
people.'[14]

When General Sir Alexander Cunningham came to write up
his report on Bharhut he had no doubts as to the extreme
antiquity of the stupa's railing and gateways: 'The absolute
identity of the forms of the Bharhut characters with those of
the *Asoka* period is proof sufficient that they belong to the
same age.' This was not a judgement based on pure sentiment.
A few years earlier Cunningham had examined a hoard of silver
coins found in a field near the Jwalamukhi temple in Kangra
in the Western Himalayas. It had included some thirty coins
of Apollodotus Soter, ruler of an Indo-Greek kingdom that
stretched from Taxila to (modern) Gujarat, his rule extending
from about 175 BCE to 160 BCE. These appeared freshly
minted, suggesting that they had been buried in the early part
of that reign. However, the greater part of the hoard was made
up of Indian coins, including those of a king named Amogha-
buti, whose dating was known to be mid-second century BCE.
The Brahmi lettering on all these Indian coins showed a
number of modifications from the Brahmi used in Ashoka's

time, suggesting that these had been introduced not earlier than 175 BCE.

Cunningham's judgement had also been swayed by his reading of the most important of the site's many inscriptions, carved prominently on one a pillar of the Bharhut stupa's East Gateway. With the help of the Calcutta Sanksritist Babu Rajendra Lal Mitra, Cunningham read this inscription as: 'In the kingdom of Sugana this *toran*, with its ornamental stonework and plinth, was caused to be made by King Dhanabhuti, son of Vacchi and Aga Raja son of Goti, and grandson of Visa Deva son of Gagi'. Both Cunningham and Mitra took the word *suganam* to be a reference to the minor kingdom of Srughna, a feudatory of the greater Mauryan empire. In addition, some of the other names matched those Cunningham had earlier found on a Buddhist railing at Mathura. It led him to declare that the Bharhut gateways and railings had been erected between 240 and 210 BCE – in other words, in the last years of Ashoka's reign and just after.

The general consensus today is that the word *suganam* in the gateway inscription refers to the Shungas, the dynasty established some fifty years after Ashoka's death when the last Mauryan ruler was assassinated by his commander-in-chief, Pushyamitra Shunga. The original brick stupa at Bharhut was indeed raised in Ashoka's time, as at Sanchi and elsewhere, but the surrounding railings and gateways probably went up no earlier than 180 BCE – though there are diehards who still argue that Cunningham was right to subtitle his publication on the Bharhut stupa *A Buddhist Monument ornamented with numerous Sculptures illustrative of Buddhist Legend and History of the Third Century B.C.*

What Cunningham might have asked himself was why, if the

Bharhut stupa had been built at or so soon after Ashoka's time, there were no Ashokan memorials here – no Ashokan pillar and no images of Ashoka? The probable answer is that there were very good political reasons why Dharmashoka should not be directly represented at Bharhut, for the ruling dynasty in power when the gateways and colonnade were built were the Shungas, and the founding father of that dynasty was Pushyamitra Shunga, the general who had killed the last of the Mauryas and embarked on a round of anti-Buddhist destruction.

And yet there may very well be an act of homage to Ashoka at Bharhut – in the person of the carved figure that Cunningham describes simply as 'one royal relic bearer on an elephant'. He can be seen astride his elephant in a prominent position on the front of a railing post beside one of the pillars of the East Gateway, flanked by two outsiders on smaller elephants and escorted by two standard bearers on horseback (see p. 251 and also p. 362). He clutches a relic casket tightly to his chest.

The Bharhut sculptures, along with those at Sanchi and Amaravati, are very much part of Ashoka's legacy, in that they grew out of what Ashoka started. They also provide us with the best images we are ever likely to see of how people lived and worshipped as Buddhists in the Ashokan and post-Ashokan era.

13
Corpus Inscriptionum Indicarum

The inscribed central portion of the elephantine Girnar rock,
beside the path leading to the top of Girnar Hill, by D. H. Sykes
in 1869. (APAC, British Library)

Jaugada is not an easy place to find. A two-hour drive south from Bhubaneshwar on the coastal road brings you to Ganjam and the mouth of the Rushikulya River. There you turn inland and follow the river's twists and turns as far as Purushottampur village. Nobody here has heard of Jaugada. But continue to follow the river and just where it seems you have no option but to cross it on a narrow bridge, a narrow track plunges off the road and leads to Pandia hamlet. Here they know exactly what you want and are eager to show you the way. The track ends at the foot of the piled-up rocks of Jaugada hill. Now it becomes a case of scouting for the most likely boulder – and there it is – looming elephant-like against the skyline, its lower flank covered by a hideous construction of concrete and iron bars, like a zoo cage.

What is today known as the Jaugada Rock Edict had first been reported by Captain Markham Kittoe back in the mid-1830s. He had written to James Prinsep of reports of 'an inscription covering 270 square feet'[1] but had failed to find it. A quarter of a century passed before Kittoe's inscription was tracked down to Jaugada hill, in what was then part of the Madras Presidency and is now in south Orissa. The rediscoverer was most probably the Madras civil servant Walter Elliot, who afterwards kept very quiet about it and with good reason.

Elliot is best remembered today as the man who 'saved' the Amaravati marbles. He entered the Madras Civil Service in 1820 and passed most of his career in the Madras Presidency, where an early interest in hunting soon gave way to more serious pursuits that included zoology, Indian languages and ancient remains. In 1845 Elliot took over the Guntur Division south of the Krishna River, where he found himself responsible for the ruins of the Great Stupa at Amaravati. This had suffered further depredations since Colonel Colin Mackenzie's day. Many of the carved slabs drawn by Mackenzie's draughtsmen had been lost to the lime-pit and the Collector of Masulipatam had removed a further thirty-three slabs to decorate his new town square. Elliot's account of his own excavation of the Amaravati stupa site was subsequently lost at sea but not the marbles he despatched to Madras. In 1859 121 pieces of 'Elliot's marbles' were shipped to London, where they lay forgotten in an old coachhouse before being tracked down by the architectural historian James Fergusson.

Walter Elliot has to be the prime suspect in the defacing of the Jaugada Rock Edict. In the early 1850s he visited the site in the company of another Madras civil servant twenty years his junior. The rock was at that time said to be 'more perfect'

The first five edicts of the Jaugada Rock Edict showing some of the damage inflicted by a 'European gentleman'. (From Alexander Cunningham, *Inscriptions of Aśoka*, 1877)

than it was found to be later. In 1854 Elliot left the area and it
then became known that a European gentleman and a civilian – the noun used at that time to describe a member of the
Indian Civil Service (ICS) – had visited the Jaugada rock and
had tried to prise off its inscription, with disastrous results.
According to the local villagers, he 'threw a quantity of hot
tamarind juice and water on the rock, and then beat it with
hammers, the result being that he broke off a large portion of
rock on which the inscription was carved'.[2]

Not surprisingly, the vandal remained silent, so that it was
not until 1872 that the Jaugada Rock Edict was officially
reported on, by a district officer named W. F. Grahame. By the
time Grahame's report appeared in the first issue of the *Indian
Antiquary*, Sir Walter Elliot, KCIE, had retired from India and
had become a leading member of the Royal Asiatic Society.
The question of the identity of the Jaugada 'civilian' was not
pursued.

The Jaugada inscription proved to be another of Emperor
Ashoka's major Rock Edict sites, the fifth so far discovered after
Girnar, Dhauli, Shahbazgarhi and Kalsi. In common with the
other edict rocks, it had been inscribed with REs 1–10 and 14.
However, REs 11–13 had been replaced by two other edicts:
the so-called Separate Rock Edicts (SREs 1 and 2). These had
been set apart from the main edicts in two boxes and were
relatively undamaged.

This was precisely what James Prinsep had found on the
Dhauli Rock Edict outside Bhubaneshwar, and its discovery
helped to explain why it was that REs 11–13 had been omitted
both here and at the Dhauli rock, for both these sites lay within
the boundaries of ancient Kalinga, one in the north, the other
in the south. The three missing Rock Edicts were those in

which Emperor Ashoka had described his conquest of Kalinga and his subsequent remorse at the suffering he had caused. In Kalinga itself those remarks had been deliberately omitted, presumably to spare the feelings of the already traumatised people of Kalinga.

The two SREs that had replaced REs 11–13 at Jaugada and Dhauli are addressed to Ashoka's *mahamatras* or special religious officers at Tosali (Dhauli) and Samapa (Jaugada). They are directed to carry out the emperor's instructions regarding the spiritual welfare of the people under their care and to do so justly and impartially, so that the people of Kalinga might live at peace with one another. It was in this context that Emperor Ashoka had set out what is perhaps his most famous doctrine, in which he declares that he rules for the happiness of all his subjects (modern translation): 'All men are my children. What I desire for my own children, and I desire their welfare and happiness both in this world and the next, that I desire for all men. You do not understand to what extent I desire this, and if some of you do understand, you do not understand the full extent of my desire.'[3]

SRE 2 continues in the same vein but it, too, carries a quite remarkable message, intended for 'the people of the unconquered territories'. If they are wondering what the king's intentions are towards them, Ashoka's answer is this (modern translation):

My only intention is that they live without fear of me, that they may trust me and that I may give them happiness, not sorrow. Furthermore, they should understand that the king will forgive those who can be forgiven, and that he wishes them to practise Dharma so that they can attain happiness in this world and the next. I am telling you this so that I may discharge the debts I owe, and that in instructing you, you may know that my vow and my promise will not be broken . . . Assure them [the people of the unconquered territories] that: 'The king is like a father. He feels towards us as he feels towards himself. We are to him like his own children.'

This message was for the peoples who lived south and west of Kalinga, whose territories had yet to be conquered by Ashoka. They had seen the terrible fate that had befallen Kalinga when it had resisted Ashoka's armies. Now the emperor wanted them to understand that he was a changed man who wished to conquer by force of Dharma alone.

In the event, Ashoka never did conquer the southern tip of India, any more than he conquered the island of Lanka beyond. He had no need to for, as the *Great Dynastic Chronicle* tells us, he achieved his aims by peaceful means with the spread of the Dharma.

With the discovery of the fifth edict rock a distinct pattern began to emerge. All five had been cut into the outer flank of a prominent – and elephantine – boulder set on a hillside overlooking a human settlement. Both at Jaugada and at Dhauli the edict rocks look down upon the remains of walled cities. At Dhauli the ancient city of Tosali is on the far side of the nearby River Daya, the 'River of Compassion', but its monumental mud and brick walls and outer moat are still strikingly visible. At Jaugada the hill actually merges into a corner of the walls of Samapa so as to form a sort of acropolis, as in a Greek city. Here the earthworks are less impressive but what is still visible to the naked eye is that the original town of Samapa had been laid out in a square on a north–south grid, with two gates on each side – again, very much on the Greek model. From its size and location, it must at one time have been an important administrative centre for the southern half of ancient Kalinga, with its close proximity to the river and the sea coast making it well placed to engage in trade inland and up and down the coast.

Walter Elliot carried out a cursory dig here at Jaugada in 1858 and unearthed a collection of Kushan coins dating from the first century CE. A more thorough excavation would be carried out in 1956–7 by Mrs Debala Mitra of the Archaeological Survey of India. She would show that Samapa had been founded during the reign of Ashoka in the third century CE. Punch-marked coins of the Mauryan era and a range of working and decorative materials pointed to a flourishing and prosperous community.[4] That same pattern is found at Tosali, so that both appear to have been new towns founded immediately after the conquest of Kalinga as new administrative centres of Ashoka's empire.

The Sanskritist who first examined and wrote about the Jaugada Rock Edict was an Indian: the scholar and social reformer Dr Ramakrishna Gopal Bhandarkar,[5] at this time assistant lecturer in Sanskrit at Bombay University, which by now had become the centre of Indian studies in India.

West-coast Bombay had eclipsed Calcutta – and if General Sir Alexander Cunningham was to be believed, this was because the Asiatic Society of Bengal had been taken over by what he called 'the Naturalists, who then monopolised the direction of the Museum', so much so that when he visited its museum to re-examine a Buddhist statue excavated by him at Sravasti he found it tucked away 'in the midst of a herd of stuffed deer and antelopes, [which] completely hid its inscribed pedestal from view'.[6] However, the real factor in Bombay's rise to prominence was that it was less hidebound by race and caste on both sides and it had profited from a succession of enlightened governors – among them the Orientalist Jonathan Duncan, who had died in office in Bombay in 1811 – who recognised the need to bring Indians on board.

The enterprise that had characterised Calcutta in its early days had now become Bombay's hallmark, which in the academic field found expression in the rise to prominence of Elphinstone College. It became the nucleus of Bombay University in 1860 and within a decade its Department of Oriental Studies had become a beacon of scholarship, largely thanks to the presence of Professor Georg Bühler, under whose aegis Indian epigraphy was transformed from a hobby into a discipline. Sanskrit – and in due course Pali – became a respectable subject to study at university and a new breed of college-educated Sanskritists began to appear who were no longer content to serve merely as pandits to Europeans.

A third golden age of Indology now began in which Indian scholars were able to participate on an equal footing not only with foreign-born epigraphists working in India, such as Dr Bühler and Dr John Fleet of the ICS, but with their counterparts in Europe. In Bombay the first local graduate to make his mark was Professor Bühler's protégé, the Maharashtran Brahmin Ramakrishna Bhandarkar, born in the *annus mirabilis* of 1837. When Bühler took on a more senior post in 1868 it was Dr Bhandarkar who took over his chair as Professor of Sanskrit – only to be passed over four years later when the position was given to a twenty-five-year-old Oxford scholar, Dr Peter Peterson. Despite the protests of Bühler and others, the authorities refused to back down, so Bhandarkar had no option but to serve as Peterson's assistant – a humiliation compounded by Peterson's insistence on sharing the credit for what Bhandarkar saw as his greatest achievement: his collection and editing of scores of previously unknown Sanskrit and Pali manuscripts. When it became clear that Peterson was staying put, a special post was created for Bhandarkar as Professor of Sanskrit at the Deccan College in Poona, which Dr Bhandarkar lived to see develop into the Bhandarkar Oriental Research Institute, formally opened by the Viceroy in 1917, by which time Dr Bhandarkar had himself been awarded a knighthood.

Master and pupil; *guru* and *chela*. (Left) Professor Georg Bühler, whose career was cut short by his drowning in 1898. (Right) Sir Ramakrishna Gopal Bhandarkar, KCIE, remembered in Maharashtra today as a social reformer rather than a scholar.

Dr Bhandarkar is best remembered today as someone who fought against the evils of the caste system and Brahminical orthodoxy, and for religious reforms within Hinduism. But he should also be remembered as the man who reconstructed the early political history of the Deccan, showing how the Satavahana dynasty, also known as the Andhras, had dominated central India for more than four centuries following the collapse of the Mauryas and had played an important role as patrons of Buddhism, resulting in a flowering of the greatest of the early Buddhist monuments extending from the Ellora and Ajanta caves in the west to Amaravati in the south-east.

Two other pioneer Indian Sanskritists who played their part in the unveiling of Ashoka were Dr Bhau Daji and Bhagavan Lal Indraji, the former another early alumnus of Elphinstone College, a medical practitioner who took up Sanskrit in order to familiarise himself with traditional Hindu medicine and went on to become one of the leading lights of the Bombay branch of the RAS and a regular contributor to its journal. Dr Bhau Daji's contribution to Indian studies was finally recognised in 1975 when Bombay's Victoria and Albert Museum was renamed the Bhau Daji Laud Museum. However, scant recognition has been accorded to the man who acted as Dr Bhau Daji's assistant and field-researcher, Bhagavan Lal Indraji, for it was largely thanks to the unassuming Indraji, who in the course of thirteen years travelled far and wide in India and Nepal in search of inscriptions, manuscripts and old coins, that his employer was able to contribute so extensively to the advancement of Indian epigraphy.

Indraji himself came from the princely state of Junagadh, within whose territory lay Girnar mountain and the Ashokan Rock Edict boulder at its foot. Indeed, it was this great rock that first drew Indraji to palaeography. It had long been known that the Girnar rock carried a second set of inscriptions in Brahmi, but it was the combined scholarship of Bhau Daji and Indraji that produced the first clear reading of what became known as the Rudradaman inscription, published in 1863.[7] Much of it was taken up with the glorification of the mighty conqueror Rudradaman, already identified from his coinage as the Scythian or Shaka king Rudradaman I, who had ruled Malwa towards the middle of the second century CE. The new reading showed that the inscription marked the completion of major repairs to a dam and reservoir at the foot of Mount Girnar. The dam had been breached in a storm and the task of repairing the breach had been taken on by King Rudradaman's minister and local governor Suvishakha, who described himself as 'able, patient, not wavering, not arrogant, upright, not to be bribed, who by his good government increased the spiritual merit, fame and glory of his master'.[8]

But the most striking revelation contained in the Rudradaman inscription was its statement that the original dam and reservoir had been constructed by a man named Pushagupta, a provincial governor of the Mauryan king Chandragupta. It had subsequently been 'adorned with conduits for Ashoka Maurya by the Yavana king Tushaspha while governing'. In other words, the original dam, built in Chandragupta's time, had been improved upon by King Ashoka's local governor, a Graeco-Bactrian named Tushaspha. Other remarks on the rock inscription, such as King Rudradaman's strong attachment to Dharma, his compassion and his vow to abstain from slaying men, except in battles, made it clear that here at least the name and ethos of Ashoka had survived into the second century CE.

The death of Dr Bhau Daji in 1874 left Bhagavan Lal Indraji in straitened circumstances. However, it had the effect of allowing his own scholarship to be brought out from under his employer's shadow, one example being the detective work that led to the discovery of what is known today as the Sopara Rock Edict.[9]

In 1882, acting on information received from the Collector of Thana District, Indraji travelled by train up the coast from Bombay to Sopara, situated beside a creek a few miles from the ruins of the Portuguese settlement of Bassein. From the Collector's account Indraji suspected that what he had described as a fort was actually a Buddhist stupa, which proved to be the case. An artificial pool was identified as a harbour from the days when Sopara had its own port, and here Indraji found a block of polished stone bearing a few lines of Brahmi that he identified on sight as part of RE 7. According to the local townspeople, this had been part of a much larger stone covered in writing that had disappeared only very recently.[10]

Indraji felt sure that a search of some of the religious buildings in the area would bring to light more pieces of the edict rock, but for political reasons no such examinations were permitted. However, in 1955 a second piece of polished stone would be discovered at Sopara, this time bearing part of RE 9. It would confirm Indraji's claim that one of Ashoka's major Rock Edicts had been placed here. The Greek geographer Ptolemy had spoken of a seaport named Sopara, as had various Arab geographers, and everything Indraji had read indicated that this had once been the capital of Aparanta, the coastal region north of Bombay. 'It appears as a holy city in Buddhist, Brahmanical and Jain books,' he wrote. 'Asoka sent to Aparanta one of his missionaries, Dhammarakhita the Yona or Yavana, that is the Greek or Bactrian ... I believe Dhammarakhita made Sopara the centre of his missionary efforts, and that it was from Sopara that Buddhism spread over Western India.'

Meanwhile, in Bengal local Sanskritists had also found a role model in the multi-talented linguist Rajendra Lala Mitra, a Bengali from the Kayastha sub-caste who in 1846 was appointed Librarian and Assistant Secretary of the Asiatic Society of Bengal. Mitra went on to become Secretary of the Society and served as its vice-president for nineteen years before finally becoming its first Indian president, in the meantime contributing no less than 114 learned articles to the *JRAS*. Mitra is best remembered today as the 'uncompromising crusader' who used the press to promote nationalist causes and campaigned to improve working conditions in the indigo plantations of Bihar and Bengal. However, he was an equally outspoken advocate for the preservation of India's past and in the late 1860s secured the backing of the government of Bengal for a systematic investigation of all the ancient buildings, temples and 'tumuli' (burial mounds, but in fact Buddhist stupas) of the province of Orissa, the fruits of which afterwards appeared in two large volumes as *The Antiquities of Orissa*, one of the first publications in India to use photographs as illustrations. From this time onwards Mitra and General Sir Alexander Cunningham were in frequent correspondence, with the latter frequently seeking Mitra's opinions on issues ranging from architectural styles to his readings of early inscriptions.

Much of the fieldwork that the general had previously undertaken in North India was now being carried out by his two assistants, Joseph Beglar and Archie Carllyle. The former identified the remains of at least two early stupa complexes – at Deoria, on the eastern border of the United Provinces (Uttar Pradesh), and at Beshnagar, a few miles north of Vidisha and Sanchi hill – both with sculptured railings and gateways similar to those found at Bharhut but so severely damaged as to suggest deliberate iconoclasm.

Archie Carllyle's chance to shine had come in the course of
the two Cold Weather seasons of 1874–5 and 1875–6, during
which he revisited many of the Buddhist sites in North Bihar
first noted by Francis Buchanan. This included a re-evaluation
of its several Ashokan pillars and it was while Carllyle was
engaged in taking a new impression of the Lauriya-Araraj Pillar
Edict that he was approached by a group of Tharu forest-
dwellers, the original inhabitants of the sub-Himalayan forest
belt known as the Tarai.

The Tharus reported the existence of a very similar pillar
some distance to the north – 'a stone sticking in the ground
which they called Bhim's Lat, and which they said resembled
the top of the capital at Laoriya'.[11] Guided by the Tharus,
Carllyle entered what was still considered to be wild and dangerous country due to its jungle and the fatal miasmas that
killed all strangers who ventured into those parts and stayed on
after nightfall. Outside the village of Rampurva, close to the
border with Nepal, Carllyle came upon the top of a pillar 'sticking out of the ground in a slanting position, and pointing
towards the north'. Nearby were the remains of its capital in the
form of a seated lion, with supporting abacus and bell attached,
broken in half just above its paws. Round the sides of the
abacus were pairs of geese with lowered heads similar in stance
and style to those found on the pillars at Sanchi and Lauriya-
Nandangarh.

With the help of the Tharus, Carllyle succeeded in exposing
just enough of the column, as it lay buried diagonally in the
swampy ground, to reveal the upper half of an inscription
incised in Brahmi. It was too waterlogged to go any deeper so
Carllyle had to make do with a rough impression, achieved
only by his men standing up to their waists in water. This was

good enough to identify the inscription as yet another set of the Pillar Edicts, making it the fifth so far discovered.

Sticking out of the ground some three hundred yards south of the lion pillar was the stump of a second pillar. Since Carllyle and his men were anxious to get back to safer country this had to be left to a later generation of archaeologists, who would find a capital in the form of a hump-backed bull complete with bell and abacus, displaying that characteristic Mauryan sheen and in almost perfect condition. The head and upper torso of Carllyle's lion capital was also located, its face damaged but otherwise in good order.

The excavation of Carllyle's first Rampurva pillar, accomplished in 1907 under the direction of Dr Day Ram Sahni. The lion capital can just be seen on the upper left. (APAC, British Library)

The Rampurva bull capital now stands on a plinth on the verandah of Rashtrapati Bhavan in New Delhi, the official residence of the President of India, where it is almost as impossible to visit and photograph as is the Ashokan pillar in Allahabad Fort.

Carllyle's discovery of the two Rampurva pillars close to the border with Nepal and the Himalayan foothills led him to speculate that they had been erected by Emperor Ashoka to mark some sort of royal pilgrimage: 'Four different pillars of Asoka are now known to be situated along the line of the old north road which led from Magadha to Nipal ... I should therefore expect to find another pillar, or else a rock-cut inscription, still further north somewhere in the Nipal Tarai.' More than two decades were to pass before the accuracy of Carllyle's prediction was confirmed.

Carllyle's single greatest coup was his excavation at Kasia of the colossal Nirvana statue of the Buddha described long ago by Xuanzang, confirming that this was the site of ancient Kushinagara where Sakyamuni Buddha had died. His excavations here, at the great Kesariya stupa nearby, and at other sites in North Bihar, showed how widespread had been the stupa cult in this region, a practice that had transformed the landscape of Bihar and owed its origin to Ashoka, even if it was his successors – the Shungas, Kushans and Guptas – who had taken it to its full fruition.

Archibald Carllyle continued to perform sterling work for Cunningham and the Archaeological Survey of India for several more years, particularly in the field of Indian prehistory, where his pioneering work on cave-paintings in the central India highlands and microliths in Bundelkhand and Bhagelkhand entitles him to be listed among palaeontology's founding fathers.[12]

His reports are fascinating to read but not always for the best reasons, for he never held back from expressing thoughts best left unsaid, not least his views on race, which were that the British, along with the Parsis, were the cream of the Aryans, and Hindus but the 'coffee dregs'. By 1885 Carllyle's eccentricity had tipped over into paranoia and Cunningham was forced to pension him off. By then Alexander Cunningham had himself reached the age of seventy but justified his non-retirement on the grounds that he was indispensable, which indeed he was.

The fieldwork undertaken by Beglar and Carllyle allowed Cunningham to work on the bigger picture of Indian archaeology. This he did in close consultation with the leading epigraphists of the day, authorities such as Georg Bühler and Ramakrishna Gopal Bhandarkar in Bombay, Rajendra Lal Mitra in Calcutta, Max Müller in Oxford and the brilliant young scholar Émile Senart in Paris. It was this collaboration that enabled Cunningham to publish in 1877 his *Inscriptions of Aśoka*, being Volume I of the *Corpus Inscriptionum Indicarum* – a mammoth project that James Prinsep had dreamed of initiating as early as 1836. Here for the first time in one volume were assembled all the known Ashokan inscriptions, each with its several translations, from the first to the most recent and authoritative.

The tally of known Ashokan inscriptions now amounted to six Rock Edict sites, seven Minor Rock Edict sites, seven Pillar Edicts and fifteen cave inscriptions. They represented, in Cunningham's view, but a fraction of the many edicts that must originally have been inscribed on Ashoka's orders. Even the Pillar Edicts, he reckoned, must at one time have been numerous, although probably confined for obvious logistical reasons to 'the very heart of Asoka's dominions, from the Jumna to the Gandak [Gandaki River]', since they would have had to be transported by a system of barges very much as Sultan Firoz Shah had demonstrated.[15]

By combining all the known evidence, extending from the dating of the Mauryas given in the *Puranas*, the Ceylon chronicles, the *Legend of King Ashoka* and the *Divine Stories*, and the travel accounts of Faxian and Xuanzang, to the information given on the Rock and Pillar Edicts, Cunningham now felt able to assemble a chronology for the key events in the life of Ashoka and his Mauryan forebears:

478 BCE Death of Sakyamuni Buddha.

316 BCE Anointing of Chandragupta Maurya, reigns for twenty-four years.

292 BCE Anointing of Bindusara Maurya, reigns for twenty-eight years.

277 BCE Prince Ashoka appointed governor of Ujjain.

276 BCE Birth of Mahinda.

264 BCE Death of Bindusara. Ashoka begins four-year struggle with brothers.

260 BCE Anointing of Ashoka Maurya as Piyadasi.

257 BCE Ashoka's conversion to Buddhism.

256 BCE Ashoka's treaty with Antiochos.

255 BCE Ashoka's eldest son Mahinda ordained.

251 BCE Earliest date of Rock Edicts.

244 BCE Third Synod under Moggaliputta Tissa.

243 BCE Mahinda leads mission to Ceylon.

234 BCE Pillar Edicts issued.

231 BCE Queen Asandhimitra dies.

228 BCE Ashoka marries Queen Tishyarakshita.

226 BCE Queen Tishyarakshita attempts to destroy the Bodhi tree.

225 BCE Ashoka becomes an ascetic.

224 BCE Death of Ashoka.[14]

But even before Cunningham's *Inscriptions of Aśoka* had been published these datings had been thrown into doubt by the scholarship of the Dutch Professor Johann Hendrik Kern, who had briefly held the post of Professor of Sanskrit in the 1860s at the Sanskrit and Queen's Colleges in Benares before moving on to Leiden University.[15] Kern argued that Sakyamuni had died not in 478 BCE but in 388 BCE, and that the gap between his Great Final Extinguishing and Ashoka's inauguration was 118 years, therefore Ashoka's anointing had taken place in the year 270 BCE. In short, Cunningham was out by ten years in his datings for Ashoka.

'I need hardly say that I dissent from this conclusion altogether,' Cunningham wrote.[16] But Cunningham was (probably) wrong and Kern (probably) right – at least in so far as his dating for Ashoka was concerned. That view is widely shared by later scholars, with the following dates representing the general consensus today:

322–299 BCE Reign of Chandragupta.

299–274 BCE Reign of Bindusara.

302 BCE Birth of Ashoka.

285 BCE Birth of Ashoka's eldest son Mahinda.

282 BCE Birth of Ashoka's eldest daughter Sanghamitta.

274–270 BCE Four-year interregnum.

270 BCE Ashoka's anointing.

265 BCE Ashoka converts to become a lay Buddhist.

Begins Buddhist building programme.

263 BCE Ashoka conquers Kalinga.

260 BCE Ashoka issues first Minor Rock Edicts, makes first tour of Buddhist sites, begins his stupa-building programme, his queen Padmavati gives birth to Kunala.

259 BCE Ashoka issues Kalinga Rock Edicts.

258 BCE Ashoka issues the Rock Edicts, grants Barabar caves to the Ajivikas.

253 BCE Ashoka inaugurates Third Buddhist Council.

252 BCE Mahinda goes to Lanka. Ashoka institutes missionary programme.

252 BCE Ashoka goes on second pilgrimage tour, including Lumbini.

243–242 BCE Ashoka issues Pillar Edicts.

240 BCE Ashoka celebrates the five-year *pancavarsika* festival.

239 BCE Death of Ashoka's queen Asandhimitra.

235 BCE Ashoka marries Queen Tishyarakshita. Ashoka's son and heir Kunala sent to Taxila.

234 BCE Kunala blinded. Queen Tishyarakshita leads anti-Buddhist faction at court and is executed. Ashoka becomes increasingly infirm. Kunala's infant son Samprati appointed heir-apparent.

233 BCE Ashoka dies.

General Sir Alexander Cunningham kept up his Cold Weather tours. In 1882–3 he returned to the holy city of Mathura, much damaged by Muslim iconoclasm, where a number of ancient mounds were in the process of giving up their secrets, revealing a wealth of magnificent Buddhist and Jain sculpture from the Kushan period. But earlier Buddhist sculpture was also recovered, including a colossal male figure more than seven feet in height, much battered but retaining traces of a high polish. It carried a crudely cut inscription on the base written in early Ashokan Brahmi characters, allowing Cunningham to date it to the third century BCE – the earliest statue yet found in India. He speculated in his report that it might be a yaksha demi-god but omitted to mention that the figure was remarkably corpulent, which is not an attribute of yakshas except for those of the dwarf variety, and that he had a very round face, its features all but obliterated.

The mysterious Parkham giant, identified by the inscription on its base as Mauryan. (APAC, British Library)

Cunningham's last contribution to Ashokan studies was his work on what is now known as the Mahabodhi temple at Bodhgaya and its restoration. This began in 1877 in the wake of a botched attempt at restoration carried out by Burmese work-men under the orders of the king of Burma. Rajendra Lal Mitra was asked by the government of Bengal to report on the situ-ation and was appalled by what he found: 'The mischief they have done by their misdirected zeal has been serious,' he wrote in a damning report. 'The demolitions and excavations already completed by them have swept away most of the old land-marks and nothing of ancient times can now be traced on the area they have worked on.'[17] The Burmese were ordered off the premises and the task was handed over to the ASI, Joseph Beglar assuming onsite control, with Mitra as his adviser. The complex history of the Mahabodhi temple and its sur-rounds was painstakingly revealed, suggesting that the original Mauryan shrine and protective railings enclosing the Bodhi tree had been replaced by a grander structure and surround at the time of the Kushan king Huvishka in the second century CE. More sections of the original Ashokan railing were recov-ered, including parts of the four pillars that had supported the original Ashokan shrine and – most dramatic of all – the slab of the Diamond Throne placed by Ashoka at the base of the Bodhi tree. All these features corresponded to the first depictions of Bodhgaya as shown on a number of bas-reliefs at Bharhut.

Today the decorated upper surface of Ashoka's Diamond Throne is usually concealed under ornate coverings, while the plinth's lower sections are completely buried under earth as a result of the Bodhi tree's growth. However, it is usually possi-ble to catch glimpses of the repeated pattern of acanthus leaves

(Above) Emperor Ashoka's Diamond Throne at the base of the Bodhi tree, enclosed within a protective pavilion raised on four pillars, one surmounted with an elephant capital. Detail of a panel from the Bharhut stupa. (Cunningham, *The Stupa of Bharhut*, 1879) (Overleaf) Emperor Ashoka's Diamond Throne after the restoration of the Mahabodhi temple in the 1880s, showing the Bodhi tree some years after its replanting by Alexander Cunningham. The seated figure is Angarika Dharmapala, a pivotal figure in the Buddhist reform movement that began following his visit to Bodhgaya in 1891. (Theosophical Society of India)

that decorates the sides of the plinth, echoing the motifs found on several of Ashoka's pillar capitals.

With the help of an early stone model of the Mahabodhi temple recovered from the ruins, Cunningham, Mitra and

Beglar made the best of a bad job. By the time Sir Alexander
Cunningham was finally persuaded to step down he was aged
seventy-one. He sailed from Bombay in September 1885 on
board the steamship *Indus*, which soon afterwards struck a rock
off Ceylon and foundered, taking with it much of Cunningham's collection of coins. Cunningham himself got to shore
unscathed and was able to congratulate himself on having previously sent on ahead his best gold and silver pieces, now in
the British Museum. He died in South Kensington eight years
later, by which time almost all the missing pieces in the
Buddhist jigsaw he had tried to fill with the help of Faxian and
Xuanzang had been found – almost but not quite.

14

India after Cunningham

The Lumbini pillar with its inscription barely visible below ground level, soon after its excavation by General Sumsher Khadga Rana in 1896. Photograph by Dr Anton Führer. (APAC, British Library)

Sir Alexander Cunningham's brief never extended to the Madras and Bombay Presidencies. In 1873 Dr James Burgess, editor of the *Indian Antiquary* and chief disciple of James Fergusson, had been appointed Archaeological Surveyor for Western India. Two years later, following intense lobbying from James Fergusson, Sir Walter Elliot and other grandees in England, Burgess was given the additional charge of archaeology in south India. Following Cunningham's retirement he was appointed Surveyor General for the whole of India and his triumph over his former rival appeared to be absolute, even if Cunningham's senior assistant Joseph Beglar continued to challenge his authority as Archaeological Surveyor for Bengal.

Burgess's interests were very different from those of Cunningham, focusing on architecture rather than archaeology and, in particular, the Buddhist cave temples of western India and their inscriptions. This may account for his failure to take due notice of what Cunningham had always considered to be a prime archaeological site but which he himself had never been allowed to examine: Amaravati.

The result was that Amaravati continued to suffer the assaults of amateur archaeologists and locals in search of building material, culminating in an order from the governor of Madras to clear the site. It meant that when Burgess finally got around to excavating there himself in 1882 he found little more than what he himself described as 'a large pit'.[1]

Burgess's only achievement at Amaravati was to note that a number of the remaining stone slabs had been carved on both sides and that the stupa had apparently suffered some violent destruction at an early stage, probably in the second century BCE when the Satavahana dynasty was in the process of moving in to fill the vacuum left by the Mauryas. It had then been restored and greatly enlarged when the nearby city of Dhanyakataka had become the capital of the Satavahana rulers of Andra. However, Burgess has to be given some credit for his subsequent survey of the archaeological sites upstream of Amaravati and his discovery of the Jaggayyapeta bas-relief (see illustration p. 93).

The Jaggayyapeta slab excited little interest then and it has been largely overlooked since. Yet taken together with the surviving Wheel-turning Monarch scenes from Amaravati, it demonstrates that the cult of the Chakravartin was now well established within India, from where it would spread to China and beyond.

Burgess's authority never extended to the two largest princely states in South India: Hyderabad and Mysore. Here it was left to local enthusiasts to advance the cause of Ashokan studies, most notably Benjamin Lewis Rice, who had been born in Bangalore (also in the *annus mirabilis* of 1837) and had returned there in the early 1860s to be the headmaster of a high school. Bangalore was then the British administrative centre for the princely state of Mysore and in due course Rice was made Inspector of Schools and Director of Public Instruction for Mysore State. In the course of his duties he toured the state on horseback and became increasingly interested in the many inscribed stones he came across in the course of his travels. With the help of Sanskrit and Kannada pandits he began to collect and decipher these ancient scripts, eventually amassing over nine thousand inscriptions. On his retirement he was appointed Mysore State's director of archaeology, a position he held until he finally left India in 1906 at the age of seventy.

Lewis Rice's memorial is his twelve-volume *Epigraphia Carnatica*, but his biggest coup came in 1892, when he discovered no less than three Ashokan Minor Rock Edicts in Mysore

State: the Brahmagiri, Jatinga-Ramesvara and Siddapur MREs –
all found in close proximity beside the River Chinna Hagari in
the Chitaldroog (Chitradurga) District of what is now Karnataka,
about 150 miles north of Bangalore. All three were the work of
the same hand, who had signed himself 'Capada' in Kharosthi
and had described himself as a 'scribe', suggesting to Lewis
Rice that he had probably come from the Taxila region: 'The
inference is that the scribe may have been an official transferred from the extreme north to the extreme south of the
empire, which implies a freer inter-communication than has
been generally supposed to exist at that period.'

Shortly before Lewis Rice's departure he presided over an
even greater discovery when a Brahmin from Tanjore presented
the newly opened Mysore Oriental Library with a collection of
palm-leaf texts in Sanskrit. It included a copy of the *Arthashastra*,
or 'Treatise on State Economy', which set out in fifteen chapters
how a ruler should be selected, educated and directed to govern
a well-ordered kingdom. This was a work of almost legendary
status that was said to have been in wide circulation until the
Hindu kingdoms were overwhelmed by the Muslim sultanates,
after which all copies had apparently disappeared. It was then
presumed lost – until this one surviving copy was identified by
Shama Shastry, the Librarian of the Mysore Oriental Library.

In its surviving form the *Treatise on State Economy* was
ascribed to an editor or redactor named Vishnugupta, writing
in the early Gupta era, but the original work had always been
credited to the Brahman Chanakya, also known as Kautilya,
the 'crow-like'. This was the hero of *The Minister's Signet Ring*
political drama and of the *Puranas* who in the fourth century
BCE had overthrown the base-born King Nanda and placed
his protégé Chandragupta on the throne. Indeed, Chanakya's

authorship was confirmed within the text itself, for in its penultimate paragraph he had written that this was the work of 'one who forcibly and quickly achieved the liberation of the mother-country, of its culture and learning (and) its military power, from the grip of the Nanda kings'.[2]

The *Treatise on State Economy* had initially been passed by oral transmission by Chanakya to his disciples and they to theirs until finally committed to paper. When it resurfaced in Mysore in the early twentieth century it was quickly recognised for what it was: a highly sophisticated, practical – and in its own time, revolutionary – treatise on statecraft and government that had underpinned the administration of Chandragupta and his immediate successors.

Its revolutionary aspect came from the claim by its author that the key to good government lies not in prayers, sacrifices to the gods or offerings to Brahmans but in trained leadership. The skills of kingship could be taught, but only to those who already possessed the desire and ability to learn, the capacity to retain and to draw the right inferences from what they learned, and the willingness to show obedience to their teachers. Through association with learned teachers the future ruler learned self-discipline by their example, which led to increased self-possession and greater efficiency in acquiring knowledge. Only by being disciplined, learned, conscious of the welfare of all beings and devoted to just government, could a king hope to rule unopposed. 'In the happiness of his subjects lies the king's happiness,' runs perhaps the most famous passage in Chanakya's *Treatise*, 'in their welfare his welfare. He shall not consider as good only that which pleases him but treat as beneficial to him whatever pleases his subjects.' These were sentiments that would be reflected in stone in the edicts of

Chandragupta's grandson, who would have been steeped in the contents of the *Treatise* as part of his princely education.

Kingship was the standard polity of the Aryans in India, going right back to the quasi-mythical King Prithu, imposed on anarchic humankind by the gods and infused with divinity. However, Chanakya challenged this tradition by arguing that the first king was Manu, elected by the people as the person most fit to rule, and who ruled not by divine right but by virtue of a contract between ruler and ruled. So long as he guaranteed the welfare of the people the king had the right to enforce law and order. Being of Kshatriya birth was a prerequisite, certainly, but no king was fit to rule unless he possessed the highest qualities of intellect, leadership, resolution and self-discipline. He had also to take the advice of his ministers and respect his chief minister as a son his father. That chief minister was, of course, a Brahman, and in the *Treatise on State Economy* he is glorified as the only person of equal standing to the king – with the right to depose him should the king became a tyrant or if he impoverished his people.

As his title suggests, Chanakya laid great stress on the responsibility of the ruler to build a sound economy, since good government requires a well-ordered administration with high ethical standards that allow trade, business and agriculture to flourish. However, side by side with these high ideals, Chanakya stressed the importance of learning the cruder aspects of kingship: how to secure and hold a kingdom; what tactics to employ in invading an enemy's territory and capturing an enemy fortress; the use of spy networks; and the seven strategies for dealing with and overcoming neighbouring powers, which included appeasement, punishment, bribery, deceit, deception and dividing the opposition.

It was this aspect of the *Treatise* that caught the public attention when it became the subject of much discussion in political and academic circles in India in the 1920s. It became fashionable to describe Chanakya as the Indian Machiavelli, a glib comparison that the future Prime Minister of India Jawaharlal Nehru rejected when writing his *Discovery of India* in a British jail. Machiavelli, after all, was a failed theoretician, whereas Chanakya was an extremely successful one who had carried his ideas through into fruition:

> Bold and scheming, proud and resourceful, never forgetting a slight, never forgetting his purpose, availing himself of every device to delude and defeat the enemy, he sat with the reins of empire in his hands and looked upon the emperor more as a loved pupil than as a master ... There was hardly anything Chanakya would have refrained from doing to achieve his purpose; he was unscrupulous enough, yet he was also wise enough to know that this very purpose might be defeated by means unsuited to the end.[3]

Chanakya, it seems, was as much a role model for Pandit Nehru as he was for the grandson of the man he made king. It is an indication of Nehru's high regard for the author of the *Treatise on State Economy* that when he became Prime Minister of India he ordered the new diplomatic enclave being laid out in New Delhi to be named Chanakyapuri or 'the city of Chanakya'.

The reappearance of the *Treatise* in the first decade of the twentieth century came in the wake of a raft of scholarly publications, all of which shed further light on the Mauryas. Dr Émile Senart's *Inscriptions de Piyadassi* (1881) improved on Cunningham's work and was itself improved upon by Dr Eugen (Ernst) Hultzsch, whose revised edition of *Inscriptions of Aśoka* (1925) remains the standard work on the subject. In Britain Edward Cowell,[4] former principal of the Sanskrit College in Calcutta before becoming the first Professor of Sanskrit at the University of Cambridge, contributed to Professor Max Müller's *Sacred Books of the East* series and joined with Robert Alexander Neil, translator of the Buddhist *Jataka Tales*, to produce the *Divyavadana* or 'Buddhist Tales'. In Ceylon the pioneering work by George Turnour was taken up by two of a later generation of Ceylon Civil Service administrators: Robert Caesar Childers and Thomas Rhys Davids. In 1872 Childers became Sub-librarian at the India Office and in that same year published the first part of his *Dictionary of the Pali Language*. He subsequently became the first Professor of Pali at London University but died in 1876, whereupon Rhys Davids then assumed his mantle, going on to form the Pali Text Society in 1881.

Within the Indian subcontinent the Archaeological Survey of India went through another bad patch as local provinces sought to reassert themselves. The two Afghan Wars had ensured that Afghanistan remained out of bounds and a very similar state of affairs existed in Nepal, where its Rana rulers remained deeply suspicious of the British government in India and its intentions. However, that situation changed when in the mid-1890s reports began to be received of an inscribed pillar known locally as *Bimasenaki nigali* or 'Bhim Sen's smoking pipe', said to have been seen by the Nepalese governor of Western Nepal. In March 1895 Dr Anton Führer, archaeological surveyor to the government of the North-West Provinces and Oude (today Uttar Pradesh), was authorised to cross the border on an elephant. He duly located two sections of a monumental pillar, the shorter and lower shaft of which bore a short inscription in Brahmi, slightly damaged but readable.

The Nigliva Sagar inscription, erected by Emperor Ashoka twenty years after his consecration. Photographed by Anton Führer in 1895. (APAC, British Library)

Führer sent a copy of the inscription to his mentor and patron Dr Georg Bühler, by then Professor of Sanskrit at the University of Vienna, who showed it to be a hitherto unknown form of Ashokan memorial. It reads (in a modern translation by Professor Harry Falk):

When king Priyadarsin, dear to the gods, was consecrated for this 14th regal year he enlarged the stupa of Buddha Konagamana to double its size. When he was consecrated for his 20th [?] regnal year he came in person and paid homage and had a stone pillar erected.[5]

The inscription showed that in the fourteenth year of his reign as anointed ruler – or about the year 256 BCE – Ashoka had ordered the enlarging of an existing memorial to Buddha Konagamana, one of the Buddhas said to have preceded Buddha Sakyamuni. He had then visited the site himself six years later, in about 250 BCE. The Chinese traveller Xuanzang had seen just such a stupa together with an Ashokan pillar south-east of the city of Kapilavastu.

Despite their best efforts, Cunningham and his colleagues had failed to locate both Kapilavastu, the city where Sakyamuni had been raised as Prince Siddhartha, and Lumbini, the nearby garden in which he had been born.

Führer's discovery initiated a race to find that fabled city and the Lumbini Garden, because Xuanzang and his compatriot Faxian had both placed Lumbini near Kapilavastu, and Kapilavastu several days' journey east of Sravasti, located by Alexander Cunningham back in 1863. The full story of the race to find these two prime Buddhist sites has been told elsewhere.[6] It tells how in November 1896 Dr Führer was again allowed to enter Nepalese territory, only to be escorted to the camp of the local governor, General Khadga Shumsher Rana, and shown a standing pillar with a prominent crack running down from the top. The general's sappers then dug round the base of the pillar to a depth of about five feet to uncover four and a half lines of beautifully cut Brahmi, perfectly preserved.

When Führer read the phrase at the end of the second line – *hida budhe jate sakyamuni,* or 'here the Buddha was born, the sage of the Sakyas' – the significance of these four and a half lines at once became apparent. He knew he had found Lumbini. Xuanzang had described Ashoka's pillar as split in half by a dragon, and here was that split very much in evidence on what remained of the pillar (see illustration, p. 303). Scholars continue to dispute the exact meaning of the last sentence but there is nothing ambiguous about the rest (Professor Falk's translation):

When king Priydarsin, dear to the gods, was consecrated for this 20th regnal year he came in person and paid reverence. Because the Buddha, the Sakyamuni, was born at this place, he had a stone railing made and a stone pillar erected. Because the Lord (of the world) was born at this place, he exempted the village of Lumbini from taxes and granted it the eight shares.[7]

The Lumbini and Nigliva Sagar pillars and their inscriptions were patently by-products of the same royal tour made by Emperor Ashoka in about 250 BCE. A third pillar, surviving only as a stump on its original foundations and located by Dr Führer a few miles south-west of the Nigliva pillar, almost certainly dated from the same royal visit. Together they proved beyond doubt that Ashoka had done what Xuanzang and the *Legend of King Ashoka* had claimed for him, which was to make an extensive pilgrimage to the holy places of Buddhism, beginning with the Lumbini Grove and moving on to Kapilavastu nearby, where he had erected a number of memorial stupas and pillars.[8]

Unfortunately for Führer and Indian archaeology, the German archaeologist had made wild claims in his report on his first foray into Nepal. In a desperate bid to locate the ancient city of Kapilavastu, which he had claimed to have seen in all its glory, Führer dug himself almost literally into a hole, which grew all the deeper when it emerged that he had been selling bogus relics to a Buddhist monk from Burma. Führer was sacked but his antics appear to have preyed on the mind of his patron Georg Bühler, who in April 1898 disappeared while out rowing late at night on Lake Constance. That tragedy and the suspicions of fakery overshadowed the last phase of archaeological discoveries made in Bihar in the last decade of the nineteenth century, of which three are of particular importance in the Ashoka story.

The first was a find rather than an excavation, made in 1892 by Dr William Hoey, commissioner of Gorakhpur Division in North Bihar. Hoey was a keen antiquarian and in the course of exploring a series of mounds beside the Rapti River he got talking to an old man from the village of Sohgaura and learned that in his youth the old man had dug up a small copper plate, which he had presented to the local *zamindar* or 'land-owner'. Hoey made enquiries and some months later the son of the landowner turned up at his office with the plate and presented it to him.

The Sohgaura plate turned out to be bronze rather than copper, which was itself remarkable. It was no more than 2½ inches long and 1¾ inches wide and in astonishingly good condition. Even more remarkably, it bore both symbols and letters, moulded in such high relief that they were easy to make out.

The writing consisted of four lines of early Ashokan Brahmi. Above it was a line of seven distinct symbols: two different species of trees set behind railings, two triple-storey buildings with pillars and thatch roofs, a single spear-like object, a globe topped by a taurine symbol and, at the centre, a 'stupa' pyramid of three semi-circular domes topped by a horned moon. Apart from the two buildings, all were symbols found on early Indian punch-marked coins.

The Mauryan Sohgaura plate, presented by Dr William Hoey to the Asiatic Society of Bengal and subsequently lost or stolen. (*JASB*, 1894)

Quite by chance, one of the ICS officers serving under Hoey was Vincent Smith, a great admirer of Sir Alexander Cunningham and who a decade later would retire to Oxford to write the first biography of Ashoka and the first edition of the *Oxford History of India*. Hoey and Smith presented a joint paper to the Asiatic Society of Bengal on the Sohgaura plate but were unable to shed much light beyond declaring it to be of the Mauryan period. Fortunately, they took photographs and sent a copy to Professor Bühler, who showed that the language was Prakrit and that it was an order from the religious officers at Sravasti declaring that two storehouses at Vamsagrama were in urgent need of supplies of grain, pulses and other foods, and that these supplies were not to be withheld. The symbols were as much of a mystery to Dr Bühler then as they are to epigraphers today.

Claims have been made that the Sohgaura plate represents a key moment of transition from pictographs to a proper written language, rather in the manner of a miniature Rosetta Stone. This has given rise to much wild speculation about India's lost Saraswati writing, best left to the internet. What is more relevant is that in 1931, while archaeologists were starting preliminary excavations at the great walled city of Mahasthan in East Bengal, first noted by Buchanan back in 1808 and very briefly explored by Cunningham in 1879, a local villager uncovered a small stone slab very like the Sohgaura plate. Its seven lines of Brahmi carried a message similar in general form, in that it was an order from an unnamed ruler of Magadha – maddeningly, the first part of the top line is too damaged to be readable – to the religious officer of a town named Pundranagara telling him to take measures to relieve the distress of the Samvamgiya people caused by superhuman agency and – curiously – parrots, and to replenish the granary and the treasury.[9]

These two finds are almost certainly contemporaneous and Mauryan. They point to the existence of a highly sophisticated administrative system that employed an equally sophisticated message system. Because of the references to famine relief, it has been suggested that they may date from Chandragupta's time when a twelve-year famine raged. But the Greeks who reported on Chandragupta's kingdom would surely have mentioned such a sophisticated communications system had it existed. All the evidence points to these two messages being Ashokan in their dating. Indeed, it has been argued that the central symbol on the Sohgaura plate of the stupa overlooked by *chandra*, the moon, may have been the personal seal of Ashoka himself. The brass plate was itself the product of a manufacturing system requiring great skill in casting, using a wax technique not seen again in India until the eighth century CE.

Dr Hoey presented the Sohgaura plate to the Asiatic Society

of Bengal. So chaotic was the curating at this low period in the fortunes of the ASB that some years passed before it was officially admitted that the Sohgaura plate had been lost. It may turn up one day, perhaps lodged behind one of the many cupboards lining the walls at No. 1 Park Street, Calcutta, where the ASB had its headquarters. In the meantime, its loss can only be described as incalculable. It is the oldest bronze plate found in India and nothing like it has been found since.

The second Ashokan discovery took place in Patna, which had so far proved a graveyard of archaeological hopes. Cunningham had explored the town and surrounds and had come away disappointed, convinced that the great capital city of Pataliputra as seen and reported on by the Greeks in the days of Chandragupta had long since been washed away. It fell to Dr L. A. Waddell of the Indian Medical Service to prove him wrong. Waddell was an unlikeable character, quick to take offence and unscrupulous in the pursuit of his own goals.[10] He considered himself to be the true discoverer of Lumbini and Kapilavastu, and he did his best to destroy the career of a fellow archaeologist, Babu Purna Chandra Mukherji, who found the city of Kapilavastu in the jungle at Tilaurakot just west of Nigliva Sagar.[11]

Like so many of his contemporaries, Waddell pored over the writings of the Chinese pilgrim travellers. In 1892 he came to Patna from his medical post in Darjeeling on two days' leave, armed with a sketch map based on the information supplied by Faxian and Xuanzang. This suggested to him that some of the monuments visited by the Chinese travellers lay within what was now the oldest quarter of Patna city, and that Ashoka's palace and the great Ashokarama monastery built by Ashoka would be found south of the railway line, which at that time marked the southern limits of the city. 'I was surprised to find', he afterwards wrote, 'that most of the leading landmarks of Asoka's palaces, monasteries, and other monuments remained so very obvious that I was able in the short space of one day to identify many of them beyond all doubt, by taking the itineraries of the Chinese pilgrims as my guide.'[12]

Waddell's findings involved a lot of wishful thinking but he was on the right track. The first site he examined was in the city about half a mile south of Patna College: an artificial mound made of brick about twenty feet high and about a quarter of a mile in circuit (long since covered over). In Waddell's time it was known by the suggestive title of *Bhikna pahari*, or 'Monk hill', and, according to Waddell, it matched Xuanzang's description and location of the hermitage built by Ashoka for his younger brother Tissa.

Equally speculative was Waddell's identification of Ashoka's notorious 'Hell', the prison in which captives were said to have been tortured to death in his pre-Buddhist years as Fierce Ashoka. This Waddell located in an ancient well, known as the *Agam kuan* or 'bottomless well', sited just outside the boundary of the city formed by the railway line (just southwest of today's Gulzarbagh railway station). The well had been restored and covered by a roof in Emperor Akbar's time but Waddell found – or claimed to have found – that it was associated with evil, so much so that no one ever drank from it.

More importantly, the well was adjacent to the Hindu temple of Shitala Devi, goddess of smallpox. Alexander Cunningham had come here in 1879 in search of Mauryan yakshi fertility goddesses, having read that three such sculptures had been found in the area back in the 1820s. Two had been transported downriver to the Asiatic Society of Bengal's museum but the third figure had been left behind – to be rediscovered by Cunningham at the shrine of Shitala Devi, but now an object of worship too sacred to be moved.

Waddell found Cunningham's goddess (in fact, two goddesses back to back) half-buried in the temple courtyard and was struck immediately by how similar they were to the yakshi figures excavated by Cunningham at Bharhut. He made enquiries and learned that the pillar had originally come from another site entirely, half a mile to the west. He would afterwards claim that it was Xuanzang's trail that he was following, but it was the yakshi pillar that led him to the village of Kumrahar.

A Buddhist railing pillar in the form of a pair of *yakshis* at the shrine of Shitala Devi beside Patna's 'bottomless well', photographed by Alexander Caddy in 1895. (APAC, British Library)

This entire village belonged to a local landowner named Shaikh Akram-ul-Haq, and what Waddell learned from the Shaikh and saw for himself convinced him that he had found the site of King Ashoka's palace.

The Shaikh's story was that a number of pagan statues had been found here in the past, the most recent having been dug up in the courtyard of his own house in his father's time and taken away by the Hindus. Indeed, Shaikh Akram-ul-Haq was happy to hand over to Waddell parts of a Buddhist railing and a few other sculptured stones that he or his ancestors had unearthed in digging wells or house foundations. Waddell's own searches produced more fragments of stone pillars and railings, showing that an early Ashokan-style Buddhist stupa had once stood in the vicinity. He also learned that whenever wells were dug in or near Kumrahar village the diggers struck a barrier at a depth of fifteen or twenty feet, usually in the form of massive wooden beams or palisades. This put Waddell in mind of 'the old wooden walls of the city as described by Megasthenes'.

Greatly encouraged by this brief reconnaissance, Waddell petitioned the government of Bengal for funds and in 1896 returned to Patna to supervise the digging of trenches at Kumrahar and at three other sites. At a depth of about fifteen feet, close to the railway line, he found a section of wooden palisade, as well as a magnificent capital of a 'distinctly Greek type ... manifestly of Asoka's period or soon after it'. At Kumrahar village itself Waddell uncovered broken fragments of 'a gigantic pillar of Ashoka ... one of those polished colossal monoliths which that emperor set up and inscribed with his edicts'.

A 'magnificent capital of a distinctly Greek type', combining
Ashokan and Graeco-Persian motifs. (From Waddell's *Report on
the Excavations at Pataliputra (Patna)*, 1903)

Waddell's further ground survey of the area south of
Kumrahar identified low-lying areas that were dried-out river
beds, showing that at some time in the past the Sone River had
divided into two channels just before it joined the Ganges.
The main channel had run through what was now the British
Civil Lines district, known as Bankipur, upstream of Patna
town, while the lesser channel had joined the Ganges just
south of Patna, so creating the island upon which the city of
Pataliputra had been built. When Waddell discovered the
wooden piers of what he surmised was some kind of landing
stage at the southern edge of Kumrahar village it seemed to
confirm that this was indeed the case.

Waddell returned to the Kumrahar site in 1897 to continue
his excavations but to his dismay found a professional archaeologist already at work. This was Babu P. C. Mukherji, from the

Indian Museum in Calcutta. To make matters worse, Mukherji had already found parts of six separate Ashokan pillars at Kumrahar, all buried among a thick layer of ashes and embers – pointing to what he believed had been a deliberate attempt to split the pillars by heat.

Waddell was furious at this intrusion and mounted an unsuccessful campaign to have Mukherji dismissed. Two years later when Mukherji was appointed to continue the archaeological survey of the Nepal Tarai begun by the disgraced Dr Führer, Dr Waddell again intervened in a bid to have the Bengali archaeologist removed. It is a pleasure to report that it was Mukherji who had the last laugh – by discovering the true site of ancient Kapilavastu at Tilaurakot while Waddell was pursuing a false lead elsewhere.

Yet Dr Waddell's pioneering work at Patna deserves to be remembered, as does his discovery of two more fertility goddesses courtesy of information supplied by Shaikh Akram-ul-Haq. He tracked these wonderful, lustrous creatures down to a temple at Naya Tola, half a mile to the west of Kumrahar (today Rajendra Nagar railway station). As at the Shitala Devi shrine, the yakshis stood back to back supporting a pillar, but were infinitely superior in execution. Just short of life-size and naked but for waist-belts, each raises a polished hand above a polished breast to grasp the branch of a tree.

Magnificent as this sculpture is, it has to give pride of place to another goddess in Patna Museum's magnificent collection of Mauryan and Shungan sculptures: the so-called Didarganj Yakshi, unquestionably one of the finest artworks of the Mauryan era yet discovered. Made of the same light sandstone in which the Ashokan pillars had been carved, and probably from the same quarry, she has the characteristic polish of the

(Above left) One of Dr Waddell's lustrous Naya Tola tree-goddesses, superbly sculpted but outclassed by the Didarganj Yakshi (above right) more correctly a *chowri dharani*, or 'fly-whisk holder'. (Both photos courtesy of Namit Arora of Shunya)

pillars and the best Ashokan sculptures. Like Waddell's tree-goddesses, she has prominent, globular breasts, a trim waist and curvaceous hips, with two soft rolls of flesh on her tummy – all glowing with a magnificent sheen. As well as the traditional *shringar patti* jewellery on her head (just as worn by Indian brides today) she wears earrings, a necklace, bangles down to her elbow and heavy, ornate anklets. She carries a *chowrie* or fly-whisk over her right shoulder, showing that she was one of a pair of attendants flanking what must have been a colossal and quite magnificent central Buddha figure. She has been called the Venus de Milo of Indian art, which does her no favours, for she has far more allure, even if she shares her Greek sister's modesty in wearing a drape, which hangs from her waist in delicate folds, just about held up by an intricately carved chain-belt. She was carved at least a century and a half before the Greek Venus – and by an artist every bit as good as Praxitiles.

The Didarganj Yakshi owes nothing to Dr Waddell. She was found in 1917 by a villager of Didarganj, sticking up out of the mud beside the Ganges just west of Bankipur, very probably washed downstream when the River Sone burst its banks at some time in the distant past when its course was nearer to Pataliputra.

The work begun by Waddell and Mukherji at Kumrahar was completed by an American archaeologist, Dr David Spooner, who had cut his teeth excavating Kushan Buddhist sites in and around the Vale of Peshawar. In 1913 Spooner came to Kumrahar and conducted the first large-scale and systematic excavation on the site, thanks to funding from the Parsi industrialist Sir Ratan Tata. Under a Gupta level of brick buildings he came upon the same thick layer of burned wood and ashes that Mukherji had first noted, among which were the fragments of at least seventy-two sandstone pillars set fifteen feet apart in eight rows of ten pillars. These were the remains of a pillared hall built on a truly grand scale, covering an area of more than 18,000 square feet. The pillars had originally stood on supporting wooden rafts which, Dr Spooner conjectured, must have gradually sunk into the soft subsoil under the combined weight of the pillars and the hall's roof. Nothing like it had ever been found in India, the only comparable structure being the great pillared hall at Persepolis built by the Achaeminid kings and partially destroyed by Alexander's fire.

Part of David Spooner's excavation at Kumrahar, showing (above) an Ashokan pillar and the fragments of many more lying in individual heaps, and (below) workmen clearing some of the wooden rafts supporting the pillars of Ashoka's Great Assembly Hall at Pataliputra. (APAC, British Library)

Also uncovered at an even greater depth than the supporting rafts was a wooden stairway leading directly from the Great
Assembly Hall down to the riverside. Everything found here
by Spooner was from the Mauryan era or after, showing that
the Great Hall had been constructed on open ground just outside the city of Pataliputra. It could only have been the work
of a very powerful ruler, and had clearly been built not to serve
as a palace but as a meeting hall.

The obvious answer is that this was the scene of Ashoka's
Third Buddhist Council, a convention regarded by him as so
important that he chose to build India's first monumental
building of stone, very probably importing architects and
stonemasons from Persia to do the job. Dr Spooner certainly
thought so but then rather spoiled his case by going on to argue
that the Mauryan rulers may themselves have been Persian in
origin.[11] John Marshall was quick to downplay Spooner's
Persian claims, which had not gone down well in Patna, a
centre of Indian nationalist feeling. Yet outside influence there
undoubtedly was, as displayed in the capital found by Waddell,
which is incontestably Graeco-Persian in inspiration if not in
manufacture.

The last important Ashokan discovery of the nineteenth
century took place in North Bihar in 1898, in the wake of Dr
Führer's announcement that he had discovered the birthplace
of the Buddha at Lumbini and his home city of Kapilavastu. In
January 1898 – just as Dr Führer was desperately trying to save
his reputation at an excavation just a few miles away – a local
landowner named William Claxton Peppé opened the largest
of a number of stupa mounds on his estate at Piprahwa. Its
location was significant: just half a mile south of the Nepal
border, 10 miles south-west of Lumbini and its Ashokan pillar,

17 miles south of the Nigliva Sagar Ashokan pillar, 12 miles south-east of the Gotihawa Ashokan pillar, and 15 miles south-east of Tilaurakot, the site of ancient Kapilavastu.

At a depth of twenty-four feet, at the very centre and base of the stupa, Peppé found a large sandstone coffer, weighing some three-quarters of a ton, within which were five soapstone reliquaries, a crystal bowl and a mass of small jewels shaped like flowers, semi-precious stones and other offerings. Overlooked in the initial excitement were some ashes and bone fragments, afterwards presented to the King of Siam, and a short inscription in Brahmi lettering crudely inscribed round the top of one of the soapstone vases.

The Piprahwa reliquary vase (centre) showing part of the Brahmi inscription carved round its lid. (Photo courtesy of Neil Peppé)

That inscription was first read by Vincent Smith and then by Dr Führer, who sent a hand-drawn copy to Professor Georg Bühler in Vienna. Like so many epigraphists since, Bühler was baffled by three letters that spelled out *su ki ti*, but the general import of the rest of the inscription seemed quite clear:

> This relic shrine of the divine Buddha (is the donation) of the Sakya Sukiti brothers, associated with their sisters, sons and wives.

It was Professor Bühler's belief that what William Peppé had found was the Sakya clan's share of the relics of Sakyamuni Buddha, making it the oldest inscription yet found in India.[14] So it was initially assumed that what Peppé had opened was a brick stupa raised by Ashoka over the original mud stupa that had covered the Buddha's ashes, as recounted in the *Legend of King Ashoka* and by Xuanzang. Moreover, a second excavation of the same site conducted in 1972–3 by K. M. Srivastiva showed that the stupa was of the Kushan era, built over an earlier mud stupa. But what also came to light was an earlier deposition of relics two feet below the place where the stone coffer had stood, with evidence that this had been disturbed at the time the stone coffer with its reliquaries and reliquary offerings were added.

Because of Peppé's links with Führer and the subsequent death of Bühler, doubts continue to be raised about the authenticity of the Piprahwa site and its inscription. Yet, except for those on the lunatic fringe of Buddhist studies, there can be no question but that the Piprahwa inscription is a genuine document and a very early one at that.

To date, approximately fifty Buddha relic inscriptions have been found on the Indian subcontinent, mainly from the region of ancient Gandhara in or close to Afghanistan but with a second big cluster in and around Sanchi in central India. Only one has been discovered in the Buddhist heartland of Magadha itself – at Piprahwa. Here alone the relics are referred to as *salilanidhane budhasa bhagavate sakiyanam*, or 'relic receptacle of the blessed Buddha of the Sakyas', and nowhere else is the term *nidhane* used for the term 'reliquary' rather than the more usual *samudaga* or *manjusa* found elsewhere. Yet this only points to the greater authenticity of the inscription. 'The Piprahwa inscription rings true in all regards,' the epigraphist Professor Richard Salomon has argued. 'Its language is a good specimen of Ardhamagadhi [early Magadhan Prakrit] ... It would have taken a very brilliant linguist to come up with such an excellent imitation of this little-documented language over one hundred years ago.'[15]

So who put the Piprahwa inscription there and when? The simplicity of its lettering points either to an early date in the evolution of Brahmi – or to a rustic interpretation of Brahmi as conceived in this distant corner of Magadha. But that takes no account of the unique stone coffer in which the reliquary was found and the sheer quantity and quality of the relic offerings – amounting to more than 1400 individual items in all – which include lapidary work of an order found in no other reliquary deposition. Somebody very important ordered these grave goods and stone coffer, this last probably hewn from the very same quarry at Chunar on the Ganges from which Ashoka's other monumental works had come.

From the combined evidence of the two excavations at Piprahwa it is possible to construct a scenario in which members of the Sakya clan buried their share of the relics of their distinguished family member near Kapilavastu city – relics that were subsequently disturbed by Emperor Ashoka or his representative as part of his Sakya relic redistribution programme as described in the *Legend of King Ashoka*, Xuanzang's account and other sources. The emperor then ordered the reburial of some part of the sage's relics with due ceremony and added his own simple stupa on top, which was afterwards enlarged by the Kushans.

Among those caught up in the Lumbini-Kapilavastu-Piprahwa controversy in the last months of the nineteenth century were Vincent Smith in India and the Pali scholar T. W. Rhys Davids, by then Secretary of the Royal Asiatic Society in London. By 1900 Smith had had enough and took early retirement to become a full-time historian. His *Asoka, the Buddhist Emperor of India* appeared a year later. It so happened that T. W. Rhys Davids had also been working on a book on Ashoka, which illness had prevented him from completing. His response was to write *Buddhist India*, published in 1903. These two books brought the name of Ashoka out of the scholarly closet and into the world domain. After two thousand years of obscurity India's emperor was once more a public figure.

15
Ashoka in the Twentieth Century

The Ashokan lion capital at Sarnath, with the inscribed pillar in the foreground. Only fragments were found of the Wheel of the Moral Law, which the four lions had originally supported. Photographed by Madho Prasad in 1905. (APAC, British Library)

It seems entirely appropriate that the man who introduced modern archaeological methods to India should have had the same name as the first British Orientalist, John Marshall – and that the man who appointed him, Lord Curzon, should have been almost alone among British proconsuls in India in sharing Warren Hastings's fascination for Indian culture and history. It was Curzon who declared that 'the sacredness of India haunts me like a passion' and it was this empathy for Indian culture that led him to insist that the Archaeological Survey of India (ASI) should be thoroughly overhauled, centralised and equipped with enough funds to do its job properly. He refused to countenance the appointment of a local man to head the ASI and saw to it that a professional trained in the latest techniques was brought in, even if he was a twenty-six-year-old who had never set foot in Asia.

This second John Marshall arrived in India 238 years after the first. In the course of the next twenty-six years he transformed the entire archaeological scene in India and the ASI with it. 'Even at that early date', he wrote some years after his retirement, 'it was patent to me that the future of archaeology in India must depend more and more on the degree of interest taken in it by Indians themselves, and that the surest way of strengthening my own Department was to provide it with an increasing number of Indian recruits.'[1] Marshall began by setting up government scholarships, the first person to win one being Daya Ram Sahni, who subsequently followed Marshall as Director-General, and the second R. D. Banerjee, whose excavations at Mohenjo-Daro in 1922 revealed the existence of the pre-Aryan Indus Civilisation. Initially, however, Marshall had to make the best use of what European experts were available, some highly qualified, and others who were no more than local enthusiasts – the last in a long line of amateurs.

John Marshall and his wife seated on the slopes of a stupa mound at Rajgir, Bihar, *c.*1918. (APAC, British Library)

One of the latter was Mr F. O. Oertal, executive engineer of Benares Division, whose only archaeological qualification was that he had spent some years in Burma in the Public Works Department (PWD). In the Cold Weather of 1904–5, with John Marshall's permission and acting on his advice, Oertal conducted his own excavation at Sarnath, exposing an area west of the great Dharmekh stupa that Cunningham had left relatively untouched. It proved to be the site's main shrine, a square temple constructed during the Gupta period but overlaying an earlier structure, which included polished monolithic railings cut from Chunar sandstone that were unmistakably Ashokan.

Immediately to the west of the shrine Oertal uncovered the lower section of an Ashokan column still embedded on its base but broken just at the point where the fourth line of the oldest of its three sets of inscriptions had been cut (see illustration, p. 331). Three inscribed fragments of pillar found nearby were enough for most of the inscription to be read. It was another of Emperor Ashoka's Schism Edicts, directed at the monks and nuns of the Buddhist Sangha, warning them against dividing their community.

At Sanchi the pillar had been capped by a magnificent but damaged capital made up of four lions back to back, brought to light by Cunningham and Maisey in 1851. It now fell to Oertal to improve upon that at Sarnath. He disinterred his lion capital a few yards away from the pillar upon which it had stood when Xuanzang came to the Deer Park in about the year 637 (see illustration, p. 331). To the delight of all who witnessed the discovery, it was not only in much better condition than the Sanchi capital but of far superior artistry, suggesting that here was the original and the other a copy. Where the two capitals also differed was in the abacus. At Sanchi this had been decorated with pairs of geese, whereas here the frieze showed four perfectly modelled animals: a lion with twitching tail, an elephant, a bull and a galloping horse, interspersed with the twenty-four-spoked Wheel of the Moral Law.

Each of these four animals has its place as a symbol of Buddhism: the lion represents Sakyasimha, lion of the Sakya clan, with the voice of a lion; the elephant signifies Sakyamuni entering the womb of his mother Mayadevi in her dream, but also Sakyamuni as the tamer of wild elephants; the horse, besides being a symbol of temporal royalty, is the vehicle that carried Prince Siddhartha on his journey of renunciation;

finally, the bull is the great inseminator, here symbolising the Buddha's teaching, the Dharma. The horse and elephant together support the Wheel-turning Monarch.

Both at Sarnath and Sanchi the four lions had originally supported a large Wheel of the Moral Law, and in both places that wheel had been smashed into too many pieces to attempt a reconstruction. At Sanchi Cunningham had concluded that an earthquake or some other natural cause had brought down pillar and capital, but here it seemed more likely that human violence had been responsible.

There is no finer demonstration of the state of sculpture at the time of Ashoka than the Sarnath lion capital. It is no exaggeration to speak of it as the work of a Mauryan Michelangelo, a craftsman whose mastery over his material was as complete as anything produced by the Assyrians, the Persians or the Greeks – and who could well have been the same genius who sculpted the Didarganj Yakshi. Yet he and his school, which would include those who produced the few surviving Ashokan pillar capitals, bells and drums, appear as if from nowhere. They have no known precedents in India other than the clumsy monumental figures found by Cunningham's assistants at Parkham and Besnagar. This new fluency had to come from somewhere, and the surviving works themselves point to Seleucid Bactria and its Graeco-Persian craftsmen, which is entirely plausible given Ashoka's family ties, his grandfather's and father's known links with their Western neighbours, and his own ties as set down on the Rock Edicts. It points to the arrival of a group of sculptors and stonemasons and a dramatic move away from working in wood to stone, a very costly break with tradition only made possible by royal command and patronage.

But if this same master sculptor enjoyed the patronage of Ashoka, why is it that we have no sculptures of his employer? Ashoka would have been aware of the cult of royal personality on the Persian and Greek models exemplified by their coinage, yet it seems that he declined to follow suit. No iconic images of the Buddha himself were permitted in Ashoka's lifetime so it may be that the Mauryas extended this prohibition to images of themselves. But what is equally feasible is that images of Ashoka were indeed made in his lifetime but that none have survived – unless that massive stone figure of a supposed demi-god found by Cunningham at Parkham is actually the statue of a Mauryan king.

Whoever those first sculptors and stonemasons were, they appear to have come from the north-west and set up one work-shop under royal patronage at Mathura and possibly another at Varanasi, which laid the foundations for an increasingly indige-nous Indian school of sculpture whose works subsequently graced Bharhut, Sanchi, Amaravati and many other Buddhist and Jain monuments now lost and forgotten.

On seeing what Oertal had dug up at Sarnath, Marshall reog-nised that it was too important a site to be left to the PWD. So extensive were his subsequent finds and of such outstanding quality that Marshall asked for and secured funds to build India's first onsite museum to house them. He went on to do the same at Sanchi and Taxila, returning to these last two sites again and again over the next twenty-five years.

In the meantime more Rock Edicts continued to be dis-covered, mostly of the Minor Rock Edict (MRE) category, with a notable cluster in Mysore State: at Maski in Raichur District, Karnataka, in 1915; at Erragudi in Anantapur District, Andhra Pradesh, in 1928 – this one found in close proximity to a major

Rock Edict site bearing REs 1–13 spread over five boulders, now known as the Erragudi Rock Edict; at Govimath, in Raichur District, Karnataka, in 1931; at Palkigundu, also in Raichur District, Karnataka, in 1931; and at Rajula-Mandagiri, Kurnool District, Andhra Pradesh, in 1946.

Of these, one stood out from the rest: the Maski MRE, discovered by a gold prospector. The lettering was severely damaged in parts but it was still possible to see that in place of the standard opening found on the other MREs the Maski MRE begins:

$$\text{ʒδⵏ⊂⊥⅄⅄+⅄}$$

De va na pi ya sa A sho ka sa

To this day the Rupnath MRE remains the only place where Ashoka's name has been found carved in stone on one of his edicts, although it is quite possible that other such examples have yet to be discovered, just as others have probably been lost for ever, destroyed either by human activity or the forces of nature.

In Afghanistan the distrust of the British engendered by the First and Second Afghan Wars continued well into the twentieth century. It meant that when Afghanistan finally began to open up to the West in the 1920s, under the modernising King Amanullah, it was the French who won exclusive rights to conduct excavations in Afghanistan under the leadership of Dr Alfred Foucher, who had studied at the Sanskrit College in Benares and, courtesy of John Marshall, had cut his teeth at excavations in India's North-West Frontier Province and at Sanchi. It was Foucher who invented the term 'Graeco-Buddhist' to describe the religious art produced in Gandhara, and who argued, like Cunningham before him, that the influence of classical Gandharan art penetrated deep into India and beyond.[2] Foucher spent months following the trails of Alexander the Great and Xuanzang across Afghanistan, leading to the discovery of numerous archaeological sites. Under his aegis, the excavation of the Gandharan summer capital of Kapisha at Begram, begun in 1936, and the subsequent unearthing of the Begram Treasure, proved to be the first of a series of spectacular discoveries that provided ample evidence of Gandhara's dominant role as an international crossroads and as a major catalyst for change in the region before, during and after the Mauryan era.

In the course of these excavations numerous texts written in Greek, Aramaic and Brahmi script were discovered, but only one of these could be directly linked to Ashoka: a triangular fragment of rock inscribed in Aramaic, found in the Laghman region just west of the town of Jalalabad in 1930. This turned out to contain elements of both Ashoka's Rock and Pillar Edicts in Prakrit language but transliterated into Aramaic script. No further Ashokan finds were made until 1958, when an inscribed rock boulder was spotted by chance at the foot of a ridge beside the ancient highway leading out of Kandahar westwards to Herat. It was a bilingual Ashokan edict, written in Greek and Aramaic. The two texts differed slightly but both carried the same message from Ashoka, his name being written in Greek as 'Piodasses'. It was dated from the tenth year after Ashoka's consecration and echoed the prohibitions against killing and respect for others to be found in a number of the Rock and Pillar Edicts.

Five years later a second inscribed rock was found not far from the first in the ruins of ancient Kandahar. This was entirely in Greek and carried the end of RE 12 and the beginning of RE 13. In that same year part of a quite different inscription was picked up in Kandahar bazaar: a scrap of rock inscribed with part of PE 7, written in Aramaic. These finds show that a number of Ashoka's Rock Edicts and Pillar Edicts or their amalgams, had at one time been erected in ancient Gandhara at least as far west as Kandahar – which is approximately 1300 miles from Patna.

It is John Marshall's restoration work that makes Sanchi such a delight to visit today. He kept being drawn back to the site, in 1918 writing to a friend that Sanchi was 'just as beautiful and fascinating as ever – nay, more so than it ever was in the old days'.[3] Part of this fascination lay in the fact that his old friend Alfred Foucher – 'a first rate scholar and a Frenchman of the nicest type' – had realised that the gateways of the Great Stupa of Sanchi and the single gateway of Stupa 2 were essentially memorials to the spread of the Dharma.[4]

At the end of the Great War Marshall resigned on doctor's advice, leaving his unfinished work at Sanchi with a long sigh of regret. The sweetener of a knighthood helped to change his mind and after some months' leave he returned reinvigorated and ready to serve as Director-General of the ASI for another decade. This extra term allowed Marshall to work intermittently with Foucher at Sanchi for another two years until the latter was made director of the Délégation Archéologique Française en Afghanistan in 1921. It meant that almost two decades passed before their joint masterwork, the massive three-volume *The Monuments of Sanchi*, was ready for publication, not helped by the death of their third collaborator, killed while providing new readings of the Sanchi inscriptions by robbers who believed him to be digging for buried treasure. Another Marshall protégé, the Sanskritist N. G. Majumdar, stepped in and a limited printing of the book appeared at the outbreak of war in 1939, with a second and equally limited printing in 1947, just as India was in the throes of independence and partition.

Marshall and Foucher showed in *The Monuments of Sanchi* that the Buddhist stupa cult could be traced back directly to the relic stupas erected by Emperor Ashoka and that his stupas and his Rock and Pillar Edicts 'came to be invested with a peculiar sanctity of their own ... as accepted emblems of the Faith'. They further demonstrated that the Great Stupa's four gateways were Ashokan in spirit and in kind – in particular, the South Gateway, the first to be completed and in their estimation the finest of the four despite its damage.

The South Gateway had been erected beside Ashoka's pillar and was itself intrinsically Ashokan, beginning with the two lion capitals on its two pillars, patently copied from the Ashokan pillar's lion capital right down to the geese and acanthus leaves on the drum. What is now the outer panel of the middle architrave shows Emperor Ashoka himself in a two-horse chariot visiting the Buddha relic stupa at Ramagrama and being met by its guardian deities, the Naga kings, here shown 'in human form with serpent hoods, worshipping at the stupa, bringing offerings, or emerging from the waters of a lotus pond'.[5] This is precisely the scene that Major Franklin and Captain Murray had drawn in the early nineteenth century (see pages 108, 159 and 240).

The middle architrave of the incorrectly restored South Gateway.
It shows Emperor Ashoka visiting the Buddha stupa at Ramagrama
to claim its relics, only to find it guarded by the Naga kings.
(Photograph by Andrew Whittome)

The story continues on the inner face of the bottom, damaged
crossbeam. This shows the other scene that Captain Murray
drew and submitted to James Prinsep back in 1837. On the right
a king stands in a chariot with an escort on an elephant, in the
centre a city is under attack, and on the left a king is shown
apparently directing the siege. This is usually interpreted
as a scene from the so-called 'War of the Relics', when eight
rulers fought over Sakyamuni Buddha's relics, other and more
clear versions of the same story occuring on the architraves of
the North, West and East Gateways. But what Murray had
failed to show in his drawing is that the giant elephant is actually carrying away a relic casket, which a turbaned raja rests on
his head as shown on Lieutenant Fred Maisey's later drawing.

A detail from Fred Maisey's finished drawing of the inner panel of the bottom architrave on the South Gateway at Sanchi, showing King Ashoka seated on a giant elephant bearing away the Buddha relics from Rajgir. (From Maisey, *Sanchi and its Remains*, 1892)

What is actually being portrayed here is Ashoka's attack on the city of Rajgir with a 'fourfold army' and his removal of its Buddha relics back to Pataliputra, as related in the *Legend of King Ashoka*. He then proceeded to the Ramagrama stupa, which was originally shown on the panel immediately above but was accidentally reversed during restoration so that it now appears on the outer side. It is no coincidence that the scene portrayed on the inner side of the top architrave shows a row of stupas and Bodhi trees being worshipped by a Naga king, a yakshi fertility goddess and, on the left, a human king, presumably King Ashoka (see original photo of fallen South Gateway on p. 239).

Other scenes portrayed on the same South Gateway strengthen the case for its being raised specifically as an act of homage to King Ashoka; in particular, two adjacent panels on its west pillar. Again a king is shown riding a two-horse chariot preceded by a giant guard holding a club. The same king then reappears on the next panel, now flanked by his two queens. They stand directly underneath the Bodhi tree at Bodhgaya and the pavilion constructed around it by Ashoka. His posture, his right arm over one queen while the other queen holds his right arm, is most unusual. 'There we see only a royal personage apparently supported by two of his queens,' writes Alfred Foucher of this crucial scene. 'But ... he can only be Aśoka. Hence we cannot fail to be reminded, by his tottering attitude, either of the immense grief which overcame him when he was told that his beloved tree was perishing – he declared that he would not be able to survive it – or, in another simpler version of the pilgrimage, of the emotion which seized him at sight of a spot so sacred.'

A modern photograph of this scene shows what Lieutenant Maisey's drawing from 1851 (see p. 241) failed to show, which is that the Ashoka here is short and fat, with a balloon-like head. The sculptor could not have seen Ashoka himself but memories of Ashoka would still have been green in the area, which suggests that this image is based on the emperor's actual physical appearance. It is surely no coincidence that the Brahmi inscription carved on the panel immediately below records that this was the work of the ivory workers of the nearby town of Vidisha.

Other gateways show more Ashokan scenes. At the East Gateway the outer panel on the bottom architrave again

Emperor Ashoka faints into the arms of his queens at the sight
of the Bodhi tree. A modern photograph capturing the detail
that earlier depictions missed. (Photo by Andrew Whittome)

shows Ashoka paying homage to the Bodhi tree. 'He is wearily
getting off his elephant, supported by his first queen,' writes
Foucher. 'Then both go forward in devout posture towards the
same Bodhi-tree surrounded by the same stone-enclosure ...
From the other side, to the sound of music, people are advancing in procession to the tree; and the figures in the foreground
are plainly carrying pitchers for watering it.'

Foucher leaves it to John Marshall to provide the explanation: 'This is the ceremonial visit which Aśoka and his queen
Tishyarakshita paid to the Bodhi tree, for the purpose of watering it and restoring its pristine beauty after the evil spell which
the queen in a fit of jealousy had cast upon it.'

On the West Gateway several panels may represent Ashoka

A modern photograph of the outer panel of the bottom architrave on the East Gateway shows Emperor Ashoka (standing)
with his queen (kneeling) as they worship the Bodhi tree,
having dismounted from an elephant. On the left side of the
panel musicians play and standard bearers watch as pitchers of
milk are brought to pour over the Bodhi tree to revive it. The
tree itself is depicted within the enclosure built for it by Ashoka,
which also covers the Diamond Throne. Carved on the supports
above are three distinctive Ashokan symbols: (left to right) an
edict pillar topped by a four-lion capital; the Wheel of the Moral
Law symbol; and the Bodhi tree. (Detail of a photo by Andrew
Whittome)

on his pilgrimage to the holy places of Buddhism, one showing
the same corpulent figure as that depicted fainting at the Bodhi
tree on the South Gateway, here seen praying beside a much
simpler Bodhi tree. Fred Maisey unwittingly drew this same
scene back in 1851 (see p. 242). The panorama on the back of
the middle architrave shows another of the 'War of the Relics'

scenes, which can equally be read as representing Ashoka collecting his Buddha relics – an interpretation strengthened by the fact that one end of that same beam shows a melon-faced king riding in a chariot, and the other end that same king looking exhausted and resting on a very modern-looking chair. He is being looked after by a bevy of women attendants and holds in his right hand what looks like a ball or fruit. Neither Marshall nor Foucher were prepared to speculate on what this might be intended to represent, but it is tempting to see it as the dying Ashoka and his last possession, the myrobalan or cherry plum fruit.

Because of its delays and bad timing, the revelations contained in Marshall and Foucher's *The Monuments of Sanchi* were largely overlooked by a generation of historians in India – and continue to be viewed with suspicion by those who find Foucher's views on Greek influence too much for their patriotic sentiments.

Indeed, it is striking – even downright disheartening – how this quintessentially Indian monarch still fails to be accorded a wholehearted welcome in the land of his birth more than a century after he first emerged as a subject fit for biography. To start with, Ashoka was ill-served by the English historian Vincent Smith who in writing *Asoka: The Buddhist Emperor of India* (1901) rejected the two prime Buddhist sources as 'the silly fictions of mendacious monks'. This work was swiftly denounced by the Welsh Pali scholar T. W. Rhys Davids, whose own book *Buddhist India* (1903) reflected a growing fascination with Buddhism in the West. That in turn led the writer and social reformer H. G. Wells to declare in his popular work *The Outline of History* that Ashoka was the very paradigm of the model ruler:

In the history of the world there have been thousands of kings and emperors who called themselves 'their highnesses,' 'their majesties,' and 'their exalted majesties' and so on. They shone for a brief moment, and as quickly disappeared. But Ashoka shines and shines brightly like a bright star, even unto this day.

Indian nationalists, looking for pre-colonial models of government, were quick to seize on this idea, among them Dr Radhakumud Mookerji, whose lectures on early Indian history at Lucknow University in the early 1920s became the basis for the first truly scholarly account of Ashoka and his times. He, too, sought to put Ashoka in a wider historical context:

In his efforts to establish a kingdom of righteousness after the highest ideals of a theocracy, he has been likened to David and Solomon of Israel in the days of its greatest glory; in his patronage of Buddhism, which helped to transform a local into a world religion, he has been compared to Constantine in relation to Christianity; in his philosophy and piety he recalls Marcus Aurelius; he was a Charlemagne in the extent of his empire and, to some extent, in the methods of his administration, too; while his Edicts, 'rugged, uncouth, involved, full of repetitions,' read like the speeches of Oliver Cromwell in their mannerisms. Lastly, he has been compared to Khalif Omar and Emperor Akbar, whom also he resembles in certain aspects.[6]

Hot on Mookerji's heels came a new wave of home-grown Ashokan scholarship that continued into the post-independence era. Almost without exception these Indian historians took a patriotic line, presenting Ashoka as untainted by foreign influences, his philosophy totally in keeping with the ideals of *ahimsa*, or 'non-violence', and *satyagraha*, or 'soul-force', promoted by the political and spiritual leader M. K. Gandhi as the moral basis of the freedom struggle against the British Raj. Perhaps for the same reason these same historians tended also to downplay Pali sources in favour of Sanskrit, with more than a hint of Brahminical bias. They also ignored the new evidence presented by Sir John Marshall and Alfred Foucher of Emperor Ashoka's commemoration on the Sanchi gateways.

Since independence three more Ashokan edict sites have been found in Karnataka State: Minor Rock Edicts at Nittur and Udegolam, found in 1977 and 1978, and a Rock Edict at Sannati in 1989. All are sited near major rivers, the first two beside the Tungabhadra River, the third on a bend of the River Bhima in Gulbarga District of South Karnataka. This last came to light when an abandoned Hindu shrine beside the village's Candralamba temple was being cleared for restoration. When the workmen came to remove a large stone slab upon which the deity had stood, they found it inscribed on both sides: parts of Ashoka's RE 12 and RE 14 on one side and the Kalinga Separate Rock Edicts 1 and 2 on the other. It was clear that the slab had originally stood upright along with other slabs carrying the remaining edicts but now missing. To date no more such slabs have been found.

Up to that point these particular major edicts had only been found carved on large rock boulders, hence their naming as Rock Edicts, but here was evidence that in some parts of Ashoka's empire these same edicts had been carved on slabs as well as boulders.

Mention must also be made of four Minor Rock Edict sites discovered in northern and central India in the post-war period: at Gujarra in the Datia District of Madhya Pradesh in 1953; at Ahraura, in Mirzapur District, Bihar, in 1961; at Bahapur in the east of Kailash District in New Delhi in 1965; and at Panguraria, Sehore District, Madhya Pradesh, in 1971. This last site has to be considered as very special indeed.

Panguraria is the name of a tiny hamlet sited on the northern bank of the River Narmada, which the British knew as the Nerbuddha. This is one of the largest rivers in India, and because it flows westwards for some eight hundred miles across the subcontinent's widest point, it has traditionally been seen as a natural boundary between North and South India. It helps that the Narmada flows along a rift valley with the Vindhya mountain range to the north and the Satpuras on the south. Panguraria village lies within this rift, between the river and a spur jutting out from the main Vindhya range. These hills contain a great many natural caves and rock shelters, and in this instance the find was made by a survey party of archaeologists from the Nagpur Circle of the ASI, who were looking for evidence of early human settlement.

What drew them to the Panguraria site were the remains of nine small stupas placed along the spine of a low ridge overlooking a side valley. The largest of these stupas was the highest, and just above it was a rock shelter, in which was found an Ashokan inscription in the form of a Minor Rock Edict crudely cut into the rock face. The MRE's opening preamble is only partly readable, but enough survives to show it to be significantly different from the usual opening statements of other MREs in that it was addressed by Ashoka to a prince named Samva. Whether this Prince

Samva – the word means 'concord' in Sanskrit – was one of Ashoka's sons is open to speculation, since the name is found nowhere else. From all the surviving evidence, the monastery at Panguraria over which Prince Samva was placed in authority was a typical early monastic centre where the monks slept in rock shelters rather than monastic cells. Yet the place clearly had a very special significance for Emperor Ashoka, for just to the left of the cave containing the MRE is a second rock shelter set into the same low cliff, and on its brow is another, shorter inscription, set high up on the rock face in big bold letters.

Unlike the MRE next door, this inscription has not been incised using a mallet and chisel but clumsily tapped out, probably by the writer standing on a rock and using a chisel attached to a stick. It is not so much a planned edict as a piece of casual graffiti, albeit one carried out on the orders of a powerful ruler. According to one of the outstanding epigraphists of our own times, Professor Harry Falk, it reads:

Piyadasi nama
rajakumara va
samvasamane
imam desam papunitha
vihara(y)atay(e)

This Falk translates as:

The king, who (now after consecration) is called Piyadassi, (once) came to this place on a pleasure tour while he was still a (ruling) prince, living together with his unwedded consort.[7]

Panguraria is just forty-five miles due south of Vidisha, the
district in which Sanchi and its surrounding Buddhist sites
falls – and from which Ashoka's first wife hailed. Ashoka's graffiti at Panguraria is a sort of informal memento, placed there
when the emperor returned to a place he had visited in his
youth, when as viceroy of Ujjain he had toured these parts with
his girlfriend, the woman who would bear him his eldest son
and daughter Mahinda and Sanghamitta. It is a touchingly
human document that shows the emperor with his guard down.

Panguraria may also mark the moment when Ashoka first
began to use the new Brahmi alphabet to spread his edicts
across the land, beginning with his Minor Rock Edicts, which
in nearly every instance tell us – most obligingly – that this
process was initiated two and a half years after he had converted
to Buddhism and while he was on tour: 'This proclamation (was
issued by me) on tour. Two hundred and fifty-six nights (had
then been) spent on tour.'[8]

To date sixteen complete and incomplete sets of MREs have
been found, well spread out but with a cluster of eleven in the
Karnataka region of South India. Together they form the oldest
certain examples of Brahmi writing – and thus the oldest examples
of written Prakrit, precursor of Pali and Sanskrit. They represent
the first wave of Ashoka's proclamations set in stone. Although the
order went out while Ashoka was out on tour, it seems logical to
suppose that the earliest of these MREs went up in the Magadha
region and the Gangetic plains, as at Ahraura and Sassaram. And
indeed, only at Ahraura, Sassaram and Rupnath do the MREs
actually state how Ashoka's commands are to be spread: 'And
cause ye this matter to be engraved on rocks. And where there
are stone pillars here (in my dominions), there also cause (it) to
be engraved.'[9] The later MREs have dropped this order.

Nearly all of these sixteen known MRE sites are associated with caves or rock shelters on rocky outcrops or small hills, and always away from population centres, even if close to roads or river crossings. Ashoka may have chosen these sites deliberately as places where crowds might gather at annual religious fairs, so that his promotion of Buddhism might become associated with local cults.[10] It can equally be argued that Ashoka in the early days of his conversion to Buddhism chose not to challenge directly the powerful forces of the Brahman establishment, who would have been concentrated in the big towns. However, we have no idea to what degree Ashoka's monumental decrees were targeted by those who came after him. If they were attacked, the first to be pulled down or broken up would have been those sited in or near population centres. His pillars would have made the most visible targets and would have been the first to go. The edicts we see today – with considerable difficulty since the majority are so isolated – must be seen as the survivors of many.

This first round of Ashokan edicts – the Minor Rock Edicts – were followed by the Schism Edicts, starting with the Bairat-Calcutta Schism Edict, which is addressed directly to the Sangha and not to the mahamatras or religious officers, who have been placed in charge of the Buddhist Church by the time the Sanchi and Sarnath Schism Edict pillars go up. The next to be set in stone were the Separate or Kalinga Rock Edicts at Dhauli and Jaugada in Orissa and Sannati in South Karnataka, which also anticipate the creation of the special cadre of religious officers. They would have been followed by the remaining Rock Edicts, of which fourteen have been identified to date, ranging from Karnataka to Kandahar in Afghanistan.

Only five of the Ashokan columns carrying the emperor's Pillar

Edicts can be described as complete or nearly so. The remains of another eleven or possibly twelve survive as fragments. These were erected twenty-six years after Ashoka's anointing as bold public statements, no longer tucked away on hillsides or among monastic communities but placed at or near population centres or major thoroughfares, and in many cases beside well-constructed wells where people would gather. PE 7 is the last to go up, dated to the twenty-seventh year after his coronation, and found only on Firoz Shah's Lat.

The largest of these magnificent columns stands 46 feet high and weighs more than 50 tons, with its capital, bell and abacus adding another 6 feet and 3 more tons – major achievements in themselves, requiring not only a school of skilled monumental masons but also equally skilled engineers capable of transporting them across land and water, to say nothing of their erection. Their size must have presented a logistical headache to those charged with transporting them, so it is easy to see why they were confined to the Mauryan heartland, with the Ganges and its tributaries providing the means of transportation. No Ashokan pillars have been found south of Sanchi, although it has been argued that the Amaravati stupa had such a pillar that was destroyed soon after its erection, parts of which were then recycled.[11] They would have been obvious targets for those who considered Buddhism to be heretical or who saw them as manifestations of idolatry, so we can only speculate as to how many such monuments were actually cut from the quarry at Chunar, upstream of Benares, and possibly also from the quarry at Pabhosa, across from Kausambi on the River Jumna.[12]

What is equally remarkable is that Emperor Ashoka's edicts appear out of nowhere, fully formed. The probability is that the first Kharosthi and Brahmi scripts were tried out on palm leaves, perhaps even bits of cloth as Alexander's admiral, the Greek Nearchos, seemed to suggest – probably beginning at Taxila.[13] Taking his cue from the Persian Achaemenids and the Greeks, Ashoka initiated the practice of writing monumental inscriptions on stone, using lettering inspired from outside but locally determined to better convey his own local spoken Magadhan Prakrit, so that these inscriptions should be read throughout his empire and for posterity.

Despite the best efforts of bigots, iconoclasts and the elements, Ashoka's song has survived the vicissitudes of some 2270 years. And yet, for all his brave words and despite all the Buddhist tales about Dharmashoka, the Wheel-turning Monarch, the man himself still remains intangible, more myth than real personage, little known and little valued, a subject seemingly fit only for academics and not the wider world.

This is particularly – especially – the case in India itself. The nation that adores Rama – the mythical warrior-hero of the epic *Ramayana*, who fought the demon king Ravanna before returning to be crowned king of Ayodhya and rule over India for eleven thousand years as the perfect monarch – has little time for the real thing: the man who first forged India into a single nation state, and thus has a real claim to be its founding father; the first Indian ruler with a distinctive, identifiable voice; the pre-Gandhian pioneer of non-violence, the first proponent of conquest by moral force alone, whose words remain absolutely, unequivocally, unique among rulers as a statement of governing principles.

Those stirring sentiments reached and helped shape the culture in the furthest corners of Asia. Yet today in India itself they are shown scant respect – and the monuments upon which they are inscribed receive only cursory protection from the ASI.

Why this indifference? It cannot be put down to ignorance. In 1927, writing from his prison cell to his fourteen-year-old daughter Indira – whom he had also named Priyadarshini in direct homage to the emperor who liked to call himself *Priyadasi*, or 'Beloved-of-the-Gods' – the Harrow-educated secularist Pandit Jawaharlal Nehru put Ashoka on a par with Jesus Christ as a source of inspiration in his non-violent struggle against the British rulers of India. Two decades later, when Nehru became a more modern father of the nation as independent India's first Prime Minister, he selected as the symbols of the new India two images directly linked to Emperor Ashoka: the twenty-four-spoked wheel known as the *chakra*, or 'Wheel of Law', which was set at the centre of the Indian tricolour; and, for its national emblem, the Ashokan capital excavated at Sarnath in 1904–5 showing four lions standing guard over four chakras, representing the 'lion's roar of the Buddha' spreading to the cardinal directions.

These symbols were expressly chosen to represent the new, secular India, free of any specific religious affiliation, as the author and journalist Gita Mehta remembers: 'As children, we were often told by our parents that these 2300-year-old symbols were not mere deference to antiquity; they were to inspire us to create a country governed by righteousness.'[14] There was also the romance associated with the name of Ashoka, a great conqueror who had become a great teacher, as Mehta goes on to explain:

At the very pinnacle of his glory as a conqueror Emperor Ashoka embraced the philosophy of *ahimsa*, 'nonviolence', declaring, 'Instead of the sound of the war drum, the sound of Dharma will be heard.'

Two-and-a-half millennia later, the sound of Dharma would once again be heard when Mahatma Gandhi used nonviolence to expel the British from India. In the newly liberated nation, Ashoka's Dharma Chakra, the Wheel of Law, would be given pride of place in the centre of free India's flag. Ashoka's pillar crowned with four lions facing the four points of the compass and denoting the peaceful coexistence of Dharma would become free India's national symbol – a constant reminder to India of what government should be.

Nehru's choice of two Ashokan symbols was also a very deliberate riposte to the thinking of his great co-liberator, M. K. Gandhi. The Mahatma's vision of a free India was very different from his own, being based on the ideal of *Ram Raj*, of a return to the mythical Hindu golden age of Rama wherein life would revolve around the spinning wheel, the bullock cart and the village well, with local councils of elders and a benevolent but distant government – rooted in tradition but somehow free of caste and gender oppression. To Nehru this was a fantasy. He wanted an India free of the 'communal malaise' that had prevented it from keeping pace with the modern world, which only a strong, secular and centralised government could deliver. In Ashoka's India he found his model.

In the event, Nehru's dilemma and Gandhi's dream ended with the latter's assassination at the hands of a Hindu fundamentalist in the grounds of Birla House, New Delhi, on 30 January 1948. So it came about that in the first, idealistic decades of the secular Indian Republic, 'Ashok' and 'Ashoka' were the buzz words, symbolised by the building in the 1960s of the mammoth four-star hotel in New Delhi known as the Ashok, which became the flagship of a group of government-run hotels scattered across India. A cast was made of the great granite boulder at the foot of the Girnar hill inscribed with Ashoka's fourteen Rock Edicts and a bronze replica placed in the grounds of Jai Singh's Observatory in New Delhi. Ashoka – or, more usually, Ashok – also became a popular boy's name, not because it had Buddhist associations but because it seemed in accordance with the spirit of the times, an India 'without sorrow'. More importantly, India's new constitution, drafted by the Dalit (untouchable caste) Minister of Justice Dr Bhimrao Ramji Ambedkar and made law on 26 November 1949, provided constitutional guarantees for a wide range of civil liberties that included freedom of religion and the outlawing of all forms of caste discrimination.

Sadly for India, this spirit of idealism failed to move the reactionaries – in particular, that noisy minority of sectarians and chauvinists whose rallying-cry was *Hindutva* or 'Hinduness'. To them a good Indian was a Hindu Indian, which was an underhand way of getting at members of India's large Muslim population and, to a lesser degree, its Christians, Parsis – and its increasingly politicised Dalit underclass. Six weeks before his death in December 1956, a disillusioned Dr Ambedkar had organised a mass conversion of himself and many thousands of his followers to Buddhism, arguing that caste discrimination was still entrenched in Indian society and that large numbers of India's Dalits were in fact the descendants of Buddhists who had been driven out of society. These Dalits today constitute a quarter of India's population, and in the last two decades Dalit power has become a political reality, challenging but also threatening the traditional conjoined authority of India's Brahmin and Kshatriya ruling classes.

One of the pillars of the Hindutva movement is its rejection of what its theorists term the 'Aryan Invasion theory' in favour of 'Out of India': the belief that Indian civilisation was rooted in the subcontinent and owed nothing to external influences. That rejection somehow extends to include Buddhism and Emperor Ashoka, portrayed in some circles as un-Indian by virtue of his rejection of Brahmanist religion in favour of Buddhism – this despite the fact that the Dharma he set out on his Rock and Pillar Edicts took as much from Hindu and Jain ethics as it did from Buddhism.

A prominent target of the Hindutvas in the late 1990s was Professor Romila Thapar, whose reading of the early history of India as set down in the national school syllabus was altered in what she saw as an attempt to replace mainstream history with a 'Hindutva version of history'.[15] Thapar's protests led to her being accused of being anti-Hindu and, after she took up an appointment at the US Library of Congress in 2003, of betraying India. There was a double irony here of which Thapar's accusers were probably unaware, in that the emperor she wrote about was himself a victim of Hindutvaism in one of its earliest historical manifestations. Fortunately, it now appears that the tide has turned and that the voices of unreason are no longer finding an audience.

Meanwhile the search for Ashoka continues. Almost every year some new piece of the jigsaw comes to light. In 1982 it was the discovery by Dr P. K. Mishra, superintending archaeologist of the Nagpur Circle of the ASI, of a monastic complex at Deorkothar, close to the highway linking Allahabad to Rewa, that pre-dates the Bharhut and Sanchi stupas. Dr Mishra's later excavations in 1999 and 2000 revealed that two of the stupas had been enclosed by a rudimentary stone railing with the simplest of ornamental designs, perhaps marking the transition from working in wood to stone. In Mishra's view, the outstanding discovery of the dig was the recovery of a colossal polished pillar 'which alludes to the times of Asoka in the 3rd century B.C. having *Chakra* on the abacus'.[16] This pillar lay in more than fifty pieces alongside the railings, which themselves had been broken into smithereens. Everywhere there was evidence of 'systematic annihilation', which Mishra ascribed to the first quarter of the second century BCE.

When pieced together, the pillar fragments were found to carry a six-line inscription in Brahmi of what appears to be a dedication of the pillar to Lord Buddha, placed there not by Ashoka Maurya but by the Buddhist elder Upagupta of Mathura and his followers. If this reading is confirmed – and doubts have been raised as to whether it really is Upagupta's name on the inscription – it would give credence to the *Ashokavadana*'s and Xuanzang's claims that it was Upagupta, patriarch of the Sarvastivada school of Buddhism at the time of Ashoka, who converted the emperor to Buddhism and guided his progress thereafter.

The violent destruction at Deorkothar also gives credence to the claim that it was the Brahman general Pushyamitra Shunga who brought the Mauryan dynasty to a violent end and then set about destroying Buddhist sites – although it has always to be borne in mind that defaced sculptures and smashed columns may equally be the victims of earthquakes and accidental fires – just as Ashokan pillars serving as lingams, Buddhist icons worshipped as Hindu deities, and Buddhist shrines converted into or built over by Hindu temples may in many cases be nothing more than examples of the human propensity to put what is found to best use.

Currently the most exciting work in the field of Ashokan archaeology is coming from northern Orissa and the Langudi Hills, where the ruins of the Great Monastery of Pushpagiri, where Xuanzang spent a year studying and teaching, have been identified. They extend over three adjoining hills. On one there stands a simple brick stupa dated to the third century BCE, encircled by twenty-six railing pillars, plain and simple for the most part. Nearby is a rock-cut elephant very similar in style and dating to that found by Markham Kittoe guarding the Dhauli Rock Edict.

The Langudi rock-cut elephant, similar in design and dating to the Ashokan elephant guarding the Dhauli Rock Edict. This was uncovered during excavations that in 2011 are still ongoing at the site of the Great Monastery of Pushpagiri in ancient Kalinga, visited by the Chinese pilgrim Xuanzang in the seventh century. (Courtesy of the American Committee of South Asian Arts)

In the Cold Weather of 2000–1 a team led by Dr D. R. Pradhan, curator of Orissa State Archaeology, uncovered at Langudi two small stone sculptures. What has so excited students of Indian history is that both of these sculptures carry inscriptions in Brahmi lettering that appear to refer to Ashoka by that name. The smaller of the two is the head and shoulders of a man with long piled-up hair and large earrings. According to Professor B. N. Mukherjee of Calcutta University, the accompanying inscription reads: '*Chhi* [*shri*, honoured] *karena ranja ashokhena*'. The word *karena* can be read as 'bestowal', which suggests that the statue is a portrait of a donor named 'King Ashoka'.

The second sculpture is slightly larger, some twenty inches across, and shows a man seated on a throne flanked by two standing queens or female attendants. He sits with his legs crossed and his hands on his knees, and wears a turban and pendulous earrings, with numerous bangles from his wrists up to his elbows. Here the inscription is a little longer:

ama upaska ashokasa samchiamana agra eka stupa.

This Professor Mukherjee has provisionally translated as:

A lay worshipper Ashoka with religious longing is associated in the construction of a prominent stupa.[17]

The reference to Ashoka as a lay Buddhist would appear to date this image to about 265–263 BCE – about the time of the conquest of Kalinga.

So the story of the Lost Emperor continues to unfold.

16

The Rise and Fall of Ashokadharma

An overlooked detail from the front of the pillar beside the East Gateway at Bharhut. It shows a king bearing a Buddhist relic casket on an elephant. The accompanying donor inscription declares this to be the gift of 'Chapa Devi, wife of Revati Devi of Vidisha', the town close to Sanchi where Ashoka's first wife lived. (Courtesy Benoy K. Behl)

The story of Ashoka begins with his grandfather – and the man who placed him on the throne of Magadha: the Brahman Chanakya, nicknamed Kautilya, the 'crow-like'. Chanakya was a product of Taxila,[1] absorbed into the Achaemenid empire at the time of Cyrus the Great and by the fourth century BCE a centre of learning that drew high-caste youths from all over India – Brahmans to study law, medicine and military science, Kshatriyas the art of warfare. But Taxila was also a crossroads of cultures where men came together to exchange ideas and goods – a crucial factor when considering the influences that shaped the thinking of Chanakya and the early Mauryan rulers.

One of Chanakya's teachers at Taxila may have been the grammarian Panini,[2] who laid down the rules of classical Sanskrit. Yet the sole medium available to Panini and his colleagues in which to set down their thoughts was Aramaic, a poor vehicle for the Prakrit spoken languages of northern India. It forced them to think long and hard as to why they had nothing comparable – or better – but it also required the authority of a ruler strong enough to challenge tradition and willing to listen to good advice.

Chanakya's period of study at Taxila preceded Alexander the Great's arrival by a couple of decades. He then followed the example of Panini in travelling east to Pataliputra and presenting himself to King Dhana Nanda, a bid that failed so disastrously that he had to flee for his life, helped first by Ajivikas and later by Jains who supported him with funds. He then began a search for a candidate 'entitled by birth to be raised to sovereign power', a quest that led him to the boy Chandragupta.

But who was Chandragupta? Was he Dhana Nanda's son by

his equally low-caste queen Mura, grandson of a keeper of peacocks? Or was he a Kshatriya descended from surviving Sakyas who had settled in Champaran in eastern Magadha, famous for its peacocks? Or could he have been the son of the chieftain of a hill-town named Moriyanaga, 'peacock mountain'? The last is the most credible. The Mauryas may well have had a link with peacocks as a tribal totem, but the family most probably had its origins in the mountain region of Mer or Meru on India's north-western border, dominated by the Mer-Koh or Mahabun massif, Alexander's Mount Aornos. It explains why Ashoka's two major Rock Edicts at Shahbazgarhi and Mansehra are sited where they are, as gateways to the Mahabun region. It also means that Chandragupta was one of the Greeks' Assakenoi, the Ashvakan horse-people of the Chandravanshi lunar dynasty who offered their services to Alexander as mercenary cavalrymen.

That Chandragupta was a horseman of the Vaisya caste[3] is supported by the story that his mother placed him in the care of a cattle herdsman, where he was spotted by Chanakya, who set about moulding him very much as the great Aristotle taught the young Alexander of Macedon. It is a remarkable coincidence that two of the ancient world's most powerful men should have received their education at more or less the same time at the hands of two of the ancient world's greatest thinkers. But Alexander soon abandoned his Aristotelian ethics, whereas Chandragupta never shook off his teacher until he abdicated as ruler of Magadha. Chanakya seems to have clung to him like a leech, remaining at his elbow even after Chandragupta had become the most powerful man that India had ever known, providing the guiding hand and the restraining influence that prevented power going to his protégé's head.

All the Indian records agree that Chanakya secured the removal of the last of the Nanda line and replaced him with Chandragupta, the Moon-Protected. The Greeks tell us only that Chandragupta fought his way to power, initially as the leader of a mercenary rebellion against their Greek patrons, but there is no reason to doubt that this was achieved with Chanakya as his strategic advisor. That Chanakya afterwards felt secure enough to write his *Treatise on State Economy* is the best possible proof that this primer grew out of his own experience of grooming Chandragupta and then guiding his ascent – a training that almost certainly began at Chanakya's old alma mater of Taxila.

His training over, the teenage Chandragupta then put Chanakya's teaching into practice, accomplished with such dash that he was soon commanding a band of mercenaries, first offering his services to Bessos, satrap of Bactria, before switching sides to join the advancing Alexander the Great. According to the Greeks, Chandragupta was a stripling when he met Alexander but it is hard to believe that so experienced a warrior could then have been any younger than seventeen, which would put his year of birth at or around 343 BCE, making him thirteen years younger than Alexander.

Alexander knew him as Sisikottos – Sashigupta, the Moon-Protected – Indian mercenary and leader of cavalry. And as Sashigupta, the young Chandragupta played a key role in Alexander's subjugation of Chandragupta's own mountain people, helping the Greeks conquer his former homeland in return for the governorship of Mount Aornos (Mahabun). As Meroes 'the mountain man', Chandragupta further justified Alexander's faith in him by bringing King Poros over to Alexander's side. He stayed his hand until Alexander and his army had moved down the Indus but may well have been implicated in the murder of Alexander's governor Philippos. By the time Eudemos took over, Chandragupta appears to have united the local tribes, forming an alliance with King Parvataka of Himavatkuta, probably Kashmir.

The Greek accounts date their withdrawal as completed in 317 BCE, but the evidence points to the loss of all Greek territory east of the Indus within a year or two of Alexander's death in 323 BCE, at which point Chandragupta can have been no more than twenty-two. With Chanakya as his chario-teer – surely a metaphor for guide and mentor – he attempted a lightning strike against Dhana Nanda and was soundly defeated. Then comes the popular story of the demoralised Chandragupta overhearing a woman admonish her son for eating only the centre of a hot chapatti and throwing away the rest. Whether a chapatti was involved or not, Chandra-gupta and Chanakya abandoned direct confrontation in favour of diplomacy. Virtually all the peoples listed in the *Mudrarakshasa* as joining Chandragupta as his allies – the Yavanas (Greeks), Sacas (Scythians), Cambojans (Kambojans of Gandhara) and Ciratas (Nepalese or Kashmiris) – came from the Indian north-west or beyond, greatly strengthening the case for this being the young man's homeland.

The subsequent defeat of Dhana Nanda left Chandragupta and his principal ally Parvataka as undisputed rulers of north-ern India. Both took daughters of the defeated Nanda king as their trophy wives, only for Parvataka to be poisoned: 'Thereafter the Himalayan chief died', declares *The Lives of the Jain Elders*, 'and the whole empire passed intact to Chandragupta. Thus Chandragupta became king 155 years after the *Mukti* [final liberation] of Sri Mahavira [founder of

Jainism].'⁴ The Jain belief is that Mahavira died in the year 527 BCE but scholarly opinion regards that date as too early by half a century, giving a date of about 322 BCE for Chandragupta's anointing as king of Magadha. He adopted the epithet of *Priyadasi*, or 'Beloved-of-the-Gods', in recognition of the good fortune that had accompanied his rapid rise to power.⁵

Parvataka's death left Chandragupta undisputed master of northern India and with a vast standing army. He absorbed his deceased ally's territories to the north and acquired further kingdoms to the south of the Vindhya mountain range, stopping short of modern Karnataka, the country to which he later retired to die.

For the duration of his twenty-four-year reign Chandragupta's army remained invincible, so that when in 305 BCE Seleukos the Victor, the new ruler of Babylon and Persia, took it into his head to reclaim Alexander's lost Greek territories east of the Indus, Chandragupta repulsed his forces with ease, launching a counter-attack that drove Seleukos back across the Indus and deep into his own lands. Chandragupta was then wise enough to call a halt, no doubt on the advice of Chanakya – who devotes an entire chapter in his *Treatise on State Economy* on how to deal with a powerful enemy and how to respond to overtures of peace. The outcome was an unequal treaty that required Seleukos to give up Gandhara south of the Hindu Kush mountain range, including what is now modern Kabul, Ghazni, Kandahar, Herat and Baluchistan. In return, Chandragupta handed over five hundred war elephants and their drivers; a calculated act of friendship since there is evidence that the gifted pachyderms were past their sell-by date. Even so, their arrival gave Seleukos a decisive advantage in his struggles against his fellow Successors. At least four hundred

Indian elephants took part in the battle of Ipsus in 301 BCE, which resulted in Alexander's empire being carved up between Ptolemy, Lysimachus and Seleukos.[6]

The third element of the peace treaty was the marriage. The most likely arrangement is that the bridegroom was Chandragupta and the bride one of the two daughters of Seleukos by his marriage to the Persian princess at Susa in 322 BCE. These girls would have been of marriageable age in 304 BCE and Chandragupta about forty years old. Whoever was the bridegroom, the offspring of that marriage would have been tainted in Indian eyes. Alexandrian in spirit it may have been but any child would have been regarded as outcaste and ineligible as a royal heir. Yet the subsequent impact of a Graeco-Persian queen and her entourage on Pataliputra must have been considerable.

As a successful raja Chandragupta would already have taken a number of wives, including his first trophy wife, Dhana Nanda's daughter. Only one of these early wives is known by name: his maternal cousin Dhurdara, who bore his son and heir Bindusara, and was the unlucky subject of a bizarre story in the *Great Dynastic Chronicle* in which she unwittingly takes poison while in the the last stages of pregnancy, forcing Chanakya to lop off her head, cut open her womb and keep the embryonic Bindusara wrapped in a succession of freshly slaughtered goats until he is strong enough to survive on his own. Hence the boy becomes known as *Bindusara*, or 'Blood-Spotted'. The essence of the story seems to be that Dhurdara suffered complications at the birth, necessitating a fatal Caesarean with a successful outcome for her child – who may possibly have had some form of skin blemish, so giving rise to his curious name.

The fourth element of the Chandragupta–Seleukos alliance

was the exchange of ambassadors, a policy continued after Chandragupta's death when Seleukos sent his man Deimachos to Chandragupta's son Amitrochates, a rendering of the Sanskrit *Amitraghata*, or 'slayer of enemies' – a title known to have been used by Bindusara. Thanks to Chanakya's *Treatise* and Megasthenes' *India*, we have two perspectives on early Mauryan India. From the *Treatise* we can assume that Chandragupta ruled as a 'Defender of Dharma' – but Dharma in this context meaning the moral foundation underpinning the laws of the universe and the duties of caste. He acknowledged the immutable laws drawn up by Manu the Lawgiver, but applied a penal code drawn up by his ministers, led by Rakshasa Katyayan, the chief minister who gave his name to the verse drama *Mudrarakshasa* that so excited Sir William Jones when he first came across it in the 1780s. Chanakya played a more discreet role as the king's *éminence grise*, but his influence clearly remained paramount.

If Chandragupta or his descendants followed Chanakya's advice to the letter they must have followed a very strict regime indeed. The king would be awoken by music in the early hours for a period of meditation on political matters, followed by consultations with his ministers and spies, then morning prayers. His mornings were divided into four periods devoted in turn to receiving reports, public audiences, the allotment of tasks and to writing letters and receiving reports from his spies; his afternoons given over to inspecting his troops and conferring with his generals; and his evening to prayers before a bath and retirement to his bedchamber.

Megasthenes' *India* describes Mauryan society as rigidly defined by caste, governed by a monarch who brooked no dissent, with widespread respect for the law: 'Truth and virtue they hold in esteem … The simplicity of their laws and their contracts is proved by the fact that they seldom go to law. They have no suits about pledges or deposits, nor do they require either seals or witnesses.'[7] Nevertheless, Chandragupta took no risks, Megasthenes reporting that the king entrusted the care of his person only to women, and changed beds every night for fear of assassination. And whenever Chandragupta left his palace, security was paramount: 'Crowds of women surround him and on the outside are spearmen. The road is marked off with ropes, and it is death for a man or even a woman to pass within the ropes … At his side stand two or three armed women.' Bas-reliefs from Sanchi and elsewhere confirm that women attendants and bodyguards were the norm.

What Megasthenes was better able to observe was the smooth running of an administration run by a cadre of civil officers remarkably similar in their duties and responsibilities to the Indian Civil Service established more than two thousand years later. All were drawn from the Brahman caste, who served as priests but also provided an inner elite of counsellors: 'This class is small in number, but in wisdom and justice excels all the others. From them are chosen their rulers, governors of provinces, deputies, treasurers, generals, admirals, controllers of expenditure, and superintendents of agriculture.' Every city was administered by thirty civil officers, divided into five sections, each with specific responsibilities ranging from taxation to looking after strangers. Similar groups administered the provinces.

Such a sophisticated system of government required an equally sophisticated system of written communications, which meant adopting the unsuitable Aramaic alphabet in the north-western regions before Kharosthi and then Brahmi were devised as a better written medium for Prakrit. Kharosthi probably came into use in about 300 BCE when Ashoka was still a child and Brahmi after he himself had come to power. Chanakya, the spider at the web's centre, was surely involved in the development of this pan-Indian script.

King Chandragupta's achievement was to unite northern and central India under one royal umbrella and a centralised government run by a professional civil service. With law and order came improved communications, better trading links, the growth of urban centres and the development of a monetary economy, all of which helped the mercantile castes to grow and prosper, while reducing the authority of the Brahmans. Silver punch-marked coins had already been circulating in India for more than a century but now a concerted effort was made to standardise coinage throughout the Mauryan empire in terms of weight, shape, material, symbols and the number of punch-marks – usually four or five. Arguments continue to rage among numismatists over which of the symbols found on punch-marked coinage is specifically Mauryan or identifies a particular ruler, but these coins always carried two specific symbols: one representing the sun and the other – a central dot and circle with three arrows radiating outwards interspersed with three hornlike objects, known as the *sadarchakra* – probably representing universal kingship. Two other symbols commonly associated with the early Mauryas are the 'three eggs in a row' and the 'three hills and horned moon', the first made up of three ovals linked by a central band, the second made up of a pyramid formed by three arched mounds with a semi-circle above, almost certainly representing – as James Prinsep first proposed – a Buddhist stupa surmounted by the new moon – *chandra*:

Despite Megasthenes' service as ambassador to the courts of both Chandragupta and Bindusara, nothing survives from *India* on the transition of power. It appears to have been effected smoothly and peacefully, entirely in accordance with Chanakya's advice in his *Treatise on State Economy* that internal strife within a royal family is to be avoided. But, highly unusually, this handover took place while Chandragupta was still alive. The Jain texts all agree that he abdicated to follow the Jain saint Bhadrabahu, who led a migration south following a twelve-year famine in the Magadha country.[8] His death from self-starvation in a cave at Sravana Belgola in Mysore took place twelve years after the death of his guru Bhadrabahu.

Chandragupta's mentor Chanakya cannot have been happy at this turn of events. Yet he evidently transferred his allegiance to Bindusara and went on to act as his advisor until his own death some fifteen years later. Chanakya's grandson and pupil Radhagupta is said to have presided over his cremation, having followed his grandfather to become chief minister at court in succession to Rakshasa Katyayan. This same Radhagupta then appears to have played the key role in helping Ashoka take the throne from his older half-brother. By these means Chanakya continued to shape Mauryan polity long after Chandragupta's departure and his own death.

With the Jains weakened by the migration south, the Brahmans became the dominant power at court, a dominance greatly resented by the oppressed Buddhist community. The tenth-century Indo-Tibetan *Manjusri-mula-tantra*, or 'The Root of the Doctrine of Manjusri', a chronicle masquerading as prophesy after the manner of the *Puranas*, declares that King Bindusara will be a wise and courageous monarch but that 'Canakya, the minister of the king Candagupta and after him his son Bindusara, will depart to hell'. Taranatha's *History of Buddhism in India* takes the same line, attributing to Chanakya demonic powers that he employed to kill the kings and ministers of sixteen major kingdoms, as a result of which he caught a foul disease which 'decomposed his body into pieces.'[9]

The *Puranas* seem undecided as to whether Bindusara reigned for twenty-four or twenty-eight years, presumably due to confusion over when his father abdicated. He justified his title of 'Enemy-Slayer' by extending his father's empire across the Deccan to include the Mysore region – but failed to take the powerful kingdom of Kalinga to the east. These victories would have strengthened the position of Bindusara's Kshatriya army, threatening the supremacy of the Brahmans at court.

Little else is known about Bindusara's rule other than that he maintained links with his western neighbours, favoured the Ajivikas and had a great many queens and concubines, who in turn produced a great many sons: 101 by Buddhist accounts, of whom the oldest was Sumana (Sushima in the Northern tradition) and the youngest Tissa (Vitashoka). According to the Southern tradition, the mother of Bindusara's son Ashoka was Dharma, whose father was an Ajivika elder named Janasana. This would explain why Ashoka was a known patron of the Ajivika sect at least up to his twelfth year as ruler. However, according to the more favoured Northern tradition, Ashoka's mother was Subhadrangi, daughter of a Brahman of Champaran, who also bore his younger brother Tissa/Vitashoka.

There is no mention of further marriage alliances with the Seleucids, but there was a continuing Graeco-Persian presence at court through Ashoka's step-grandmother by marriage. Her brother Antiochos I became ruler of the Seleucid Empire in 281 BCE, which would surely have made her a very powerful presence in the palace until his death in 261 BCE.

It is unlikely that Ashoka was born before 302 BCE, his mother being among the most junior of the royal wives. One popular story has the boy Ashoka winning the affection of his grandfather the king though his intelligence and fighting skills, but then Chandragupta becomes a Jain and throws his sword away, which Ashoka finds and keeps, despite Chandragupta's admonitions. However, it is doubtful that Ashoka could have been known to his grandfather as anything other than a toddler. Since Bindusara patronised the Ajivikas, it is reasonable to suppose that his children were brought up with Ajivika beliefs.[10]

Bindusara's first-born son Sushima was the heir-apparent and treated as such, whereas the boy Ashoka was not only near the bottom of the princely pecking order but suffered from some form of skin condition – 'rough and unpleasant to touch' – that made him so unattractive that his father wanted nothing to do with him. There are no less than three further references to Ashoka's ugliness in the Northern tradition, which accounts for it with a tale about Ashoka meeting the Buddha in a previous life as a little boy and unwittingly offering him some earth. The *Legend of King Ashoka* also tells how the unreformed Wrathful Ashoka burns his entire harem on hearing that they disliked caressing his skin. Some versions of the *Legend of King Ashoka* include an account of the court diviner declaring that Ashoka's body bears certain inauspicious marks, which he tries to remove by performing meritorious deeds.[11] Further supporting evidence for Ashoka's ugliness comes from the panel on Sanchi's South Gateway showing the emperor fainting into the arms of his queens before the Bodhi tree (see illustration, p. 344) Instead of a tall and handsome king, as portrayed by Shah Rukh Khan in the recent Bollywood movie, the artist has shown Ashoka as short, paunchy and with a grossly pumpkin-like face.

This fainting episode is one of several such instances described in Lanka's *Great Dynastic Chronicle*, suggesting either that Ashoka was a highly emotional type or that he suffered from something like epilepsy – the 'falling sickness' of antiquity. All in all, Prince Ashoka appears to have been physically afflicted to a degree that disqualified him as a potential heir to the throne.

Yet even as an unwanted prince Ashoka was educated as a son of the most powerful ruler India had yet known. Everything we know about Ashoka points to the continuing influence of Chanakya through his grandson Radhagupta – and perhaps Kautilya, the 'crow-like', was someone with whom the ugly prince could identify. A point much emphasised by Chanakya in his *Treatise on State Economy* is the importance of associating with learned men, and this Ashoka seems to have taken to heart, for he certainly had powerful friends at court, including Bindusara's chief minister Radhagupta, who appears to have led a conspiracy to exclude the heir-apparent Sushima in favour of Ashoka. Bindusara may have got wind of this, which would explain why at an unreasonably early age Ashoka was despatched to Taxila to put down a local rebellion, although it could be that even in his early teens Ashoka was seen as the most capable of the king's male offspring as well as the most dangerous. After all, his early nickname was *canda*, 'wrathful' or 'storm-like', and this appellation may well have predated Ashoka's supposed cruelties as ruler. Certainly, his very appearance at Taxila seems to have been enough to restore order.

Taxila in 287 BCE or thereabouts was still very much the international crossroads where Greek, Persian and Aramaic were as much spoken as Indian Prakrit. Prince Ashoka was welcomed as the grandson of the local hero Chandragupta, liberator and vanquisher of Seleukos the Victor, and that welcome seems to have left its mark on the teenager. Renewed family ties with leaders of the mountain tribes stood him in good stead a decade later.

Prince Ashoka's reward for the pacification of Taxila was to be sent south as his father's viceroy to Ujjain, the capital of Avanti (today Madhya Pradesh). This continuing exile set Ashoka among Buddhists and it was here that he met Devi, the daughter of a merchant from Vidisha. That she was a *Sakyakumari*, a princess claiming descent from the family of Sakyamuni Buddha, may be a pious fiction, but she was undoubtedly a devout Buddhist. We have the touching evidence of the tapped-out message on the rock shelter at Panguraria that this was a close, loving relationship unlike the usual dynastic arrangement. Devi gave Ashoka his first two children – the boy Mahendra/Mahinda, born in about the year 285 BCE, and the girl Sanghamitta, born about three years later.

Yet Devi failed to convert Ashoka to her faith and he left her and their children in Vidisha when finally recalled to Pataliputra. It would have been unfitting for a prince of the house of Maurya to have a merchant's daughter for a spouse, and a more suitable wife was found for him in Asandhimitra, afterwards his chief queen. She probably came from a little

kingdom in what is now East Haryana north of Delhi, for it
seems more than coincidence that the little town of Assandh
boasts what it claims to be the biggest Ashokan stupa in India,
80 feet high and 250 feet in diameter.

In about the year 274 BCE a second revolt broke out in Taxila
and this time the crown prince was sent to deal with it. It was
more serious than the first and Prince Sushima was forced to
stay on. In the meantime, King Bindusara fell seriously ill and
ordered Sushima's recall, with Ashoka to replace him – whereupon Ashoka's ally at the palace, the minister Radhagupta,
stepped in to suppress the royal order. Ashoka himself bought
time by feigning illness but then confronted his father to
demand that he declare him his temporary regent – an act
so shocking that it brought on an apoplectic fit that killed
Bindusara. Sushima returned to Pataliputra to find his young
half-brother in occupation and the gates defended by Greek
giants – presumably mercenaries with such a fearful reputation
that they inspired terror or even a continuing echo of Sikander,
whose name was still evoked to shush naughty children right
up into the nineteenth century. The continuing presence of
Greek mercenaries in India is exemplified in the Greek warrior
figure uncovered by Cunningham at Bharhut.

The killing of Sushima at Pataliputra's eastern gate was the
first round in a four-year war of succession that the Northern
Buddhists (those following what became the Mahayana school
of Buddhism) afterwards remembered as the dark period of
Ashoka the Wrathful, when all sorts of horrors were perpetrated
in Ashoka's name, including the killing of his ninety-nine
remaining half-brothers and Ashoka's Hell; most likely exag-
gerations of real events embroidered by the writers of the
Legend of King Ashoka to present Ashoka as an evil-doer

transformed by conversion. Yet even the milder *Great Dynastic Chronicle* admits that Ashoka fought his way to the throne and that four years passed before he felt able to proclaim himself ruler of Magadha.

Ashoka then did what the strongest contenders have always done when no social constraints are there to hold them back, which was to eliminate all rivals in the male line, his uterine brother Tissa/Vitashoka being the exception. Only when all threats had been removed did Ashoka feel able to undergo the ceremony of cleansing, anointing and consecration by Brahman priests that made him a king by divine authority. He thereupon took the title *Devanamapriya*, 'Beloved-of-the-Gods', first used by his grandfather and subsequently used by his grandson Dasharatha, and the regnal name of *Priyadasi*, 'beloved-to-behold' – perhaps to make up for his physical shortcomings. His younger brother became vice-regent, a position he abused before being made to see the error of his ways by Ashoka and resigning his office to become a Buddhist hermit – a convoluted story that may be the glossing over of the enforced exile of a beloved but troublesome younger brother.

The consecrated Devanamapriya Priyadasi began his rule in or around 270 BCE by following his father in supporting a large number of Brahmans at court. He patently had no time for the Buddhists at this stage. The Northern tradition speaks of both Ashoka and his queen as heretics who attempted to destroy the Bodhi tree, with Ashoka using his troops to destroy other sites associated with the Buddha. This seems unlikely for a man whose first wife was a Buddhist, but it may represent his indifference to his senior queen's overt hostility towards Buddhism.

Within four or five years of his anointing, Ashoka took the

first steps that would shape the remainder of his life and his rule, and here we should not discount the likelihood that Ashoka, once secured on the throne at Pataliputra, summoned the wife and two children left behind in Vidisha – all three brought up in the Buddhist faith. That his conversion was prompted either by the example of the young novice monk Samudra, who underwent torture at Ashoka's Hell (Northern tradition), or by the little boy-monk Nigrodha, son of the older half-brother he had killed (Southern tradition), can be taken as pious fiction overlying a grain of truth: that Ashoka's authority was restricted by the power of the Brahmans at court and he responded by transferring his patronage to a less threatening group, the Buddhists – as a result of which the latter's influence expanded dramatically by virtue of their access to the king.

The king had at least six named wives, besides concubines, and fathered at least eleven sons and three daughters.[12] Only the *Great Dynastic Chronicle* mentions Ashoka's two eldest children by his first wife, Mahinda and Sanghamitta, but the early dating of its source, the *Dipavamsa*, or 'Island Chronicle', predating all others, and its soundness in other respects, demand that we take it seriously. The Minor Rock Edicts inform us Ashoka became a lay Buddhist in or about 265 BCE, even if by his own confession he did not take this conversion seriously for the first two and a half years. A year or two after their father's nominal commitment to Buddhism, Mahinda and Sanghamitta became fully ordained as initiate monk and nun. The boy would then have been about eleven or twelve and his sister Sanghamitta about eight or nine – although serious doubts remain over Sanghamitta's early commitment, since she apparently went on to marry a husband and bear him a son, both of whom followed her into the Sangha.

In about 263 BCE Ashoka launched his attack on Kalinga, the only significant kingdom within the subcontinent that had resisted his father. With Kalinga's subjugation and the effective subordination of the remaining unconquered territory to the south, Ashoka could now regard himself as ruler of all India, truly an emperor and more powerful than either his father or his grandfather had ever been. A *Pax Ashokanica* then descended on the subcontinent, which enjoyed an unbroken peace for the next three decades. Nothing like it would occur again in India until the *Pax Britannica* of the British Raj.[13]

But as RE 13 at Girnar, Kalsi, Shahbazgarhi, Mansehra and Erragudi proclaims, the brutality of the conquest of Kalinga had a devastating impact both on the people of Kalinga and on Ashoka himself. It may have taken him two or three years to accept this fact and act upon it, but the Kalinga war does indeed seem to have been a tipping point, the decisive factor that turned him from a nominal lay Buddhist into a devout one and a pacifist – a genuine case of the convert finding refuge in the Dharma, as Buddhists like to put it. From this time onwards the emperor directed all his efforts into forging a system of government based on a new morality loosely based on the Buddhist interpretation of Dharma.

This new agenda was only possible because of Kalinga and the terror it inspired. And yet the fact remains that in the process of graduating from king to emperor of all India, Priyadasi ceased to be Ashoka the Wrathful and became Ashoka Dharma, a transformation without precedent and of such breathtaking originality that it was bound to fail.

The first of Emperor Ashoka's public pronouncements went up three years after Kalinga, about 260 BCE, in the form of his Minor Rock Edicts. In them the emperor required it to be known that he was now a committed lay Buddhist, had visited the Sangha and that the gods and men had drawn closer thanks to his endeavours. What these endeavours were he did not spell out, but he desired all his subjects to do the same, and to this end he was making this announcement wherever he went on tour, these words to be inscribed on rocks and pillars wherever available.

We may imagine this royal tour moving across the landscape like an advancing army: the emperor and royal family surrounded by an inner cordon of courtiers, officials, household staff and female bodyguards, with an outer ring made up of thousands of camp-followers and troops; a vast tented camp springing up at each new location, its inhabitants exhausting each region's resources before moving on. Like all good monarchs, Ashoka made himself available to his subjects, but his spoken words can only have been heard by a privileged few. Ashoka wanted them to be heard by all – and for those words to endure. Hence his need for a written language and a medium that would survive.

Ashoka's own spoken tongue of Prakrit, the spoken language of Magadha, was now set down in a newly formalised alphabet designed to give it better expression than Kharosthi. It was still less than perfect, so that when after centuries of oblivion the value of each character was once more understood, the exact meaning of the words they spelled out would remain tantalisingly ambiguous. Yet these words are unmistakably those of an autocrat not quite sure what he is trying to say but determined to say it, dictated to a scribe who dare not question them. They may have come straight from the heart, but they are naive, incoherent and egotistical.

The emperor's early reference to pillars and rocks shows that both were employed from the start, even if only the latter have survived – unless we include another early set of Ashokan edicts: the so-called Schism Edicts. These are undated but the no-nonsense manner in which Ashoka takes it upon himself to tell the Sangha's monks and nuns how to behave, what to wear and what to read makes it plain that he saw himself as head of the Buddhist Church in the manner of Henry VIII in Tudor England. These Schism Edicts provide the earliest documented evidence of the growing divisions within the Buddhist Sangha that would lead to its fragmentation into eighteen different schools and the great divide between the Northern and Southern traditions.

From this point onwards Ashoka's public life became increasingly focused on how to express his Buddhist faith and how best to support the Buddhist Church. The touring he refers to in his Minor Rock Edicts may refer to the first of at least two pilgrimages to the holy places of Buddhism, made under the guidance of a senior elder of the Buddhist Sangha. But which elder? Readers of the *Great Dynastic Chronicle* are left in no doubt that the dominant figure in Ashoka's religious life was the elder Moggaliputta Tissa of the Sthaviravada (later Therevada) school of Buddhism, some of whose ashes were recovered by General Cunningham at Sanchi. However, in the *Legend of King Ashoka* the book's great hero is Upagupta, the dominant figure of the rival Sarvastivadas school of Mathura (later Mahayana). Just to confuse the issue further, the Tibetan historian Taranatha puts forward his candidate: the elder Yashah, abbot of the Kukkutarama, or 'Cock' monastery, outside Pataliputra, also known as the Ashokarama, founded and funded by Ashoka. Yashah is patently not Upagupta, who in the same text has died long before Ashoka is born. Indeed, Upagupta does seem to be the intruder here, resurrected to give greater authority to the Mahayana case. These contradictory accounts point to bitter in-fighting within the Buddhist community as each faction sought to place its dogmas and practices at the heart of the emperor's established church.

It is possible to pick a path through this religious minefield with the help of the Ashokan edicts, the second tranche of which began to appear in about 259 BCE, probably starting in the conquered territories of Kalinga and working north from there – although it remains a mystery why no Rock Edict has ever been found in the Gangetic basin. The best guess is that such edicts did go up in that region, inscribed on pillars rather than rocks, and that none have survived.

The great advance between the Minor Rock Edicts and the Rock Edicts is summed up in the word Dharma. It appears in the first sentence of the first Rock Edict, to be repeated many times thereafter. It had now become the bedrock of Ashoka's political philosophy, and a strategy for the propagation of Dharma had now been worked out, involving the specially created cadre of religious administrators-cum-commissars: the Dharma Mahamatras, charged with spreading the Dharma and promoting the moral welfare of the people.

A new tone can be heard in the Rock Edicts. As the opening phrase of every edict made clear, the emperor is still very much in charge, but he wants people to know how he had changed, and not simply in relation to the remorse he felt about Kalinga. Perhaps for the first time in his life Ashoka has begun to understand the real meaning of humility, to the extent that he feels obliged to tell his subjects of the efforts being made to improve the way state business is transacted and how he himself attends to it. 'Truly I consider the welfare of all to be my duty', he tells his subjects, 'and the root of this is exertion and the prompt despatch of business. There is no better work than promoting the welfare of all the people.'[14]

It was now twelve or thirteen years since his anointing and Emperor Ashoka was approaching his mid-forties. He had committed his government to a revolutionary programme of social and religious reform that struck at the heart of the old order. It had three main goals: non-violence as a means of achieving ends, allowing conquest by Dharma only; freedom of religious expression with respect for the views of others; and the promotion of the 'essentials of all religions' based on proper behaviour, consisting of purity of heart, self-control, firm devotion, respect for each other, generosity, good deeds, gratitude, restraint, impartiality, not injuring or harming others, and forgiving those who do wrong 'where forgiveness is possible'.

This was not Dharma as understood by the Buddhists – or by Brahmans, for that matter. There was no specific reference either to Sakyamuni or to the Sangha as the source of this Dharma. And with good reason, for the Rock Edicts were directed at the entire nation and not exclusively at the Buddhist community, in line with Ashoka's declaration that all men were his children. This would explain why they contain moral rather than religious precepts. The only reference to gods is in Ashoka's own regnal name and title, and the only time he mentions religious ceremonies it is in a distinctly negative context, when in RE 2 he refers to 'vulgar and worthless ceremonies'. Even though Ashoka repeatedly calls for the Brahman caste to be shown respect, that phrase must surely have rankled in Brahmanical circles, for who else could it have been aimed at?

Neither here nor in the later edicts is there any reference to the massive stupa-building programme ascribed to Ashoka in the Southern tradition, said to have been completed within three years. One explanation is that this took place between the cutting of the Rock Edicts in about 259–258 BCE and the erection of the Pillar Edicts in 243–242 BCE. That stupa and monastery building on a subcontinental scale did indeed take place is unquestionable, supported by the remains of hundreds of Buddhist monastic settlements built around stupas scattered across India and extending deep into Afghanistan, as far west as Herat. These ruins show mostly Kushan or Gupta stupas, but in many cases they overlie rudimentary Mauryan structures. There is no denying the existence of a stupa cult within early Buddhism that underwent a dramatic expansion at the time of Ashoka.

Before Ashoka no religious structure had been constructed of anything other than wood and mud and plaster, and now structures of bricks and mortar and stone were springing up all over the land. This sudden transformation of the religious landscape of India must have had a profound impact, for whatever may have been Ashoka's intentions, the message these buildings conveyed was unmistakable. It was not the universal Dharma of the Rock Edicts that was being promoted here, but the Dharma of Buddhism.

Ashoka's stupa cult went hand in hand with Bodhi-tree worship and Wheel of the Moral Law worship. As soon as the first sculptures appear on Buddhist monuments these three symbols are displayed as quintessential icons of the Buddhist faith, all three owing their predominance in Buddhist iconography to Ashoka. Tree worship and the closely allied worship of fertility goddesses had always been an important element of Indian folk religion but was now given new importance thanks to

Emperor Ashoka's increasing fixation on the Bodhi tree at Bodhgaya in the last years of his rule. As for the Wheel of the Moral Law, how was this to be understood by non-Buddhists – as a symbol of the Vedic pan-Indian Dharma or as Sakyamuni Buddha's Dharma? In promoting the one Ashoka was subverting the universality of the other.

Ashoka would have been approaching fifty when he began his stupa-building programme. It drew him into the very heart of the Buddhist Sangha and its elders, and yet the rivalries and discord within and without the Buddhist Church continued to dog his rule. In about 254 BCE a minister was despatched to sort out a dispute between the Buddhists and a sect of naked ascetics known as the Nirgranthas but made matters worse by killing some monks. Ashoka's younger brother Tissa/Vitashoka somehow got caught up in the business and was killed. These events appear to have been the catalyst that led the emperor to summon the entire Buddhist monastic community to his Kukkutarama/Ashokarama monastery outside Pataliputra. According to the Southern tradition, it ended with the expulsion of those who refused to accept the doctrines of the more conservative elders, followed by a great council to codify what the victors of the dispute held to be doctrinally correct, after which a major programme of proselytising was started, with missionaries despatched to every quarter, including Prince Mahinda's mission to Lanka.

The Northern tradition has not a word to say about such a council or missionary programme, suggesting it was they who came off the worst. Since no reference to the Third Buddhist Council can be found in the Ashokan edicts it has been argued that this major event was a Southern fabrication. But there is the striking archaeological evidence of such a council in the

Great Hall of columns discovered in stages by Waddell, Mookerji and Spooner beside the railway line outside Patna City. This unique structure, with its flight of wooden steps and jetty, was purpose-built outside the city as a grand assembly hall, accessible both from Pataliputra and from the surrounding countryside. It could not have housed all the supposed sixty thousand participants of the Third Buddhist Council but would have provided shelter for their representatives.

Equally impressive is the validity of the *Great Dynastic Chronicle*'s tale of the missionaries sent to Lanka, the far corners of India and beyond, for how can one doubt the veracity of the names of the missionaries it lists when the named relics of several of their number were found by Cunningham and Maisey at Sanchi. Indeed, it can be argued that Sanchi hill is a memorial to the spreading of the Dharma, initially by Sakyamuni within India, then under Ashoka to the world beyond

From the time of the Third Buddhist Council onwards the Northern accounts become seriously fractured, in marked contrast to the Lankan *Great Dynastic Chronicle*. For the Northern tradition, what really mattered was demonstrating Emperor Ashoka's subordinate relationship to the Buddhists of Mathura, so he is portrayed prostrating himself before Upagupta, being helped by Upagupta in his stupa building, being led by Upagupta on his pilgrimages, supporting Upagupta's faction through his increasingly generous offerings to the church. This reading is validated to some degree by pillar inscriptions at Lumbini and nearby Nigliva Sagar, and the royal highway of Ashokan pillars in North Bihar. The undoubted portrayals of Ashoka at Sanchi also confirm the emperor's collecting of Buddha relics, his stupa building and his growing devotion to the Bodhi tree, one of the few areas where the two traditions are in agreement.

They also lend some credence to the portrayal of Ashoka in the last phase of his life, given in the *Legend of King Ashoka*, as someone so obsessed with his promotion of the Sangha as to have little time for anything else.

The Pillar Edicts, erected twenty-six years after Ashoka's anointing, provide a counterbalance to the picture promoted in both Buddhist traditions of a ruler utterly devoted to the sponsorship of Buddhism. They show that Emperor Ashoka and his ministers presided over an administration both efficient and benevolent to a degree rarely seen before or since, glimpses of which can be seen in such reforms as the abolition of animal sacrifices, animal fights, hunting and the eating of meat (RE 1); the provision of hospitals, botanical gardens, wells and the planting of shade trees along roads (RE 2); the supply of medical aid to the border areas and among neighbouring countries (RE 2); the institution of five-year touring circuits for religious and administrative officers (RE 3); independent jurisdiction granted to governors regarding law and order, and reforms relating to stays of execution for those sentenced to death (PE 4). If all the reforms listed in the Rock Edicts were fully implemented then it can be argued that Ashokan rule was the first welfare state in history, even if the archaeological supporting evidence to date is slight. Recent surveys of the Sanchi region have uncovered evidence of an extensive dam and irrigation network dating from Mauryan times, and elsewhere Ashokan pillars and wells seem to have gone hand in hand.

That such reforms were carried through is shown by Ashoka's last public statement, as contained in the seventh Pillar Edict statement added to the Firoz Shah's Lat. This is a summation of what Emperor Ashoka had achieved in the thirty-seven years of his reign. It listed the good works that he and his religious officers had carried out in the name of the Dharma and what effect this had had, concluding that what progress had been effected had been achieved by regulations and by persuasion, but chiefly through the latter. However, much as Ashoka's personal devotion to Buddhism had grown, in matters of state he continued to maintain an even hand – 'I have honoured all religions with various honours'[15] (PE 6), and 'My Dharma Mahamatras too are occupied with various good works among the ascetics and householders of all religions' (PE 7) – still promoting a Dharma based on ethics rather than anything that might be described as religious practice. As in the Rock Edicts, it is public and private morality that is being promoted here, not religion or religious practice. In PE 2 Ashoka even asks rhetorically, 'What constitutes Dharma?' and sums it up as 'little evil, much good, kindness, generosity, truthfulness and purity' – to which he adds, from RE 1, 'much self-examination, much respect, much fear (of evil) and much enthusiasm'. Not so much as a word about prayers, offerings, sacrifices, rituals or gods.

The emperor ends PE 7 with closing words that still have the power to stir after so many centuries:

Concerning this, Beloved-of-the-Gods says: Wherever there are stone pillars or stone slabs, there this Dharma edict is to be engraved so that it may long endure. It has been engraved so that it may endure as long as my sons and great-grandsons live and as long as the sun and the moon shine, and so that people may practise it as instructed. For by practising it happiness will be attained in this world and the next. This Dharma edict has been written by me twenty-seven years after my coronation.

These last words were inscribed in or about the year 242 BCE, by which time Emperor Ashoka would be approaching sixty – an old man by the norms of his time.

Ashoka's final years were surrounded by closing darkness and confusion. All the evidence points to the emperor becoming increasingly fervent in his devotion to Buddhism and his support for the Buddhist Sangha, even to the point where it tipped over into religious mania. This overenthusiasm seems to have begun with a growing obsession with the Bodhi tree at Bodhgaya, perhaps arising from guilty feelings over his assault on the tree in the early years of his rein. The Bodhi tree looms large in every account of Ashoka's last years. 'His faith was particularly roused by the Bodhi tree', declares the *Legend of King Ashoka*, which has the emperor declare: 'When I looked at the king of trees, I knew that even now I was looking at the Self-Existent Master.' The *Great Dynastic Chronicle* devotes folios to the process by which Ashoka selected and despatched his cutting from the Bodhi tree for his new ally King Devanama-piyatissa of Lanka, to say nothing of the manner in which the wicked queen Tishyarakshita caused the tree to wither and die – an act, of course, that leaves the newly planted Bodhi tree in Lanka as the sole living representative of Buddha's Enlightenment.

The last phase of Ashoka's life begins with his staging of the *pancavarsika* or 'quinquennial rainy season assembly', which may have had its roots in pre-Buddhist festivals but nevertheless set a pattern for other Buddhist or pro-Buddhist monarchs to follow. More than eight centuries later the Chinese traveller Xuanzang witnessed just such a festival organised by the great monarch Harsha at Prayag (Allahabad), at which he gave away quantities of gold, silver and other gifts to the thousands of priests and monks assembled there, representing all the wealth accumulated over the previous five years. Even by Xuanzang's Buddhist-oriented account, Harsha ensured that all religions were represented and equally treated – whereas it seems that Ashoka's pancavarsika was exclusively for the Buddhists, in that he offers everything from his kingship to his son Kunala to the Sangha.[16]

It is quite possible, of course, that the writer of the *Legend of King Ashoka* and Taranatha in his *History* overegged the Buddhist pudding, but in the absence of any hint of inclusiveness we have to assume that Ashoka acted as the Northern tradition has it. Such blatant favouritism cannot have gone down well with the Brahmans, Jains, Ajivikas and other non-Buddhist sections of the community. This favouring of Buddhism impacted most directly on the orthodox Brahmans because it was chiefly from their ranks that the Buddhist monks were drawn. Sakyamuni Buddha's first disciples were Brahmans and this trend had continued, so that the more Brahmans who converted to Buddhism the weaker their community became. A reaction was inevitable.

Ashoka's first quinquennial festival ended with Ashoka mounting a special platform built round the Bodhi tree in order to bathe it 'with milk scented with sandalwood, saffron, and camphor [poured from] five thousand pitchers of gold, silver, crystal, and cat's eye, filled with different kinds of perfumes' – very much as shown on the outer panel of the bottom architrave on the East Gateway of the Great Stupa at Sanchi (see illustration, p. 345). This event most probably took place in about 240 BCE and, since it was traditionally held every five years, a second such festival would have been scheduled for 235 BCE.

But in 239 BCE Ashoka lost his wife Asandhimitra, the chief queen who had born him his beloved heir-apparent Kunala of the beautiful eyes. Her place was filled four years later – so about 235 BCE – by Tishyarakshita, who in both Northern and Southern traditions is portrayed as a wicked heretic who conspires against Buddhism. Her first act is to cause the Bodhi tree to wither. Her next is more serious, when she sets out to destroy Kunala when he rejects her advances. Her chance comes when Kunala is sent to deal with a rebellion in Taxila and she cures Ashoka's mysterious stomach ailment. She then brings about the blinding of Kunala by the king's supposed order, but is discovered and put to death when Kunala manages to make his way back to Pataliputra to tell his story. Kunala's blinding makes him ineligible to rule and his son Samprati (Sampadin) becomes the heir-apparent.

Much of this story can be dismissed as embroidery.[17] The essential element seems to be that the new queen headed a non-Buddhist faction at court which opposed the Buddhist heir-apparent Kunala and which grew in strength while Kunala was away acting as governor of Taxila. The anti-Buddhists succeeded in blinding Kunala but were subsequently crushed, resulting in the execution of the queen and the break-up of the anti-Buddhist faction. In support of this thesis, Xuanzang provides a detail not found in other versions of the story, which is that having executed his queen, Ashoka 'reproached his ministers and denounced his assistants at court, who were dismissed, or banished, or relegated, or executed, and many powerful and wealthy families were deported to the desert to the north-east of the Snowy Mountains'.

These events may have been contemporaneous with some bizarre happenings at Pataliputra, as the fading emperor sought to stage a second pancavarsika festival, only to be thwarted by his ministers. The *Legend of King Ashoka* more or less sums it up in one paragraph:

Ashoka had already built the 84,000 dharmarajikas [stupas], and had made a donation of 100,000 pieces of gold to each of them. Then, he had given 100,000 thousand to the place of the Buddha's birth, to the Bodhi tree, to the place where he set in motion the Wheel of the Dharma, and to the site of his parinirvana. Then he had held a great quinquennial festival and spent 400,000 on the entertainment of 300,000 monks ... Also, he had offered to the arya sangha ... 400,000 pieces of gold.[18] Thus, his total gift to the Teaching of the Blessed One amounted to 96 *kotis* [1 koti = 10 million]. Presently, however, Ashoka became ill, and thinking that he would soon pass away, he became despondent.

The sick emperor's determination to send yet more gold coins to his Kukkutarama/Ashokarama monastic centre seems to have been the last straw for his ministers. They turned to the new heir-apparent, Prince Samprati, who ordered the state treasury to cease disbursing any more funds to the king's order. This was a blatant act of lese-majesty, a direct challenge to the authority of the emperor amounting to treason. But Ashoka was too weak to respond and no one came to his aid. He had, to all intents, ceased to rule. So Samprati became the de facto ruler of Magadha and the country, backed by Radhagupta and the other ministers – but opposed by the Buddhist Sangha, which had much to lose.

It was against this backdrop of growing dissension that the dying emperor passed his last days, as Xuanzang recounts in the course of describing his visit to the ruins of Ashoka's Kukkutarama monastery: 'When King Aśoka was ill on his deathbed, he knew that he was incurable and he intended to give up his gems and jewels for the performance of good deeds. But his influential ministers had seized power and would not allow him to do what he desired.'[19] There follows the pathetic story of the cherry plum fruit, with Ashoka declaring that he now has sovereign power over just half a fruit and orders it to be offered to the monks of Kukkutarama, where it is mashed and served up as soup. Then in his last moments the emperor presents the whole earth to the Sangha, has this declaration set down in a document, seals it with his teeth and expires.

In all accounts, Ashoka's demise and his subsequent cremation by his ministers is described in the briefest terms and with no protestations of sorrow. In the Northern tradition the minister Radhagupta appears as the key player, resolving the problem of Ashoka's last donation by taking four kotis from the state treasury and presenting them to the Sangha in order to buy back the earth. The ministers then consecrate Samprati as the new king.

There are serious weaknesses in this Northern scenario, such as the continuing presence of Radhagupta, the chief minister, who manages to preside over Ashoka's claiming of the throne as well as his deposition forty-one years later. It is equally hard to believe that Kunala's son Samprati could have played any active part in this deposition since he must have been a minor at the time. What is more credible is the anti-Buddhist faction making some form of reparation to buy off the Buddhists.

However, the most surprising element here is the absolute

silence of the Southern tradition regarding the circumstances surrounding the death of their favourite monarch, the Wheel-turning friend of Lanka who brought the Dharma to their island. The *Island Chronicle*, the *Great Dynastic Chronicle* and *Great Dynastic Chronicle* gloss have absolutely nothing to say on Ashoka's demise or the succession. This silence is deafening. At the very least, it suggests dismay and grave disapproval of whatever did happen, which can only have been a major set-back to the Buddhist cause.

Equally revealing is the disagreement among the *Puranas* over who succeeds Ashoka. The only names which appear twice and in the same order are Dasharatha and Samprati (as Samgata) – and all we know for certain is that Dasharatha was the author of the three Ajivika cave dedications in the Nagarjuni Hills. Perhaps crucially, *The Lives of the Jain Elders* names Samprati as Ashoka's grandson and describes him as a convert to Jainism who ruled from two capitals: Pataliputra and Ujjain.

The best reading of these events is that in 235 BCE the Buddhist crown prince Kunala, having voiced his disapproval of the new queen and her anti-Buddhist faction, was sent away to govern Taxila, leaving his infant son Samprati behind as the usual hostage. In that same year Ashoka began to organise his second quinquennial festival in the face of growing opposition led by his queen with the tacit support of his ministers, increasingly concerned at his draining of the state treasury to support the Buddhists. Fearing for his own future, Prince Kunala made his own bid for power – a rebellion that failed, leading to his blinding and removal from the line of succession in favour of his infant son Samprati, but also to the break-up of the queen's anti-Buddhist faction and her execution. All these events besmirched Ashoka's name as a righteous king of Dharma and were damaging to his son Kunala's reputation as a Buddhist saint and so had to be excised from the Buddhist record. It would explain why in three of the *Puranas* Kunala appears as Ashoka's successor, his length of rule unspecified.

The death of the great emperor was followed by a free-for-all as his sons competed to wrestle his throne from the appointed heir, the minor Samprati. The initial winner was probably Dasharatha, who may have been appointed regent during Samprati's minority, but whose support for the Ajivikas made him unpopular both with the Buddhists and the Brahmans. Dasharatha ruled for eight years at best, at which point a second power struggle ensued, with the Buddhists rallying round Ashoka's chosen heir, the teenage Samprati, who let them down by turning to the Jains, resulting in his being ousted from Pataliputra, possibly by his cousin or nephew Shalishuka, and forced to set up his new capital in Ujjain.

Whether this was part of a Brahman backlash or not, it seems pretty certain that within a decade of Ashoka's death his mighty empire had fragmented into as many as four or five regional kingdoms each ruled by his sons or grandsons, among them Jalauka in Kashmir, who reversed his father's policies in favour of Shaivism and led a successful campaign against the Graeco-Bactrians, themselves seeking to take advantage of the power vacuum in north-west India to reclaim Taxila.

The confusion of Mauryan names continues for some forty years until Shatadhanvan emerges to become what all the *Puranas* agree was the penultimate ruler in the Mauryan dynasty, although his kingship may not have extended beyond the bounds of Magadha. The *Puranas* are equally in agreement that the last Maurya ruler of Magadha was Brihadratha, whose death at the hands of his Shunga general Pushyamitra came in or about the year 183 BCE, fifty years after the death of Ashoka.

Pushyamitra Shunga set out to restore central Brahmanical authority, gaining a reputation as a violent anti-Buddhist by destroying a number of prominent Ashokan Buddhist sites that included the Cock monastery, Deorkothar, Bharhut and Sanchi. However, either he or his immediate successor Agnimitra (c.150–142 BCE), who was viceroy of Vidisha during his father's reign, very soon reversed that policy to become a patron of Buddhism – as were several later Shunga rulers.

But even before the rise of the Shungas, other local kingdoms had used the confusion following Ashoka's death to break away, the most successful of these being the Satavahanas from the country south and west of Kalinga. From about 180 BCE the sixth Satavahana king Satakarni (180–124 BCE) began to push back the Shungas, the Kalingas and the Greeks to establish his dynasty as the supreme power across all central and South India. At least some of the Satavahanas were demonstrably Buddhists or patrons of Buddhism.

It is thanks to the tolerance of some of these Shunga and Satavahana rulers that we have the glories of the Bharhut, Amaravati and Sanchi sculptures. At Bharhut, Ashoka has no overt presence, hardly surprising since it was the founder of the Shunga dynasty who had brought the Mauryan dynasty to a violent end – although the sculpted figure of the king bearing a Buddha relic on an elephant on the front pillar beside the Bharhut stupa railing's East Gateway (see illustration, p. 362) may well be a covert homage to Ashoka.

Sanchi had also been destroyed by a Shunga before being repaired and enlarged under one of his successors, but here the Satavahanas had followed and it was with the blessing of Raja

Satakarni Satavahana that its four magnificent gateways went
up. It is unlikely that those masterpieces were created before
150 BCE, by which time memories of Ashoka would be at
second hand at best, but still fresh enough for his frailties to
be remembered and to show him as he really was: a stumpy,
fat-faced and fragile king with a tendency to faint under stress.
At Amaravati, however, Emperor Ashoka survives not as he
really was but as the idealised Wheel-turning Monarch who
bestows his blessings on the world. Here the fainting monarch
has been transformed into the all-conquering Dharmarajah.

Ashoka transformed. At Sanchi (left) the emperor is shown as
a vulnerable and imperfect human being. Two centuries later
at Amaravati (right) he had become an all but perfect Wheel-
turning Monarch, the embodiment of the Buddhist Dharma on
earth. (Andrew Whittome / British Museum)

Despite the disaster of his last years, the triumph of Ashoka was
that he made the ideal of rule by moral force acceptable, a concept

that still pervades much of Asia. Some would argue that his greatest achievement was that by adopting Buddhism, funding it, helping it through a period of crisis, propagating it throughout the subcontinent and beyond, even reshaping it to some degree, Ashoka transformed a minor sect into a world religion. For the next six to seven centuries Buddhism blossomed in large parts of India, becoming the predominant faith for much of the population. Wherever its monastic centres enjoyed the patronage of local rulers and the support of the trading community, Buddhism more than held its own. It survived the persecutions of the Huna kings and Brahman rulers such as Simhavarma, Trilochana, and Sassanka of Bengal – whose tyranny was ended by Harsha the Great, perhaps the last of the Indian rulers who aspired to emulate Dharmashoka as a Wheel-turning Monarch.

But like the Bodhi tree at Bodhgaya, Buddhism needed new soil to grow, which it found in Lanka, Nepal, Gandhara and north of the Himalayas. It was here that the Ashokan ideal of the Wheel-turning Monarch governing by moral force lived on. In India itself Buddhism surrendered to the fatal embrace of tantrism and was to all intents a spent force by the time Adi Shankaracharya began his *digvijaya* or 'tour of conquest' at the start of the eighth century. It is unlikely that violence against Buddhists was ever part of this great reformer's agenda, really because there was no need for it. Brahmanism had learned much from Buddhism and had itself evolved into the Hinduism we recognise today. Priest-led blood and fire sacrifices had given way to *bhakti*, or personal devotion; the ancient unapproachable gods and goddesses had evolved into the kinder deities, such as Krishna, so beloved of Hindus today; and even the Buddha himself had been brought on board as the ninth (and somewhat unfriendly) avatar of Lord Vishnu, a recognition that Buddhism shared with ancient *Vedanta* the belief that man's ultimate goal is to transcend self and achieve unity with the first principle, whether it be called Brahma or Nirvana. The downside for Buddhism was that in India its holy places were absorbed, its history excised and those who clung to its heresies declared untouchable. For in the wake of Shankaracharya's 'tour of conquest', and in South India in particular, the Brahmin (as we should now call him) himself remained inviolate, as did the curse of caste, which continues to blight India's progress to this day.

In August 2010 a highly unusual bill was placed before the Indian Parliament enabling the formation of Nalanda International University, to be built beside the ruins of ancient Nalanda in Bihar. A consortium involving representatives from India, China, Japan, Singapore and other South and South-East Asian nations is now engaged in raising one billion US dollars to build and run the university, which will be residential like its predecessor and made up of five schools: a School of International Relations and Peace; a School of Languages and Literature; a School of Environmental Studies and Ecology; a School of Business Management and Development; and a School of Buddhist Studies. Pledges of government and international support have been received and plans are now well advanced for building to begin in 2011 and for classes to open in the following year.

The Ashokan ideals, so often trampled on, live on.

Acknowledgements

In researching this book I have sat on the shoulders of giants – generations of scholars of whom only the most prominent have found a mention in my main text. Here my expressions of gratitude must be confined to the living – the many good persons who assisted me, either directly or indirectly, in the research and writing of this book, some in terms of scholarly advice, some in more material ways. Of the former, my first thanks to: the Ven. Shravasti Dhammika, spiritual adviser to the Buddha Dhamma Mandala Society in Singapore, for allowing me to quote extensively from his translation of the Ashokan Edicts (by kind permission of the Buddhist Publications Society); the Ven. P. C. Chandasiri, abbot of the Wat Thai in Vaisali, Bihar, and the Ven. Waskaduwe Mahindawansa Maha Nayaka Thera, abbot of the Rajaguru Sri Subuthu Viharya in Waskaduwa, Sri Lanka, for their hospitality; and the Buddhist Society, London, for its continuing support.

Among academics and scholars abroad my special thanks to: Professor Dr Harry Falk, Institut für Indische Philologie und Kunstgeschichte, Freie Universität, Berlin, for allowing me to quote a number of his translations of Ashokan Edicts – I have also relied heavily on his *Aśokan Sites and Artefacts*; Professor Richard Salomon, Associate Professor of Sanskrit, Dept. of Asian Languages and Literature, University of Washington, for allowing me to quote from an unpublished paper on the Piprahwa inscription – I have also relied heavily on his *Indian Epigraphy*; Professor Sheldon Pollock, Professor of Sanskrit and South Asian Studies, Columbia University, for allowing me to quote from a lecture given at Cambridge in 2010; Dr John Strong, Faculty of Religious Studies, Bates College, for allowing me to quote (by kind permission of Princeton University Press) from his translations of the *Ashokavadana* in his *The Legend of King Asoka*, on which I have drawn heavily; Dr Imtiaz Ahmad, Director of the Khada Baksh Oriental Public Library, Patna, for making available to me the illustrated copy of *Sirat-i Firoz Shahi*; Gita Mehta, for allowing me to quote from an article published in *Tricycle: The Buddhist Review* in 1998; Dr Om Prakash Kejariwal, former Director, Nehru Museum, New Delhi, for advice and suggestions on James Prinsep; Dr G. M. Kapur, Convenor INTACH for West Bengal and Kolkata, for advice on Jones, Prinsep and the Asiatic Society in Calcutta, Raymond Bickson and staff of the Taj Group for their continuing support and hospitality in India; Rohan and Sujata Samarajiva in Colombo and Geoffrey Dobbs in Galle for their support and hospitality in Sri Lanka; Dr Jona Lendering, Vrije Universitat, Amsterdam, author of *Alexander de Grote*, extracts of which she has translated and placed on the website *Livius*; Dr Gautam Sengupta, Director General, Archaeological Survey of India, New Delhi; N. Taher, Supt. Archaeologist, Bhopal Circle, ASI, and staff; A. K. Patel, Supt. Archaeologist, Bhubaneshwar Circle, ASI, and staff; Sanjay Manjul, Supt. Archaeologist, Patna Circle, ASI.

Closer to home, my thanks to: Professor Richard Gombrich, President, Oxford Centre for Buddhist Studies, Oxford, for advice on datings – I have relied most heavily on his *Theravada*

Buddhism among his many published works; Professor Max Deeg, Cardiff School of History, Archaeology and Religion, Cardiff University, for making a number of his papers available to me; Professor Mike Franklin, University of Swansea, for making available to me a paper on Jones – I have also relied heavily on his *Sir William Jones* and other texts; Dr Ann Buddle, National Galleries of Scotland, for making available the papers of the late Dr John Irwin, and for advice and suggestions; Dr Andrew Grout, Centre of Research Collections, Edinburgh University Library, for making available unpublished Prinsep letters; Dr Jennifer Howes, Curator India Office Prints, Drawings and Photographs, APAC, British Library, for tracking down the Jaggayyapeta Chakravartin and for advice on Colin Mackenzie and Amaravati; and her colleague John Falconer, Curator of Photography at the British Library, for his invaluable help and advice; Kathy Lazenblatt, Librarian, Royal Asiatic Society, and Library Assistants Alice McEwan and Helen Porter, for unstinting help extending over many months; Andrew Whittome for his Sanchi photographs.

My thanks for the continuing support of the publishing team at Little, Brown, most particularly Tim Whiting and Iain Hunt; also to my agent Vivien Green at Sheil Land; and to my fellow traveller Liz. A final thanks also to the Society of Authors for the writing award that made it possible for me to stretch my Ashokan travels that little bit further.

A note on bibliography

I have tried to list my main sources in my Notes. For those seeking a full Ashokan bibliography I can do no better than point them to the extensive bibliography given in Harry Falk, *Aśokan Sites and Artefacts*, 2006.

Appendix

The Rock and Pillar Edicts of King Ashoka

Taken from Venerable Shravasti Dhammika's *The Edicts of King Asoka*, 2009

This rendering is based heavily on Amulyachandra Sen's English translation, which includes the original Magadhi and a Sanskrit and English translation of the text. I have also consulted the translations of C. D. Sircar and D. R. Bhandarkar and in parts favoured their interpretations. Any credit this deserves is due entirely to the labours and learning of these scholars. For the complete rendering, including the Minor Rock Edicts, Schism Edicts and others, together with my introduction and notes see http://www.accesstoinsight.org/lib/authors/dhammika/wheel386.html.

Venerable S. Dhammika

The Fourteen Rock Edicts

These fourteen edicts, with minor differences, are found at Girnar, Kalsi, Shahbazgarhi and Mansehra, with fragments at Sopara and Erragudi. This version is from the Girnar Rock Edict. In two other places, Dhauli and Jaugada, they are found minus REs 11, 12 and 13 (see Kalinga Rock Edicts below).

1

Beloved-of-the-Gods, King Piyadasi, has caused this Dharma edict to be written. Here in my domain no living beings are to be slaughtered or offered in sacrifice. Nor should festivals be held, for Beloved-of-the-Gods, King Piyadasi, sees much to object to in such festivals, although there are some festivals that Beloved-of-the-Gods, King Piyadasi, does approve of.

Formerly, in the kitchen of Beloved-of-the-Gods, King Piyadasi, hundreds of thousands of animals were killed every day to make curry. But now with the writing of this Dharma edict only three creatures, two peacocks and a deer, are killed, and the deer not always. And in time, not even these three creatures will be killed.

2

Everywhere within Beloved-of-the-Gods, King Piyadasi's domain, and among the people beyond the borders, the Cholas, the Pandyas, the Satiyaputras, the Keralaputras, as far as Tamraparni and where the Greek king Antiochos rules, and among the kings who are neighbours of Antiochos, everywhere has Beloved-of-the-Gods, King Piyadasi, made provision for two types of medical treatment: medical treatment for humans and medical treatment for animals. Wherever medical herbs suitable for humans or animals are not available, I have had them imported and grown. Wherever medical roots or fruits are not available I have had them imported and grown. Along roads I have had wells dug and trees planted for the benefit of humans and animals.

3

Beloved-of-the-Gods, King Piyadasi, speaks thus: Twelve years after my coronation this has been ordered – Everywhere in my domain the Yuktas, the Rajjukas and the Pradesikas shall go on inspection tours every five years for the purpose of Dharma instruction and also to conduct other business.

Respect for mother and father is good, generosity to friends, acquaintances, relatives, Brahmans and ascetics is good, not killing living beings is good, moderation in spending and moderation in saving is good. The Council shall notify the Yuktas about the observance of these instructions in these very words.

4

In the past, for many hundreds of years, killing or harming living beings and improper behaviour towards relatives, and improper behaviour towards Brahmans and ascetics has increased. But now due to Beloved-of-the-Gods, King Piyadasi's Dharma practice, the sound of the drum has been replaced by the sound of the Dharma. The sighting of heavenly cars, auspicious elephants, bodies of fire and other divine sightings has not happened for many hundreds of years. But now because Beloved-of-the-Gods, King Piyadasi promotes restraint in the killing and harming of living beings, proper behaviour towards relatives, Brahmans and ascetics, and respect for mother, father and elders, such sightings have increased.

These and many other kinds of Dharma practice have been encouraged by Beloved-of-the-Gods, King Piyadasi, and he will continue to promote Dharma practice. And the sons, grandsons and great-grandsons of Beloved-of-the-Gods, King Piyadasi, too will continue to promote Dharma practice until the end of time; living by Dharma and virtue, they will instruct in Dharma. Truly, this is the highest work, to instruct in Dharma. But practising the Dharma cannot be done by one who is devoid of virtue and therefore its promotion and growth is commendable.

This edict has been written so that it may please my successors to devote themselves to promoting these things and not allow them to decline. Beloved-of-the-Gods, King Piyadasi, has had this written twelve years after his coronation.

5

Beloved-of-the-Gods, King Piyadasi, speaks thus: To do good is difficult. One who does good first does something hard to do. I have done many good deeds, and, if my sons, grandsons and their descendants up to the end of the world act in like manner, they too will do much good. But whoever amongst them neglects this, they will do evil. Truly, it is easy to do evil.

In the past there were no Dharma Mahamatras but such officers were appointed by me thirteen years after my coronation. Now they work among all religions for the establishment of Dharma, for the promotion of Dharma, and for the welfare and happiness of all who are devoted to Dharma. They work among the Greeks, the Kambojas, the Gandharas, the Rastrikas, the Pitinikas and other peoples on the western borders. They work among soldiers, chiefs, Brahmans, householders, the poor, the aged and those devoted to Dharma – for their welfare and happiness – so that they may be free from harassment. They (Dharma Mahamatras) work for the proper treatment of prisoners, towards their unfettering, and if the Mahamatras think, 'This one has a family to support,' 'That one has been bewitched,' 'This one is old,' then they work for the release of such prisoners. They work here, in outlying towns, in the women's quarters belonging to my brothers and sisters, and among my other relatives. They are occupied everywhere. These Dharma Mahamatras are occupied in my domain among people devoted to Dharma to determine who is devoted to Dharma, who is established in Dharma, and who is generous.

This Dharma edict has been written on stone so that it might endure long and that my descendants might act in conformity with it.

6

Beloved-of-the-Gods, King Piyadasi, speaks thus: In the past, state business was not transacted nor were reports delivered to the king at all hours. But now I have given this order, that at any time, whether I am eating, in the women's quarters, the bedchamber, the chariot, the palanquin, in the park or wherever, reporters are to be posted with instructions to report to me the affairs of the people so that I might attend to these affairs wherever I am. And whatever I orally order in connection with donations or proclamations, or when urgent business presses itself on the Mahamatras, if disagreement or debate arises in the Council, then it must be reported to me immediately. This is what I have ordered. I am never content with exerting myself or with despatching business. Truly, I consider the welfare of all to be my duty, and the root of this is exertion and the prompt despatch of business. There is no better work than promoting the welfare of all the people and whatever effort I am making is to repay the debt I owe to all beings to assure their happiness in this life, and attain heaven in the next.

Therefore this Dharma edict has been written to last long and that my sons, grandsons and great-grandsons might act in conformity with it for the welfare of the world. However, this is difficult to do without great exertion.

7

Beloved-of-the-Gods, King Piyadasi, desires that all religions should reside everywhere, for all of them desire self-control and purity of heart. But people have various desires and various passions, and they may practise all of what they should or only a part of it. But one who receives great gifts yet is lacking in self-control, purity of heart, gratitude and firm devotion, such a person is mean.

8

In the past kings used to go out on pleasure tours during which there was hunting and other entertainment. But ten years after Beloved-of-the-Gods had been coronated, he went on a tour to Sambodhi and thus instituted Dharma tours. During these tours, the following things took place: visits and gifts to Brahmans and ascetics, visits and gifts of gold to the aged, visits to people in the countryside, instructing them in Dharma, and discussing Dharma with them as is suitable. It is this that delights Beloved-of-the-Gods, King Piyadasi, and is, as it were, another type of revenue.

9

Beloved-of-the-Gods, King Piyadasi, speaks thus: In times of sickness, for the marriage of sons and daughters, at the birth of children, before embarking on a journey, on these and other occasions, people perform various ceremonies. Women in particular perform many vulgar and worthless ceremonies. These types of ceremonies can be performed by all means, but they bear little fruit. What does bear great fruit, however, is the ceremony of the Dharma. This involves proper behaviour towards servants and employees, respect for teachers, restraint towards living beings, and generosity towards ascetics and Brahmans. These and other things constitute the ceremony of the Dharma. Therefore a father, a son, a brother, a master, a friend, a companion, and even a neighbour should say: 'This is good, this is the ceremony that should be performed until its purpose is fulfilled, this I shall do.' Other ceremonies are of doubtful fruit, for they may achieve their purpose, or they may not, and even if they do, it is only in this world. But the ceremony of the Dharma is timeless. Even if it does not achieve its purpose in this world, it produces great merit in the next, whereas if it does achieve its purpose in this world, one gets great merit both here and there through the ceremony of the Dharma.

10

Beloved-of-the-Gods, King Piyadasi, does not consider glory and fame to be of great account unless they are achieved through having my subjects respect Dharma and practise Dharma, both now and in the future. For this alone does Beloved-of-the-Gods, King Piyadasi, desire glory and fame. And whatever effort Beloved-of-the-Gods, King Piyadasi, is making, all of that is only for the welfare of the people in the next world, and that they will have little evil. And being without merit is evil. This is difficult for either a humble person or a great person to do except with great effort, and by giving up other interests. In fact, it may be even more difficult for a great person to do.

11

Beloved-of-the-Gods, King Piyadasi, speaks thus: There is no gift like the gift of the Dharma, no acquaintance like acquaintance with Dharma, no distribution like distribution of Dharma, and no kinship like kinship through Dharma. And it consists of this: proper behaviour towards servants and employees, respect for mother and father, generosity to friends, companions, relations, Brahmans and ascetics, and not killing living beings. Therefore a father, a son, a brother, a master, a friend, a companion or a neighbour should say: 'This is good, this should be done.' One benefits in this world and gains great merit in the next by giving the gift of the Dharma.

12

Beloved-of-the-Gods, King Piyadasi, honours both ascetics and the householders of all religions, and he honours them with gifts and honours of various kinds. But Beloved-of-the-Gods, King Piyadasi, does not value gifts and honours as much as he values this – that there should be growth in the essentials of all religions. Growth in essentials can be done in different ways, but all of them have as their root restraint in speech, that is, not praising one's own religion, or condemning the religion of others without good cause. And if there is cause for criticism, it should be done in a mild way. But it is better to honour other religions for this reason. By so doing, one's own religion benefits, and so do other religions, while doing otherwise harms one's own religion and the religions of others. Whoever praises his own religion, due to excessive devotion, and condemns others with the thought 'Let me glorify my own religion' only harms his own religion. Therefore contact (between religions) is good. One should listen to and respect the doctrines professed by others. Beloved-of-the-Gods, King Piyadasi, desires that all should be well learned in the good doctrines of other religions.

Those who are content with their own religion should be told this: Beloved-of-the-Gods, King Piyadasi, does not value gifts and honours as much as he values that there should be growth in the essentials of all religions. And to this end many are working – Dharma Mahamatras, Mahamatras in charge of the women's quarters, officers in charge of outlying areas, and other such officers. And the fruit of this is that one's own religion grows and the Dharma is illuminated also.

13

Beloved-of-the-Gods, King Piyadasi, conquered the Kalingas eight years after his coronation. One hundred and fifty thousand were deported, one hundred thousand were killed and many more died from other causes. After the Kalingas had been conquered, Beloved-of-the-Gods came to feel a strong inclination towards the Dharma, a love for the Dharma and for instruction in Dharma. Now Beloved-of-the-Gods feels deep remorse for having conquered the Kalingas.

Indeed, Beloved-of-the-Gods is deeply pained by the killing, dying and deportation that take place when an unconquered country is conquered. But Beloved-of-the-Gods is pained even more by this – that Brahmans, ascetics, and householders of different religions who live in those countries, and who are respectful to superiors, to mother and father, to elders, and who behave properly and have strong loyalty towards friends, acquaintances, companions, relatives, servants and employees – that they are injured, killed or separated from their loved ones. Even those who are not affected (by all this) suffer when they see friends, acquaintances, companions and relatives affected. These misfortunes befall all (as a result of war), and this pains Beloved-of-the-Gods.

There is no country, except among the Greeks, where these two groups, Brahmans and ascetics, are not found, and there is no country where people are not devoted to one or another religion. Therefore the killing, death or deportation of a hundredth, or even a thousandth part of those who died during the conquest of Kalinga now pains Beloved-of-the-Gods. Now Beloved-of-the-Gods thinks that even those who do wrong should be forgiven where forgiveness is possible.

Even the forest people, who live in Beloved-of-the-Gods' domain, are entreated and reasoned with to act properly. They are told that despite his remorse Beloved-of-the-Gods has the power to punish them if necessary, so that they should be ashamed of their wrong and not be killed. Truly, Beloved-of-the-Gods desires non-injury, restraint and impartiality to all beings, even where wrong has been done.

Now it is conquest by Dharma that Beloved-of-the-Gods considers to be the best conquest. And it (conquest by Dharma) has been won here, on the borders, even six hundred yojanas away, where the Greek king Antiochos rules, beyond there where the four kings named Ptolemy, Antigonos, Magas and Alexander rule, likewise in the south among the Cholas, the Pandyas, and as far as Tamraparni. Here in the king's domain among the Greeks, the Kambojas, the Nabhakas, the Nabhapamkits, the Bhojas, the Pitinikas, the Andhras and the Palidas, everywhere people are following Beloved-of-the-Gods' instructions in Dharma. Even where Beloved-of-the-Gods' envoys have not been, these people too, having heard of the practice of Dharma and the ordinances and instructions in Dharma given by Beloved-of-the-Gods, are following it and will continue to do so. This conquest has been won everywhere, and it gives great joy – the joy which only conquest by Dharma can give. But even this joy is of little consequence. Beloved-of-the-Gods considers the great fruit to be experienced in the next world to be more important.

I have had this Dharma edict written so that my sons and great-grandsons may not consider making new conquests, or that if military conquests are made, that they be done with forbearance and light punishment, or better still, that they consider making conquest by Dharma only, for that bears fruit in this world and the next. May all their intense devotion be given to this which has a result in this world and the next.

14

Beloved-of-the-Gods, King Piyadasi, has had these Dharma edicts written in brief, in medium length, and in extended form. Not all of them occur everywhere, for my domain is vast, but much has been written, and I will have still more written. And also there are some subjects here that have been spoken of again and again because of their sweetness, and so that the people may act in accordance with them. If some things written are incomplete, this is because of the locality, or in consideration of the object, or due to the fault of the scribe.

The Kalinga Rock Edicts (also known as the Separate Rock Edicts)

These are found only at Dhauli and Jaugada in Orissa, where they replace REs 11, 12 and 13, and in incomplete form at Sannati in Karnataka.

1

Beloved-of-the-Gods says that the Mahamatras of Tosali who are judicial officers in the city are to be told this: I wish to see that everything I consider to be proper is carried out in the right way. And I consider instructing you to be the best way of accomplishing this. I have placed you over many thousands of people that you may win the people's affection.

All men are my children. What I desire for my own children, and I desire their welfare and happiness both in this world and the next, that I desire for all men. You do not understand to what extent I desire this, and if some of you do understand, you do not understand the full extent of my desire.

You must attend to this matter. While being completely law-abiding, some people are imprisoned, treated harshly and even killed without cause so that many people suffer. Therefore your aim should be to act with impartiality. It is because of these things – envy, anger, cruelty, hate, indifference, laziness or tiredness – that such a thing does not happen. Therefore your aim should be: 'May these things not be in me.' And the root of this is non-anger and patience. Those who are bored with the administration of justice will not be promoted; (those who are not) will move upwards and be promoted. Whoever among you understands this should say to his colleagues: 'See that you do your duty properly. Such and such are Beloved-of-the-Gods' instructions.' Great fruit will result from doing your duty, while failing in it will result in gaining neither heaven nor the king's pleasure. Failure in duty on your part will not please me. But done properly, it will win you heaven and you will be discharging your debts to me.

This edict is to be listened to on Tisa day, between Tisa days, and on other suitable occasions, it should be listened to even by a single person. Acting thus, you will be doing your duty.

This edict has been written for the following purpose: that the judicial officers of the city may strive to do their duty and that the people under them might not suffer unjust imprisonment or harsh treatment. To achieve this, I will send out Mahamatras every five years who are not harsh or cruel, but who are merciful and who can ascertain if the judicial officers have understood my purpose and are acting according to my instructions. Similarly, from Ujjayini, the prince will send similar persons with the same purpose without allowing three years to elapse. Likewise from Takhasila [Taxila] also. When these Mahamatras go on tours of inspection each year, then without neglecting their normal duties, they will ascertain if judicial officers are acting according to the king's instructions.

2

Beloved-of-the-Gods speaks thus: This royal order is to be addressed to the Mahamatras at Samapa. I wish to see that everything I consider to be proper is carried out in the right way. And I consider instructing you to be the best way of accomplishing this. All men are my children. What I desire for my own children, and I desire their welfare and happiness both in this world and the next, that I desire for all men.

The people of the unconquered territories beyond the borders might think: 'What is the king's intention towards us?' My only intention is that they live without fear of me, that they may trust me and that I may give them happiness, not sorrow. Furthermore, they should understand that the king will forgive those who can be forgiven, and that he wishes to encourage them to practise Dharma so that they may attain happiness in this world and the next. I am telling you this so that I may discharge the debts I owe, and that in instructing you, that you may know that my vow and my promise will not be broken. Therefore acting in this way, you should perform your duties and assure them (the people beyond the borders) that: 'The king is like a father. He feels towards us as he feels towards himself. We are to him like his own children.'

By instructing you and informing you of my vow and my promise I shall be applying myself in complete fullness to achieving this object. You are able indeed to inspire them with confidence and to secure their welfare and happiness in this world and the next, and by acting thus, you will attain heaven as well as discharge the debts you owe to me. And so that the Mahamatras can devote themselves at all times to inspiring the border areas with confidence and encouraging them to practise Dharma, this edict has been written here.

This edict is to be listened to every four months on Tisa day, between Tisa days, and on other suitable occasions, it should be listened to even by a single person. Acting thus, you will be doing your duty.

The Pillar Edicts

These are the edicts on the stone columns found at Firoz Shah's Lat (originally from Topra), Delhi Ridge (originally from Meerut), Allahabad (originally from Kausambi), Lauriya-Nandangarh, Lauriya-Araraj and Rampurva. Only the first of these carries RE 7. The so-called Queen's Edict found at Allahabad has not been included.

1

Beloved-of-the-Gods speaks thus: This Dharma edict was written twenty-six years after my coronation. Happiness in this world and the next is difficult to obtain without much love for the Dharma, much self-examination, much respect, much fear (of evil), and much enthusiasm. But through my instruction this regard for Dharma and love of Dharma has grown day by day, and will continue to grow. And my officers of high, low and middle rank are practising and conforming to Dharma, and are capable of inspiring others to do the same. Mahamatras in border areas are doing the same. And these are my instructions: to protect with Dharma, to make happiness through Dharma and to guard with Dharma.

2

Beloved-of-the-Gods, King Piyadasi, speaks thus: Dharma is good, but what constitutes Dharma? (It includes) little evil, much good, kindness, generosity, truthfulness and purity. I have given the gift of sight in various ways. To two-footed and four-footed beings, to birds and aquatic animals, I have given various things including the gift of life. And many other good deeds have been done by me.

This Dharma edict has been written that people might follow it and it might endure for a long time. And the one who follows it properly will do something good.

3

Beloved-of-the-Gods, King Piyadasi, speaks thus: People see only their good deeds saying, 'I have done this good deed.' But they do not see their evil deeds saying, 'I have done this evil deed' or 'This is called evil'. But this (tendency) is difficult to see. One should think like this: 'It is these things that lead to evil, to violence, to cruelty, anger, pride and jealousy. Let me not ruin myself with these things.' And further, one should think: 'This leads to happiness in this world and the next.'

4

Beloved-of-the-Gods speaks thus: This Dharma edict was written twenty-six years after my coronation. My Rajjukas are working among the people, among many hundreds of thousands of people. The hearing of petitions and the administration of justice has been left to them so that they can do their duties confidently and fearlessly and so that they can work for the welfare, happiness and benefit of the people in the country. But they should remember what causes happiness and sorrow, and being themselves devoted to Dharma, they should encourage the people in the country (to do the same), that they may attain happiness in this world and the next. These Rajjukas are eager to serve me. They also obey other officers who know my desires, who instruct the Rajjukas so that they can please me. Just as a person feels confident having entrusted his child to an expert nurse thinking, 'The nurse will keep my child well', even so, the Rajjukas have been appointed by me for the welfare and happiness of the people in the country.

The hearing of petitions and the administration of justice have been left to the Rajjukas so that they can do their duties unperturbed, fearlessly and confidently. It is my desire that there should be uniformity in law and uniformity in sentencing. I even go this far, to grant a three-day stay for those in prison who have been tried and sentenced to death. During this time their relatives can make appeals to have the prisoners' lives spared. If there is none to appeal on their behalf, the prisoners can give gifts in order to make merit for the next world, or observe fasts. Indeed, it is my wish that in this way, even if a prisoner's time is limited, he can prepare for the next world, and that people's Dharma practice, self-control and generosity may grow.

5

Beloved-of-the-Gods, King Piyadasi, speaks thus: Twenty-six years after my coronation various animals were declared to be protected – parrots, mainas, *aruna*, ruddy geese, wild ducks, *nandimukhas*, *gelatas*, bats, queen ants, terrapins, boneless fish, *vedareyaka*, *gangapuputaka*, *sankiya* fish, tortoises, porcupines, squirrels, deer, bulls, *okapinda*, wild asses, wild pigeons, domestic pigeons and all four-footed creatures that are neither useful nor edible. Those nanny goats, ewes and sows which are with young or giving milk to their young are protected, and so are young ones less than six months old. Cocks are not to be caponised, husks hiding living beings are not to be burnt and forests are not to be burnt either without reason or to kill creatures. One animal is not to be fed to another. On the three Caturmasis, the three days of Tisa and during the fourteenth and fifteenth of the Uposatha, fish are protected and not to be sold. During these days animals are not to be killed in the elephant reserves or the fish reserves either. On the eighth of every fortnight, on the fourteenth and fifteenth, on Tisa, Punarvasu, the three Caturmasis and other auspicious days, bulls are not to be castrated, billy goats, rams, boars and other animals that are usually castrated are not to be. On Tisa, Punarvasu, Caturmasis and the fortnight of Caturmasis, horses and bullocks are not be branded.

In the twenty-six years since my coronation prisoners have been given amnesty on twenty-five occasions.

6

Beloved-of-the-Gods speaks thus: Twelve years after my coronation I started to have Dharma edicts written for the welfare and happiness of the people, and so that not transgressing them they might grow in the Dharma. Thinking, 'How can the welfare and happiness of the people be secured?' I give attention to my relatives, to those dwelling near and those dwelling far, so I can lead them to happiness and then I act accordingly. I do the same for all groups. I have honoured all religions with various honours. But I consider it best to meet with people personally.

This Dharma edict was written twenty-six years after my coronation.

7

Beloved-of-the-Gods speaks thus: In the past kings desired that the people might grow through the promotion of the Dharma. But despite this, people did not grow through the promotion of the Dharma. Beloved-of-the-Gods, King Piyadasi, said concerning this: 'It occurs to me that in the past kings desired that the people might grow through the promotion of the Dharma. But despite this, people did not grow through the promotion of the Dharma. Now how can the people be encouraged to follow it? How can the people be encouraged to grow through the promotion of the Dharma? How can I elevate them by promoting the Dharma?' Beloved-of-the-Gods, King Piyadasi, further said concerning this: 'It occurs to me that I shall have proclamations on Dharma announced and instruction on Dharma given. When people hear these, they will follow them, elevate themselves and grow considerably through the promotion of the Dharma.' It is for this purpose that proclamations on Dharma have been announced and various instructions on Dharma have been given and that officers who work among many promote and explain them in detail. The Rajjukas who work among hundreds of thousands of people have likewise been ordered: 'In this way and that encourage those who are devoted to Dharma.' Beloved-of-the-Gods speaks thus: 'Having this object in view, I have set up Dharma pillars, appointed Dharma Mahamatras, and announced Dharma proclamations.'

Beloved-of-the-Gods, King Piyadasi, says: Along roads I have had banyan trees planted so that they can give shade to animals and men, and I have had mango groves planted. At intervals of eight *krosas*, I have had wells dug, rest-houses built, and in various places I have had watering-places made for the use of animals and men. But these are but minor achievements. Such things to make the people happy have been done by former kings. I have done these things for this purpose, that the people might practise the Dharma.

Beloved-of-the-Gods, King Piyadasi, speaks thus: My Dharma Mahamatras too are occupied with various good works among the ascetics and householders of all religions. I have ordered that they should be occupied with the affairs of the Sangha. I have also ordered that they should be occupied with the affairs of the Brahmans and the Ajivikas. I have ordered that they be occupied with the Niganthas. In fact, I have ordered that different Mahamatras be occupied with the particular affairs of all different religions. And my Dharma Mahamatras likewise are occupied with these and other religions.

Beloved-of-the-Gods, King Piyadasi, speaks thus: These and other principal officers are occupied with the distribution of gifts, mine as well as those of the queens. In my women's quarters, they organise various charitable activities here and in the provinces. I have also ordered my sons and the sons of other queens to distribute gifts so that noble deeds of Dharma and the practice of Dharma may be promoted. And noble deeds of Dharma and the practice of Dharma consist of having kindness, generosity, truthfulness, purity, gentleness and goodness increase among the people.

Beloved-of-the-Gods, King Piyadasi, speaks thus: Whatever good deeds have been done by me, those the people accept and those they follow. Therefore they have progressed and will continue to progress by being respectful to mother and father, respectful to elders, by courtesy to the aged and proper behaviour towards Brahmans and ascetics, towards the poor and distressed, and even towards servants and employees.

Beloved-of-the-Gods, King Piyadasi, speaks thus: This progress among the people through Dharma has been done by two means, by Dharma regulations and by persuasion. Of these, Dharma regulation is of little effect, while persuasion has much more effect. The Dharma regulations I have given are that various animals must be protected. And I have given many other Dharma regulations also. But it is by persuasion that progress among the people through Dharma has had a greater effect in respect of harmlessness to living beings and non-killing of living beings.

Concerning this, Beloved-of-the-Gods says: Wherever there are stone pillars or stone slabs, there this Dharma edict is to be engraved so that it may long endure. It has been engraved so that it may endure as long as my sons and great-grandsons live and as long as the sun and the moon shine, and so that people may practise it as instructed. For by practising it happiness will be attained in this world and the next.

This Dharma edict has been written by me twenty-seven years after my coronation.

Notes

Prakrit, meaning 'ordinary', is the name given to a group of Indo-Iranian vernacular languages from which both Pali and Sanskrit emerged as 'classical' languages restricted by caste and religion. The dominant form of Prakrit was that spoken across the Gangetic plains centred on the ancient kingdom of Magadha. This became the lingua franca of the subcontinent with regional variations.

Sanskrit is a classical form of Prakrit, its structure probably formalised in the fourth century BCE by the grammarian Panini, who refined the archaic Vedic Sanskrit of an earlier age to make it more cultured. Hindus, Jains and (originally) Buddhists considered Sanskrit to be a language of the gods, and thus a sacred language exclusive to the Brahman priestly caste.

Pali originated as a sophisticated form of Prakrit, probably that spoken by the educated classes in the Magadhan region at the time of Sakyamuni Buddha and his contemporary the Jain teacher Mahavira, so that when the canonical texts of the Buddhists and Jains came to be written down in the first–second century CE they were first set down in Pali. It was most probably formalised at or just before the time of Ashoka, afterwards becoming the sacred language of the Theravada or Southern tradition of Buddhism, centred on the island of Tamraparni, Singhala or Lanka (afterwards Ceylon and now Sri Lanka). Within India, however, Pali was supplanted by Sanskrit as a sacred language, and it was in Sanskrit form that the Buddhist sacred texts were exported into Tibet and along the Silk Road to China and beyond.

The Kharosthi script was developed by the Gandharans in what is today the Afghan–Pakistan border region to write not only their own Gandhari language but Prakrit. It was almost certainly developed and applied before the Brahmi alphabet was invented in India proper, most probably but not verifiably at the time of Ashoka's grandfather Chandragupta. It has obvious links with the Aramaic alphabet that entered the Gandharan region following the Achaemenid conquest but was conceived to better express the sounds of the Prakrit languages.

The Brahmi alphabet has been described as the ancestor of most of the alphabets of South-East Asia. Despite claims that proto-Brahmi writing dating back to the sixth century BCE has been found in the southern Indian state of Tamil Nadu, the general consensus today is that the Brahmi alphabet was formalised at about the time of Emperor Ashoka, possibly from a pre-existing script, but devised to give written expression to Prakrit speech and was intended to be an improvement on the Kharosthi script used in Gandhara and the Upper Punjab. Like Kharosthi, Brahmi is a script in which each letter of the alphabet represents a consonant preceding the vowel 'a', the other vowels being represented through diacritical marks added to the consonants. Its early usage appears to have been restricted initially to royal edicts and royal donors' inscriptions on religious structures.

For the full picture see Professor Richard Salomon's masterly *Indian Epigraphy: A Guide to the Study of Inscriptions in Sanskrit, Prakrit, and the other Indo-Aryan Languages*, 1998.

Preface. The King Without Sorrow

1 Built in the form of a giant chariot drawn by horses, the Surya temple at Konarak was erected by Raja Narasimhadeva in the thirteenth century to mark his victory over the forces of darkness, with the Buddhist elephant represented as a malign beast crushing man in his trunk. Pockets of Buddhism survived in what was then Kalinga and is now Orissa longer than anywhere else in India before its final extinction in the thirteenth century.

2 In his book *Orientalism*, published in 1978, Said argued that these Orientalists were inspired not by the new spirit of enquiry central to the European Enlightenment but by an intellectual imperialism that sought to control and contain subject peoples and to objectify them. Said's *Orientalism* has since been thoroughly discredited. See, for example, Robert Irwin, *The Lust for Knowing: the Orientalists and the Enemies*, 2006, and Ibn Warraq, *Defending the West: a Critique of Edward Said's Orientalism*, 2007. For a wider take on the debate in the Indian context see Sheldon Pollock, *The Language of the Gods in the World of Men: Sanskrit, Culture, and Power in Premodern India*, 2006.

3 Max Deeg, 'From the Iron-Wheel to Bodhisattvahood: Aśoka in Buddhist Culture and Memory', *Aśoka in History and Historical Memory*, Ed. P. Olivelle, 2009.

Chapter 1. The Breaking of Idols

1 Sadr-ud-din Muhammad Hasan Nizami, *Taj-ul-Masr*, in Sir Henry Elliot and John Dowson, *History of India as Told By its Own Historians*, 1867–77, Vol. II.

2 Minkaj-ud-din, *Tabakat-i-Nasiri: a General History of the Muhammadan Dynasties of Asia, including Hindustan; from A.H.194 (810 A.D.) to A.H.658 (1260 A.D.) and the irruption of the infidel Mughals into Islam*, Vol. I, trans. H. G. Raverty, 1880.

3 Sir Henry Elliot and John Dowson, *History of India as Told By its Own Historians*, Vol. II, 1867–77.

4 The last known eyewitness of the fate of Nalanda was a Tibetan monk named Dharmaswamin. Arriving at Nalanda in the year 1235, he found just

one survivor, a ninety-year-old monk named Rahul Sribhandra who was teaching a small class of acolytes from a Sanskrit grammar – the only man-uscript to have survived the great fire. Dharmaswamin stayed on to study, only for the class to break up in panic when it was reported that Turk raiders were heading their way. Dharmaswamin carried his elderly teacher into hiding, and when the two returned to Nalanda they found the rest of the class had fled. Having taught Dharmaswamin all he knew, the aged monk handed him his copy of the Sanskrit grammar and told him to return to Tibet.

5   The first fire was Julius Caesar's accidental burning of the city in the Alexandrian War of 48 BCE. There were then two episodes of anti-pagan pogroms, initiated by the Christian patriarchs Theophilus and his nephew Cyril in about 390 and 410 CE. Finally there was the Arab sack of the city in 642 CE, when the last of the great library's books were used for fuel by the general Amr ibn al-As – supposedly, by order of Caliph Omar on the grounds that if they agreed with the word of God they were superfluous and if they did not they were heretical. The fairest account of the destruction of the Ptolemaic Royal Library at Alexandria is to be found in James Hannan's *Bede's Library*. The Arab sack of the library has been questioned ever since Edward Gibbon, in his *Decline and Fall of the Roman Empire*, heaped all the blame on the thirteenth-century anti-Muslim Christian Bishop Gregory Bar Hebraeus. However, this does not explain how the ear-lier Arab traveller Abd-ul-Latif al-Baghdadi, writing before Hebraeus in 1231, was able to refer in passing to Caliph Omar's ordering of the destruc-tion of the library in his *Account of Egypt*. See also Professor Bernard Lewis's letter 'The Vanished Library' in the *New York Review of Books*, 27 September 1990, where he suggests that this may have been an anti-Shia canard started by Saladin.

Chapter 2. The Golden Column of Firoz Shah

1   The pillar probably came from Kangra in the Western Himalayas. It carries a six-line inscription in Gupta Brahmi stating that it was erected on a moun-tain named Vishnupada by a king named Chandra who conquered Bengal and the Upper Punjab, probably Chandragupta II. It has to be said that this version of events contradicts the popular version in all the guidebooks, which is that Qutb built his mosque over a Hindu temple (quite possible) and around a standing Vishnu pillar (highly unlikely, given his religious orthodoxy). The late John Irwin of the V&A has written extensively and controversially on this subject in such essays as 'Islam and the Cosmic Pillar'.

2   Shams-i Siraj 'Afif, *Tarikh-i Firoz Shahi*, in Sir Henry Elliot and John Dowson, *History of India as Told By Its Own Historians*, 1867–77, Vol. III.

3   *Sirat-i Firoz Shahi*, quoted in Harry Falk, *Aśokan Sites and Artefacts: a Source-Book with Bibliography*, 2006.

4   Quoted by Samuel Purchas, *Hakluytus Posthumus; or, Purchas his pilgrimes*, 1625, ed. W. Foster, 1905–7.

5   As translated by the late Dr S. M. Askari, whose translation of the *Sirat-i-Firoz Shahi*, edited by Dr Ahmad, is to be published shortly.

6   The most complete account of these and other Ashokan columns is given in Harry Falk, *Aśokan Sites and Artefacts*, 2006.

7   Timur, *Malfuzat-I Timuri*, in Sir Henry Elliot and John Dowson, *History of India as Told By Its Own Historians*, 1867–77, Vol. II.

8   William Finch in Samuel Purchas, *Purchas His Pilgrimes*, 1613.

9   Shafaat Ahmad Khan, ed., *John Marshall in India: Notes and Observations in India 1668–1672*, 1927.

10 Sultan Qutb-ud-din Aybak's hammer Muhammad Bakhtiyar in the fourteenth century, the Sharqi rulers of Jaunpur and Sikander Lodi in the fifteenth century, and Emperor Shah Jehan early in the seventeenth century.

11 Jean-Baptiste Tavernier, *Travels in India, translated from the original French of 1676 with a biographical sketch of the author, Notes, Appendices, etc.*, by V. Ball, ed. William Crooke, 2001.

12 The local historian was none other than James Prinsep, writing in his books of sketches *Benares Illustrated*, published in 1833. He was quite unaware that the lat was an Ashokan pillar.

13 H. R. Nevill, *Banaras Gazeteer*, 1909. The *Varanasi Gazeteer* of 1965 gives a very different and wholly unwarranted version of these events, playing down the religious differences between the two communities.

14 Bishop Reginald Heber, *Journey though India, from Calcutta to Bombay with Notes upon Ceylon*, 1828.

15 Padre Marco della Tomba, de Gubernatis, 1878, trans. Hosten 1812, quoted in Harry Falk, *Aśokan Sites and Artefacts*, 2006.

16 M. Noti, *Joseph Tiefenthaler, S.J., A Forgotten Geographer of India*, 1906.

17 For more detail on William Jones's Indian career see Charles Allen, *The Buddha and the Sahibs: the Men who Discovered India's Lost Religion*, 2003; Dr Michael J. Franklin, *Sir William Jones: a Critical Biography*, 1997, and as editor, *The European Discovery of India*, 2007.

18 Sir William Jones, co-founder of the Asiatic Society of Bengal, *Letters*, 1970. See also O. P. Kejariwal, *The Asiatic Society of Bengal and the Discovery of India's Past*, 1988.

Chapter 3. Objects of Enquiry

1   Rudyard Kipling, 'The City of Dreadful Night and Other Places', 1892.

2   James Forbes, *Oriental Memoirs*, 1834.

3   Author unknown, *Calcutta Review*, Vol. VI, 1849.

4 Lord Teignmouth, *Memoirs of the Life, Writings and Correspondence of Sir William Jones*, 1804.

5 Sir William Jones to Charles Wilkins, 22 June 1784, *The Letters of Sir William Jones*, Vol. II, ed. G. Cannon, 1970. My thanks to Dr Michael Franklin for drawing my attention to this and to other aspects of Jones contained in his unpublished paper 'And the Celt Knew the Indian: Sir William Jones 1746–94', read at conference at Cardiff University on 25 May 2010.

6 Sir William Jones, 'Asiatick Orthography', *AR*, Vol. I, 1788; see also Kejariwal.

7 Sir William Jones, 'On the Chronology of the Hindus', *AR*, Vol. II, 1790.

8 Ill-health forced Law to quit India and he eventually settled down to farm near Washington in the United States of America.

9 Law's paper was never published, but is referred to in James Prinsep, 'Further particulars of the Sarun and Tirhut Laths, and account of two Bauddha Inscriptions found, the one at Bakhra, in Tirhut, the other at Sarnath, near Benares', *JASB*, Vol. IV, 1835.

10 John Harington, 'A Description of a Cave near Gaya', *AR*, Vol. I, 1788.

11 John Harrington had a stronger constitution than Law and he stayed on in Bengal, eventually retiring from India in 1822 to become President of the Board of Trade.

12 Robert Montgomery Martin, *The British Colonies: British Possessions in Asia*, Vol. XI, 1854.

13 The unfortunate Polier ran straight into the French Revolution and was stabbed to death by a mob. However, just before he left India in 1788 he sold half of his collection of five hundred Persian, Arabic and Sanskrit MSS to Edward Pote, Resident at Patna, who promptly donated most of them to his alma mater, Eton College.

14 Sir William Jones in a letter to Lieutenant William Steuart, Krishna-nagar, 13 September 1789, *The Letters of Sir William Jones*, Vol. II, ed. G. Cannon, 1970.

15 Sir Charles Ware Mallet, 'Account of Some Ancient Inscriptions at Ellora', *AR*, Vol.V, 1897.

16 Sir William Jones, 'Fourth Anniversary Discourse', delivered 15 February 1787 by the President, *AR*, Vol. II, 1790.

17 Sir William Jones, 'On the Gods of Greece, Italy and India', *AR*, Vol. I, 1788.

18 Henry Colebrooke, 'On the Sanscrit and Pracrit Languages', *AR*, Vol. VII, 1804.

19 Captain Wilford, 'Of the Kings of Magad'ha; their Chronology', *AR*, Vol. IX, 1807.

20 John Harrington, 'Introductory Remarks, Intended to Have Accompanied Captain Mahony's Paper on Ceylon', *AR*, Vol. VII, 1804.

21 William Chambers, 'Some Account of the Sculptures and Ruins at Mavalipuram', *AR*, Vol. I, 1788.

22 Charles Wilkins, 'An Inscription Copied by Mr Wilmot from a Stone at Bood-dha-Gaya', *AR*, Vol. I, 1788.

23 Quoted without source in Theon Wilkinson, *Two Monsoons*, 1976.

24 Jonathan Duncan, 'An Account of the Discovery of Two Urns in the Vicinity of Benares', *AR*, Vol. IV, 1795.

25 This happy phrase comes from one of Jones's successors, George Turnour, in the introduction to his *An Epitome of the History of Ceylon, Compiled from Native Annals: and the First Twenty Chapters of the Mahawanso*, 1836.

Chapter 4. Enter Alexander

1 In chronological order: several chapters in the *Bibliotecha Historica* of the Sicilian-Greek historian Diodoros Siculos, writing at the time of Julius Caesar; *Historiae Alexandri Magni*, written by the gladiator's son Quintus Curtius Rufus (usually referred to as 'Curtius'); *Anabasis* by Lucius Flavius Arrianus Xenophon ('Arrian'); a chapter on Alexander in *Bioi Paralleloi* or 'Parallel Lives' by Lucius Mestrius Plutarchus ('Plutarch'); and *Historiarum Philippicarum* by the fifth-century Roman historian Marcus Junianus Justinus ('Justin'), drawing heavily on an earlier and now lost forty-four-volume work on Macedonian history written by his fellow Roman Trogus Pompeius.

2 Arrian, *Anabasis*. This translation from *The Invasion of India by Alexander the Great, as described by Arrian, Quintus Curtius, Diodorus, Plutarch, and Justin*, trans. by J. W. McCrindle, 1893.

3 Ibid.

4 Quintus Curtius Rufus, *Historiae Alexandri Magni*. This translation from *The Invasion of India by Alexander the Great, as described by Arrian, Quintus Curtius, Diodorus, Plutarch, and Justin*, trans. by J. W. McCrindle, 1893.

5 Plutarch, *Parallel Lives*. This translation from *The Invasion of India by Alexander the Great, as described by Arrian, Quintus Curtius, Diodorus, Plutarch, and Justin*, trans. by J. W. McCrindle, 1893.

6 Arrian, *Anabasis*. This translation from *The Invasion of India by Alexander the Great, as described by Arrian, Quintus Curtius, Diodorus, Plutarch, and Justin*, trans. by J. W. McCrindle, 1893.

7 Arrian, *Anabasis*. This translation from *The Invasion of India by Alexander the Great, as described by Arrian, Quintus Curtius, Diodorus, Plutarch, and Justin*, trans. by J. W. McCrindle, 1893.

8 Junianus Justinus, *Historiarum Philippicarum*. This translation from *Alexander the Great: Selections from Arrian, Diodorus, Plutarch, and Quintus Curtius [Rufus]*, trans. by Pamela Mensch & James Romm, 2005.

9 It was Spitamenes who had delivered the rebel Bessos to Alexander, only to become a rebel in his turn. He had then been murdered by his wife, who had achieved some notoriety among the Macedonians by presenting herself at Alexander's tent with her husband's head.

10 Diodorus Siculos, *Library of World History*, Book XIX.

11 Appian, *History of Rome, The Syrian Wars*.

12 Junianus Justinus, *Historiarum Philippicarum*. This translation from *The Invasion of India by Alexander the Great, as described by Arrian, Quintus Curtius, Diodorus, Plutarch, and Justin*, trans. by J. W. McCrindle, 1893.

13 Plutarch, *Life of Alexander*. This translation from *The Invasion of India by Alexander the Great, as described by Arrian, Quintus Curtius, Diodorus, Plutarch, and Justin*, trans. by J. W. McCrindle, 1893.

14 Athenaios, *Deipnosophists*, quoted by J. W. McCrindle.

15 Junianus Justinus, *Historiarum Philippicarum*. This translation from *The Invasion of India by Alexander the Great, as described by Arrian, Quintus Curtius, Diodorus, Plutarch, and Justin*, trans. by J. W. McCrindle, 1893.

16 Pliny the Elder, *Natural History*, Book VI.

17 Arrian, *Indica*, from *Anabasis of Alexander, together with the Indica*, trans. E. J. Chambers, 1893.

18 Sir William Jones, 'The Tenth Anniversary Discourse, delivered 28 February 1793, by the President, on Asiatick History, Civil and Natural', *AR*, Vol. IV, 1795.

19 Patna is actually 240 miles downstream of Benares and 85 miles upstream of Monghyr, but that tallies almost exactly with Al-Biruni's proportion of 11: 3. Jones was, of course, unaware that Al-Biruni had shown in his *Al-Hind* that Pataliputra was located on the Ganges some 220 miles downstream of Benares and 60 miles upstream of Monghyr – which placed it fair and square at the modern town of Patna.

20 James Rennell's case was set out in the introduction to his *Memoir and Map of Hindoostan*, 1788.

21 Sir William Jones, 'The Tenth Anniversary Discourse, delivered 28 February 1793, by the President, on Asiatick History, Civil and Natural', *AR*, Vol. IV, 1795.

22 Sir William Jones, 'The Tenth Anniversary Discourse, delivered 28 February 1793, by the President, on Asiatick History, Civil and Natural', *AR*, Vol. IV, 1795.

23 Captain Wilford, 'Of the Kings of Magad'ha; their Chronology', *AR*, Vol. IX, 1809.

Chapter 5. Furious Orientalists

1 Sir William Jones to Lord Cornwallis, Lord Teignmouth, *Memoir of the Life, Writings and Correspondence of Sir William Jones*, Vol. II, 1804.

2 Henry Colebrooke in a letter to his father, Sir T. E. Cokebrooke, *The Life of H. T. Colebrooke*, 1873.

3 This information came from Lieutenant M. Kittoe, contained in a letter published in James Prinsep, 'Further Particulars of the Sarun and Tirhut

Laths, and Account of Two Bauddha Inscriptions Found, the One at Bakhra, in Tirhut, the Other at Sarnath, near Benares', *JASB*, Vol. IV, 1835.

4 Henry Colebrooke, 'Translation of One of the Inscriptions on the Pillar at Dehlee, Called the Lāt of Feeroz Shah', *AR*, Vol. VII, 1801.

5 Hugh Murray, 'Conquest of Mysore', *Historical and Descriptive Account of British India*, Vol. II, 1843.

6 Letter to a Mr Ballantyne dated Penag, 24 October 1805, quoted by Robert Chambers, *Biographical Dictionary of Eminent Scotsmen*, 1856.

7 Sir John Malcolm in an obituary published in the *Bombay Courier*, quoted by Chambers.

8 H. H. Wilson, 'An Essay in the Hindu History of Cashmir', *AR*, Vol. XV, 1825.

9 Francis Buchanan, 'On the Religion and Literature of the Burmas', *AR*, Vol. VI, 1800.

10 Buchanan in later years took the name of 'Hamilton', which had the effect of dispersing his achievements under three names: Buchanan, Hamilton and Buchanan-Hamilton.

11 Sir Charles D'Oyly, *Sketches of the New Road in a Journey from Calcutta to Gaya*, 1830.

12 Francis Buchanan, 'Description of the Ruins of Buddha Gaya, by Dr Francis Buchanan Hamilton, Extracted from his Report of the Survey of South Bihar', *Transactions of the Royal Asiatic Society*, Vol II, 1830, and *Journal of Francis Buchanan (afterwards Hamilton) kept during the Survey of the Districts of Patna and Gaya in 1811–12*, Ed. H. V. Jackson, 1925.

13 Montgomery Martin, *The History, Antiquities, Topography and Statistics of Eastern India*, Vol. I, 1838 (compiled from the papers of Francis Buchanan).

14 Colin Mackenzie in a letter to Sir Alexander Johnston in 1817, quoted by H. H. Wilson in his introduction to *A Descriptive Catalogue of the Oriental Manuscripts and other Articles Illustrative of the Literature, History, Statistics, and Antiquities of the South of India; Collected by the Late Lieut.-Col. Colin Mackenzie, Surveyor General of India*, 1828.

15 See Richard Fynes, trans., *The Lives of the Jain Elders*, 1998.

16 The story of Chandragupta's last years as a Jain monk at Sravana Belgola in Mysore was summed up by a later Orientalist, Bernard Lewis Rice, when he came to write the *Gazetteer* of the princely state of Mysore in the 1890s: 'Chandra Gupta continued to minister to the wants of this his guru to the last, and was the only witness of his death. According to tradition, Chandra Gupta survived for twelve years, which he spent in ascetic rites at the same place and died there ... Not only is Bhadrabahu's cave, in which he expired, pointed out on the hill at Sravana Belgola, but the hill itself is called Chandra-giri after Chandra Gupta; while on its summit, surrounded with temples, is the Chandra Gupta *basti* [temple], the oldest there, having its façade minutely sculptured

with ninety scenes from the lives of Bhadabahu and Chandra Gupta. Additional evidence is contained in the ancient rock inscriptions on the hill.' B. Lewis Rice, *Mysore: a Gazetteer Compiled for Government*, Vol. I, 1897.

17   Colin Mackenzie, 'Extracts from a Journal, dated Feb. 24 1797', *AR*, Vol. IX, 1809.

18   Colin Mackenzie, 'The Ruins of Amravutty, Depauldina, and Durnacotta', *Asiatic Journal*, May 1823.

19   Mackenzie Album (WD1061), India Office Library Prints and Drawings, British Library. See also Robert Knox, *Amaravati Sculptures at the British Museum*, 1994.

20   James Burgess, in a brief additional note at the back of *Notes on the Amaravati Stupa*, 1882.

21   The Chakravartin is defined in the Mandhata-avadana and Sudasasana sutra. See also I. Armelin, *Le Roi Détenteur de le Roue Solaire en Révolution (Carkravartin) selon le Brahmanisme et selon le Bouddhisme*, 1975. The Chakravartin king had about him seven treasures: the chakra wheel as the symbol of the Dharma, his queen, his wise councillor, his treasurer, his jewels, his horse and chariot and his elephant.

Chapter 6. The Long Shadow of Horace Hayman Wilson

1   Quoted in R. F. Young and G. P. V. Somaratna, *Vain Debates: the Buddhist-Christian Controversies of Nineteenth-Century Ceylon*, 1996.

2   Sir Alexander Johnston in a letter to the chairman of the Court of Directors of the EICo, dated 13 November 1826, reproduced in Edward Upham, *The Mahavansi, the Raja-Ratnacari and the Raja-vali, forming the Sacred and Historical Books of Ceylon*, 1833.

3   'Remarks furnished by Captain J. J. Chapman of the R.E. upon the Ancient City of Anarajapura or Anaradhepura, and the Hill Temple of Mehentale, in Ceylon', *Transactions of the Royal Asiatic Society*, Vol. III, 1834.

4   James Emerson Tennent, *Ceylon: an Account of the Island*, 1859. Tennent was Turnour's Resident in Ceylon and, by his account, one of the few members of the Ceylon Civil Service who appreciated the nature and immensity of the task he had undertaken.

5   Drawings of Sanchi by John Henry Bagnold, accession nos. 07.001–022, Royal Asiatic Society.

6   Andrew Stirling, *An Account, Geographical, Statistical, and Historical, of Orissa Proper, or Cuttack*, 1822. This was afterwards reprinted under the same title in *AR*, Vol. XV, 1825.

7   A. K. Mitra, 'A Bell-Capital from Bhuvanesvara', *Indian Historical Quarterly*, 5, 1929; and Nirmalkar Basu, 'Some Ancient Remains from Bhubaneswar', *Journal of the Bihar and Orissa Research Society*, 15, 1929.

8   Harry Falk, 'Rajula-Mandagiri', *Aśokan Sites and Artefacts*, 2006.

9   James Tod, 'Major Tod's Account of Greek, Parthian, and Hindu Medals, Found in India', *Transactions of the Royal Asiatic Society*, Vol. I, 1827.

10 James Tod, *Travels in Western India, Embracing a Visit to the Sacred Mounts of the Jains, and the Most Celebrated Shrines of Hindu Faith between Rajpootana and the Indus*, 1839.

11 James Tod, 'Major Tod's Account of Greek, Parthian, and Hindu Medals, Found in India', *Transactions of the Royal Asiatic Society*, Vol. I, 1827.

12 William Wilberforce in the debate that preceded the passing of the India Act of 1813. The same individual is on record as declaring that he held the conversion of India to Christianity to be the 'greatest of all causes, for I really place it before Abolition [of slavery]'.

13 Robert Montgomery Martin, *The British Colonies: British Possessions in Asia*, Vol. XI, 1854.

14 Despatch, 29 September 1830.

15 James Alexander, 'Notice of a Visit to the Cavern Temples of Adjunta in the East-Indies', *Transactions of the Royal Asiatic Society*, Vol. II, 1830.

16 The full background is set out in J. Prinsep, 'Facsimiles of Ancient Inscriptions, lithographed by Jas. Prinsep', *JASB*, Vol. V, 1836. It includes Mr Ralph's account of his first visit to Ajanta with Mr Gresley.

Chapter 7. Prinsep's Ghat

1   A perverse name change since Job Charnock, the founder of modern Calcutta, took the name from the village of Kalighat, the site of a riverine port since the days of the Mauryas and named as such by the Chinese monk Xuanzang in the seventh century.

2   Obituary 'The Late James Princep [*sic*]', *The Friend of India*, 30 July 1840.

3   From a letter quoted by Om Prakash Kejariwal in his introduction to James Prinsep's *Benares Illustrated*, reprinted 1996.

4   James Prinsep, 'Note on the Occurrence of the Bauddha Formula', *JASB*, Vol. IV, 1835.

5   B. H. Hogdson in a letter dated 11 August 1827 to Dr Nathaniel Wallich, quoted in Donald S. Lopez, Jr, 'The Ambivalent Exegete', essay in *The Origins of Himalayan Studies: Brian Houghton Hodgson in Nepal and Darjeeling 1820–1858*, ed. David Waterhouse, 2004.

6   B. H. Hodgson, 'Sketch of Buddhism, derived from the Bauddha Scriptures of Nipal', *Transactions of the Royal Asiatic Society*, Vol. II, 1830.

7   B. H. Hodgson, 'A Dispatch Respecting Caste by a Buddhist', *Transactions of the Royal Asiatic Society*, Vol. III, 1929.

8   B. H. Hodgson, 'Notices on the Languages, Literature, and Religion of the Bauddhas of Nepal and Bhot', *AR*, Vol. XVI, 1828.

9   H. H. Wilson, 'Description of Select Coins from Originals or Drawings in the Possession of the Asiatic Society', *AR*, Vol. XVII, 1832.

10 James Prinsep, 'Editor's Preface', *JASB*, Vol. I, 1832. See also Charles Allen, *The Buddha and the Sahibs*, 2002.

11 Dr H. Falconer, quoted in H. T. Prinsep, 'Memoir of the Author', *Essays on Indian Antiquities by James Prinsep*, 1858.

12 Dr J. G. Gerard, 'Memoir on the Topes and Antiquities of Afghanistan', *JASB*, Vol. III, 1834.

13 C. A. Court, 'Extracts Translated from a Memoir on a Map of Peshawar and the Country Comprised Between the Indus and the Hydaspes', *JASB*, Vol. V, 1836.

14 James Prinsep, 'Additions to Bactrian Numismatics, and Discovery of the Bactrian Alphabet', *JASB*, Vol. VII, 1838.

15 James Prinsep, 'Note on Lieutenant Burnes' Collection of Ancient Coins', *JASB*, Vol. II, 1833. See also Harry Falk, 'The Art of Writing at the Time of the Pillar Edicts of Asoka', *Berliner Indologische Studien*, 7, 1993; Richard Salomon, 'On the Origin of the Early Indian Scripts', *Journal of the American Oriental Society*, 115, 1995; Richard N. Frye, 'The Aramaic Alphabet in the East', *Journal of Inner Asian Art and Archaeology*, 2006.

16 James Prinsep, 'Note on the Coins, found by Captain Cautley, at Behat, near Saharanpur', *JASB*, Vol. III, 1834.

17 James Prinsep, 'On the connection of various ancient Hindu coins with the Grecian or Indo-Scythic series', *JASB*, Vol. IV, 1835.

18 Alexander Cunningham, 'Four Reports made during the years 1862–63–64–65', *ASI Report*, Vol. I, 1871.

19 Ibid.

20 James Prinsep, 'Note on Inscription No. 1 on the Allahabad Column', *JASB*, Vol. III, 1834.

21 Lieutenant T. S. Burt, 'A Description with Drawings of the Ancient Stone Pillar at Allahabad, Called Bhim Sen Gada or Club, with Accompanying Copies of Four Inscriptions Engraven Upon its Surface', *JASB*, Vol. III, 1834.

22 B .H. Hodgson, 'Notice of Some Ancient Inscriptions in the Characters of the Allahabad Column', *JASB*, Vol. III, 1834.

23 James Prinsep, 'Note on the Mathiah Lath Inscription', *JASB*, Vol. III, 1834.

24 B. H. Hodgson, 'Account of a Visit to the Ruins of Simroun, Once the Capital of the Mithila Province', *JASB*, Vol. III, 1834.

25 James Prinsep, 'Further Particulars of the Sarun and Tirhut Laths, and Accounts of Two Bauddha Inscriptions Found', *JASB*, Vol. III, 1834.

26 James Prinsep, 'Second Note on the Bhilsa Inscription', *JASB*, Vol. III, 1834. This incorporated Captain E. Fell's 'Description of an Ancient and Remarkable Monument, near Bhilsa', originally published in the *Calcutta Journal*, 11 July 1819.

27 George Turnour, 'Examination of Some Points of Buddhist Chronology', *JASB*, Vol. V 1836.

28 'Minutes of the Committee of Pares on Mr Turnour's Proposed Publication of the Mahavansi [*sic*]', JASB, Vol. V 1836.

29 George Turnour, *An Epitome of the History of Ceylon, Compiled from Native Annals: and the First Twenty Chapters of the Mahawanso, translated by the Hon. George Turnour, Esq., Ceylon, Civil Service*, 1836.

30 For reasons of greater accuracy this excerpt is not from Turnour's translation but from a later and more accurate version by Wilhelm Geiger, *The Mahavamsa: the Great Chronicle of Lanka*, translated into German and English and published in 1912. Elsewhere Turnour's original translation is given, unless otherwise stated.

31 George Turnour, *An Epitome of the History of Ceylon, Compiled from Native Annals: and the First Twenty Chapters of the Mahawanso*, 1836. This section is missing from the MSS translated by Geiger, which paraphrases this section as follows: 'When Bindusara had fallen sick Asoka left the government of Ujjeni conferred on him by his father, and came to Pupphapura [Pataliputra], and when he had made himself master of the city, after his father's death, he caused his eldest brother to be put to death and took on himself the sovereignty in the splendid city.'

32 Wilhelm Geiger, *The Mahavamsa: the Great Chronicle of Lanka*, 1912.

33 Ibid.

34 Ibid.

35 George Turnour, *An Epitome of the History of Ceylon, Compiled from Native Annals: and the First Twenty Chapters of the Mahawanso, translated by the Hon. George Turnour, Esq., Ceylon, Civil Service*, 1836.

36 Wilhelm Geiger. The excerpt is from Ch. XXII. Turnour's translation ended at Ch. XX.

Chapter 8. Thus Spake King Piyadasi

1 That same year saw the publication in France of *Foé Koué Ki*, subtitled *Relations des Royaumes Bouddhiques: voyage dans la Tarsarie, dans l'Afghanistan et dans l'Inde, exécuté, à la fin du IVe siècle, par Chy Fa Hian*. This was a posthumous work by the French sinologist, Jean-Pierre Abel-Rémusat, completed by his colleagues Jules von Klaproth and Jean-Pierre Landresse. It was the first translation outside China of an account by a Chinese Buddhist monk named Faxian of his pilgrimage across India at the start of the fifth century CE.

2 According to the Society's records, Stuart had in 1813 donated 'two slabs with inscriptions from Bhubaneshwar in Orissa'.

3 The remaining statues purloined by Stuart were auctioned by Christie's and are now in the British Museum.

4 Markham Kittoe's report is contained in James Prinsep, 'Examination of the Separate Edicts of the Aswastama Inscription at Dhauli in Cuttack', *JASB*, Vol. VII, 1838.

5 The 'passive resistance' of the Oriya peoples of Orissa that irritated Markham Kittoe in the 1830s so unnerved the Armenian archaeologist Joseph Beglar in the 1870s that he devoted pages of an archaeological report to a denunciation of the Oriyas for their 'stolid bigotry' and 'vengeful disposition'. See J. D. M. Beglar, 'Report of Tours in the South-Eastern Provinces in 1874–75 and 1875–76', *ASI Report*, Vol. XIII, 1882.

6 'Son of Drona', but in this context probably meaning 'lower mountaintop'.

7 J. Prinsep, 'Note on the Facsimiles of Inscriptions from Sanchi near Bhilsa, taken by Captain Ed. Smith, and on the Drawings of the Buddhist Monument, presented by Captain W. Murray', *JASB*, Vol. VI, 1837.

8 J. Prinsep, 'The Legends of the Saurashtra Group of Coins Deciphered', *JRAS*, VI. 1837.

9 The word that Prinsep translated as 'anointment' was *abisitena*, corresponding to the Sanskrit term *abhisheka* used to describe the ancient Vedic rite of anointing rulers, corresponding to the Western term 'coronation', which in its strictest sense implies the crowning of a monarch. The earliest representations of rulers in India show them wearing ornate turbans but without any auspicious *tilak* mark on their foreheads, so there is no reason to object to the use of the word 'coronation' in this context, as used above and in several other modern renderings of the Ashokan edicts.

10 Romila Thapar, *Aśoka and the Decline of the Mauryas*, 1973.

11 Ven. S. Dhammika, *The Edicts of King Asoka*, 2009. This translation, which draws on the earlier translations of Amulyachandra Sen, C. D. Sirkar and D. K. Bhandarkar, can be seen in full on http://www.accesstoinsight.org/lib/authors/dhammika/wheel386.html.

12 James Prinsep, 'Interpretation of the Most Ancient of the Inscriptions on the Pillar called the Lat of Firuz Shah, near Delhi, and of the Allahabad, Radhia and Mattia Pillar or Lat Inscriptions which agree herewith', *JASB*, Vol. VI, 1837.

13 George Turnour's letter is quoted in James Prinsep, 'Further Elucidation of the Lat or Silasthambha Inscriptions from Various Sources', *JASB*, Vol. VI, 1837.

14 Turnour afterwards wrote again to say that he had since found other texts which confirmed that 'Piyadaso, Piyadasino or Piyadasi ... was the name of Dharmashoka before he usurped the Indian empire; and it is of this monarch that the amplest details are given in the Pali annals.' See George Turnour, 'Further Notes on the Inscriptions on the Columns at Delhi, Allahabad, Betiah, etc', *JASB*, Vol. VI, 1837.

15 James Prinsep, 'Facsimiles of Ancient Inscriptions', *JASB*, Vol. VI, 1837.

16 James Prinsep, 'Discovery of the Name of Antiochus the Great, in Two of the Edicts of Asoka King of India', *JASB*, Vol. VII, 1838. Although published in the February issue, the discovery had been made late in 1837 following the despatch of Kittoe's new facsimile of the Dhauli inscription.

17 Markham Kittoe, 'Mr Kittoe's Journal of his Tour in the Province of Orissa', *JASB*, Vol. VII, 1838.

18 James Prinsep, 'Discovery of the Name of Antiochus the Great, in Two of the Edicts of Asoka King of India', *JASB*, Vol. VII, 1838. Although published in the February issue, the discovery had been made late in 1837 following the despatch of Kittoe's new facsimile of the Dhauli inscription.

19 James Prinsep, 'On the Edicts of Piyadasi, or Asoka, the Buddhist Monarch of India, Preserved on the Girnar Rock in the Gujerat Peninsula, and on the Dhauli Rock in Cuttack, with the Discovery of Ptolemy's Name therein', *JASB*, Vol. VII, 1838.

20 Ven. S. Dhammika, *The Edicts of King Asoka*, 2009.

21 Ibid.

22 Prinsep's summary is quoted in Alexander Cunningham, *Inscriptions of Aśoka*, 1877.

23 James Prinsep, 'Discovery of the Name of Antiochus the Great, in Two of the Edicts of Asoka, King of India', *JASB*, Vol. VII,1838.

24 Ven. S. Dhammika, *The Edicts of King Asoka*, 2009.

25 George Turnour, *JASB*, Vol. VII, 1838.

Chapter 9. Brian Hodgson's Gift

1 Undated letter from his biographer W. W. Hunter quoted in David Waterhouse, Ed. *The Origins of Himalayan Studies: Brian Houghton Hodgson in Nepal and Darjeeling 1820–1858*, 2004.

2 B. H. Hodgson in a letter to W. W. Hunter, dated 1 November 1867, quoted in David Waterhouse, ed. *The Origins of Himalayan Studies: Brian Houghton Hodgson in Nepal and Darjeeling 1820–1858*, 2004.

3 Except up in India's north-west borders and beyond where, as James Prinsep had discovered, a local 'Bactrian' was spoken and written, better known today as Kharosthi.

4 John S. Strong, *The Legend of King Aśoka: a Study and Translation of the Aśokavadana*, 1983.

5 V. P. Vasiliev, Introduction to the Russian translation of Taranatha's *History of Buddhism in India*, 1869.

6 The *Avadana-Kalpalata* and *Magadhai-pandita sa-dban-bzan-po*, the last being the work of a Pandit Ksemendrabhadra of Magadha.

7 Lama Chimpa and Alaka Chattopadhyaya, *Taranatha's History of Buddhism in India*, 1970.

8   There was a dynasty of Candra kings who ruled in Arakan and the eastern fringes of Bengal from about 350 CE to 600 CE. The later Candras were Buddhists with close ties to Lanka, so it is possible that Taranatha heard of them and muddled them up with Ashoka's family.

9   The full title is *Foé Koué Ki, ou Relations des Royaumes Bouddhiques: voyage dans la Tarsarie, dans l'Afghanistan et dans l'Inde, exécuté, à la fin du IVe siècle, par Chy Fa Hian, traduit du chinois et commenté par Abel Rémusat. Ouvrage Posthume. Revu, complété et augmenté d'éclaircissements nouveaux par MM. Klaproth et Landresse*, 1836.

10 This was afterwards followed by a more complete translation by Julien of Xuanzang's travels under the title of *Memoires sur les Contrées Occidental, traduits du Sanscrit en Chinois en l'an 648, par Hiouen-tsang*, published in two volumes in 1857 and 1858.

Chapter 10. Records of the Western Regions

1   The full story is told in Sun Shuyun, *Ten Thousand Miles Without a Cloud*, 2004.

2   James Legge, *A Record of Buddhistic Kingdoms; being an Account by the Chinese Monk Fa-Hien of his Travels in India and Ceylon (AD 399–414) in Search of the Buddhist Books of Discipline*, 1886.

3   For a full account of Ashoka in China see Max Deeg, 'From the Iron-Wheel to Bodhisattvahood: Aśoka in Buddhist Culture and Memory', *Aśoka in History and Historical Memory*, ed. P. Olivelle, 2009; 'Mapping Common Territory – Mapping Other Territory', *Acta Orientalia Vilnensia*, Vol. VIII, Issue 1, 2007; and 'Writing for the Emperor: Xuanzang between Pietry, Religious Propaganda, Intelligence, and Modern Imagination', *Indica et Tibetica*, Vol. 52, 2009.

4   The vigilant reader will have spotted that I have taken a liberty here. Legge, writing after Ashoka's identity had become known in the West, speaks of Aśoka rather than Wuyou Wang, as do later translators of Xuanzang. But to do so here would be out of context – and it spoils the story!

5   James Legge, *A Record of Buddhistic Kingdoms, being an Account by the Chinese Monk Fa-Hien of Travels in India and Ceylon (AD 399–414) in Search of the Buddhist Books of Discipline*, 1886.

6   Max Deeg, 'From the Iron-Wheel to Bodhisattvahood: Aśoka in Buddhist Culture and Memory', *Aśoka in History and Historical Memory*, ed. P. Olivelle, 2009.

7   Xuanzang, *Datang Xiguo-ji, The Geat Tang Dynasty Record of the Western Regions*, trans. Li Rongxi, 1996.

8   Again I have taken the liberty of preserving the Chinese original, with apologies to the translator, Li Rongxi.

9 Beginning with *Examen critique de quelques pages de Chinois relative à l'Inde, traduites couple MG Pauthier, accompagné de discussions grammaticales sur certain rules de position qui, a Chinois, jouent le même role que les inflexions dans les autres langues, par M. Stanislas Julien,* 1841.

10 Alexander Cunningham, 'An Account of the Discovery of the Ruins of the Buddhist City of Samkassa – by Lieut. Alexander Cunningham of the Bengal Engineers, in a letter to Colonel Sykes', *JRAS*, Vol. VII, 1843.

11 Alexander Cunningham, 'Proposed Archaeological Excavation', *JASB*, Vol. XVII, 1848.

12 Markham Kittoe, 'Note on the Inscription found near Bhabra', *JRAS*, Vol. IX, 1840.

13 M. E. Burnouf, *Le Lotus de la Bonne Loi*, 1852.

14 It was subsequently published in Calcutta in 1848 under the title of *The Pilgrimage of Fa Hian*.

15 Markham Kittoe in a letter to Cunningham quoted in *The Bhilsa Topes*, 1853.

Chapter 11. Alexander Cunningham the Great

1 Edwin Norris, 'On the Kapur-di-Giri Rock Inscription', *JRAS*, Vol. VIII, 1846, and Charles Masson, 'Narrative of an Excursion from Peshawar to Shah-baz-Ghari', *JRAS*, Vol. VIII, 1846.

2 Ibid.

3 Edwin Norris, 'On the Kapur-di-Giri Rock Inscription', *JRAS*, Vol. VIII, 1846.

4 The story of Lumsden and the Corps of Guides is told in Charles Allen, *Soldier Sahibs: the Men who Made the North-West Frontier*, 2001.

5 Alexander Cunningham, *Inscriptions of Aśoka*, 1877.

6 The story of the 'Hindustani fanatics' is told in Charles Allen, *God's Terrorists: the Wahhabi Cult and the Roots of Modern Jihad*, 2004.

7 James Abbott, 'Gradus ad Aornon', *JRAS*, Vol. XIX, 1856.

8 Abbott's thesis was afterwards taken apart by Aurel Stein in 1905, after the latter became the first European to examine the Mahabun massif from an archaeological point of view, albeit hurriedly and under tribal escort. Stein's view was that the real Aornos lay further north. Stein, *Report of Archaeological Survey Work in the North-West Frontier Provinces and Baluchistan for the period from January 2nd 1904 to March 31st 1905*, 1905.

9 The story of Abbott and Bellew is told in Charles Allen, *Soldier Sahibs: the Men who Made the North-West Frontier*, 2001.

10 Dr Henry Bellew, *A General Report on the Yusufzais*, 1864.

11 Alexander Cunningham, *The Bhilsa Topes*, 1854.

12 John Marshall translates this as 'Ananda, son of Vasithi, foreman of the artisans of Raja Siri Satakarni', John Marshall, *A Guide to Sanchi*, 1918.

13 Alexander Cunningham, *The Bhilsa Topes*, 1854.

14 James Mill, *History of British India*, 1818.

Chapter 12. Sir Alexander in Excelsis

1 Thomas Watters, *On Yuan Chwang's Travels in India* AD *629–645*, 1904.

2 Alexander Cunningham, 'A-yu-to, or Ayodhya', *ASI Report*, Vol. I, 1871. See also Harry Falk, *Aśokan Sites and Artefacts*, 2006.

3 Alexander Cunningham, 'Four Reports Made During the Years 1862–63–64–65', *ASI Report*, Vol. I,1871.

4 Alexander Cunningham, *Mahabodhi or the Great Buddhist Temple under the Bodhi Tree at Buddha-gaya*, 1892.

5 Xuanzang quoted in Thomas Watters, *On Yuan Chwang's Travels in India* AD *629–645*, 1904.

6 Alexander Cunningham, 'Four Reports Made During the Years 1862–63–64–65', *ASI Report*, Vol. I, 1871.

7 Sakyamuni's mother Mayadevi had dreamed of a white elephant implanted in her womb and the elephant was thereafter regarded as the vehicle of the *chakravarti*, or universal monarch, a position that Buddhists claimed for Sakyamuni and which Ashoka may even have claimed for himself.

8 Ven. S. Dhammika, 'The Edicts of King Asoka', *Access to Insight*, 7 June 2009.

9 Ibid.

10 Mookerji and Dhammika give no translations of these lines, so I have turned to the earlier translation by Professor Eugen Hultzch, *Inscriptions of Aśoka*, 1925.

11 When Daya Ram Sahni carried out further excavations at the Bairat site in 1935–6 he found the fragments of two Ashokan pillars.

12 Sir Alexander Cunningham, *Inscriptions of Asoka*, 1877.

13 Alexander Cunningham, *The Stupa of Bharhut: a Buddhist Monument Ornamented with Numerous Sculptures Illustrative of Buddhist Legend and History of the Third Century* B.C., 1879.

14 Alexander Cunningham, *The Stupa of Bharhut*, 1879.

Chapter 13. Corpus Inscriptionum Indicarum

1 Markham Kittoe quoted in James Prinsep, 'Further Elucidation of the Lat or Silasthambha Inscriptions from Various Sources', *JASB*, Vol. VI, 1837, p. 708.

2 W. F. Grahame, 'Rock Inscriptions in Ganjam District', *Indian Antiquary*, Vol. I, 1872.

3 Ven. S. Dhammika, *The Edicts of King Asoka*, 2009.

4 Benudhar Patra, 'Jaugadha: an Early Historical Fort Town of Orissa', *Orissa Review*, Jan 2007.

5 Ramakrishna Gopal Bhandarkar, 'Note on the Ganjam Rock Inscription', *IA*, Vol. I, 1872.

6 Cunningham's acerbic comments on the ASB are to be found in his preface to *The Stupa of Bharhut*, 1879.

7 Bhau Daji, 'Rudraman inscription', *JBBRAS*, Vol. VII, 1863.

8 *Epigraphica Indika*, Vol. II, 1881.

9 Bhagwanlal Indraji, 'Antiquarian remains at Sopara and Padana', *JBBRAS*, Vol XV, 1882.

10 James Burgess, *Notes on a Visit to Gujarat*, 1870.

11 Archibald Carllyle, 'Discovery of a new Edict Pillar of Asoka at Rampurwaparsa in the Tarai, 32½ miles to the North of Betiya', *ASI Report*, Vol. XXII, 1885.

12 See J. Cook and H. E. Martingell, 'The Carllyle Collection of Stone Age Artefacts from Central India', *British Museum Occasional Paper 95*, 1994.

13 Alexander Cunningham, *Inscriptions of Aśoka*, 1877.

14 This chronology is taken from Alexander Cunningham, *Inscriptions of Aśoka*, 1877.

15 J. H. C. Kern, 'On the Era of Buddha and the Asoka inscriptions', *Indian Antiquary*, 1874, and *Concerning the Chronology of the Southern Buddhists*, 1876,

16 Alexander Cunningham, *Inscriptions of Aśoka*, 1877.

17 Rajendra Lala Mitra, letter to the Secretary to the Government of Bengal dated 31 October 1877, OIOC, BL, quoted in Upinder Singh, *The Discovery of Ancient India*, 2004.

Chapter 14. India after Cunningham

1 James Burgess, *Notes on the Amaravati Stupa*, 1882.

2 R. Shama Shastry trans., *Kautilya's Arthashastra*, 1915, quoted in R. K. Mookerji in his 'Appendix I. Chanakya and Chandragupta Traditions (from Buddhist Sources)', *Chandragupta Maurya and his Times*, 1943.

3 Jawaharlal Nehru, *Discovery of India*, 1946.

4 Today Cowell is probably best remembered as the man who while rummaging through the library of the Asiatic Society of Bengal found a manuscript of a *rubaiyat* or 'collection of quatrains' by a twelfth-century Persian mathematician, astronomer and sometime poet named Omar Khayyam, which he translated and published in the *Calcutta Review* – but which he also had copied and sent to one of his former students, Edward Fitzgerald.

5 Harry Falk, *Aśokan Sites and Artefacts*, 2006.

6 Charles Allen, *The Buddha and Dr Führer: an Archaeological Scandal*, 2008.

7 Harry Falk, *Aśokan Sites and Artefacts*, 2006.

8 Parts of an abacus and a decorated bell retaining the forepaws of a lion were found in Basti District, just south of the Nepal border in 1955, perhaps originating from a village known as Dharamsinghwa (Dharma-lion) or from the temple of Palta Devi, said to contain a large pillar worshipped as a Shiva lingam. Part of another Ashokan pillar may well be the object of worship in the Shaiva temple in the centre of Taulihawa town, on the Nepal side of the border. See Harry Falk, *Aśokan Sites and Artefacts*, 2006.

9 R. Mukerji, S. K. Maitry, 'A Fortunate Find of 1931', *Corpus of Bengal Inscriptions*, 1967.

10 The various episodes of Waddell's life have been charted by Charles Allen in *The Buddha and the Sahibs*, 2002; *Duel in the Snows: the True Story of the Younghusband Mission to Lhasa*, 2004; and *The Buddha and Dr Führer*, 2008.

11 Mukherji's story is told in Charles Allen, *The Buddha and Dr Führer: an Archaeological Scandal*, 2008.

12 Dr L. A. Waddell, *Report on the Excavations at Pataliputra (Patna), the Palibothra of the Greeks*, 1903.

13 See Mary Stewart, 'The Persepolitan Legacy in India', *Circle of Ancient Iranian Studies* website, 1998.

14 Letter from G. Bühler to P. C. Peppé dated 21 February 1898, Peppé Collection, RAS.

15 Quoted in Charles Allen, *The Buddha and Dr Führer: an Archaeological Scandal*, 2008. The author has drawn on Dr Salomon's expertise here.

Chapter 15. Ashoka in the Twentieth Century

1 Sir John Marshall, 'The Story of the Archaeological Department in India', *Revealing India's Past*, 1939.

2 A. Foucher, *L'art gréco-bouddique du Gandhâra: Étude sur les origines de l'influence classique dans l'art bouddhique de l'Inde et de l'Extrême-Orient*, Vol. I 1905, Vol. II 1922, Vol. III 1951.

3 John Marshall in an unpublished letter to a friend dated Sanchi, 28 December 1918. Courtesy of John Wilson of John Wilson Manuscripts, Cheltenham.

4 A. Foucher, *La Porte Orientale du Stupa de Sanchi*, 1910.

5 Sir John Marshall, *A Guide to Sanchi*, 1918.

6 Radhakumud Mookerji, *Asoka*, 1927.

7 Harry Falk, 'The Preamble at Panguraria', P. Kieffer-Pulz and J. Hartmann, eds., *Bauddhavidyasudhakarah*, 1997. This section owes much to Professor Falk's remarks in *Aśokan Sites and Artefacts*, 2006.

8 From the Sahasram MRE, as translated by Eugen Hultsch, *Inscriptions of Aśoka*, 1925.

9 Ibid.

10 This argument has been put forward by Harry Falk in his *Aśokan Sites and Artefacts*, 2006.

11 D. C. Sirkar, 'Minor Rock and Pillar Edicts at Kandahar and Amaravati', *Ashokan Studies*, 1979. In 1959 a sandstone washing-stone in a house in Amaravati town was seen to have some Brahmi characters inscribed on its side face. It bore traces of the characteristic Ashokan polish and appeared to have been cut down a section of pillar so as to make a rectangular slab. Because of the way it has been cut it carries only a few letters from each of

seven lines, with letters lost on either side. What appear to be words like *paratra*, 'in the future world', and *abhisita*, 'anointed', are characteristically Ashokan as found on the Girnar Rock Edict.

12 The case for and against Pabhosa as an Ashokan quarry is given in Harry Falk, *Aśokan Sites and Artefacts*, 2006.

13 It may be that this started not in Taxila, as long assumed, but the island of Lanka. Excavations at Anuradhapura in the late 1980s and 1990s, under the direction of the British archaeologists Raymond Allchin and Robin Coningham, have produced potsherds bearing short inscriptions scratched in Brahmi lettering – not in itself surprising, except that radiocarbon dating has placed them in the fourth century BCE; that is to say, before Ashoka and perhaps even pre-dating his grandfather Chandragupta. See R. A. E. Coningham, R. Allchin, C. M. Batt and D. Lucy, 'Passage to India? Anuradhapura and the Early Use of the Brahmi Script', *Cambridge Archaeological Journal*, Vol. VI, 1996.

14 Gita Mehta, 'In the Footsteps of the Buddha', *Tricycle: the Buddhist Review*, Winter 1998.

15 Romila Thapar, 'Propaganda as History Won't Sell', *Hindustan Times*, 9 December 2001.

16 P. K. Mishra, 'Deorkother: a Milestone of History', *Govt. of India Press Release*, 4 February 2003. See also Mishra, 'Excavations at the Buddhist Site of Deorkjothar (Barhat) District Rewa, Madhya Pradesh, India 1999–2001', *CIAA Newsletter*, Issue 13, June 2001.

17 B. N. Mukherjee, 'A Fragmentary Inscription Referring to Aśoka', in *Journal of the Epigraphical Society of India*, forthcoming. Most regrettably, no clear photographs of the two sculptures or their inscriptions have been as yet published.

Chapter 16. The Rise and Fall of Ashokadharma

1 The *Mahavamsa* gloss states that Chanakya was a native of Taxila, where Chandragupta spent several years as his pupil. Although this commentary is comparatively late there seems no reason to doubt its veracity in this context.

2 Although traditionally dated to earlier centuries, the fact that Panini uses the word *yavanani*, or 'Greek script', in his *Ashtadhyayi* points to the fourth century BCE. His mention of King Ambhi, who ruled before and after Alexander, narrows him down to that same era. The unreliable *Manjusri-mula-tantra* specifically links Panini to Nanda: 'The king Virasena will rule for 70 years and will be succeeded by the king Nanda. The latter's reign will endure 56 years and his friend will be the Brahman Panini. Then there will appear the king Chandragupta . . .'

3 The word *gupta* is commonly understood to mean 'preserved' or 'protected',

but it is also the name of a clan belonging to the Vaisya caste, such as those who many centuries later established the Gupta dynasty. That matches the detail of Chandragupta being, as Justinus puts it, 'born in humble life'.

4 *Parisishtaparvan of Hemachandra*, trans. P. L. Bhargava.

5 W. W. Tarn, *The Greeks of Bactria and India*, 1938.

6 Within twenty years all but a handful were dead, and so played no decisive role in the final battle of the Wars of the Successors, fought in 281 BCE, in which the elderly Seleukos faced his old friend and rival Lysimachus on the battlefield of Corupedium and saw him slain. The last survivors of these Mauryan war elephants were deployed in 279 BCE by Alexander's cousin Pyrrhus in his 'pyrrhic' victory against the Romans.

7 Strabo in *Ancient India as Described in Classical Literature*, trans. J. W. McCrindle, 1901.

8 These migrants were *Digambara*, or 'sky-clad' (i.e. naked), Jains, who at this time broke away from the less austere Swetambaras to form their own sub-sect.

9 Taranatha, *History of Buddhism in India*, trans. Lama Chimpa Alaka Chattopadhyaya, 1970.

10 Gosala, founder of the Ajivika sect, taught that man's fate was pre-determined and since nothing could be done to alter the outcome, life should be suffered with indifference. However, what little is known about the Ajivikas comes mainly from Jain and Buddhist sources, and since the founders of both these religions were initially influenced by Gosala but went on to reject his doctrines, those sources must be regarded as suspect.

11 See the appendix in John S. Strong, *The Legend of King Aśoka*, 1983.

12 The Queen's Edict appended to Ashoka's edicts on the Allahabad Pillar Edict names Karuvaki as 'second queen, mother of Tivara'; the *Great Dynastic Chronicle* names Ashoka's chief queen as Asandhimitra, who died in the thirtieth year of Ashoka's reign; the *Divine Stories* names queen Padmavati, mother of Dharmavivardhana, also known as Kunala; and the *Great Dynastic Chronicle*, the *Divine Stories* and Taranatha's *History* are in rare agreement in naming Ashoka's last 'chief queen' as Tissarakkha, or Tishyarakshita. As for offspring, the Ashokan edicts speak of four unnamed *kumaras*, or 'princes', ruling as viceroys in different regions of the Indian subcontinent; Taranatha states that Ashoka had eleven sons, the best being Kunala, and names Ashoka's successor as his son Virasena; the *Legend of King Ashoka* names Kunala's son, who ruled in his father's place because of his blindness, as Sampadin; Faxian names a son of Ashoka ruling in Taxila as Dharmavivardhana; and Kalhana's Kashmir chronicle speaks of a son of Ashoka who ruled there after his death as Jalauka. A daughter named Charumati is said to have married Khattiya Devapala in Nepal, the two of them presiding over two monasteries in what is today the town of Patan.

Only the *Great Dynastic Chronicle* mentions Ashoka's two eldest children by his first wife, Mahinda and Sanghamitta.

13 Akbar the Great spent most of his five decades as emperor of India waging a succession of campaigns and never conquered the southern tip. Even the ninety-year *Pax Britannica* from 1857 to 1947 took place with two-fifths of India sub-contracted to several hundred Indian maharajas, rajas and nawabs.

14 RE 10, as rendered by Ven. S. Dhammika, *The Edicts of King Asoka*, 2009.

15 Ven. S. Dhammika, *The Edicts of King Asoka*, 2009.

16 John S. Strong, *The Legend of King Aśoka*, 1983.

17 One intriguing alternative reading of this episode is that Ashoka's son Kunala was actually sent to Taxila for his education and that the emperor's message in Brahmi was altered by his son's enemies, the word *adhya*, for 'educate', being altered by the addition of a dot to read *andhya*, meaning 'blind'.

18 It seems a shame to point out that not a single gold piece from the Mauryan era has been found.

19 Li Rongxi trans., *The Great Tang Dynasty Record of the Western Regions*, 1996.

Index